English Novel Explication

Criticisms to 1972

Compiled by

HELEN H. PALMER

&

ANNE JANE DYSON

THE SHOE STRING PRESS, INC.   1973

Library of Congress Cataloging in Publication Data

Palmer, Helen H
    English novel explication.

    1. English fiction—History and criticism—
Bibliography—Indexes. I. Dyson, Anne Jane, 1912–
joint author. II. Title.
Z2014.F5P26   016.823'009   73-410
ISBN 0-208-01322-9

© 1973 by The Shoe String Press, Inc.
Hamden, Connecticut 06514

Printed in The United States of America

_18974_

CONTENTS

INTRODUCTION

Since the checklist, The English Novel by Inglis F. Bell and
Donald Baird, of twentieth century criticisms, published in
1959, covered published criticisms only through 1957, the need
for up-to-date information has become important. Rather than
redo the work covered by Bell and Baird, we have assumed its
availability and in this book cover criticisms from 1958 to 1972
with a few entries we discovered which had been published
earlier and had not been included in the Bell and Baird book.

This comprehensive listing is of criticisms which have ap-
peared in books and periodicals, in English and foreign languages.
Only articles concerned with the novel as a whole, or with a large
or important part of it, are included. References to a word, line,
or one or two lines have been omitted.

The quality of the articles was not considered; the primary
criterion has been that critical material relating to a certain
novel could be found in a particular book or journal.

The arrangement is alphabetical by author, with the novels
alphabetized under the author's name and the sources of criticisms in alphabetical order under the titles. There are cross
references from foreign to English titles and also from full titles
to short titles. Cross references are also listed for pseudonyms
and joint authors.

We have indicated some novels by their group title; i.e.,
Anthony Powell's Music of Time, which includes A Buyer's Market, A Question of Upbringing, The Acceptance World, and others,
Durrell's Alexandria Quartet, Lessing's Children of Violence,
and others. "SEE ALSO" references are included. These individual novels have also been listed in some cases. Dates of publication are listed with the title of the novel. An alphabetical index
listing authors (with their vital statistics) and novels has been
included, as well as a listing of books indexed and journals indexed.

We have based this work on items appearing in the following
bibliographies: Bulletin Signalétique, Essay and General Literature Index, Social Science and Humanities Index, PMLA Bibliography, Reader's Guide, and other books and periodicals not
listed in the above.

It is inevitable that errors will appear, but we have endeavored
to be as accurate as possible. Both the authors and the publisher
will be grateful if omissions and such errors as appear are drawn
to their attention so that corrections can be incorporated into
future supplements.

We are indebted to our husbands for their support and encour-
agement and to Mr. T. N. McMullan, Director of the Louisiana
State University Library and Mr. George J. Guidry, Jr., Associate
Director of the Louisiana State University Library for lending
support, cooperation and assistance.

Helen H. Palmer and Anne Jane Dyson
Louisiana State University

July 1972

Publisher's Note: In composition the quotation marks setting off
titles of articles in journals were inadvertently omitted. Since
we feel that, after the first brief strangeness, this will in no way
affect the usefulness of the volume, we decided to proceed with
printing. We ask the reader's indulgence.

RICHARD ALDINGTON

Death of a Hero, 1929

Bergonzi, Bernard, Heroes' Twilight; a Study of the Literature of the Great War. 1966. p 171—97

KINGSLEY AMIS

The Anti-Death League, 1966

Bergonzi, Bernard, The Situation of the Novel. 1970. p. 171—74

Ross, T. J., Manners, Morals, and Pop; On the Fiction of Kingsley Amis, Studies in the Twentieth Century (Fall 1969), #4:61—73

I Like It Here, 1958

Colville, Derek, The Sane New World of Kingsley Amis, Bucknell Review (March 1960), 9:46—57

Hopkins, R. H., Satire of Kingsley Amis's "I Like It Here," Critique (Spring 1966), 8:62—70

Hurrell, John D., Class and Conscience in John Braine and Kingsley Amis, Critique; Studies in Modern Fiction (Spring—Summer 1958), 2:39—53

Lebowitz, Naomi, Kingsley Amis: The Penitent Hero, Perspective (Summer—Autumn 1957—59), 10:129—36

Lodge, David, The Modern, the Contemporary, and the Importance of Being Amis, Critical Quarterly (1963), 5:335—54

Taking It Easy, London, Times Literary Supplement (Jan. 17, 1958), p. 30

Lucky Jim, 1954

Alsop, Kenneth, Angry Decade; A Survey of the Cultural Revolt of the Nineteen Fifties. 1959. p. 43—95

Boyle, Ted E. and Terence Brown, The Serious Side of Kingsley Amis's "Lucky Jim," Critique; Studies in Modern Fiction (1967), 9:100—07

Brophy, Brigid, Don't Never Forget; Collected Views and Reviews. 1967. p. 217—22

Conquest, Robert, Christian Symbolism in "Lucky Jim," Critical Quarterly (Spring 1965), 7:87—92

Feldman, Gene and Max Gartenberg, eds., Beat Generation and the Angry Young Men. 1958. p. 339—41

Harkness, Bruce, The Lucky Crown—Contemporary British Fiction, English Journal (October 1958), 47:387—97

Hurrell, John D., Class and Conscience in John Braine and
Kingsley Amis, Critique; Studies in Modern Fiction (Spring–
Summer 1958), 2:39–53

Kvam, Ragnar, Teddy-Boys og Nietzsche-Boys, Vinduet (1958),
12:179–87

Lebowitz, Naomi, Kingsley Amis; The Penitent Hero, Perspective (Summer–Autumn 1957–59), 10:129–36

Lodge, David, The Modern, the Contemporary, and the Importance of Being Kingsley Amis, Critical Quarterly (1936),
5:335–54

Noon, William T., Satire: Poison and the Professor, English
Record (Fall 1960), 11:53–56

Ward, Anthony, Jimsday, Spectator (Jan. 24, 1964), #7074:112

My Enemy's Enemy, 1962

Gross, John, Makes you Sober: "My Enemy's Enemy," New
Statesman (Sept. 21, 1962), 64:363–64

One Fat Englishman, 1963

Hamilton, Kenneth, Kingsley Amis, Moralist, Dalhousie Review
(Autumn 1964), 44:339–47

Powell, Anthony, Kingsley's Heroes, Spectator (Nov. 29, 1963),
#7066:709–10

Soule, George, The High Cost of Plunging, Carleton Miscellany
(Fall 1964), 5:106–11

T. L. S. Essays and Reviews from the Times Literary Supplement. 1964. Vol. 2 p. 107–09

Ward, Anthony, Jimsday, Spectator (Jan. 24, 1964), #7074:112

Take a Girl Like You, 1961

Bergonzi, Bernard, The Situation of the Novel. 1970. p. 165–
68

Coleman, John, King of Shaft, Spectator (Sept. 23, 1960),
#6900:445–46

Lodge, David, The Modern, the Contemporary, and the Importance of Being Amis, Critical Quarterly (1963), 5:335–54

Moers, Ellen, Still Angry, Commentary (June 1961), 31:542–44

Parker, R. B., Farce and Society: The Range of Kingsley
Amis, Wisconsin Studies in Contemporary Literature (Fall
1961), 2:27–38

Ross, T. J., Lucky Jenny, or Affluent Times, New Republic
(March 27, 1961), 144:21–22

Sissman, L. E., Kingsley Amis at Halfway House, New Yorker
(April 26, 1969), 45:163–70

That Uncertain Feeling, 1955

Hurrell, John D., Class and Conscience in John Braine and
Kingsley Amis, Critique; Studies in Modern Fiction (Spring-
Summer 1958), 2:39-53
Lebowitz, Naomi, Kingsley Amis; The Penitent Hero, Per-
spective (Summer-Autumn 1957-59), 10:129-36

FRANCES BURNEY D'ARBLAY

SEE

FANNY BURNEY

JANE AUSTEN

Emma, 1816

Booth, Wayne, C., Point of View and the Control of Distance
in "Emma," Nineteenth Century Fiction (1961), 16:95-116
Bradbury, Malcolm, Jane Austen's "Emma," Critical Quarterly
(Winter 1962), 4:335-46
Bramer, George R., The Setting in "Emma," College English
(Dec. 1960), 22:150-56
Brower, Reuben Arthur and William Richard Poirrier, eds.,
In Defense of Reading; A Reader's Approach to Literary
Criticism. 1962. p. 235-55
Brown, Lloyd, W., The Comic Conclusion in Jane Austen's
Novels, Modern Language Association. Publications (1969),
84:1582-87
Collins, Thomas J., Some Mutual Sets of Friends: Moral
Monitors in "Emma" and "Our Mutual Friend," Dickensian
(Jan. 1969), 65:32-34
Corsa, Helen S., A Fair but Frozen Maid: A Study of Jane
Austen's "Emma," Literature and Psychology (1969), 19:
101-24
Dolezel, Lubomir and Richard W. Bailey, eds., Statistics and
Style. 1969. p. 197-213
Drew, Elizabeth A., The Novel; A Modern Guide to Fifteen
English Masterpieces. 1963. p. 792-821
Duckworth, Alistair M., The Improvement of the Estate; A
Study of Jane Austen's Novels. 1971. p. 145-78
Elsbree, Langdon, Jane Austen and the Dance of Fidelity and
Complaisance, Nineteenth Century Fiction (Sept. 1960), 15:
113-36
Gooneratne, Yasmine, Jane Austen. 1970. p. 136-65

Harper, Howard M., Jr., and Charles Edge, eds., The Classic
    British Novel. 1972. p. 51–64
Harris, Harold J., A Note on Snobbishness in "Emma," Ball
    State Teachers College Forum (Spring 1964), 5:55–57
Harvey, W. J., The Plot of "Emma," Essays in Criticism
    (Jan. 1967), 17:48–63
Hellstrom, Ward, Francophobia in "Emma," Studies in English
    Literature, 1500–1900 (Autumn 1966), 5:607–17
Hughes, R. E., The Education of Emma Woodhouse, Nineteenth
    Century Fiction (June 1961), 16:69–74
Jones, Evan, Characters and Values: "Emma" and "Mansfield
    Park," Quadrant (1968), 12:35–45
Karl, Frederick Robert, An Age of Fiction; The Nineteenth
    Century British Novel. 1964. p. 27–62
Knoeplmacher, U. C., Importance of Being Frank: Character
    and Letter-Writing in "Emma," Studies in English Literature
    (Autumn 1967), 7:639–58
Kooiman-Van Middendorp, Gerarda M., The Hero in the Femi-
    nine Novel. 1966. p. 49–59
Latham, Jacqueline E. M., Head Versus Heart; The Role of
    Miss Bates in "Emma," English (Spring 1965), 15:140–43
Lawry, J. S., "Decided and Open": Structure in "Emma,"
    Nineteenth Century Fiction (June 1969), 24:1–15
Marshall, Sarah Latimer, Rationality and Delusion in Jane
    Austen's "Emma," University of Mississippi Studies in
    English (1968), 9:57–67
Martin, W. R., "Emma": A Definition of Virtue, English
    Studies in Africa (March 1960), 3:21–30
Minter, David Lee, "Aesthetic Vision and the World of "Emma,"
    Nineteenth Century Fiction (June 1966), 21:49–59
Moore, E. Margaret, "Emma" and Miss Bates: Early Experi-
    ence of Separation and the Theme of Dependency in Jane
    Austen's Novels," Studies in English Literature (Autumn
    1969), 9:573–85
Schorer, Mark, The Humiliation of Emma Woodhouse, Liter-
    ary Review (1959), 2:547–63
Shenfield, Margaret, Jane Austen's Point of View, Quarterly
    Review (July 1958), 296:298–305
Sherry, Norman, Jane Austen. 1969. p. 76–83
Simon, Irene, Jane Austen and the Art of the Novel, English
    Studies (1962), 43:225–39
Tomlinson, T. B., Jane Austen's Originality: "Emma,"
    Critical Review (1966), 9:22–37

Trilling, Lionel, Beyond Culture; Essays on Literature and
Learning. 1965. p. 31–55
Trilling, Lionel, Emma, Encounter (1957), 8:49–59
White, Edward M., "Emma" and the Parodic Point of View,
Nineteenth Century Fiction (June 1963), 18:55–63

Lady Susan, 1871

Kronenberger, Louis, The Polished Surface; Essays in the
Literature of Worldliness. 1969. p. 127–50
Levine, Jay A., "Lady Susan": Jane Austen's Character of
the Merry Widow, Studies in English Literature, 1500–1900
(Autumn 1961), 1:23–34

Love and Friendship, 1790

Griffin, Cynthia, The Development of Realism in Jane
Austen's Early Novels, ELH (1963), 30:36–52

Mansfield Park, 1814

Brown, Lloyd W., The Comic Conclusion in Jane Austen's
Novels, Modern Language Association. Publications (1969),
84:1582–87
Brown, Lloyd W., Jane Austen and the Sublime: A Note on
"Mansfield Park," Studies in Burke and His Time (Fall 1968),
10:1041–48
Burroway, Janet, The Irony of the Insufferable Prig: "Mans-
field Park," Critical Quarterly (Summer 1967), 9:127–38
Carroll, D. R., "Mansfield Park," "Daniel Deronda" and
Ordination," Modern Philology (1965), 62:217–26
Chanda, S. M., The New Vein in "Mansfield Park," Indian
Journal of English Studies (1960), 1:96–99
Colby, Robert Alan, Fiction with a Purpose; Major and Minor
Nineteenth Century Novels. 1967. p. 66–104
Donohue, J. W., Ordination and the Divided House at "Mans-
field Park," ELH (June 1965), 32:169–78
Draffan, Robert A., "Mansfield Park": Jane Austen's Bleak
House, Essays in Criticism (Oct. 1969), 19:371–84
Duckworth, Alistair M., The Improvement of the Estate; A
Study of Jane Austen's Novels. 1971. p. 35–80
Edge, Charles E., "Mansfield Park" and Ordination, Nineteenth
Century Fiction (1961), 16:269–74
Edwards, Thomas R., Jr., The Difficult Beauty of "Mansfield
Park," Nineteenth Century Fiction (June 1965), 20:51–67
Ellis, David, The Irony of "Mansfield Park," Melbourne

Critical Review (1969), 12:107-19

Fleisman, Avrom, "Mansfield Park" in Its Time, Nineteenth
Century Fiction (June 1967), 22:1-18

Fryxell, Donald R., Lovers' Vows in "Mansfield Park," Midwest Review (1961), 2:75-78

Gooneratne, Yasmine, Jane Austen. 1970. p. 104-135

Henfrey, Norman, Mansfield Park, Delta (Summer 1966),
#39:4-11

Jones, Evan, Characters and Values; "Emma" and "Mansfield
Park," Quadrant (1968), 12:35-45

Kaul, A. N., The Action of English Comedy; Studies in the
Encounter of Abstraction and Experience from Shakespeare
to Shaw. 1970. p. 231-36

Kooiman-Van Middendorp, Gerarda M., The Hero in the Feminine Novel. 1966. p. 49-59

Lodge, David, Language of Fiction; Essays in Criticism and
Verbal Analysis of the English Novel. 1966. p. 94-113

Lodge, David, A Question of Judgment; The Theatricals at
Mansfield Park, Nineteenth Century Fiction (Dec. 1962),
17:275-82

Lynch, P. R., Speculation at Mansfield Parsonage, Notes and
Queries (Jan. 1967), 14:21-22

Magee, William H., Romanticism on Trial in "Mansfield Park,"
Bucknell Review (March 1966), 14:44-59

Martin, W. R., "Ordination" in "Mansfield Park," English
Studies in Africa (Sept. 1966), 9:146-57

Porteous, Alexander, The Beast in the Park: Some Features
of Jane Austen's Work, Melbourne Critical Review (1964),
7:66-77

Rathburn, Robert C. and Martin Steinman, eds., From Jane
Austen to Joseph Conrad; Essays Collected in Memory of
James T. Hillhouse. 1958. p. 23-34

Rosenfeld, Sybil, Jane Austen and Private Theatricals, Essays
and Studies (1962), 15:40-51

Schneider, Sister M. Lucy, The Little White Attic and the East
Room: Their Function in "Mansfield Park," Modern Philology
(Feb. 1966), 63:227-35

Sherry, Norman, Jane Austen. 1969. p. 70-76

Simon, Irene, Jane Austen and the Art of the Novel, English
Studies (1962), 43:225-39

Trilling, Lionel, Opposing Self; Nine Essays in Criticism,
1955. p. 206-30

White, Edward M., A Critical Theory of "Mansfield Park,"

Studies in English Literature, 1500-1900 (Autumn 1967),
7:659-77

Wiltshire, John, "Mansfield Park" and Fanny Price, Melbourne
Critical Review (1965), 8:121-28

Zimmerman, Everett, Jane Austen and "Mansfield Park": A
Discrimination of Ironies, Studies in the Novel (Fall 1969),
1:347-56

Northanger Abbey, 1818

Brown, Lloyd W., The Comic Conclusion in Jane Austen's
Novels, Modern Language Association. Publications (1969),
84:1582-87

Chillman, Dawes, Miss Morland's Mind: Sentiment, Reason,
and Experience in "Northanger Abbey," South Dakota Review
(Dec. 1963), 1:37-47

Duckworth, Alistair M., The Improvement of the Estate; A
Study of Jane Austen's Novels. 1971. p. 81-85, 91-102

Emden, Cecil S., The Composition of "Northanger Abbey,"
Review of English Studies (Aug. 1968), 19:279-87

Gallon, D. N., Comedy in "Northanger Abbey," Modern
Language Review (Oct. 1968), 63:802-09

Gooneratne, Yasmine, Jane Austen. 1970. p. 49-62

Gornall, F. G., Marriage, Property, and Romance in Jane
Austen's Novels, Hibbert Journal (1907), 65:151-56

Griffin, Cynthia, The Development of Realism in Jane Austen's
Early Novels, ELH (1963), 30:36-52

Kaul, A. N., The Action of English Comedy; Studies in the Encounter of Abstraction of Experience from Shakespeare to
Shaw. 1970. p. 206-13

Kearful, Frank J., Satire and the Form of the Novel: The
Problem of Aesthetic Unity in "Northanger Abbey," ELH
(1965), 32:511-27

Mathison, John K., "Northanger Abbey" and Jane Austen's
Conception of the Value of Fiction, ELH (1957), 24:138-52

Rathburn, Robert C. and Martin Steinman, eds., From Jane
Austen to Joseph Conrad: Essays Collected in Memory of
James T. Hillhouse. 1958. p. 35-45

Rubinstein, E., "Northanger Abbey": The Elder Morlands and
"John Homespun," Papers in Language and Literature (1969),
5:434-40

Shenfield, Margaret, Jane Austen's Point of View, Quarterly
Review (July 1958), 296:298-306

Sherry, Norman, Jane Austen. 1969. p. 46-56

Sørensen, Knud, Johnsonese in "Northanger Abbey": A Note
    on Jane Austen's Style, English Studies (1969), 50:390–97
Zimmerman, Everett, Function of Parody in "Northanger
    Abbey," Modern Language Quarterly (March 1969), 30:53–63

Persuasion, 1818

Bowen, Elizabeth, Persuasion, London Magazine (1957), 4:
    47–51
Bradbury, Malcolm, "Persuasion" Again, Essays in Criticism
    (Oct. 1968), 18:383–96
Crane, Ronald Simon, The Idea of the Humanities and Other
    Essays Critical and Historical. 1967. Vol. 2. p. 283–302
Duckworth, Alistair M., The Improvement of the Estate; A
    Study of Jane Austen's Novels. 1971. p. 179–208
Gomme, Andor, On Not Being Persuaded, Essays in Criticism
    (April 1966), 16:170–84
Gooneratne, Yasmine, Jane Austen. 1970. p. 166–94
Kaul, A. N., The Action of English Comedy; Studies in the
    Encounter of Abstraction of Experience from Shakespeare
    to Shaw. 1970. p. 237–49
Martin, W. R., Sensibility and Sense; A Reading of "Persua-
    sion," English Studies in Africa (Sept. 1960), 3:119–30
Page, Norman, Categories of Speech in "Persuasion," Modern
    Language Review (Oct. 1969), 64:734–41
Sherry, Norman, Jane Austen. 1969. p. 83–88
Simon, Irene, Jane Austen and the Art of the Novel, English
    Studies (1962), 43:225–39
Zeitlow, Paul N., Luck and Fortuitous Circumstance in
    "Persuasion": Two Interpretations, ELH (1965), 32:179–95

Pride and Prejudice, 1813

Babb, Howard S., Dialogue with Feeling: A Note on "Pride and
    Prejudice," Kenyon Review (Spring 1958), 20:203–16
Brogan, Howard O., Science and Narrative Structure in Austen,
    Hardy, and Woolf, Nineteenth Century Fiction (March 1957),
    11:276–87
Brown, Lloyd W., The Comic Conclusion in Jane Austen's
    Novels," Modern Language Association. Publications (1969),
    84:1582–87
Bush, Douglas, Engaged and Disengaged. 1966. p. 20–26
Dooley, D. J., Pride, Prejudice and Vanity in Elizabeth Bennet,
    Nineteenth Century Fiction (Sept. 1965), 20:185–88
Drew, Philip, A Significant Incident in "Pride and Prejudice,"

Nineteenth Century Fiction (March 1959), 13:356–58

Duckworth, Alistair M., _The Improvement of the Estate; A Study of Jane Austen's Novels_. 1971. p. 115–43

Ebiike, Shunji, "Pride and Prejudice" and "First Impressions," _Studies in English Literature_ (1965), English #:31–45

Elsbree, Langdon, Jane Austen and the Dance of Fidelity and Complaisance, _Nineteenth Century Fiction_ (Sept. 1960), 15:113–36

Fox, Robert C., Elizabeth Bennet: Prejudice or Vanity?, _Nineteenth Century Fiction_ (Sept. 1962), 17:185–87

Gooneratne, Yasmine, _Jane Austen_. 1970. p. 81–103

Griffin, Cynthia, The Development of Realism in Jane Austen's Early Novels, _ELH_ (1963), 30:36–52

Halliday, E. M., Narrative Perspective in "Pride and Prejudice," _Nineteenth Century Fiction_ (June 1960), 15:65–71

Karl, Frederick Robert, _An Age of Fiction; The Nineteenth Century British Novel_. 1964. p. 27–62

Kaul, A. N., _The Action of English Comedy; Studies in the Encounter of Abstraction and Experience from Shakespeare to Shaw_. 1970. p. 218–31

Kooiman-Van Middendorp, Gerarda M., _The Hero in the Feminine Novel_. 1966. p. 49–59

Kronenberger, Louis, _The Polished Surface; Essays in the Literature of Worldliness_. 1969. p. 127–50

McCann, Charles J., Setting and Character in "Pride and Prejudice," _Nineteenth Century Fiction_ (June 1964), 19:65–75

Maugham, William Somerset, _Art of Fiction; An Introduction to Ten Novels and Their Authors_. 1955. p. 55–78

Marcus, Mordecai, A Major Thematic Pattern in "Pride and Prejudice," _Nineteenth Century Fiction_ (Dec. 1961), 16:274–79

Moler, Kenneth L., "Pride and Prejudice": Jane Austen's "Patrician Hero," _Studies in English Literature, 1500–1900_ (Summer 1967), 7:491–508

Nash, Ralph, The Time Scheme for "Pride and Prejudice," _English Language Notes_ (1967), 4:194–98

Shapiro, Charles, ed., _Twelve Original Essays on Great English Novels_. 1960. p. 69–85

Sherry, Norman. _Jane Austen_. 1969. p. 63–69

Ten Harmsel, Henrietta, The Villain-Hero in "Pamele" and "Pride and Prejudice," _College English_ (Nov. 1961), 23:104–08

Zimmerman, Everett, "Pride and Prejudice in "Pride and Prejudice," _Nineteenth Century Fiction_ (June 1968), 23:64–73

Sense and Sensibility, 1811

> Brown, Lloyd W., The Comic Conclusion in Jane Austen's
> Novels, Modern Language Association. Publications (1969),
> 84:1582-87
> Cecil, Lord David, Fine Art of Reading; And Other Literary
> Studies. 1957. p. 149-60
> Duckworth, Alistair M., The Improvement of the Estate; A
> Study of Jane Austen's Novels. 1971. p. 81-91 and 102-14
> Gillie, Christopher, "Sense and Sensibility": An Assessment,
> Essays in Criticism (Jan. 1959), 9:1-9
> Gooneratne, Yasmine, Jane Austen. 1970. p. 63-80
> Gornall, F. G., Marriage, Property, and Romance in Jane
> Austen's Novels, Hibbert Journal (1967), 65:151-56
> Griffin, Cynthia, The Development of Realism in Jane Austen's
> Early Novels, ELH (1963), 30:36-52
> Kaul, A. N., The Action of English Comedy; Studies in the En-
> counter of Abstraction of Experience from Shakespeare to
> Shaw. 1970. p. 213-18
> Kooiman-Van Middendorp, Gerarda M., The Hero in the Femi-
> nine Novel. 1966. p. 49-59
> McKillop, Alan D., The Context of "Sense and Sensibility,"
> Rice Institute Pamphlets (1957), 44:65-78
> Sherry, Norman, Jane Austen. 1969. p. 56-63

JOHN BARCLAY

Argenis, 1621

> Coleridge, Samuel Taylor, Coleridge on the Seventeenth Cen-
> tury. 1955. p. 433-36
> Schulz-Behrend, G., Opitz' Übersetzung von Barclays
> "Argenis," Modern Language Association. Publications
> (1955), 70:455-73

Euphomormionis Satyricon, 1603

> Fleming, David A., Barclay's "Satyricon": The First Satirical
> Roman à Clef, Modern Philology (1967), 65:95-102
> Fleming, David A., Names in Allegorical Satire: Barclay's
> "Satyricon," Names (1968), 16:347-56

BEACONSFIELD, BENJAMIN DISRAELI, FIRST EARL OF

SEE

BENJAMIN DISRAELI

SAMUEL BECKETT

How It Is, 1961

Kostelanetz, Richard, On Contemporary Literature; An
Anthology of Critical Essays on the Major Movements and
Writers of Contemporary Literature. 1964. p. 255–61
T. L. S., Essays and Reviews From the Times Literary Sup-
plement, 1964–1965. 1965–1966. Vol. 3–4, p. 45–47

L'Innommable, SEE The Unnamable

Malone Dies, 1951

Barnard, G. C., Samuel Beckett; A New Approach. 1970. p.
45–56
Barrett, William, How I Understand Less and Less Every
Year, Columbia University Forum (Winter 1959), 2:44–48
Bersani, Leo, Balzac to Beckett; Center and Circumference
in French Fiction. 1970. p. 300–27
Bruns, Gerald L., The Storyteller and the Problem of Language
in Samuel Beckett's Fiction, Modern Language Quarterly
(1969), 30:265–81
Cmarada, Geraldine, "Malone Dies": A Round of Conscious-
ness, Symposium (1960), 14:199–212
Chambers, Ross, Samuel Beckett and the Padded Cell, Meanjin
(Dec. 1962), 21:451–62
Freidman, Melvin J., The Novels of Samuel Beckett, Compara-
tive Literature (Winter 1960), 12:47–58
Frye, Northrup, The Nightmare Life in Death, Hudson Review
(Autumn 1960), 13:442–49
Glicksburg, Charles J., Samuel Beckett's World of Fiction,
Arizona Quarterly (Spring 1962), 18:32–47
Goldberg, Gerald Jay, The Search for the Artist in Some
Recent British Fiction, South Atlantic Quarterly (Summer
1963), 62:387–401
Hamilton, Carol, Portrait in Old Age; The Image of Man in
Beckett's Trilogy, Western Humanities Review (Spring 1962),
16:157–65
Hamilton, Kenneth, Boon or Thorn? Joyce Cary and Samuel
Beckett on Human Life, Dalhousie Review (Winter 1959), 38:
433–42
LeSage, Laurent, The French New Novel; An Introduction and
a Sample. 1962. p. 47–54

Oates, J. C., The Trilogy of Samuel Beckett, Renascence
(Spring 1962), 14:160-65

Robinson, Michael, The Long Sonata of the Dead; A Study of
Samuel Beckett. 1969. p. 140-48 and 170-90

Vold, Jan Erik, Samuel Becketts Romaner, Samtiden (Spring
1965), 74:441-47

Webb, Eugene, Samuel Beckett; A Study of His Novels. 1970.
p. 143-46

Malone Meurt, SEE Malone Dies

Molloy, 1951

Barnard, G. C., Samuel Beckett; A New Approach. 1970. p.
32-44

Barrett, William, How I Understand Less and Less Every
Year, Columbia University Forum (Winter 1959), 2:44-48

Bersani, Leo, Balzac to Beckett; Center and Circumference
in French Fiction. 1970. p. 300-27

Bruns, Gerald L., The Storyteller and the Problem of Language in Samuel Beckett's Fiction, Modern Language Quarterly (1969), 30:265-81

Chambers, Ross, Samuel Beckett and the Padded Cell, Meanjin
(Dec. 1962), 21:451-62

Freidman, Melvin J., Molloy's "Sacred" Stones, Romance
Notes (1967), 9:8-11

Freidman, Melvin J., The Novels of Samuel Beckett, Comparative Literature (Winter 1960), 12:47-58

Frye, Northrup, The Nightmare Life in Death, Hudson Review
(Autumn 1960), 13:442-49

Gerard, Martin, Molloy Becomes Unnamable, X, A Quarterly
Review (October 1960), 1:314-19

Glicksburg, Charles I., Samuel Beckett's World of Fiction,
Arizona Quarterly (Spring 1962), 18:32-47

Goldberg, Gerald Jay, The Search for the Artist in Some
Recent British Fiction, South Atlantic Quarterly (Summer
1963), 62:387-401

Hamilton, Carol, Portrait in Old Age; The Image of Man in
Beckett's Trilogy, Western Humanities Review (Spring
1962), 16:157-65

Hamilton, Kenneth, Boon or Thorn? Joyce Cary and Samuel
Beckett on Human Life, Dalhousie Review (Winter 1959),
38:433-42

Hamilton, Kenneth, Negative Salvation in Samuel Beckett,
Queen's Quarterly (Spring 1962), 69:102-11

Kern, Edith, Moran-Molloy: The Hero as Author, Perspective (Autumn 1959), 11:183-93

LeSage, Laurent, The French New Novel; An Introduction and a Sample. 1962. p. 47-54

Oates, J. C., The Trilogy of Samuel Beckett, Renascence (Spring 1962), 14:160-65

Pingaud, Bernard, "Molloy" Douze ans Après, Temps Modernes (1963), 18:1283-1300

Robinson, Michael, The Long Sonata of the Dead; A Study of Samuel Beckett. 1969. p. 140-69

Shapiro, Barbara, Toward a Psychoanalytic Reading of Beckett's "Molloy," Literature and Psychology (1969), 19:71-86 and 15-30

Solomon, Philip H., The Imagery of "Molloy" and Its Extension into Beckett's Other Fiction, Dissertation Abstracts (1968), 28:3198A-99A

Solomon, Philip H., Samuel Beckett's "Molloy": A Dog's Life, French Review (1967), 41:84-91

Sutherland, William O. S., ed., Six Contemporary Novels; Six Introductory Essays in Modern Fiction. 1962. p. 90-112

Vold, Jan Erik, Samuel Becketts Romaner, Samtiden (Sept. 1965), 74:441-47

Webb, Eugene, Samuel Beckett; A Study of His Novels. 1970. p. 113-15 and 140-43

Murphy, 1938

Barnard, G. C., Samuel Beckett; A New Approach. 1970. p. 9-15

Chambers, Ross, Samuel Beckett and the Padded Cell, Meanjin (Dec. 1962), 21:451-62

Cooney, Seamus, Beckett's "Murphy," Explicator (Sept. 1966), 25:Item 3

Freidman, Melvin J., The Novels of Samuel Beckett, Comparative Literature (Winter 1960), 12:47-58

Frye, Northrup, The Nightmare Life in Death, Hudson Review (Autumn 1960), 13:442-49

Hamilton, Kenneth, Negative Salvation in Samuel Beckett, Queen's Quarterly (Sept. 1962), 69:102-11

Hesla, David H., The Shape of Chaos; An Interpretation of the Art of Samuel Beckett. 1971. p. 30-58

Mintz, Samuel I., Beckett's "Murphy": A "Cartesian" Novel, Perspective (Autumn 1959), 11:156-65

Robinson, Michael, The Long Sonata of the Dead; A Study of

Samuel Beckett. 1969. p. 82–99

Webb, Eugene, Samuel Beckett; A Study of his Novels. 1970.
p. 43–55

The Unnamable, 1953

Bajomée, Daniella, Lumière Ténèbres et Chaos dans "L'Innommable" de Samuel Beckett, Les Lettres Romanes (1969), 23:
139–58

Barnard, G. C., Samuel Beckett; A New Approach. 1970. p.
57–66

Barrett, William, How I Understand Less and Less Every
Year, Columbia University Forum (Winter 1959), 2:44–48

Bersani, Leo, Balzac to Beckett; Center and Circumference
in French Fiction. 1970. p. 300–27

Bruns, Gerald L., The Storyteller and the Problem of Language in Samuel Beckett's Fiction, Modern Language
Quarterly (1969), 30:265–81

Chambers, Ross, Samuel Beckett and the Padded Cell, Meanjin
(Dec. 1962), 21:451–62

Freidman, Melvin J., The Novels of Samuel Beckett, Comparative Literature (Winter 1960), 12:47–58

Frye, Northrup, The Nightmare Life in Death, Hudson Review
(Autumn 1960), 13:442–49

Glicksburg, Charles I., Samuel Beckett's World of Fiction,
Arizona Quarterly (Spring 1962), 18:32–47

Hamilton, Carol, Portrait in Old Age: The Image of Man in
Beckett's Trilogy, Western Humanities Review (Spring 1962),
16:157–65

Hamilton, Kenneth, Boon or Thorn? Joyce Cary and Samuel
Beckett on Human Life, Dalhousie Review (Winter 1959), 38:
433–42

Hamilton, Kenneth, Negative Salvation in Samuel Beckett,
Queen's Quarterly (Spring 1962), 69:102–11

Oates, J. C., The Trilogy of Samuel Beckett, Renascence
(Spring 1962), 14:160–65

Rickels, Milton, Existentialist Themes in Beckett's "Unnamable," Criticism (Spring 1962), 4:134–47

Robinson, Michael, The Long Sonata of the Dead; A Study of
Samuel Beckett. 1969. p. 190–207 and 294–97

Vold, Jan Erik, Samuel Becketts Romaner, Samtiden (Sept.
1965), 74:441–47

Webb, Eugene, Samuel Beckett; A Study of His Novels. 1970.
p. 123–28

Watt, 1953

Barnard, G. C., Samuel Beckett; A New Approach. 1970. p. 16-30

Cohn, R., "Watt" in the Light of "The Castle," Comparative Literature (Spring 1961), 13:154-66

Freidman, Melvin J., The Novels of Samuel Beckett, Comparative Literature (Winter 1960), 12:47-58

Greenberg, Alvin, The Death of the Psyche; A Way to the Self in the Contemporary Novel, Criticism; A Quarterly for Literature and the Arts (Winter 1966), 8:1-18

Hesla, David H., The Shape of Chaos; An Interpretation of the Art of Samuel Beckett. 1971. p. 59-85

Hoefer, Jacqueline, Watt, Perspective (Autumn 1959), 11:166-82

Kenner, Hugh, Flaubert, Joyce and Beckett; The Stoic Comedians. 1962. p. 67-107

Lombardi, Thomas W., Who Tells Who "Watt,"? Chelsea (June 1968), 22/23:170-79

Robinson, Michael, The Long Sonata of the Dead; A Study of Samuel Beckett. 1969. p. 100-31

Senneff, Susan Field, Song and Music in Samuel Beckett's "Watt," Modern Fiction Studies (1964), 10:137-49

Warhaft, Sidney, Threne and Theme in "Watt," Wisconsin Studies in Contemporary Literature (1963), 4:261-78

Webb, Eugene, Samuel Beckett; A Study of His Novels. 1970. p. 56-71

WILLIAM BECKFORD

Vathek, 1786

Borges, Jorge Luis, Other Inquisitions, 1937-1952. 1964. p. 137-40

Folsom, James K., Beckford's "Vathek" and the Tradition of Oriental Satire, Criticism (1964), 6:53-69

Gemmett, Robert J., The Caliph Vathek from England and the Continent to America, American Book Collector (1968), 18:12-19

Grimm, Reinhold, "Vathek" in Deutschland: Zwei Zwischenfälle ohne Folgen? Revue de Littérature Comparée (1964), 38:127-35

Mouret, François J. L., "Le Vathek" de William Beckford et le "Voyáge d'Urien" de André Gide, Modern Language Review (Oct. 1969), 64:774-76

Rieger, James Henry, "Au Pied de la Lettre": Stylistic Un-
certainty in "Vathek," Criticism (1962), 4:302-12
Steeves, Harrison Ross, Before Jane Austen; The Shaping of
the English Novel in the Eighteenth Century. 1965. p. 226-
42

APHRA BEHN

Oroonoko, 1688

Ramsaran, J. A., "Oroonoko": A Study of Factual Elements,
Notes and Queries (1960), 7:142-45

ARNOLD BENNETT

Clayhanger, 1910

Hepburn, James G., The Two Worlds of Edwin Clayhanger,
Boston University Studies in English (1961), 5:246-55

Lord Raingo, 1926

Kennedy, James G., Reassuring Facts in "The Pretty Lady"
and "Lord Raingo," English Literature in Transition (1880-
1920) (1964), 7:131-42

Old Wives' Tale, 1908

Tillyard, Eustace Mandeville Wetenhall, Epic Strain in the
English Novel. 1958. p. 168-86

The Pretty Lady, 1918

Kennedy, James G., Reassuring Facts in "The Pretty Lady"
and "Lord Raingo," English Literature in Transition (1880-
1920) (1964), 7:131-42

Riceyman Steps, 1923

Durkin, Brian, Some New Lights on "Riceyman Steps," English
Literature in Transition (1880-1920) (1967), 10:66-80
Hepburn, James G., Some Curious Realism in "Riceyman
Steps," Modern Fiction Studies (Summer 1962), 8:116-26

ENOCH ARNOLD BENNETT

SEE

ARNOLD BENNETT

RICHARD DODDRIDGE BLACKMORE

Lorna Doone, 1869

   Budd, Kenneth, "Lorna Doone," a "Christian Novel," Blackmore Studies (1969), #1:2

ERIC BLAIR

SEE

GEORGE ORWELL

GEORGE HENRY BORROW

Lavengro, 1851

   Wethered, Herbert Newton, The Curious Art of Autobiography;
   From Benvenuto Cellini to Rudyard Kipling. 1956. p. 119-34

ELIZABETH BOWEN

Death of the Heart, 1938

   Bogan, Louise, Selected Criticism: Prose, Poetry. 1955. p.
   125-28
   Greene, George, Elizabeth Bowen: Imagination as Therapy,
   Perspective (Spring 1965), 14:42-52
   Heath, William, Elizabeth Bowen; An Introduction to Her
   Novels. 1961. p. 83-102
   Heinemann, Alison, The Indoor Landscape in Bowen's "The
   Death of the Heart," Critique; Studies in Modern Fiction
   (1968), 10:5-12
   Van Duyn, Mona, Pattern and Pilgrimage: A Reading of "The
   Death of the Heart," Critique; Studies in Modern Fiction
   (Spring-Summer 1961), 4:52-66

Eva Trout, 1969

   Elizabeth Bowen's New Novel, Times Literary Supplement
   (Jan. 30, 1969), p. 101
   Taylor, Elizabeth, The Progress of Eva, New Statesman (Jan.
   24, 1969), p. 119
   Wyndham, Francis, Eva Trout, London Magazine (March 1969),
   8:89-91

Friends and Relations, 1931

> Heath, William, Elizabeth Bowen: An Introduction to Her
> Novels. 1961. p. 51–58

The Heat of the Day, 1949

> Dorenkamp, Angela G., "Fall of Leap": Bowen's "The Heat of
> the Day," Critique: Studies in Modern Fiction (1968), 10:13–
> 21
> Greene, George, Elizabeth Bowen; Imagination as Therapy,
> Perspective (Spring 1965), 14:42–52
> Heath, William, Elizabeth Bowen; An Introduction to Her
> Novels. 1961. p. 108–24
> Marković, Vida E., The Changing Face; Disintegration of Per-
> sonality in the Twentieth Century British Novel, 1900–1950.
> 1970. p. 112–22

The Hotel, 1927

> Heath, William, Elizabeth Bowen; An Introduction to Her
> Novels. 1961. p. 21–33

The House in Paris, 1930

> Greene, George, Elizabeth Bowen; Imagination as Therapy,
> Perspective (Spring 1965), 14:42–52
> Heath, William, Elizabeth Bowen; An Introduction to Her
> Novels. 1961. p. 72–83

Last September, 1929

> Heath, William, Elizabeth Bowen; An Introduction to Her
> Novels. 1961. p. 32–46

The Little Girls, 1963

> Burgess, Anthony, Treasures and Fetters, Spectator (Feb. 21,
> 1964), #7078:254
> Greene, George, Elizabeth Bowen; Imagination as Therapy,
> Perspective (Spring 1965), 14:42–52

To the North, 1932

> Heath, William, Elizabeth Bowen; An Introduction to Her
> Novels. 1961. p. 58–70

A World of Love, 1955

> Fitzsimmons, T., World of Love, Sewanee Review (Spring
> 1955), 63:323–25

Wagner, Geoffrey, Elizabeth Bowen and the Artificial Novel,
Essays in Criticism (April 1963), 13:155-63

JOHN BRAINE

Room at the Top, 1957

Hurrell, John D., Class and Conscience in John Braine and
Kingsley Amis, Critique; Studies in Modern Fiction (Spring-
Summer 1958), 2:39-53
Schlüter, Kurt, Soziale Statussymbole und ihre Künstlerische
Verwendung in John Braines Roman "Room at the Top," Die
Neueren Sprachen (May 1963), #5:193-208

ANNE BRONTË

Agnes Grey, 1847

Craik, W. A., The Brontë Novels. 1968. p. 202-27
Gérin, Winifred, Anne Brontë. 1959. p. 125-27 and 230-33
Harrison, Ada and Derek Stanford, Anne Brontë; Her Life and
Work. 1959. p. 223-45

The Tenant of Wildfell Hall, 1848

Andrews, Sir Linton, A Challenge by Anne Brontë, Brontë
Society Transactions (1965), 14:25-30
Bell, A. Craig, Anne Brontë; A Re-Appraisal, Quarterly Re-
view (July 1966), 304:315-21
Ekeblad, Inga-Stina, "The Tenant of Wildfell Hall" and "Women
Beware Women," Notes and Queries (1963), 10:449-50
Gérin, Winifred, Anne Brontë. 1959. p. 235-58
Harrison, Ada and Derek Stanford, Anne Brontë; Her Life and
Work. 1959. p. 223-45

CHARLOTTE BRONTË

Jane Eyre, 1847

Burkhart, Charles, Another Key Word for "Jane Eyre," Nineteenth Century Fiction (Sept. 1961), 16:177-79
Bushnell, Nelson S., Artistic Economy in "Jane Eyre": A Contract with "The Old Manor House," English Language Notes
(March 1968), 5:197-202
Chesterton, Gilbert Keith, The Spice of Life and Other Essays.
1966. p. 85-89

Craik, W. A., The Brontë Novels. 1968. p. 70–122

Day, Martin S., Central Concepts of "Jane Eyre," Personalist (Autumn 1960), 41:495–505

Downing, Janay, Fire and Ice Imagery in "Jane Eyre," Paunch (Oct. 1966), #27:68–78

Ericksen, Donald H., Imagery as Structure in "Jane Eyre," Victorian Newsletter (Fall 1966), 30:18–22

Gérin, Winifred, Anne Brontë. 1959. p. 227–29

Gribble, Jennifer, Jane Eyre's Imagination, Nineteenth Century Fiction (Dec. 1968), 23:279–93

Hughes, R. E., "Jane Eyre": The Unbaptized Dionysos, Nineteenth Century Fiction (March 1964), 18:347–64

Karl, Frederick Robert, An Age of Fiction; The Nineteenth Century British Novel. 1964. p. 77–103

Knies, Earl A., The Art of Charlotte Brontë. 1969. p. 171–84 and 204–11

Knies, Earl A., The "I" of "Jane Eyre," College English (April 1966), 27:546–56

Kramer, Dale, Thematic Structure in "Jane Eyre," Papers on Language and Literature (1968), 4:288–98

Langford, Thomas, The Three Pictures in "Jane Eyre," Victorian Newsletter (Spring 1967), #31:47–48

Lodge, David, Language of Fiction; Essays in Criticism and Verbal Analysis of the English Novel. 1966. p. 114–43

Marshall, William H., The Self, the World and the Structure of "Jane Eyre," Revue des Langues Vivantes (1961), 27:416–25

Millgate, Jane, Jane Eyre's Progress, English Studies (1969), Supplement XXI–XXIX.

Millgate, Jane, Narrative Distance in "Jane Eyre": The Relevance of the Pictures, Modern Language Review (April 1968), 63:315–19

Monod, Sylvére, L'Imprécision dans "Jane Eyre," Etudes Anglaises (Jan.–March 1964), 17:21–29

Moser, Lawrence E., From Portrait to Person: A Note on the Surrealistic in "Jane Eyre," Nineteenth Century Fiction (Dec. 1965), 20:275–81

O'Neill, Judith, ed., Critics on Charlotte and Emily Brontë; Readings in Literary Criticism. 1968. p. 25–31

Prescott, Joseph, "Jane Eyre": A Romantic Exemplum with a Difference, Studies in English Literature (Oct. 1959), 36:1–13

Shannon, E. F., Jr., The Present Tense in "Jane Eyre," Nineteenth Century Fiction (1955), 10:141–45

Shapiro, Arnold, In Defense of "Jane Eyre," Studies in English

Literature, 1500–1900 (Autumn 1968), 8:681–98
Sherry, Norman, Charlotte and Emily Brontë. 1969. p. 51–70
Smith, David J., The Arrested Heart; Familial Love and Psychic Conflict in Five Mid-Victorian Novels, Dissertation Abstracts (Dec. 1966), 26:1839A
Smith, David J., Incest Patterns in Two Victorian Novels, Literature and Psychology (Summer 1965), 15:135–62
Solomon, Eric, "Jane Eyre": Fire and Water, College English (Dec. 1963), 25:215–17
Tillotson, Kathleen Mary, Novels of the 1840's. 1961. p. 257–313
Williams, Raymond, The English Novel; From Dickens to Lawrence. 1970. p. 60–74

The Professor, 1857

Craik, W. A., The Brontë Novels. 1968. p. 48–69
Gérin, Winifred, Anne Brontë. 1959. p. 224–27
Knies, Earl A., The Art of Charlotte Brontë. 1969. p. 88–98
Kooiman-Van Middendorp, Gerarda M., The Hero in the Feminine Novel. 1966. p. 60–78
Sherry, Norman, Charlotte and Emily Brontë. 1969. p. 41–50

Shirley, 1849

Briggs, Asa, Private and Social Themes in "Shirley," Brontë Society Transactions (1958), 13:203–19
Craik, W. A., The Brontë Novels. 1968. p. 123–57
Grayson, Laura, "Shirley": Charlotte Brontë's Own Evidence, Brontë Society Transactions (1963), 14:31
Holgate, Ivy, The Structure of "Shirley," Brontë Society Transactions (1962), 14:27–35
Jeffares, A. Norman, "Shirley"—A Yorkshire Novel, Brontë Society Transactions (1969), 15:281–93
Knies, Earl Allen, Art, Death and the Composition of "Shirley," Victorian Newsletter (Fall 1965), #28:122–24
Knies, Earl A., The Art of Charlotte Brontë. 1969. p. 144–67
Kooiman-Van Middendorp, Gerarda M., The Hero in the Feminine Novel. 1966. p. 60–78
Korg, Jacob, The Problem of Unity in "Shirley," Nineteenth Century Fiction (1957), 12:125–36
O'Neill, Judith, ed., Critics on Charlotte and Emily Brontë: Readings in Literary Criticism. 1968. p. 36–37
Passel, Anne W., The Three Voices in Charlotte Brontë's "Shirley," Brontë Society Transactions (1969), 15:323–26

Shapiro, Arnold, Public Themes and Private Lives: Social
Criticism in "Shirley," Papers on Language and Literature
(1968), 4:74-84

Sherry, Norman, Charlotte and Emily Brontë. 1969. p. 71-84

Tompkins, J. M. S., Caroline Helstone's Eyes, Brontë Society
Transactions (1961), 14:18-28

Villette, 1853

Brigham, Caroline, The Panzaic Principle in "Villette," Paunch
(Jan. 1965), #22:32-46

Burkhart, Charles, Brontë's "Villette," Explicator (1962), 21:
Item 8

Colby, Robert A., "Villette" and the Life of the Mind, Modern
Language Association. Publications (1960), 75:410-19

Coursen, Herbert R., Jr., Storm and Calm in "Villette," Discourse (Summer 1962), 5:318-33

Craik, W. A., The Brontë Novels. 1968. p. 158-201

Dunbar, Georgia S., Proper Names in "Villette," Nineteenth
Century Fiction (June 1960), 15:77-80

Evans, Joan, ed., The Flowering of the Middle Ages. 1966. p.
11-40

Goldfarb, Russell M., Sexual Repression and Victorian Literature. 1970. p. 139-57

Johnson, E. D. H., "Daring the Dread Glance": Charlotte
Brontë's Treatment of the Supernatural in "Villette," Nineteenth Century Fiction (March 1966), 20:325-36

Knies, Earl A., The Art of Charlotte Brontë. 1969. p. 171-
200

O'Neill, Judith, ed., Critics on Charlotte and Emily Brontë:
Readings in Literary Criticism. 1968. p. 38-47

Pascal, Roy, The Autobiographical Novel and the Autobiography, Essays in Criticism (April 1959), 9:134-50

Sherry, Norman, Charlotte and Emily Brontë. 1969. p. 85-100

Williams, Raymond, The English Novel; From Dickens to
Lawrence. 1970. p. 70-74

EMILY BRONTË

Wuthering Heights, 1847

Adams, Ruth M., Wuthering Heights: The Land East of Eden,
Nineteenth Century Fiction (June 1958), 13:58-62

Allott, Mirian, "Wuthering Heights": The Rejection of Heathcliff?, Essays in Criticism (Jan. 1958), 8:27-57

Ankenbrandt, Katherine W., Songs in "Wuthering Heights,"
  Southern Folklore Quarterly (1969), 33:92–115
Bell, Vereen M., "Wuthering Heights" and the Unforgivable
  Sin, Nineteenth Century Fiction (Sept. 1962), 17:188–91
Bell, Vereen M., "Wuthering Heights" as "Epos," College
  English (Dec. 1963), 25:199–208
Brick, Allan R., Lewe's Review of "Wuthering Heights," Nine-
  teenth Century Fiction (March 1960), 14:355–59
Brick, Allan R., "Wuthering Heights": Narrators, Audience
  and Message, College English (Nov. 1959), 21:80–86
Buchen, Irving H., Emily Brontë and the Metaphysics of Child-
  hood and Love, Nineteenth Century Fiction (1967), 22:63–70
Buchen, Irving H., Metaphysical and Social Evolution in
  "Wuthering Heights," Victorian Newsletter (Spring 1967),
  #31:15–20
Buckley, Vincent, Passion and Control in "Wuthering Heights,"
  Southern Review: An Australian Journal of Literary Studies
  (1964), 1:5–23
Carrère, Félix, "Les Hauts de Hurlevent" d'Emily Brontë:
  Histoire d'Amour?, Annales de la Faculté des Lettres d'Aix
  (1958), 32:75–89
Cecil, Lord David, Victorian Novelists; Essays in Revaluation.
  1958. p. 136–82
Champion, Larry S., Heathcliff: A Study in Authorial Tech-
  nique, Ball State University Forum (1968), 9:19–25
Cowhig, Ruth M., "Wuthering Heights": An Amoral Book?,
  Use of English (Winter 1965), 17:123–26
Craik, W. A., The Brontë Novels. 1968. p. 5–47
Davies, Cecil W., A Reading of "Wuthering Heights," Essays
  in Criticism (July 1969), 19:254–72
Dean, Christopher, Joseph's Speech in "Wuthering Heights,"
  Notes and Queries (Feb. 1960), 7:73–76
Devlin, James E., "Wuthering Heights": The Dominant Image,
  Discourse (Summer 1962), 5:337–46
Drew, Elizabeth A., The Novel; A Modern Guide to Fifteen
  English Masterpieces. 1963. p. 173–90
Drew, Philip, Charlotte Brontë as a Critic of "Wuthering
  Heights," Nineteenth Century Fiction (March 1964), 18:365–81
Fike, Francis, Bitter Herbs and Wholesome Medicines: Love
  as Theological Affirmation in "Wuthering Heights," Nine-
  teenth Century Fiction (Sept. 1968), 23:127–49
Fine, Ronald E., Lockwood's Dreams and the Key to "Wuthering
  Heights," Nineteenth Century Fiction (June 1969), 24:16–30

Ford, Boris, ed., The Pelican Guide to English Literature.
1958. Vol. 6. p. 256–73

Fraser, John, The Name of Action: Nelly Dean and "Wuthering
Heights," Nineteenth Century Fiction (Dec. 1965), 20:223–36

Gasquet, E., Structure et Point de Vue dans "Les Hauts de
Hurlevent," Études Anglaises et Americaines (1966), 3:115–
28

Gérin, Winifred, Anne Brontë. 1959. p. 226–29

Gleckner, Robert F., Time in "Wuthering Heights," Criticism
(Fall 1959), 1:328–38

Goldstone, Herbert, Wuthering Heights Revisited, English
Journal (April 1959), 48:175–85

Gose, Elliott B., Jr., "Wuthering Heights": The Heath and the
Hearth, Nineteenth Century Fiction (June 1966), 21:1–19

Grove, Robin, Wuthering Heights, Critical Review (1965), 8:
70–87

Hafley, James, The Villain in "Wuthering Heights," Nineteenth
Century Fiction (Dec. 1958), 13:199–215

Hagan, John, Control of Sympathy in "Wuthering Heights,"
Nineteenth Century Fiction (March 1967), 21:305–23

Image of the Work; Essays in Criticism by Bertram Evans and
others. 1955. p. 3–17

Jordan, John E., The Ironic Vision of Emily Brontë, Nineteenth
Century Fiction (June 1965), 20:1–18

Justus, James, Beyond Gothicism: "Wuthering Heights" and an
American Tradition, Tennessee Studies in Literature (1960),
5:25–33

Karl, Frederick Robert, An Age of Fiction; The Nineteenth
Century British Novel. 1964. p. 77–103

Kenney, Blair G., Nelly Dean's Witchcraft, Literature and
Psychology (1968), 18:225–32

Knoepflmacher, U. C., Laughter and Despair; Readings in Ten
Novels of the Victorian Era. 1971. p. 84–108

Kooiman-Van Middendorp, Gerarda M., The Hero in the Feminine Novel. 1966. p. 78–81

Langman, F. H., Wuthering Heights, Essays in Criticism (July
1965), 15:294–312

Lemon, C. H., Balthus and "Wuthering Heights," Brontë Society
Transactions (1969), 15:341–42

Lemon, Charles, Sickness and Health in "Wuthering Heights,"
Brontë Society Transactions (1963), 14:23–25

Livermore, Ann Lapraik, Byron and Emily Brontë, Quarterly
Review (July 1962), 300:337–44

McCaughey, G. S., An Approach to "Wuthering Heights,"
  Humanities Association Bulletin (1964), 15:28-34
McKay, Ruth M., Irish Heaths and German Cliffs: Study of
  the Foreign Sources of "Wuthering Heights," Brigham Young
  University Studies (Autumn 1965), 7:28-39
McKibben, Robert C., The Image of the Book in "Wuthering
  Heights," Nineteenth Century Fiction (Sept. 1960), 15:159-69
Madden, David, Chapter Seventeen of "Wuthering Heights,"
  English Record (Feb. 1967), 17:2-8
Maugham, William Somerset, Art of Fiction: An Introduction
  to Ten Novels and Their Authors. 1955. p. 215-43
Marshall, William H., Hareton Earnshaw: Natural Theology
  on the Moors, Victorian Newsletter (Spring 1962), #21:14-15
Mayne, Isobel, Emily Brontë's Mr. Lockwood, Brontë Society
  Transactions (1968), 15:207-13
Meier, T. K., "Wuthering Heights" and Violation of Class,
  Brontë Society Transactions (1968), 15:233-36
Moody, Philippa, The Challenge to Maturity in "Wuthering
  Heights," Melbourne Critical Review (1962), #5:27-39
Moser, Thomas, What Is the Matter with Emily Jane? Con-
  flicting Impulses in "Wuthering Heights," Nineteenth Century
  Fiction (June 1962), 17:1-19
Mixon, Ingeborg, A Note on the Pattern of "Wuthering Heights,"
  English Studies (Supplement 1964), 45:235-42
O'Neill, Judith, ed., Critics on Charlotte and Emily Brontë;
  Readings in Literary Criticism. 1968. p. 50-101
Pearsall, Robert Brainard, The Presiding Tropes of Emily
  Brontë, College English (1966), 27:267-73
Reynolds, Thomas, Division and Unity in "Wuthering Heights,"
  University Review (1965), 32:31-37
Shannon, Edgar F., Jr., Lockwood's Dreams and the Exegesis
  of "Wuthering Heights," Nineteenth Century Fiction (Sept.
  1959), 14:95-109
Shapiro, Arnold, "Wuthering Heights" as a Victorian Novel,
  Studies in the Novel (1969), 1:284-96
Sherry, Norman, Charlotte and Emily Brontë. 1969. p. 113-38
Smith, David J., The Arrested Heart; Familial Love and Psy-
  chic Conflict in Five Mid-Victorian Novels, Dissertation
  Abstracts (1966), 26:1839A
Smith, David, The Panelled Bed and the Unrepressible Wish of
  "Wuthering Heights," Paunch (1967), 30:40-47
Solomon, Eric, The Incest Theme in "Wuthering Heights,"
  Nineteenth Century Fiction (June 1959), 14:80-83

Thompson, Wade, Infanticide and Sadism in "Wuthering
Heights," Modern Language Association. Publications
(1963), 78:69-74

Waddington-Feather, John B., Emily Brontë's Use of Dialect
in "Wuthering Heights," Brontë Society Transactions (1966),
15:12-19

Williams, Raymond, The English Novel; From Dickens to
Lawrence. 1970. p. 63-69

Willson, Jo Anne A., "The Butterfly" and "Wuthering Heights":
A Mystic's Escatology, Victorian Newsletter (Spring 1968),
#33:22-25

Woodring, Carl, The Narrators of "Wuthering Heights," Nineteenth Century Fiction (1957), 11:298-305

Worth, George J., Emily Brontë's Mr. Lockwood, Nineteenth
Century Fiction (March 1958), 12:315-20

Wright, Austin, ed., Victorian Literature; Modern Essays in
Criticism. 1961. p. 86-97

EDWARD GEORGE EARLE BULWER-LYTTON

Eugene Aram, 1832

Hunt, Leigh, Leigh Hunt's Literary Criticism. 1956. p. 394-
400

The Last Days of Pompeii, 1834

Simmons, J. C., Bulwer and Vesuvius: The Topicality of "The
Last Days of Pompeii," Nineteenth Century Fiction (June
1969), 24:98-102

Rienzi, 1835

Rathburn, Robert C. and Martin Sternmann, Jr., eds., From
Jane Austen to Joseph Conrad. 1958. p. 66-71

A Strange Story, 1862

Fradin, Joseph I., "The Absorbing Tyranny of Every-Day Life":
Bulwer-Lytton's "A Strange Story," Nineteenth Century Fiction (June 1961), 16:1-16

JOHN BUNYAN

Pilgrim's Progress from This World to the World Which Is to
Come, 1678

Alpaugh, David J., Emblem and Interpretation in "The Pilgrim's Progress," ELH (Sept. 1966), 33:299–314

Blondel, Jacques, Allégorie et Réalisme dans "The Pilgrim's Progress" de John Bunyan, Archives des Lettres Modernes (1959), #28

Cobau, William Weinschenk, Rhetorical Modes in "The Pilgrim's Progress": John Bunyan's Quest for Literary Art, Dissertation Abstracts (1965), 26:1037–38

Downs, Robert Bingham, Molders of the Modern Mind; One Hundred Eleven Books that Shaped Western Civilization. 1961. p. 84–87

Forrest, James F., Bunyan's Ignorance and the Flatterer: A Study of the Literary Art of Damnation, Studies in Philology (Jan. 1963), 60:12–22

Jauss, Hans Robert and Dieter Schaller, eds., Medium Aevum Vivum: Festschrift für Walther Bulst. 1960. p. 279–304

Kaufmann, Urlin Milo, A Study of Bunyan's "Pilgrim's Progress" in the Light of Puritan Traditions of Meditation, Dissertation Abstracts (1965), 26:5413

Lewis, Clive Staples, Selected Literary Essays. 1969. p. 146–53

Lewis, Clive Staples, The Vision of John Bunyan: "The Pilgrim's Progress," Listener (Dec. 13, 1962), 68:1006–08

McNair, Walter Edward, John Bunyan's Use of Symbols in "The Pilgrim's Progress," Dissertation Abstracts (1959), 19:2956–57

O'Neil, Robert Morris, The Role of Christian in "Pilgrim's Progress," Dissertation Abstracts (1964), 25:2986–87

Price, Lawrence Marsden, The Pilgrim Journeys of Bunyan and Heinrich Jung-Stilling, Comparative Literature (Winter 1960), 12:14–18

Reeves, Paschal, "The Pilgrim's Progress" as a Precursor of the Novel, Georgia Review (1966), 20:64–71

Rexroth, Kenneth, Classics Revisited. 1968. p. 200–04

Rupp, Ernest Gordon, Six Makers of English Religion, 1500–1700. 1957. p. 92–101

Santa Maria, Felixberto C., An Audience Analysis of John Bunyan's "Pilgrim's Progress," Dissertation Abstracts (1962), 23:2119–20

Steeves, Harrison Ross, Before Jane Austen; The Shaping of the English Novel in the Eighteenth Century. 1965. p. 6–21

Tillyard, Eustace Mandeville Wetenhall, English Epic and Its Background. 1954. p. 386–406

ANTHONY BURGESS

Clockwork Orange, 1962

    Aggeler, Geoffrey, The Comic Art of Anthony Burgess, <u>Ari</u>-<u>zona Quarterly</u> (1969), 25:234—51
    Pritchard, William H., The Novels of Anthony Burgess, <u>Massachusettes Review</u> (Summer 1966), 7:525—39

Enderby, 1963

    Aggeler, Geoffrey, Mr. Enderby and Mr. Burgess, <u>Malahat</u> <u>Review</u> (April 1969), #10:104—10

Honey for the Bears, 1963

    Pritchard, William H., The Novels of Anthony Burgess, <u>Massachusettes Review</u> (Summer 1966), 7:525—39

Nothing Like the Sun, 1964

    Aggeler, Geoffrey, The Comic Art of Anthony Burgess, <u>Ari</u>-<u>zona Quarterly</u> (1969), 25:234—51
    McCormack, Thomas, ed., <u>Afterwords; Novelists on Their</u> <u>Novels</u>. 1968. p. 28—47

The Right to an Answer, 1960

    Bergonzi, Bernard, The Situation of the Novel. 1970. p. 180—82
    Pritchard, William H., The Novels of Anthony Burgess, <u>Massachusettes Review</u> (Summer 1966), 7:525—39

Time for a Tiger, 1956

    Aggeler, Geoffrey, The Comic Art of Anthony Burgess, <u>Ari</u>-<u>zona Quarterly</u> (1969), 25:234—51
    Pritchard, William H., The Novels of Anthony Burgess, <u>Massachusettes Review</u> (Summer 1966), 7:525—39

Tremor of Intent, 1966

    Aggeler, Geoffrey, The Comic Art of Anthony Burgess, <u>Ari</u>-<u>zona Quarterly</u> (1969), 25:234—51

The Wanting Seed, 1962

    Aggeler, Geoffrey, The Comic Art of Anthony Burgess, <u>Ari</u>-<u>zona Quarterly</u> (1969), 25:234—51
    Bergonzi, Bernard, <u>The Situation of the Novel</u>. 1970. p. 185—87

Pritchard, William H., The Novels of Anthony Burgess,
Massachusettes Review (Summer 1966), 7:525–39

FANNY BURNEY

Cecilia; or, Memoirs of an Heiress, 1796

Kooiman-Van Middendorp, Gerarda M., The Hero in the
Feminine Novel. 1966. p. 24–30
Moler, Kenneth L., Fanny Burney's "Cecilia" and Jane
Austen's "Jack and Alice," English Language Notes (1965),
3:40–42

Evelina; or, A Young Lady's Entrance into the World, 1778

Erickson, James P., "Evelina" and "Betsy Thoughtless," Texas
Studies in Literature and Language (1964), 6:96–103
Hoyt, Charles Alva, ed., Minor British Novelists. 1967. p.
3–12
Kooiman-Van Middendorp, Gerarda M., The Hero in the
Feminine Novel. 1966. p. 24–30
Malone, Kemp, "Evelina" Revisited, Papers on English Lan-
guage and Literature (Winter 1965), 1:3–19
Steeves, Harrison Ross, Before Jane Austen; The Shaping of
the English Novel in the Eighteenth Century. 1965. p. 204–
25
Swinnerton, Frank Arthur, A Galaxy of Fathers. 1966. p.
103–08

The Wanderer; or, Female Difficulties, 1814

Bugnot, S., "The Wanderer" de Fanny Burney: Essai de
Réhabilitation, (July–Sept. 1962), 15:225–32

GEORGE DOUGLAS BROWN

SEE

GEORGE DOUGLAS

SAMUEL BUTLER

The Way of All Flesh, 1903

Dyson, Anthony Edward, The Crazy Fabric; Essays in Irony.
1965. p. 112–37

Hoggart, Richard, Speaking to Each Other; Essays. Vol. 2.
    1970. p. 144-68
Howard, Daniel F., The Critical Significance of Autobiography
    in "The Way of All Flesh," Victorian Newsletter (Spring
    1960), #17:1-4
Karl, Frederick Robert, An Age of Fiction; The Nineteenth
    Century British Novel. 1964. p. 323-48
Knoepflmacher, Ulrich C., "Ishmael" or Anti-Hero? The
    Division of Self: "The Way of All Flesh," English Literature
    in Transition (1880-1920) (1961), 4:28-35
Knoepflmacher, Ulrich C., Laughter and Despair: Readings in
    Ten Novels of the Victorian Age. 1971. p. 202-39
Knoepflmacher, Ulrich C., Religious Humanism and the Victo-
    rian Novel: George Eliot, Walter Pater, and Samuel Butler.
    1965. p. 257-95
Lind, Ilse Dusoir, "The Way of All Flesh" and "A Portrait of
    the Artist as a Young Man": A Comparison, Victorian News-
    letter (1957), #9:7-10
Marshall, William H., The Use of Symbols in "The Way of All
    Flesh," Tennessee Studies in Literature (1965), 10:109-21
Marshall, William H., "The Way of All Flesh": The Dual
    Function of Edward Overton, Texas Studies in Literature
    and Language (1963), 4:583-90
Noon, William T., Three Young Men in Rebellion, Thought
    (1963), 38:559-77
Pritchett, Victor Sawdon, The Living Novel and Later Appre-
    ciation. 1964. p. 140-47
Quinn, Sister Many Bernetta, Ernest Pontifex as Anti-Hero,
    English Literature in Transition (1880-1920) (1962), 5:3-31
Schweitzer, Joan, "David Copperfield" and Ernest Pontifex,
    Dickensian (1967), 63:42-45
Zabel, Morton Danwen, Craft and Character: Texts, Methods
    and Vocation in Modern Fiction. 1957. p. 97-113

LEWIS CARROLL

Alice's Adventures in Wonderland, 1865

Egoff, Sheila, G. T. Stubbs, and L. F. Ashley, eds., Only Con-
    nect; Readings on Children's Literature. 1969. p. 150-55
Fadiman, Clifton, Party of One; The Selected Writings of
    Clifton Fadiman. 1955. p. 404-10
Holmes, Roger W., The Philosopher's "Alice in Wonderland,"
    Antioch Review (Summer 1959), 19:133-49

Leach, Elsie, "Alice in Wonderland" in Perspective, Victorian
    Newsletter (Spring 1964), #25:9–11
Lehmann, John, "Alice in Wonderland" and Its Sequel, Revue
    des Langues Vivantes (1966), 32:115–30
Levin, Harry, Wonderland Revisited, Kenyon Review (Autumn
    1965), 27:591–616
Phillips, William, ed., Art and Psychoanalysis. 1957. p. 185–
    217
Rackin, Donald, "Alice's Journey to the End of Night, Modern
    Language Association. Publications (1966), 8:313–26
Rackin, Donald, Corrective Laughter; Carroll's."Alice" and
    Popular Children's Literature of the Nineteenth Century,
    Journal of Popular Culture (1967), 1:243–55

Through the Looking-Glass, 1871

O'Brien, H. B., Alice's Journey in "Through the Looking-
    Glass," Notes and Queries (Oct. 1967), 14:380–82 and (June
    1969), 16:217–18
Priestley, James Boynton, Walrus and the Carpenter; Political
    Symbolism in "Through the Looking-Glass," New Statesman
    (Aug. 10, 1957), 54:168

JOYCE CARY

African Witch, 1936

Barba, Henry, Image of the African in Transition, University
    of Kansas City Review (March 1963), 29:215–21 and (June
    1963), 29:291–96
Collins, Harold R., Joyce Cary's Troublesome Africans,
    Antioch Review (Sept. 1953), 13:397–406
Hall, Alan, The African Novels of Joyce Cary, Standpunte
    (March–April 1958), 12:40–55
Hoffman, Charles G., Joyce Cary's African Novels, South
    Atlantic Quarterly (Spring 1963), 62:229–43
Steinbrecher, George J., Joyce Cary: Master Novelist, Col-
    lege English (May 1957), 18:387–95

Aissa Saved, 1932

Collins, Harold R., Joyce Cary's Troublesome Africans,
    Antioch Review (Sept. 1953), 13:397–406
Hall, Alan, The African Novels of Joyce Cary, Standpunte
    (March–April 1958), 12:40–55
Hoffman, Charles G., Joyce Cary's African Novels, South

Atlantic Quarterly (Spring 1963), 62:229−43
Steinbrecher, George J., Joyce Cary: Master Novelist, College English (May 1957), 18:387−95

An American Visitor, 1933

Collins, Harold R., Joyce Cary's Troublesome Africans,
Antioch Review (Sept. 1953), 13:397−406
French, Warren G., Joyce Cary's American Rover Girl, Texas
Studies in Literature and Language (Autumn 1960), 2:281−91
Hall, Alan, The African Novels of Joyce Cary, Standpunte
(March−April 1958), 12:40−55
Hoffman, Charles G., Joyce Cary's African Novels, South
Atlantic Quarterly (Spring 1963), 62:229−43
Steinbrecher, George J., Joyce Cary; Master Novelist, Col-
lege English (May 1957), 18:387−95

The Captive and the Free, 1959

Adams, Hazard, Joyce Cary: Posthumous Volumes and Criti-
cism to Date, Texas Studies in Literature and Language
(Summer 1959), 1:289−99
Cosman, Max, The Protean Joyce Cary, Commonweal (March
6, 1959), 69:596−98
Hicks, Granville, Joyce Cary's Last Novel, Saturday Review
(June 3, 1949), 42:14
Hoffmann, Charles G., "The Captive and the Free": Joyce
Cary's Unfinished Trilogy, Texas Studies in Literature and
Language (1963), 5:17−24
Watson, Kenneth, "The Captive and the Free": Artist, Child
and Society in the World of Joyce Cary, English (Summer
1966), 16:49−54

Castle Corner, 1938

Hoffmann, Charles G., "They Want to Be Happy": Joyce Cary's
Unfinished "Castle Corner" Series, Modern Fiction Studies
(Autumn 1963), 9:217−25
Stevenson, Lionel, Joyce Cary and the Anglo-Irish Tradition,
Modern Fiction Studies (Autumn 1963), 9:210−16
Weintraub, Stanley, "Castle Corner": Joyce Cary's "Budden-
brooks," Wisconsin Studies in Contemporary Literature
(Winter−Spring 1964), 5:54−63
Woodcock, George, Citizens of Babel: A Study of Joyce Cary,
Queen's Quarterly (Summer 1956), 63:236−46

Except the Lord, 1953

Bettman, Elizabeth R., Joyce Cary and the Problem of Political Morality, Antioch Review (Summer 1957), 16:266–72

Gindin, James, Harvest of a Quiet Eye; The Novel of Compassion. 1971. p. 265–70

Hoffman, Charles G., Joyce Cary: Art and Reality, University
of Kansas City Review (1960), 26:273–82

Kerr, Elizabeth M., Joyce Cary's Second Trilogy, University
of Toronto Quarterly (April 1960), 29:310–25

King, Carlyle, Joyce Cary and the Creative Imagination,
Tamarach Review (1959), #10:39–51

Mitchell, Giles, Joyce Cary's "Except the Lord," Arlington
Quarterly (Autumn 1969), 2:71–82

Steinbrecher, George, Jr., Joyce Cary: Master Novelist, College English (May 1957), 18:387–95

Teeling, John, Joyce Cary's Moral World, Modern Fiction
Studies (Autumn 1963), 9:276–83

A Fearful Joy, 1945

Eastman, Richard M., Historical Grace in Cary's "A Fearful
Joy," Novel: A Forum on Fiction (1968), 1:150–57

Gindin, James, Harvest of a Quiet Eye: The Novel of Compassion. 1971. p. 273–75

McCormick, John, Catastrophe and Imagination: A Reinterpretation of the Recent English and American Novel. 1957.
p. 151–54

Morras, Sidney, What to Do with a Drunken Sailor, Hudson
Review (Autumn 1950), 3:466–74

Pittock, Malcolm, Joyce Cary: "A Fearful Joy," Essays in
Criticism (Oct. 1963), 13:428–32

Prescott, Orville, In My Opinion. 1952. p. 180–99

Herself Surprised, 1941

Adams, Hazard, Blake and Gulley Jimson: English Symbolists,
Critique; Studies in Modern Fiction (1959), 3:3–14

Adams, Hazard, Joyce Cary's Three Speakers, Modern Fiction
Studies (1959–60), 5:108–20

Brawer, Judith, The Triumph of Defeat: A Study of Joyce
Cary's "First Trilogy," Texas Studies in Literature and Language (1969), 10:629–34

Faber, Kathleen R. and M. D. Faber, An Important Theme of
Joyce Cary's Trilogy, Discourse (1968), 11:26–31

Garant, Jeanne, Joyce Cary's Portrait of the Artist, Revue des Langues Vivantes (1958), 24:476-86

Gindin, James, Harvest of a Quiet Eye; The Novel of Compassion. 1971. p. 265-70

Hall, James, The Tragic Comedians: Seven Modern British Novelists. 1963. p. 82-98

Hamilton, Kenneth, Boon or Thorn? Joyce Cary and Samuel Beckett on Human Life, Dalhousie Review (Winter 1959), 38:433-42

Hardy, Barbara, Form in Joyce Cary's Novels, Essays in Criticism (April 1954), 4:180-90

Hoffmann, Charles G., The Genesis and Development of Joyce Cary's First Trilogy, Modern Language Association. Publications (Sept. 1963), 78:431-39

Hoffmann, Charles G., Joyce Cary and the Comic Mask, Western Humanities Review (Spring 1959), 13:135-42

Hoffmann, Charles G., Joyce Cary: Art and Reality, University of Kansas City Review (1960), 26:273-82

Johnson, Pamela Hansford, Three Novelists and the Drawing of Character, Essays and Studies by Members of the English Association (1950), n.s.3:82-99

King, Carlyle, Joyce Cary and the Creative Imagination, Tamarack Review (1959), #10:39-51

Mitchell, Giles Raymond, The Art Theme in Joyce Cary's First Trilogy, Dissertation Abstracts (1965), 26:1652

Morras, Sidney, What to Do with a Drunken Sailor, Hudson Review (Autumn 1950), 3:466-74

Mustanoja, Tauno, Two Painters: Joyce Cary and Gulley Jimson, Neuphilologische Mitteilungen (1960), 61:221-44

Oppel, Horst, ed., Der Moderne Englische Roman: Interpretationen. 1965. p. 282-300

Prescott, Orville, In My Opinion. 1952. p. 180-99

Reed, Peter John, Trial by Discard: Joyce Cary's First Trilogy, Dissertation Abstracts (1965), 26:4672

Steinbrecher, George, Jr., Joyce Cary: Master Novelist, College English (May 1957), 18:387-95

Stockholder, Fred, The Triple Vision in Joyce Cary's First Trilogy, Modern Fiction Studies (Autumn 1963), 9:231-44

Van Horn, Ruth G., Freedom and Imagination in the Novels of Joyce Cary, Midwest Journal (1952-53), 5:19-30

The Horse's Mouth, 1944

Adams, Hazard, Blake and Gulley Jimson: English Symbolists,

Critique: Studies in Modern Fiction (Spring–Fall 1959),
3:3–14

Adams, Hazard, Joyce Cary's Three Speakers, Modern Fiction
Studies (Summer 1959), 5:108–20

Adams, Robert H., Freedom in "The Horse's Mouth," College
English (March 1965), 26:451–60

Allen, Walter, Reading a Novel. 1956. p. 434–36

Alter, Robert, Rogue's Progress; Studies in the Picaresque
Novel. 1964. p. 106–32

Brawer, Judith, The Triumph of Defeat: A Study of Joyce
Cary's First Trilogy, Texas Studies in Literature and Language (1969), 10:629–34

Faber, Kathleen R. and M. D. Faber, An Important Theme of
Joyce Cary's Trilogy, Discourse (1968), 11:26–31

Garant, Jeanne, Joyce Cary's Portrait of the Artist, Revue des
Langues Vivantes (1958), 24:476–86

Gindin, James, Harvest of a Quiet Eye; The Novel of Compassion. 1971. p. 265–70

Hall, James, The Tragic Comedians; Seven Modern British
Novelists. 1963. p. 82–98

Hamilton, Kenneth, Boon or Thorn? Joyce Cary and Samuel
Beckett on Human Life, Dalhousie Review (Winter 1959),
38:433–42

Hardy, Barbara, Form in Joyce Cary's Novels, Essays in
Criticism (April 1954), 4:180–90

Hoffmann, Charles G., The Genesis and Development of Joyce
Cary's First Trilogy, Modern Language Association. Publications (Sept. 1963), 78:431–39

Hoffmann, Charles G., Joyce Cary and the Comic Mask, Western Humanities Review (Spring 1959), 13:135–42

Hoffmann, Charles G., Joyce Cary: Art and Reality, University of Kansas City Review (1960), 26:273–82

Johnson, Pamela Hansford, Three Novelists and the Drawing
of Character, Essays and Studies by Members of the English
Association (1950), n.s.3:82–99

Jones, Ernest, The Double View, Nation (Feb. 25, 1950), 170:
184–86

Karl, Frederick R., Joyce Cary: The Moralist as Novelist,
Twentieth Century Literature (Jan. 1960), 5:183–96

King, Carlyle, Joyce Cary and the Creative Imagination,
Tamarack Review (1959), #10:39–51

Marković, Vida E., The Changing Face: Disintegration of
Personality in the Twentieth Century British Novel, 1900–

1950. 1970. p. 123-37

Mitchell, Giles Raymond, The Art Theme in Joyce Cary's
First Trilogy, Dissertation Abstracts (1965), 26:1652

Morras, Sidney, What to Do with a Drunken Sailor, Hudson
Review (Autumn 1950), 3:466-74

Mustanoja, Tauno, Two Painters: Joyce Cary and Gulley
Jimson, Neuphilologische Mitteilungen (1960), 61:221-44

Oppel, Horst, ed., Der Moderne Englische Roman: Interpretationen. 1965. p. 262-300

Prescott, Orville, In My Opinion. 1952. p. 180-99

Ready, William B., Joyce Cary, Critic (June-July 1960),
18:9-10, 59-60

Reed, Peter John, Trial by Discard: Joyce Cary's First
Trilogy, Dissertation Abstracts (1965), 26:4672

Ryan, Marjorie, An Interpretation of Joyce Cary's "The
Horse's Mouth," Critique; Studies in Modern Fiction (Spring-
Summer 1958), 2:29-38

Steinbrecher, George, Jr., Joyce Cary: Master Novelist, College English (May 1957), 18:387-95

Stockholder, Fred, The Triple Vision in Joyce Cary's First
Trilogy, Modern Fiction Studies (Autumn 1963), 9:231-44

Van Horn, Ruth G., Freedom and Imagination in the Novels of
Joyce Cary, Midwest Journal (1952-53), 5:19-30

Woodcock, George, Citizens of Babel: A Study of Joyce Cary,
Queen's Quarterly (Summer 1956), 63:236-46

A House of Children, 1941

Stevenson, Lionel, Joyce Cary and the Anglo-Irish Tradition,
Modern Fiction Studies (Autumn 1963), 9:210-16

Mr. Johnson, 1939

Barba, Henry, Image of the African in Transition, University
of Kansas City Review (March 1963), 29:215-21 and (June
1963), 29:291-96

Collins, Harold R., Joyce Cary's Troublesome Africans,
Antioch Review (Sept. 1953), 13:397-406

Fyfe, Christopher, The Colonial Situation in "Mr. Johnson,"
Modern Fiction Studies (1963), 9:226-30

Gindin, James, Harvest of a Quiet Eye; The Novel of Compassion. 1971. p. 262-64

Hall, Alan, The African Novels of Joyce Cary, Standpunte
(March-April 1958), 12:40-55

Hoffmann, Charles G., Joyce Cary's African Novels, South

Atlantic Quarterly (Spring 1963), 62:229–43

Kernoli, Arthur, The European Image of Africa and the
African, Busara (1969), 2:51–53

Moore, Gerald, "Mr. Johnson" Reconsidered, Black Orpheus
(Oct. 1958), #4:16–23

Prescott, Orville, In My Opinion. 1952. p. 180–99

Raskin, Jonas, The Mythology of Imperialism. 1971. p. 294–
309

Smith, B. R., Moral Evaluation in "Mr. Johnson," Critique;
Studies in Modern Fiction (1965), 11:101–10

Steinbrecher, George, Jr., Joyce Cary: Master Novelist,
College English (May 1957), 18:387–95

Woodcock, George, Citizens of Babel: A Study of Joyce Cary,
Queen's Quarterly (Summer 1956), 63:236–46

The Moonlight, 1946

Hardy, Barbara, Form in Joyce Cary's Novels, Essays in
Criticism (April 1954), 4:180–90

King, Carlyle, Joyce Cary and the Creative Imagination,
Tamarack Review (1959), #10:39–51

Not Honour More, 1955

Battaglia, Francis J., Spurious Armageddon: Joyce Cary's
"Not Honour More," Modern Fiction Studies (Winter 1967–
68), 13:479–91

Bettman, Elizabeth R., Joyce Cary and the Problem of Political Morality, Antioch Review (Summer 1957), 17:266–72

Gindin, James, Harvest of a Quiet Eye; The Novel of Compassion. 1971. p. 265–70

Hoffmann, Charles G., Joyce Cary: Art and Reality, University of Kansas City Review (1960), 26:273–82

Kerr, Elizabeth M., Joyce Cary's Second Trilogy, University
of Toronto Quarterly (April 1960), 29:310–25

King, Carlyle, Joyce Cary and the Creative Imagination,
Tamarack Review (1959), #10:39–51

Steinbrecher, George, Jr., Joyce Cary: Master Novelist,
College English (May 1957), 18:387–95

Teeling, John, Joyce Cary's Moral World, Modern Fiction
Studies (Autumn 1963), 9:276–85

Prisoner of Grace, 1952

Bettman, Elizabeth R., Joyce Cary and the Problem of Political Morality, Antioch Review (Summer 1957), 17:266–72

Gindin, James, Harvest of a Quiet Eye; The Novel of Compassion. 1971. p. 265-70

Hoffmann, Charles G., Joyce Cary: Art and Reality, University of Kansas City Review (1960), 26:273-82

Kerr, Elizabeth M., Joyce Cary's Second Trilogy, University of Toronto Quarterly (April 1960), 29:310-25

King, Carlyle, Joyce Cary and the Creative Imagination, Tamarack Review (1959), #10:39-51

Mitchell, Giles, Joyce Cary's "Prisoner of Grace," Modern Fiction Studies (Autumn 1963), 9:263-75

Steinbrecher, George, Jr., Joyce Cary: Master Novelist, College English (May 1957), 18:387-95

Teeling, John, Joyce Cary's Moral World, Modern Fiction Studies (Autumn 1963), 9:276-83

Woodcock, George, Citizens of Babel: A Study of Joyce Cary, Queen's Quarterly (Summer 1956), 63:236-46

To Be a Pilgrim, 1942

Adams, Hazard, Joyce Cary's Three Speakers, Modern Fiction Studies (Summer 1959), 5:108-20

Brawer, Judith, The Triumph of Defeat: A Study of Joyce Cary's First Trilogy, Texas Studies in Literature and Language (1969), 10:629-34

Faber, Kathleen R. and M. D. Faber, An Important Theme in Joyce Cary's Trilogy, Discourse (1968), 11:26-31

Garrant, Jeanne, Joyce Cary's Portrait of the Artist, Revue des Langues Vivantes (1958), 24:476-86

Gindin, James, Harvest of a Quiet Eye; The Novel of Compassion. 1971. p. 265-70

Hall, James, The Tragic Comedians: Seven Modern British Novelists. 1963. p. 82-98

Hamilton, Kenneth, Boon or Thorn? Joyce Cary and Samuel Beckett on Human Life, Dalhousie Review (Winter 1959), 38:433-42

Hardy, Barbara, Form in Joyce Cary's Novels, Essays in Criticism (April 1954), 4:180-90

Hoffmann, Charles G., The Genesis and Development of Joyce Cary's First Trilogy, Modern Language Association. Publications (Sept. 1963), 78:431-39

Hoffmann, Charles G., Joyce Cary and the Comic Mask, Western Humanities Review (Spring 1959), 13:135-42

Hoffmann, Charles G., Joyce Cary: Art and Reality, University of Kansas City Review (1960), 26:273-82

Johnson, Pamela Hansford, Three Novelists and the Drawing of Character, Essays and Studies by Members of the English Association (1950), n.s.3:82-99

King, Carlyle, Joyce Cary and the Creative Imagination, Tamarack Review (1959), #10:39-51

Lyons, Richard S., Narrative Method in Cary's "To Be a Pilgrim," Texas Studies in Literature and Language (1964), 6:269-79

Mitchell, Giles Raymond, The Art Theme in Joyce Cary's First Trilogy, Dissertation Abstracts (1965), 26:1652

Morras, Sidney, What to Do with a Drunken Sailor, Hudson Review (Autumn 1950), 3:466-74

Oppel, Horst, ed., Der Moderne Englische Roman: Interpretationen. 1965. p. 262-300

Prescott, Orville, In My Opinion. 1952. p. 180-99

Reed, Peter John, Holding Back: Joyce Cary's "To Be a Pilgrim," Contemporary Literature (Winter 1969), 10:103-16

Reed, Peter John, Trial by Discard: Joyce Cary's First Trilogy, Dissertation Abstracts (1965), 26:4672

Shapiro, Stephen A., Joyce Cary's "To Be a Pilgrim": Mr. Facing-Both-Ways, Texas Studies in Literature and Language (Spring 1966), 8:81-91

Steinbrecher, George, Jr., Joyce Cary: Master Novelist, College English (May 1957), 18:387-95

Stockholder, Fred, The Triple Vision in Joyce Cary's First Trilogy, Modern Fiction Studies (Autumn 1963), 9:231-44

Van Horn, Ruth G., Freedom and Imagination in the Novels of Joyce Cary, Midwest Journal (1952-53), 5:19-30

GILBERT KEITH CHESTERTON

The Man Who Was Thursday, 1908

Albérès, R. M., Chesterton Contre le Pessimisme, Revue de Paris (March 1969), 76:60-69

WILKIE COLLINS

The Moonstone, 1868

Lawson, Lewis A., Wilkie Collins and "The Moonstone," American Imago (Winter 1962), 19:61-79

Wolfe, Peter, Point of View and Characterization in Wilkie Collins's "The Moonstone," Forum (Houston) (Summer 1965), 4:27-29

The Woman in White, 1860

    Wright, Austin, Victorian Literature; Modern Essays in
    Criticism. 1961. p. 128–35

IVY COMPTON-BURNETT

Brothers and Sisters, 1929

    May, James Boyer, Ivy Compton-Burnett: A Time Exposure,
    Trace (Summer 1963), #49:92–99

Darkness and Day, 1951

    Curtis, Mary M., The Moral Comedy of Miss Compton-Burnett,
    Wisconsin Studies in Contemporary Literature (Autumn 1964),
    5:213–21

A Family and A Fortune, 1939

    Gold, Joseph, Exit Everybody; The Novels of Ivy Compton-
    Burnett, Dalhousie Review (Summer 1962), 42:227–38
    McCarthy, Mary Therese, The Writing on the Wall and Other
    Literary Essays. 1970. p. 145–52

A God and His Gifts, 1963

    Brophy, Brigid, Don't Never Forget; Collected Views and Re-
    Reviews. 1967. p. 167–70
    McCarthy, Mary, The Inventions of Ivy Compton-Burnett,
    Encounter (November 1966), 27:19–31
    T. L. S., Essays and Reviews from the Times Literary Supple-
    ment. 1963. V. 2. p. 178–80

The Mighty and Their Fall, 1961

    Curtis, Mary M., The Moral Comedy of Miss Compton-Burnett,
    Wisconsin Studies in Contemporary Literature (Autumn 1964),
    5:213–21

Mother and Son, 1955

    Gold, Joseph, Exit Everybody: The Novels of Ivy Compton-
    Burnett, Dalhousie Review (Summer 1962), 42:227–38
    West, Anthony, Principles and Persuasions; The Literary
    Essays of Anthony West. 1957. p. 225–32

Pastors and Masters, 1925

    Gold, Joseph, Exit Everybody; The Novels of Ivy Compton-

Burnett, Dalhousie Review (Summer 1962), 42:227–38
Greenfield, Stanley B., "Pastors and Masters": The Spoils of
Genius, Criticism (1960), 2:66–80

JOSEPH CONRAD

Almayer's Folly, 1895

Allen, Jerry, Conrad's River, Columbia University Forum
(Winter 1962), 5:29–35
Altick, Richard, The Scholar Adventurers. 1950. p. 289–97
Andreas, Osborne, Joseph Conrad; A Study in Non-Conformity.
1959. p. 5–9
Baines, Jocelyn, Joseph Conrad; A Critical Biography. 1960.
p. 142–55
Dowden, Wilfred S., "Almayer's Folly" and "Lord Jim": A
Study in the Development of Conrad's Imagery, Rice Univer-
sity Studies (Winter 1965), 51:13–27
Dowden, Wilfred S., Joseph Conrad: The Imaged Style. 1970.
p. 15–21
Friedman, Alan, The Turn of the Novel. 1966. p. 75–105
Guerard, Albert J., Conrad the Novelist. 1958. p. 70–78 and
81–85
Guetti, James L., Jr., The Rhetoric of Joseph Conrad. 1960.
p. 9–16
Gurko, Leo, Joseph Conrad at the Crossroads, University of
Kansas City Review (Dec. 1958), 25:83–90
Gurko, Leo, Joseph Conrad: Giant in Exile. 1962. p. 50–57
Gurko, Leo, Conrad's First Battleground; "Almayer's Folly,"
University of Kansas City Review (1959), 25:189–94
Häusermann, H. W., The Genevese Background. 1952. p.
203–08
Hicks, John H., Conrad's "Almayer's Folly": Structure, Theme
and Critics, Nineteenth Century Fiction (June 1964), 19:17–31
Johnson, Bruce, Conrad's Models of Mind. 1971. p. 8–23
Karl, Frederick R., Joseph Conrad: A "Fin de Siècle" Novelist
—A Study in Style and Method, Literary Review (Summer
1959), 2:565–76
Karl, Frederick R., A Reader's Guide to Joseph Conrad. 1960.
p. 91–100
Kirschner, Paul, Conrad: The Psychologist as Artist. 1968.
p. 27–34
Kreisel, Henry, Joseph Conrad and the Dilemma of the Up-

rooted Man, Tamarack Review (Spring 1958), Issue 7:78–85
Moser, Thomas, Joseph Conrad: Achievement and Decline.
  1957. p. 51–54
Roussel, Royal, The Metaphysics of Darkness; A Study in the
  Unity and Development of Conrad's Fiction. 1971. p. 28–50
Squire, John C., Books in General. 1919. p. 168–72
Stawell, F. Melian, Joseph Conrad, Essays and Studies by
  Members of the English Association (1920), 6:88–111
Stein, William B., "Almayer's Folly": The Terror Time,
  Conradiana (Summer 1968), 1:27–34
Visiak, E. H., The Mirror of Conrad, 1956. p. 176–81

Arrow of Gold, 1919

Andreas, Osborne, Joseph Conrad: A Study in Non-Conformity.
  1959. p. 175–77
Baines, Jocelyn, Joseph Conrad: A Critical Biography. 1960.
  p. 410–12
Dowden, Wilfred S., Joseph Conrad: The Imaged Style. 1970.
  p. 173–76
Keating, George T., A Conrad Memorial Library. 1929. p.
  273–77
Gillon, Adam, The Eternal Solitary; A Study of Joseph Conrad.
  1960. p. 66–69
Guerard, Albert J., Conrad the Novelist. 1958. p. 7–12
Gurko, Leo, Joseph Conrad: Giant in Exile. 1962. p. 225–28
Karl, Frederick R., A Reader's Guide to Joseph Conrad. 1960.
  p. 275–80
Mansfield, Katherine, Novels and Novelists. 1930. p. 60–64
Moser, Thomas, Joseph Conrad: Achievement and Decline.
  1957. p. 180–98
Stallman, Robert Wooster, Art of Joseph Conrad: A Critical
  Symposium. 1960. p. 317–22
Toliver, Harold E., Conrad's "Arrow of Gold" and Pastoral
  Tradition, Modern Fiction Studies (Summer 1962), 8:148–58
Webster, H. T., Joseph Conrad: A Reinterpretation of Five
  Novels, College English (Dec. 1945), 7:133–34
Wilson, Arthur H., The Great Theme in Conrad, Susquehanna
  University Studies (1953), 5:77–79

Chance, 1913

Andreas, Osborne, Joseph Conrad; A Study in Non-Conformity.
  1959. p. 153–56
Baines, Jocelyn, Joseph Conrad: A Critical Biography. 1960.
  p. 382–89

Curle, Richard, Joseph Conrad and His Characters. 1957. p. 185-217

Fleischmann, Wolfgang B., Conrad's "Chance" and Bergson's "Laughter," Renascence (1962), 14:66-71

Gillon, Adam, The Eternal Solitary; A Study of Joseph Conrad. 1960. p. 70-74

Guerard, Albert J., Conrad the Novelist. 1958. p. 261-72

Gurko, Leo, Joseph Conrad: Giant in Exile. 1962. p. 200-08

Hough, Graham, "Chance" and Joseph Conrad, Listener (Dec. 26, 1957), 58:1063-1065

Hudspeth, Robert N., Conrad's Use of Time in "Chance," Nineteenth Century Fiction (Dec. 1966), 21:283-89

Johnson, J. W., Marlow and "Chance": A Reappraisal, Texas Studies in Language and Literature (1968), 10:91-105

Keating, George T., A Conrad Memorial Library. 1929. p. 217-22

Levin, Gerald H., An Allusion to Tasso in Conrad's "Chance," Nineteenth Century Fiction (Sept. 1958), 13:145-51

Levin, Gerald, The Scepticism of Marlow, Twentieth Century Literature (Jan. 1958), 3:177-84

Mack, Maynard and Ian Gregory, eds., Imagined Worlds; Essays on Some English Novels and Novelists in Honour of John Butt. 1968. p. 301-22

Moser, Thomas, Joseph Conrad; Achievement and Decline. 1957. p. 163-72

Newhouse, Neville H., Joseph Conrad. 1969. p. 67-69

Roussel, Royal, The Metaphysics of Darkness; A Study in the Unity and Development of Conrad's Fiction. 1971. p. 152-79

Smith, Curtis C., Conrad's "Chance": A Dialectical Novel, Thoth (Spring 1965), 6:16-24

Stallman, Robert Wooster, Art of Joseph Conrad; A Critical Symposium. 1960. p. 296-314

Wilson, Arthur H., The Great Theme in Conrad, Susquehanna University Studies (1953), 5:71-73

Zuckerman, Jerome, Contrapuntal Structure in Conrad's "Chance," Modern Fiction Studies (1964), 10:49-54

Lord Jim, 1900

Andreas, Osborne, Joseph Conrad: A Study in Non-Conformity. 1959. p. 55-65

Baines, Jocelyn, Joseph Conrad: A Critical Biography. 1960. p. 242-52

Bancroft, William Wallace, Joseph Conrad: His Philosophy of Life. 1931. p. 57-59

Beach, Joseph Warren, The Twentieth Century Novel: Studies in Technique. 1932. p. 353−56

Bendz, Ernest, Joseph Conrad; An Appreciation. 1923. p. 53−55

Bolton, W. F., The Role of Language in "Lord Jim," Conradiana (Summer 1969), 1:51−59

Brady, M. B., The Collector Motif in "Lord Jim," Bucknell Review (May 1968), 16:66−85

Brown, E. K., James and Conrad, Yale Review (Winter 1946), 35:265−85

Clark, Charles C., The Brierly Suicide: A New Look at an Old Ambiguity, Arlington Quarterly (Winter 1967−68), 1: 259−65

Cook, William J., Jr., "Lord Jim" as Metaphor, Conradiana (1968), 1:45−53

Curle, Richard, Joseph Conrad and His Characters. 1957. p. 29−65

Daiches, David, The Novel and the Modern World. 1960. p. 31−36

Dale, James, "One of Us": Craft and Caste in "Lord Jim," English Record (April 1965), 14:5−7

Dowden, Wilfred S., "Almayer's Folly" and "Lord Jim": A Study in the Development of Conrad's Imagery, Rice University Studies (Winter 1965), 51:13−27

Dowden, Wilfred S., Joseph Conrad: The Imaged Style. 1970. p. 56−71

Drew, Elizabeth A., The Novel; A Modern Guide to Fifteen English Masterpieces. 1963. p. 156−72

Dunn, Richard J., Conrad's "Lord Jim," Explicator (Dec. 1967), 26:Item 30

Edgar, Pelham, The Art of the Novel. 1933. p. 188−90

Ehrsam, A., Cornelius the Nazarene: Ambi-Ambiguity in "Lord Jim," English Literature in Transition (1880−1920) (1969), 12:195−96

Eschbacher, Robert L., "Lord Jim": Classical Rhetoric, and the Freshman Dilemma, College English (1963), 25:22−25

Flamm, Dudley, The Ambiguous Nazarene in "Lord Jim," English Literature in Transition (1880−1920) (1968), 11: 35−37

Ford, William J., "Lord Jim": Conrad's Study in Depth Psychology, Quarterly Bulletin (Northwestern University Medical School) (Spring 1950), 24:64−69

Fraser, G. S., "Lord Jim": The Romance of Irony, Critical

Quarterly (Autumn 1966), 8:231–41

Freislich, Richard, Marlow's Shadow Side, London Magazine (Nov. 1957), 4:31–36

Freund, Philip, How to Become a Literary Critic. 1947. p. 117–24

Gillon, Adam, Betrayal and Redemption in Joseph Conrad, Polish Review (Spring 1960), 5:18–35

Gillon, Adam, The Eternal Solitary; A Study of Joseph Conrad. 1960. p. 78–85, 92–98, 125–28, 130–32, and 155–57

Gold, Joseph, Two Romantics: Jim and Stein, CEA Critic (May 1962), 24:1 and 11–12

Gordan, John D., Joseph Conrad; The Making of a Novelist. 1940. p. 259–64

Gose, Elliott B., Jr., Pure Exercise of Imagination: Archetypal Symbolism in "Lord Jim," Modern Language Association. Publications (1964), 79:137–47

Gossman, Ann M. and George W. Whiting, The Essential Jim, Nineteenth Century Fiction (1961), 16:75–80

Greenberg, Alvin, Lord Jim and the Rock of Sisyphus, Forum (Houston) (Summer 1968), 6:13–17

Guerard, Albert J., Conrad the Novelist. 1958. p. 87–92, 126–78 and 214–17

Guetti, James L., Jr., The Rhetoric of Joseph Conrad. 1960. p. 26–34

Gurko, Leo, Joseph Conrad: Giant in Exile. 1962. p. 106–17

Haugh, Robert F., Joseph Conrad; Discovery in Design. 1957. p. 40–42, 56–77, and 133–35.

Hay, Eloise K., "Lord Jim": From Sketch to Novel, Comparative Literature (Fall 1960), 12:289–309

Hay, Eloise K., The Political Novels of Joseph Conrad. 1963. p. 61–69

Heimer, Jackson W., Betrayal, Guilt, and Attempted Redemption in "Lord Jim," Ball State University Forum (1968), 9: 31–43

Hodges, Robert R., The Four Fathers of Lord Jim, University Review (Dec. 1964), 31:103–10

Hoentzsch, Alfred, Versuch über "Lord Jim," Eckart (1957), 26:316–23

Hoffman, Stanton deVoren, "Scenes of Low Comedy": The Comic in "Lord Jim," Ball State University Forum (Spring 1964), 5:19–27

Holmes, Karen Sue, Lord Jim, Conrad's Alienated Man, Descant (Winter 1960), 4:33–40

Hunt, Kellogg W., "Lord Jim" and "The Return of the Native":
A Contrast, English Journal (Oct. 1960), 49:447–56

Johnson, Bruce M., Conrad's "Karain" and "Lord Jim,"
Modern Language Quarterly (March 1963), 24:13–20

Johnson, Bruce, Conrad's Models of Mind. 1971. p. 54–69
and 70–105

Karl, Frederick R., Conrad's Stein: The Destructive Element, Twentieth Century Literature (Jan. 1958), 3:163–69

Karl, Frederick R. and Marvin Magalaner, A Reader's Guide
to Great Twentieth Century English Novels. 1959. p. 49–56

Karl, Frederick R., A Reader's Guide to Joseph Conrad.
1960. p. 120–31

Karrfalt, David H., Accepting Lord Jim on His Own Terms: A
Structural Approach, Conradiana (Fall 1969), 2:37–47

Kirschner, Paul, Conrad: The Psychologist as Artist. 1968.
p. 48–61, 243–48

Kramer, D., Marlow, Myth and Structure in "Lord Jim,"
Criticism (Summer 1966), 8:263–79

Kramer, Cheris, Parallel Motives in "Lord Jim," Conradiana
(Fall 1969), 2:58

Krieger, Murray, The Tragic Vision; Variations on a Theme
in Literary Interpretation. 1960. p. 165–79

Levin, Gerald, The Scepticism of Marlow, Twentieth Century
Literature (Jan. 1958), 3:177–84

Lorch, Thomas M., The Barrier Between Youth and Maturity
in the Works of Joseph Conrad, Modern Fiction Studies
(Spring 1964), 10:73–80

Lord Jim's Line, Times Literary Supplement (Nov. 3, 1966),
#3375:993–94

McAlpin, E. A., Old and New Books as Life Teachers. 1928.
p. 50–65

McCann, Charles J., Lord Jim vs. the Darkness: The Saving
Power of Human Involvement, College English (1965), 27:
240–43

McDonald, Walter R., Conrad as a Novelist of Moral Conflict
and Isolation, Iowa English Yearbook (Fall 1968), #13:34–43

Madden, William A., The Search for Forgiveness in Some
Nineteenth Century English Novels, Comparative Literature
Studies (1966), 3:139–53

Malbone, Raymond Gates, "How to Be": Marlow's Quest in
"Lord Jim," Twentieth Century Literature (1965), 10:172–80

Marković, Vida E., The Changing Face; Disintegration of Personality in the Twentieth Century British Novel, 1900–1950.
1970. p. 3–17

Marković, Vida E., The Emerging Character, Northwest Review (Fall–Winter 1965–66), 7:80–97

Masbock, Frederic J., Conrad's Jonahs, College English (Feb. 1961), 22:328–33

Moore, Carliste, Conrad and the Novel as Ordeal, Philological Quarterly (Jan. 1963), 42:55–74

Moseley, Edwin M., Pseudonyms of Christ in the Modern Novel: Motifs and Methods. 1963. p. 15–35

Moser, Thomas, Joseph Conrad: Achievement and Decline. 1957. p. 39–43 and 163–72

Mroczkowski, Przemyslaw, Tajemnica "Lorda Jima," Kwartalnik Neofilologiczny (1964), 11:31–49

Mudrick, Marvin, ed., Conrad; A Collection of Critical Essays. 1966. p. 55–62

Mukherjee, Sujit K., Conrad's "Lord Jim," Explicator (Jan. 1965), 23:Item 42

Najder, Zdzislaw, "Lord Jim": A Romantic Tragedy of Honor, Conradiana (Summer 1968), 1:1–7

Newhouse, Neville H., Joseph Conrad. 1969. p. 78–81

Newman, Paul B., The Drama of Conscience and Recognition in "Lord Jim," Midwest Quarterly (Summer 1965), 6:351–66

Orvis, Mary, The Art of Writing Fiction. 1948. p. 83–85

Perry, John Oliver, Action, Vision or Voice: The Moral Dilemmas in Conrad's Tale-Telling, Modern Fiction Studies (Spring 1964), 10:3–14

Phillipson, John S., Conrad's Pink Toads: The Working of the Unconscious, Western Humanities Review (Autumn 1960), 14:437–38

Purdy, S. B., On the Relevance of Conrad: Lord Jim Over Sverdlovsk, Midwest Quarterly (Oct. 1967), 9:43–51

Raskin, Jonah, The Mythology of Imperialism. 1971. p. 162–69

Rathburn, Robert C. and Martin Steinmann, Jr., eds., From Jane Austen to Joseph Conrad. 1958. p. 281–84

Resnik, G. J., De Excentrieke Lord Jim, De Vlaamse Gids (1961), 124:178–80

Roussel, Royal, The Metaphysics of Darkness; A Study in the Unity and Development of Conrad's Fiction. 1971. p. 80–108

Schneider, D. J., Symbolism in Conrad's "Lord Jim": The Total Pattern, Modern Fiction Studies (Winter 1966–67), 12:427–38

Sherrill, Rowland A., Conrad's "Lord Jim," Explicator (March 1967), 25:Item 55

Sherry, Norman, Conrad's Eastern Port: The Setting of the Inquiry in "Lord Jim," Review of English Literature (Oct.

1965), 6:52—61

Sherry, Norman, "Lord Jim" and the "Secret Sharer," Review of English Literature (Nov. 1965), 16:378—92

Sister Estelle, S. P., Thematic and Formal Function of Gentleman Brown, Notre Dame English Journal (Spring 1962), 1:26—28

Spalding, Alex, "Lord Jim": The Result of Reading Light Holiday Literature, Humanities Association Bulletin (Winter 1968), 19:14—22

Squire, J. C., Life Letters. 1921. p. 153—60

Stallman, Robert Wooster, Art of Joseph Conrad; A Critical Symposium. 1960. p. 140—54

Stallman, Robert Wooster, Conrad and "The Great Gatsby," Twentieth Century Literature (April 1955), 1:5—12

Tanner, J. E., The Chronology and the Enigmatic End of "Lord Jim," Nineteenth Century Fiction (March 1967), 21: 369—80

Tanner, Tony, Butterflies and Beetles: Conrad's Two Truths, Chicago Review (Winter—Spring 1963), 16:123—40

Weber, D. C., Conrad's "Lord Jim," Colby Library Quarterly (1950), Series 2:266—68

Wohlfarth, Paul, Joseph Conrad and Germany, German Life and Letters (Jan. 1963), 16:81—87

Wright, Walter F., How Conrad Tells a Story, Prairie Schooner (Fall 1947), 21:290—95

Nigger of the "Narcissus," 1897

Andreas, Osborne, Joseph Conrad: A Study in Non-Conformity. 1959. p. 16—22

Baines, Jocelyn, Joseph Conrad: A Critical Biography. 1960. p. 180—87

Bancroft, William Wallace, Joseph Conrad: His Philosophy of Life. 1931. p. 11—13

Beach, Joseph Warren, The Twentieth Century Novel: Studies in Technique. 1932. p. 348—52

Bernard, Kenneth, Conrad's Fools of Innocence in the "Nigger of the 'Narcissus,'" Conradiana (Fall 1969), 2:49—57

Bradbrook, M. C., Joseph Conrad: Poland's English Genius. 1942. p. 15—20

Crankshaw, Edward, Joseph Conrad: Some Aspects of the Art of the Novel. 1936. p. 148—51

Daiches, David, The Novel and the Modern World. 1960. p. 27—29

Dowden, Wilfred, Joseph Conrad: The Imaged Style. 1970.
p. 48–56

Echerno, W. J. C., James Wait and "The Nigger of the 'Narcissus,'" English Studies in Africa (Spring 1965), 8:166–80

Frances, Sister Marian, Corruption as an Agent in the "Narcissus," English Journal (May 1967), 56:708–15

Friedman, Norman, Criticism and the Novel: Hardy, Hemingway, Crane, Woolf, and Conrad, Antioch Review (Fall 1958), 18:343–70

Green, Jesse D., Diabolism, Pessimism, and Democracy: Notes on Melville and Conrad, Modern Fiction Studies (Autumn 1962), 8:287–305

Guerard, Albert J., Conrad the Novelist. 1958. p. 100–25

Guerard, Albert J., The Nigger of the "Narcissus," Kenyon Review (1957), 19:205–32

Guetti, James L., Jr., The Rhetoric of Joseph Conrad. 1960.
p. 17–25

Gurko, Leo, Death Journey in "The Nigger of the 'Narcissus,'" Nineteenth Century Fiction (March 1961), 15:301–11

Gurko, Leo, Joseph Conrad: Giant in Exile. 1962. p. 68–79

Haugh, Robert F., Joseph Conrad: Discovery in Design. 1957.
p. 3–24

Hay, Eloise Knapp, The Political Novels of Joseph Conrad. 1963. p. 230–35

Hollingsworth, Alan M., Freud, Conrad and the Future of an Illusion, Literature and Psychology (Nov. 1955), 5:78–83

Illinois University English Department, Studies by Members of the English Department, University of Illinois, in Memory of John Jay Parry. 1955. p. 219–23

Johnson, Bruce, Conrad's Models of the Mind. 1971. p. 24–40

Johnson, Bruce, Joseph Conrad and Crane's "Red Badge of Courage," Papers of the Michigan Academy of Science, Arts and Letters (1963), 48:649–55

Karl, Frederick R., Reader's Guide to Joseph Conrad. 1960.
p. 108–17

Kerf, René, "The Nigger of the 'Narcissus'" and the MS Version of "The Rescue," English Studies (1963), 44:437–43

Kinney, Arthur F., Jimmy Wait: Joseph Conrad's Kaleidoscope, College English (March 1965), 26:475–78

Kirschner, Paul, Conrad: The Psychologist as Artist. 1968.
p. 102–09, 200–05

Levine, Paul, Joseph Conrad's Blackness, South Atlantic Quarterly (Spring 1964), 63:198–206

Martin, W. R., The Captain of the "Narcissus," English
  Studies in Africa (1963), 6:191–97
Masbock, Frederic J., Conrad's Jonahs, College English
  (Feb. 1961), 22:328–33
Moorthy, P. Rama, The Nigger of the "Narcissus," Literary
  Criterion (1965), 7:49–58
Morgan, Gerald, Narcissus Afloat, Humanities Association
  Bulletin (1964), 15:45–57
Mudrick, Marvin, The Artist's Conscience and "The Nigger of
  the 'Narcissus,'" Nineteenth Century Fiction (1957), 11:
  288–97
Mudrick, Marvin, ed., Conrad: A Collection of Critical
  Essays. 1966. p. 17–36
Nelson, Harland S., Eden and Golgotha; Conrad's Use of the
  Bible in "The Nigger of the 'Narcissus,'" Iowa English Year-
  book (Fall 1963), #8:63–67
Newhouse, Neville H., Joseph Conrad. 1969. p. 40–43
Roussel, Royal, The Metaphysics of Darkness: A Study in the
  Unity and Development of Conrad's Fiction. 1971. p. 72–79
Scrimgeour, Cecil, Jimmy Wait and the Dance of Death:
  Conrad's "Nigger of the 'Narcissus,'" Critical Quarterly
  (Winter 1965), 7:339–52
Smith, David R., "One Word More" about "The Nigger of the
  'Narcissus,'" Nineteenth Century Fiction (1968), 23:201–16
Stallman, Robert Wooster, Art of Joseph Conrad; A Critical
  Symposium. 1960. p. 108–39
Torchiana, Donald T., "The Nigger of the 'Narcissus'": Myth,
  Mirror, and Metropolis, Wascana Review (1967), 2:29–41
Wilson, Arthur H., The Great Theme in Conrad, Susquehanna
  University Studies (1953), 5:53–55
Wright, Walter F., Romance and Tragedy in Joseph Conrad.
  1949. p. 7–9, 40–44, 171–74, and 204–05
Yates, Morris W., Social Comment in "The Nigger of the
  'Narcissus,'" Modern Language Association. Publications
  (1964), 79:183–85
Zabel, Morton Dauwen, Craft and Character in Modern Fiction:
  Texts, Methods, and Vocation in Modern Fiction. 1957. p.
  168–86

Nostromo, 1904

Andreas, Osborne, Joseph Conrad: A Study in Non-Conformity.
  1959. p. 86–96
Bache, William B., "Nostromo" and "The Snows of Kilimanjaro,"

Modern Language Notes (1957), 72:32-34

Baines, Jocelyn, Joseph Conrad: A Critical Biography. 1960.
p. 297-315

Bantock, G. H., Conrad and Politics, ELH (June 1958), 25:
122-36

Becker, Miroslav, Virginia Woolf's Appraisal of Joseph Conrad, Studia Romanica et Anglica Zagrabiensia (Dec. 1961),
#12:17-22

Cox, Roger Lindsay, Conrad's Nostromo as Boatswain,
Modern Language Notes (1959), 74:303-06

Cox, Roger Lindsay, Master and Man: A Study of Conrad's
"Nostromo," Dissertation Abstracts (1961), 22:255

Curle, Richard, Joseph Conrad: A Study. 1914. p. 37-40,
129-34, and 147-49

Curle, Richard, Joseph Conrad and His Characters. 1957. p.
67-107

Daiches, David, The Novel and the Modern World. 1960. p.
42-54

Dowden, Wilfred S., Joseph Conrad: The Imaged Style. 1970.
p. 94-102

Fleishman, Avrom, The English Historical Novel; Walter Scott
to Virginia Woolf. 1971. p. 225-32

Freemason, Rosemary, Conrad's "Nostromo": A Source and
Its Use, Modern Fiction Studies (1961), 7:317-26

Friedman, Alan, The Turn of the Novel. 1966. p. 75-105

Fuchs, Carolyn, Words, Action and the Modern Novel,
Kerygma (Winter 1964), 4:3-11

Garnett, Edward, Friday Nights. 1922. p. 78-84

Gillon, Adam, Betrayal and Redemption in Joseph Conrad,
Polish Review (Spring 1960), 5:29-32

Guerard, Albert J., Conrad the Novelist. 1958. p. 175-217

Guetti, James L., Jr., The Rhetoric of Joseph Conrad. 1960.
p. 35-43

Guidi, Augusto, Struttura e Linguaggio di "Nostromo,"
Convivium (1967), 35:289-306

Gurko, Leo, Joseph Conrad: Giant in Exile. 1962. p. 122-43

Hainsworth, J. D., An Approach to "Nostromo," The Use of
English (Spring 1959), 10:181-86

Harper, Howard M., Jr. and Charles Edge, eds., The Classic
British Novel. 1972. p. 166-82

Harris, Wendell V., Of Time and the Novel, Bucknell Review
(1968), 16:114-29

Haugh, Robert F., Joseph Conrad: Discovery and Design.
1957. p. 147-63

Hay, Eloise Knapp, The Political Novels of Joseph Conrad.
1963. p. 161–216

Heimer, Jackson W., Betrayal, Confession, Attempted Redemption and Punishment in "Nostromo," Texas Studies in Literature and Language (1967), 8:561–79

Hoffman, Frederick J., The Mortal No: Death and the Modern
Imagination. 1964. p. 57–64

Johnson, Bruce, Conrad's Models of Mind. 1971. p. 106–125

Karl, Frederick R. and Marvin Magalaner, A Reader's Guide
to Great Twentieth Century English Novels. 1959. p. 47–99

Karl, Frederick R., Reader's Guide to Joseph Conrad. 1960.
p. 145–88

Kenner, Hugh, Gnomon: Essays on Contemporary Literature.
1958. p. 165–67

Kimpel, Ben and T. C. Duncan Evans, The Geography and
History of "Nostromo," Modern Philology (Aug. 1958), 56:
45–54

Lindstrand, Gordon, Joseph Conrad's "Nostromo": The Trans-
mission of the Text, Dissertation Abstracts (1968), 28:3149A

Lynskey, Winifred, Conrad's "Nostromo," Explicator (Oct.
1954), 13:Item 6

McCann, Charles and Victor Comerchero, Setting as a Key to
the Structure and Meaning of "Nostromo," Research Studies
(June 1966), 34:66–84

McDonald, Walter R., Conrad as a Novelist of Moral Conflict
and Isolation, Iowa English Yearbook (Fall 1968), #13:34–43

Mack, Maynard and Ian Gregor, eds., Imagined Worlds;
Essays on Some English Novels and Novelists in Honour of
John Butt. 1968. p. 323–41

McLauchlan, Juliet, The Politics of "Nostromo," Essays in
Criticism (1968), 18:475–77

Michel, Lois A., The Absurd Predicament in Conrad's
Political Novels, College English (Nov. 1961), 23:131–36

Moser, Thomas, Joseph Conrad: Achievement and Decline.
1957. p. 87–90

Mudrick, Marvin, ed., Conrad: A Collection of Critical
Essays. 1966. p. 83–101

Muller, Herbert J., Modern Fiction: A Study of Values. 1937.
p. 259–61

Newhouse, Neville H., Joseph Conrad. 1969. p. 116–24

Oppel, Horst, ed., Der Moderne Englische Roman: Interpretationen. 1965. p. 49–77

Raskin, Jonah, "Nostromo": The Argument from Revision,
Essays in Criticism (1968), 18:183–92

Rosenfield, Claire, An Archetypal Analysis of Conrad's
   "Nostromo," Texas Studies in Literature and Language
   (1962), 3:510-34
Roussel, Royal, The Metaphysics of Darkness; A Study in the
   Unity and Development of Conrad's Fiction. 1971. p. 109-31
Schorer, Mark, ed., Modern British Fiction. 1961. p. 85-109
Smith, David R., Nostromo and the Three Sisters, Studies in
   English Literature, 1500-1900 (1962), 2:497-508
Stallman, Robert Wooster, Art of Joseph Conrad; A Critical
   Symposium. 1960. p. 198-27
Tick, Stanley, The Gods of "Nostromo," Modern Fiction
   Studies (Spring 1964), 10:15-26
Tillyard, Eustace Mandeville Wetenhall, Epic Strain in the
   English Novel. 1958. p. 126-67
Tomlinson, Maggie, Conrad's Integrity: "Nostromo,"
   "Typhoon," and "The Shadow Line," Melbourne Critical
   Review (1962), #5:40-53
Unterecker, John, ed., Approaches to the Twentieth Century
   Novel. 1965. p. 108-52
Vickery, John B., ed., Myth and Literature; Contemporary
   Theory and Practice. 1966. p. 315-34
Vidan, Ivo, Perspective of "Nostromo," Studia Romanica et
   Anglica Zagrabiensia (1962), #13-14:43-54
Vidan, Ivo and Juliet McLauchlan, The Politics of "Nostromo,"
   Essays in Criticism (1967), 17:392-406
Vidan, Ivo, Rehearsal for "Nostromo," Studia Romanica et
   Anglica Zagrabiensia (Dec. 1961), #12:9-16
Warger, Howard N., The Unity of Conrad's "Nostromo": Irony
   as Vision and Instrument, Dissertation Abstracts (1965), 26:
   3931
Warren, Robert Penn, Selected Essays. 1958. p. 31-58
Webster, H. T., Joseph Conrad: A Reinterpretation of Five
   Novels, College English (Dec. 1945), 7:128-30
Whitehead, Lee M., "Nostromo": The Tragic Idea, Nine-
   teenth Century Fiction (March 1969), 23:463-75
Wilding, M., Politics in "Nostromo," Essays in Criticism
   (Oct. 1966), 16:441-56, (July 1967), 17:392-406, and (April
   1968), 18:183-92, 234-36, and 475-77
Williams, Raymond, The English Novel; From Dickens to
   Lawrence. 1970. p. 149-54

Outcast of the Islands, 1896.

Altick, Richard, The Scholar Adventurers. 1950. p. 289-97
Andreas, Osborne, Joseph Conrad: A Study in Non-Confor-

mity. 1959. p. 10-15
Baines, Jocelyn, Joseph Conrad: A Critical Biography. 1960.
    p. 161-65
Bendz, Ernst, Joseph Conrad; An Appreciation. 1923. p. 40-43
Dowden, Wilfred S., Joseph Conrad: The Imaged Style. 1970.
    p. 21-29
Gillon, Adam, Betrayal and Redemption in Joseph Conrad,
    Polish Review (Spring 1960), 5:18-35
Guerard, Albert J., Conrad the Novelist. 1958. p. 78-84
Guetti, James L., Jr., The Rhetoric of Joseph Conrad. 1960.
    p. 9-16
Gurko, Leo, Conrad's First Battleground, University of Kan-
    sas City Review (March 1959), 25:190-94
Gurko, Leo, Joseph Conrad: Giant in Exile. 1962. p. 57-64
Johnson, Bruce, Conrad's Models of the Mind. 1971. p. 8-23
Karl, Frederick R., Joseph Conrad: A "Fin de Siècle"
    Novelist—A Study in Style and Method, Literary Review
    (Summer 1959), 2:565-76
Karl, Frederick R., A Reader's Guide to Joseph Conrad. 1960.
    p. 101-07
Kirschner, Paul, Conrad: The Psychologist as Artist. 1968.
    p. 34-40
Kreisel, Henry, Joseph Conrad and the Dilemma of the Up-
    rooted Man, Tamarack Review (Spring 1958), Issue 7:78-85
Moser, Thomas, Joseph Conrad: Achievement and Decline.
    1957. p. 54-58
Newhouse, Neville H., Joseph Conrad. 1969. p. 38-40
Roussel, Royal, The Metaphysics of Darkness; A Study in the
    Unity and Development of Conrad's Fiction. 1971. p. 52-55

The Rescue, 1920

Andreas, Osborne, Joseph Conrad: A Study in Non-Conformity.
    1959. p. 178-84
Baines, Jocelyn, Joseph Conrad: A Critical Biography. 1960.
    p. 417-20
Bruccoli, Matthew J. and Charles Rheault, Jr., Imposition
    Figures and Plate Gangs in "The Rescue," Studies in Bibliog-
    raphy: Papers of the Bibliographic Society of the University
    of Virginia (1961), 14:258-62
Dowden, Wilfred B., Joseph Conrad: The Imaged Style. 1970.
    p. 181-97
Guerard, Albert J., Conrad the Novelist. 1958. p. 84-87
Gurko, Leo, Joseph Conrad: Giant in Exile. 1962. p. 228-34

Hay, Eloise K., The Political Novels of Joseph Conrad. 1963.
p. 83-107
Johnson, Bruce, Conrad's Models of Mind. 1971. p. 177-204
Karl, Frederick R., A Reader's Guide to Joseph Conrad.
1960. p. 281-90
Mansfield, Katherine, Novels and Novelists. 1930. p. 222-26
Mégroz, R. L., Joseph Conrad's Mind and Method: A Study of
Personality and Art. 1931. p. 158-60
Moser, Thomas, Joseph Conrad: Achievement and Decline.
1957. p. 145-57 and 172-78
Roussel, Royal, The Metaphysics of Darkness; A Study in the
Unity and Development of Conrad's Fiction. 1971. p. 55-62
Stallman, Robert Wooster, Art of Joseph Conrad; A Critical
Symposium. 1960. p. 323-31
Wright, Walter F., Conrad's "The Rescue" from Serial to
Book, Research Studies of the State College of Washington
(1945), 13:203-24

The Rover, 1923

Andreas, Osborne, Joseph Conrad: A Study in Non-Confor-
mity. 1959. p. 185-87
Baines, Jocelyn, Joseph Conrad: A Critical Biography. 1960.
p. 423-26
Boyles, John, Joseph Conrad's "The Rover," Use of English
(Winter 1966), 18:124-28
Bradbrook, M. C., Joseph Conrad: Poland's English Genius.
1942. p. 70-76
Dowden, Wilfred S., Joseph Conrad: The Imaged Style. 1970.
p. 176-80
Fleishman, Avrom, Conrad's Last Novel, English Literature
in Transition (1880-1920) (1969), 12:189-94
Fleishman, Avrom, The English Historical Novel; Walter
Scott to Virginia Woolf. 1971. p. 215-21
Guerard, Albert J., Conrad the Novelist. 1958. p. 284-87
Gurko, Leo, Joseph Conrad: Giant in Exile. 1962. p. 234-39
Hay, Eloise K., The Political Novels of Joseph Conrad. 1963.
p. 315-18
Higdon, David L., Conrad's "The Rover": The Grammar of a
Myth, Studies in the Novel (Spring 1969), 1:17-26
Karl, Frederick R., A Reader's Guide to Joseph Conrad.
1960. p. 292-96
Keating, George T., A Conrad Memorial Library. 1929. p.
326-36

Kellett, E. E., Reconsiderations: Literary Essays. 1928. p. 248-61

Lehmann, John, The Open Night. 1952. p. 54-62

Martin, R. W., Allegory in Conrad's "The Rover," English Studies in Africa (1967), 10:186-94

Moser, Thomas, Joseph Conrad: Achievement and Decline. 1957. p. 198-203

Stallman, Robert Wooster, Art of Joseph Conrad; A Critical Symposium. 1960. p. 331-35

Warner, Oliver, Joseph Conrad. 1951. p. 126-32

Wright, Elizabeth Cox, The Defining Function of Vocabulary in Conrad's "The Rover," South Atlantic Quarterly (Spring 1960), 59:265-77

Wright, Walter F., Romance and Tragedy in Joseph Conrad. 1949. p. 34-36

The Secret Agent, 1907

Andreas, Osborne, Joseph Conrad: A Study in Non-Conformity. 1959. p. 102-06

Baines, Jocelyn, Joseph Conrad: A Critical Biography. 1960. p. 329-40

Bancroft, William Wallace, Joseph Conrad: His Philosophy of Life. 1931. p. 69-71

Bantock, G. H., Conrad and Politics, ELH (June 1958), 25: 122-36

Curle, Richard, Joseph Conrad: A Study. 1914. p. 40-43, 34-37, and 49-51

Curle, Richard, Joseph Conrad and His Characters. 1957. p. 109-44

Daiches, David, The Novel and the Modern World. 1960. p. 54-57

Davis, Harold E., Conrad's Revisions of "The Secret Agent": A Study in Literary Impressionism, Modern Language Quarterly (Sept. 1958), 19:244-54

Dowden, Wilfred S., The "Illuminating Quality": Imagery and Theme in "The Secret Agent," Rice Institute Pamphlets (Oct. 1960), 47:17-33

Dowden, Wilfred S., Joseph Conrad: The Imaged Style. 1970. p. 112-23

Fleishman, Avrom, The Symbolic World of "The Secret Agent," ELH (1965), 32:196-219

Fradin, Joseph I., Anarchist, Detective and Saint: The Possibilities of Action in "The Secret Agent," Modern Language

Association. Publications (1968), 83:1414-22

Fradin, Joseph I., Conrad's "Everyman": "The Secret Agent,"
Texas Studies in Literature and Language (1969), 11:1023-38

Fradin, Joseph I. and Jean E. W. Creighton, The Language of
"The Secret Agent": The Art of Non-Life, Conradiana (Fall
1968), 1:23-35

Gilmore, Thomas B., Jr., Retributive Irony in Conrad's "The
Secret Agent," Conradiana (Summer 1969), 1:41-50

Goetsch, Paul, Joseph Conrad: "The Secret Agent," Die
Neueren Sprachen (March 1963), #3:97-110

Gose, Elliott B., Jr., "Cruel Devourer of the World's Light":
"The Secret Agent," Nineteenth Century Fiction (June 1960),
15:39-51

Guerard, Albert J., Conrad the Novelist. 1958. p. 218-31

Gurko, Leo, Joseph Conrad: Giant in Exile. 1962. p. 164-78

Gurko, Leo, "The Secret Agent": Conrad's Vision of Mega-
lopolis, Modern Fiction Studies (1958), 4:307-18

Haugh, Robert F., Joseph Conrad: Discovery in Design. 1957.
p. 136-46

Hertz, Robert, The Scene of Mr. Verloc's Murder in "The
Secret Agent," Personalist (Spring 1962), 43:214-25

Hoffman, Frederick J., The Mortal No: Death and the Modern
Imagination. 1964. p. 50-57

Holland, Norman, Style as Character: "The Secret Agent,"
Modern Fiction Studies (1966), 12:221-31

Karl, Frederick R., Conrad's Waste Land: Moral Anarchy in
"The Secret Agent," Four Quarters (Jan. 1960), 9:29-36

Karl, Frederick R., A Reader's Guide to Joseph Conrad.
1960. p. 191-206

Klingopoulos, G. D., The Criticism of the Novels, The Use of
English (June 1955), 3:85-90

Kilroy, James, Conrad's "Succès de Curiosité": The Dramatic
Version of "The Secret Agent," English Literature in Transition (1880-1920) (1967), 10:81-88

Kirschman, Paul, Conrad: The Psychologist as Artist. 1968.
p. 78-88

Knoepflmacher, U. C., Laughter and Despair: Readings in Ten
Novels of the Victorian Age. 1971. p. 240-74

Kocmanová, Jessie, The Revolt of the Workers in the Novels
of Gissing, James, and Conrad, BRNO Studies in English
(1959), 1:119-39

Kubal, David L., "The Secret Agent" and the Mechanical
Chaos, Bucknell Review (Dec. 1967), 15:65-77

Lee, Robin, "The Secret Agent": Structure, Theme Mode, English Studies in Africa (1968), 11:185–93

Luecke, Sister Jane Marie, Conrad's Secret and Its Agent, Modern Fiction Studies (Spring 1964), 10:37–48

McDonald, Walter R., Conrad as a Novelist of Moral Conflict and Isolation, Iowa English Yearbook (Fall 1968), #13:34–43

Magnuson, Harold M., Anarchism in Conrad's "The Secret Agent," Wisconsin Studies in Literature (1967), #4:75–88

Mann, Thomas, Past Masters and Other Papers. 1933. p. 231–47

Marsh, D. R. C., Moral Judgments in "The Secret Agent," English Studies in Africa (March 1960), 3:57–70

Meyers, Jeffry, The Agamemnon Myth and "The Secret Agent," Conradiana (1968), 1:57–59

Michael, Marion, Conrad's Definite Intention in "The Secret Agent," Conradiana (Summer 1968), 1:9–17

Michel, Lois A., The Absurd Predicament in Conrad's Political Novels, College English (Nov. 1961), 23:131–36

Morley, Patricia A., Conrad's Vision of the Absurd, Conradiana (Fall 1969), 2:59–68

Moser, Thomas, Joseph Conrad: Achievement and Decline. 1957. p. 90–94

Mudrick, Marvin, ed., Conrad; A Collection of Critical Essays. 1966. p. 103–10

Newhouse, Neville H., Joseph Conrad. 1969. p. 34–37 and 125–32

Nash, Christopher, More Light on "The Secret Agent," Review of English Studies (August 1969), 20:322–27

O'Grady, Walter, On Plot in Modern Fiction: Hardy, James and Conrad, Modern Fiction Studies (Summer 1965), 11:107–15

Pritchett, V. S., Books in General. 1953. p. 216–22

Roussel, Royal, The Metaphysics of Darkness; A Study in the Unity and Development of Conrad's Fiction. 1971. p. 132–34

Sherry, Norman, The Greenwich Bomb Outrage in "The Secret Agent," Review of English Studies (Nov. 1967), 18:412–28

Sherry, Norman, Sir Ethelred in "The Secret Agent," Philological Quarterly (1969), 48:108–15

Spector, Robert D., Irony as Theme; Conrad's "The Secret Agent," Nineteenth Century Fiction (June 1958), 13:69–71

Stallman, Robert Wooster, Art of Joseph Conrad; A Critical Symposium. 1960. p. 111–30 and 227–54

Stallman, R. W., Time and "The Secret Agent," Texas Studies in Literature and Language (1959), 1:101-22

Tillyard, Eustace M. W., Essays, Literary and Educational. 1962. p. 144-53

Tillyard, Eustace M. W., "The Secret Agent" Reconsidered, Essays in Criticism (1961), 11:309-18

Walton, James H., The Background of "The Secret Agent" by Joseph Conrad; A Biographical and Critical Study, Dissertation Abstracts (1967), 27:2164A-65A

Walton, James, Conrad and Naturalism: "The Secret Agent," Texas Studies in Literature and Language (Summer 1967), 9:289-301

Walton, James, Conrad and "The Secret Agent": The Genealogy of Mr. Vladimir, Polish Review (1967), 12:28-42

Wiesenfarth, Joseph, Stevie and the Structure of "The Secret Agent," Modern Fiction Studies (1967), 13:513-17

Williams, Raymond, The English Novel; From Dickens to Lawrence. 1970. p. 147-49

Zuckerman, Jerome, The Motif of Cannibalism in "The Secret Agent," Texas Studies in Literature and Language (1968), 10:295-99

Suspense, 1925

Aubry, G. Jean, The Inner History of Conrad's "Suspense," Bookman's Journal (Oct. 1925), 13:3-10

Chew, Samuel, et al, Essays on "Suspense," Saturday Review of Literature (Nov. 14, 1925), 2:289-91

DeGruyten, J., A Master of English, English Studies (Dec. 1925), 7:169-75

Fleishman, Avrom, The English Historical Novel; Walter Scott to Virginia Woolf. 1971. p. 221-25

Guerard, Albert J., Conrad the Novelist. 1958. p. 287-92

Karl, Frederick R., A Reader's Guide to Joseph Conrad. 1960. p. 295-97

Keating, George T., A Conrad Memorial Library. 1929. p. 351-57

Moser, Thomas, Joseph Conrad; Achievement and Decline. 1957. p. 202-06

Stallman, Robert Wooster, Art of Joseph Conrad; A Critical Symposium. 1960. p. 331-35

Wood, Miriam H., A Source of Conrad's "Suspense," Modern Language Notes (June 1935), 1:390-94

Under Western Eyes, 1911

Andreas, Osborne, Joseph Conrad; A Study in Non-Conformi-
ty. 1959. p. 127-34
Baines, Jocelyn, Joseph Conrad; A Critical Biography. 1960.
p. 360-73
Bantock, G. H., Conrad and Politics, ELH (June 1958), 25:
122-36
Curle, Richard, Joseph Conrad; A Study. 1914. p. 43-45 and
137-39
Curle, Richard, Joseph Conrad and His Characters. 1957. p.
145-83
Daiches, David, The Novel and the Modern World. 1960. p.
57-62
Dowden, Wilfred S., Joseph Conrad: The Imaged Style. 1970.
p. 123-31
Eagleton, Terry, Exiles and Émigrés; Studies in Modern
Literature. 1970. p. 21-32
Guerard, Albert J., Conrad the Novelist. 1958. p. 218-21
and 231-53
Gurko, Leo, Joseph Conrad: Giant in Exile. 1962. p. 182-96
Gurko, Leo, "Under Western Eyes": Conrad and the Question
of "Where To?," College English (1960), 21:445-52
Hagan, John, Conrad's "Under Western Eyes": The Question
of Razumov's "Guilt" and "Remorse," Studies in the Novel
(Fall 1969), 1:310-22
Haugh, Robert F., Joseph Conrad; Discovery in Design. 1957.
p. 119-35
Häusermann, H. W., The Genevese Background. 1952. p.
207-13
Hay, Eloise K., The Political Novels of Joseph Conrad. 1963.
p. 265-313
Heimer, Jackson W., The Betrayer as Intellectual: Conrad's
"Under Western Eyes," Polish Review (1967), 12:57-68
Johnson, Bruce, Conrad's Models of Mind. 1971. p. 140-58
Johnson, Bruce, "Under Western Eyes": Politics as Symbol,
Conradiana (1968), 1:35-44
Karl, Frederick R. and Marvin Magalaner, A Reader's Guide
to Great Twentieth Century English Novels. 1959. p. 47-99
Karl, Frederick R., A Reader's Guide to Joseph Conrad.
1960. p. 211-28
Karl, Frederick R., The Rise and Fall of "Under Western
Eyes," Nineteenth Century Fiction (1959), 13:313-27

Kenner, Hugh, Gnomon: Essays on Contemporary Literature. 1958. p. 163-65

Kirschner, Paul, Conrad: The Psychologist as Artist. 1968. p. 88-101, 175-77, and 249-52

Kocmanová, Jessie, The Revolt of the Workers in the Novels of Gissing, James and Conrad, BRNO Studies in English (1959), 1:119-39

Michel, Lois A., The Absurd Predicament in Conrad's Political Novels, College English (Nov. 1961), 23:131-36

Moser, Thomas, Joseph Conrad: Achievement and Decline. 1957. p. 94-96

Mudrick, Marvin, ed., Conrad; A Collection of Critical Essays. 1966. p. 111-44

Newhouse, Neville H., Joseph Conrad. 1969. p. 100-04 and 132-34

Robson, W. W., The Politics of Solitude, London Magazine (Nov. 1957), 4:26-31

Roussel, Royal, The Metaphysics of Darkness; A Study in the Unity and Development of Conrad's Fiction. 1971. p. 132-34, 140-51, 152-59, and 182-88

Saagpakk, Paul F., Psychopathological Elements in British Novels from 1890-1930, Dissertation Abstracts (Sept. 1966), 27:782A

Stallman, Robert Wooster, Art of Joseph Conrad; A Critical Symposium. 1960. p. 259-75

Tanner, Tony, Nightmare and Complacency; Razumov and the Western Eyes, Critical Quarterly (Autumn 1962), 4:197-214

Tyrmand, Leopold, ed., Kultura Essays. 1970. p. 174-91

Wright, Walter F., Romance and Tragedy in Joseph Conrad. 1949. p. 97-101

Zabel, Morton Dauwen, Craft and Character; Texts, Methods and Vocation in Modern Fiction. 1957. p. 187-207

Victory, 1915

Andreas, Osborne, Joseph Conrad; A Study in Non-Conformity. 1959. p. 163-68

Baines, Jocelyn, Joseph Conrad; A Critical Biography. 1960. p. 394-400

Beebe, Maurice, Ivory Towers and Sacred Founts; The Artist as Hero in Fiction from Goethe to Joyce. 1964. p. 114-71

Beebe, Maurice, The Masks of Conrad, Bucknell Review (Dec. 1963), 11:35-53

Bendz, Ernst, Joseph Conrad; An Appreciation. 1923. p. 55-57

Bluefarb, S., Samburan: Conrad's Mirror Image of Eden, Conradiana (Summer 1969), 1:89-94

Brown, E. K., James and Conrad, Yale Review (Winter 1946), 35:265-85

Curle, Richard, Joseph Conrad and His Characters. 1957. p. 219-54

Curle, Richard, Mr. Joseph Conrad and "Victory," Fortnightly (Oct. 1915), 104:670-78

Dike, Donald A., The Tempest of Axel Heyst, Nineteenth Century Fiction (1962), 17:95-113

Downing, Francis, The Meaning of Victory in Joseph Conrad, Commonweal (March 28, 1952), 55:613-14

Goens, Mary B., The "Mysterious and Effective Star": The Mythic Worldview in Conrad's "Victory," Modern Fiction Studies (1967), 13:455-63

Greenberg, Robert A., The Presence of Mr. Wang, Boston University Studies in English (Autumn 1960), 4:129-37

Gross, Seymour L., The Devil in Samburan: Jones and Ricardo in "Victory," Nineteenth Century Fiction (1961), 16:81-85

Guerard, Albert J., Conrad the Novelist. 1958. p. 254-61

Gurko, Leo, Joseph Conrad: Giant in Exile. 1962. p. 212-21

Haugh, Robert F., Joseph Conrad: Discovery in Design. 1957. p. 102-16

Heimer, Jackson W., "Look On—Make No Sound"; Conrad's "Victory," Studies in the Humanities (1969), 1:8-13

Jaffe, Adrian and Herbert Weisinger, eds., The Laureate Fraternity: An Introduction to Literature. 1960. p. 267-70

Johnson, Bruce, Conrad's Models of Mind. 1971. p. 159-76

Kaehéle, Sharon and Howard German, Conrad's "Victory": A Reassessment, Modern Fiction Studies (Spring 1964), 10: 55-72

Karl, Frederick R. and Marvin Magalaner, A Reader's Guide to Great Twentieth Century English Novels. 1959. p. 47-99

Karl, Frederick R., A Reader's Guide to Joseph Conrad. 1960. p. 246-67

Kirschner, Paul, Conrad: The Psychologist as Artist. 1968. p. 155-66 and 193-98

Kreisel, Henry, Joseph Conrad and the Dilemma of the Uprooted Man, Tamarack Review (Spring 1958), Issue 7:78-85

Krieger, Murray, The Tragic Vision; Variations on a Theme

in Literary Interpretation. 1960. p. 154-94
Lodge, David, Conrad's "Victory" and "The Tempest": An
   Amplification, Modern Language Review (1964), 59:195-99
Lordi, R. J., The Three Emissaries of Evil: Their Psycho-
   logical Relationship in Conrad's "Victory," College English
   (1961), 23:136-40
Moser, Thomas, Joseph Conrad: Achievement and Decline.
   1957. p. 116-19, 155-56, and 158-59
Pilecki, Gerard A., Conrad's "Victory," Explicator (1965),
   23:Item 36
Reck, Rima D., ed., Exploration of Literature. 1966. p. 70-80
Resnik, G. J., Axel Heyst and the Second King of the Cocos
   Islands, English Studies (1963), 44:443-47
Shapiro, Charles, ed., Twelve Original Essays on Great En-
   glish Novels. 1960. p. 203-31
Stallman, Robert Wooster, Art of Joseph Conrad; A Critical
   Symposium. 1960. p. 314-16
Tanner, Tony, Conrad's "Victory": An Answer to Schopen-
   hauer, London Magazine (July 1965), 5:85-90
Webster, H. T., Joseph Conrad: A Reinterpretation of Five
   Novels, College English (Dec. 1945), 7:125-34
Widmer, Kingsley, Conrad's Pyrrhic "Victory," Twentieth
   Century Literature (Oct. 1959), 5:123-30
Wohlfarth, Paul, Joseph Conrad and Germany, German Life
   and Letters (Jan. 1963), 16:81-87

JOSEPH CONRAD AND FORD MADOX FORD

The Inheritors, 1901

Bender, Todd K., Fictional Time and the Problem of Free
   Will, Wisconsin Studies in Literature (1968), #5:12-22

MARY ANN EVANS CROSS

SEE

GEORGE ELIOT

DANIEL DEFOE

Captain Singleton, 1720

Scrimgeour, Gary J., The Problem of Realism in Defoe's
   "Captain Singleton," Huntington Library Quarterly (1963),
   27:21-37

The Fortunate Mistress Roxanna, SEE Roxanna

The Fortunes and Misfortunes of the Famous Moll Flanders, SEE Moll Flanders

The History of Colonel Jack, 1722

>McBurney, William H., "Colonel Jack": Defoe's Definition of the Complete Gentleman, Studies in English Literature, 1500–1900 (Summer 1962), 2:321–36

The Life and Strange Surprising Adventures of Robinson Crusoe of York, Mariner, SEE Robinson Crusoe

The Life of Captain Singleton, SEE Captain Singleton

Moll Flanders, 1722

>Alter, Robert, Rogue's Progress; Studies in the Picaresque Novel. 1964. p. 35–57
>Brooks, Douglas, "Moll Flanders": An Interpretation, Essays in Criticism (Jan. 1969), 19:46–59 and (July 1969), 19:351–54
>Butt, John, ed., Of Books and Humankind: Essays and Poems Presented to Bonamy Dobrée. 1964. p. 55–67
>Columbus, Robert R., Conscious Artistry in "Moll Flanders," Studies in English Literature, 1500–1900 (Summer 1963), 3:415–32
>Donoghue, Denis, The Values of "Moll Flanders," Sewanee Review (Spring 1963), 71:287–303
>Drew, Elizabeth A., The Novel; A Modern Guide to Fifteen English Masterpieces. 1963. p. 23–38
>Frye, Bobby J., The Twentieth Century Criticism of "Robinson Crusoe" and "Moll Flanders," Dissertation Abstracts (1967), 27:3007A–08A
>Goldberg, M. A., "Moll Flanders": Christian Allegory in a Hobbesian Mode, University Review (June 1967), 33:267–78
>Howson, G., Who Was Moll Flanders?, Times Literary Supplement (Jan. 18, 1967), #3438:63–64
>Koonce, Howard L., Moll's Muddle: Defoe's Use of Irony in "Moll Flanders," ELH (1963), 30:377–94
>Macey, S. L., Who Was Moll Flanders?, Notes and Queries (Sept. 1969), 16:336–37
>Martin, Terence, The Unity of "Moll Flanders," Modern Language Quarterly (July 1961), 22:115–24
>Mauriac, F., En Relisant "Moll Flanders," Quand le Romancier s'Anéantit dans son Personnage, Figaro Littéraire (July 1957), 20:1, 4

Novak, Maximillian E., Conscious Irony in "Moll Flanders":
Facts and Problems, College English (1964), 26:198-204

Novak, Maximillian E., Moll Flanders' First Love, Papers of
the Michigan Academy of Science, Arts and Letters (1961),
46:635-43

Piper, William B., "Moll Flanders" as a Structure of Topics,
Studies in English Literature, 1500-1900 (Summer 1969),
9:489-502

Price, Martin, To the Palace of Wisdom; Studies in Order and
Energy from Dryden to Blake. 1964. p. 263-84

Shinagel, Michael, The Maternal Theme in "Moll Flanders":
Craft and Character, Cornell Literary Journal (1969), 7:3-23

Starr, G. A., Defoe and Casuistry. 1971. p. 111-64

Taube, Myron, Moll Flanders and Fanny Hill: A Comparison,
Ball State University Forum (1968), 9:76-80

Watson, Francis, Moll, Mother of the Group, Guardian (Feb.
6, 1965), p. 8

Watson, Tommy G., Defoe's Attitude Toward Marriage and the
Position of Women as Revealed in "Moll Flanders," Southern
Quarterly (Oct. 1964), 3:1-8

Watt, Ian, The Recent Critical Fortunes of "Moll Flanders,"
Eighteenth Century Studies (1967), 1:109-26

Robinson Crusoe, 1719

Arnold, Heinz Ludwig, "Robinson Crusoe": Notizen zu einer
Illusion, Antaios (1965), 6:611-20

Ayers, Robert W., "Robinson Crusoe": "Allusive Allegorick
History," Modern Language Association. Publications (1967),
82:399-407

Biles, Jack I. and Carl R. Kropf, The Cleft Rock of Conversion:
"Robinson Crusoe" and "Pincher Martin," Studies in the Literary Imagination (Oct. 1969), 2:17-43

Clifford, James Lowry, ed., Eighteenth Century English Literature; Modern Essays in Criticism. 1959. p. 158-79

Downs, Robert Bingham, Molders of the Modern Mind; One
Hundred Eleven Books that Shaped Western Civilization.
1961. p. 108-11

Echerno, Michael J., "Robinson Crusoe," "Purchas his Pil-
grimes," and the "Novel," English Studies in Africa (1967),
10:167-77

Frye, Bobby J., The Twentieth Century Criticism of "Robinson
Crusoe" and "Moll Flanders," Dissertation Abstracts (1967),
27:3007A-08A

Grief, M. J., Conversion of Robinson Crusoe, Studies in English Literature (Summer 1966), 6:551–74

Halewood, William H., Religion and Invention in "Robinson Crusoe," Essays in Criticism (Oct. 1964), 14:339–51

Hayden, Donald E. and E. Alworth, eds., Classics in Semantics. 1965. p. 103–28

Hearne, John, Naked Footprint: An Enquiry into Crusoe's Island, Review of English Literature (Oct. 1967), 8:97–107

Hunter, J. Paul, Friday as a Convert: Defoe and the Accounts of Indian Missionaries, Review of English Studies (Aug. (1963), 14:243–48

Laird, John, Philosophical Incursions into English Literature. 1962. p. 21–33

Mack, Maynard and Ian Gregor, eds., Imagined Worlds; Essays on Some English Novels and Novelists in Honour of John Butt. 1968. p. 68–89

Michel-Michot, Paulette, The Myth of Innocence, Revue des Langues Vivantes (1962), 28:510–20

Novak, Maximillian E., Crusoe the King and the Political Evolution of his Island, Studies in English Literature, 1500–1900 (Summer 1962), 2:337–50

Novak, Maximillian E., The Problem of Necessity in Defoe's Fiction, Philological Quarterly (1961), 40:513–24

Novak, Maximillian E., "Robinson Crusoe" and Economic Utopia, Kenyon Review (1963), 25:474–90

Novak, Maximillian E., Robinson Crusoe's Fear and the Search for Natural Man, Modern Philology (1961), 58:238–45

Novak, Maximillian E., Robinson Crusoe's "Original Sin," Studies in English Literature, 1500–1900 (1961), 1:19–29

Price, Martin, To the Palace of Wisdom; Studies in Order and Energy from Dryden to Blake. 1964. p. 263–84

Shapiro, Charles, ed., Twelve Original Essays on Great English Novels. 1960. p. 1–21

Steeves, Harrison Ross, Before Jane Austen; The Shaping of the English Novel in the Eighteenth Century. 1965. p. 22–42

Stein, William Bysshe, Robinson Crusoe: The Trickster Tricked, The Centennial Review of Arts and Science (1965), 9:271–88

Swados, Harvey, A Radical's America. 1962. p. 133–54

Swados, Harvey, Robinson Crusoe—The Man Alone, Antioch Review (1958), 18:25–40

Tillyard, Eustace Mandeville Wetenhall, Epic Strain in the English Novel. 1958. p. 25–50

Watson, Francis, Robinson Crusoe: An Englishman of the
Age, History Today (Nov. 1959), 9:760—66
Watson, Francis, Robinson Crusoe: Fact and Fiction,
Listener (1959), 62:617—19
Weimann, Robert, Robinson Crusoe: Wirklichkeit und Utopie
im Neuzeitlichen Roman, Sinn und Form (1969), 21:453—84

Roxanna, 1724

Novak, Maximillian E., Crime and Punishment in Defoe's
"Roxanna," Journal of English and Germanic Philology (July
1966), 65:445—65
Oda, Minoru, Allegory and History; A Study of Daniel Defoe's
"Roxanna," Memoirs of Osaka Gakugei University (1966),
15:62—87
Starr, G. A., Defoe and Casuistry. 1971. p. 165—89

NIGEL DENNIS

Cards of Identity, 1955

Bergonzi, Bernard, The Situation of the Novel. 1970. p. 71—74
Karl, Frederick R., The Contemporary English Novel. 1962.
238—53
Peake, Charles, "Cards of Identity": An Intellectual Satire,
Literary Half-Yearly (Jan. 1960), 1:49—57
Tynan, Kenneth, Curtains; Selections from the Drama Criti-
cism and Related Writings. 1961. p. 138—40

CHARLES DICKENS

Barnaby Rudge, 1841

Dyson, A. E., "Barnaby Rudge": The Genesis of Violence,
Critical Quarterly (Sept. 1967), 9:142—60
Dyson, A. E., The Inimitable Dickens; A Reading of the Novels.
1970. p. 47—70
Fleishman, Avrom, The English Historical Novel; Walter Scott
to Virginia Woolf. 1971. p. 102—14
Folland, Harold F., The Doer and the Deed; Theme and Pattern
in "Barnaby Rudge," Modern Language Association. Publica-
tions (1959), 74:406—17
Gibson, Frank A., The Love Interest in "Barnaby Rudge," The
Dickensian (Winter 1958), 54:21—23
Gibson, Frank A., A Note on George Gordon, The Dickensian

(May 1961), 57:81−85
Gottshall, James K., Devils Abroad: The Unity and Signifi-
cance of "Barnaby Rudge," Nineteenth Century Fiction
(1961), 16:133−46
Monod, Sylvère, Rebel with a Cause; Hugh of the Maypole,
Dickens Studies (1965), 1:4−26
O'Brien, Anthony, Benevolence and Insurrection: The Con-
flicts of Form and Purpose in "Barnaby Rudge," Dickens
Studies (1969), 5:26−44

Bleak House, 1852−53

Andersen, Sally S., Dickens and the Problem of Maturity:
"Dombey and Son," "David Copperfield," "Bleak House,"
"Great Expectations," and "Our Mutual Friend," Dissertation
Abstracts (1968), 28:3135A
Axton, William, Esther's Nicknames: A Study in Relevance,
The Dickensian (Sept. 1966), 62:158−63
Axton, William F., Religious and Scientific Imagery in "Bleak
House," Nineteenth Century Fiction (March 1968), 22:349−59
Axton, William F., The Trouble with Esther, Modern Language
Quarterly (1965), 26:545−57
Blount, Trevor, "Bleak House" and the Sloane Scandal of 1850
Again, Dickens Studies (1967), 3:63−67
Blount, Trevor, The Chadbands and Dickens' View of Dissent-
ers, Modern Language Quarterly (1964), 25:295−307
Blount, Trevor, Chancery as Evil and Challenge in "Bleak
House," Dickens Studies (1965), 1:112−20
Blount, Trevor, Dickens' Slum Satire in "Bleak House," Mod-
ern Language Review (July 1965), 60:340−51
Blount, Trevor, The Documentary Symbolism of Chancery in
"Bleak House," The Dickensian (1966), 62:47−52, 106−11,
and 167−74
Blount, Trevor, The Graveyard Satire of "Bleak House" in the
Context of 1850, Review of English Studies (Nov. 1963), 14:
370−78
Blount, Trevor, The Importance of Place in "Bleak House,"
The Dickensian (Sept. 1965), 61:140−49
Blount, Trevor, The Ironmaster and the New Acquisitiveness:
Dickens' Views on the Rising Industrial Classes as Exempli-
fied in "Bleak House," Essays in Criticism (Oct. 1965), 15:
414−27
Blount, Trevor, Poor Jo, Education and the Problem of Juve-
nile Delinquency in Dickens' "Bleak House," Modern Philol-

ogy (1965), 62:325-39

Blount, Trevor, Sir Leicester Dedlock and "Deportment" Tur-
veydrop: Some Aspects of Dickens' Use of Parallelism in
"Bleak House," Nineteenth Century Fiction (Sept. 1966), 21:
149-65

Boo, Sister Mary Richard, Jo's Journey Toward Light in
"Bleak House," Cithara (1965), 5:15-22

Brogunier, Joseph, The Funeral Pyre and Human Decency;
The Fate of Chancery in "Bleak House," The Dickensian
(Jan. 1965), 61:57-62

Burke, Alan R., The Strategy and Theme of Urban Observa-
tion in "Bleak House," Studies in English Literature, 1500-
1900 (Autumn 1969), 9:659-76

Butt, John, "Bleak House" Once More, Critical Quarterly
(1959), 1:302-07

Collins, Philip, Dickens' Detectives: Fact and Fiction,
Police College Magazine (Autumn 1961), 7:17-27

Coolidge, Archibald, Dickens' Complex Plots, The Dickensian
(Autumn 1961), 57:174-82

Cooperman, Stanley, Dickens and the Secular Blasphemy:
Social Criticism in "Hard Times," "Little Dorrit," and
"Bleak House," College English (December 1960), 22:156-60

Craig, David, Fiction and the Rising Industrial Classes,
Essays in Criticism (Jan. 1967), 17:64-74

Crompton, Louis, Satire and Symbolism in "Bleak House,"
Nineteenth Century Fiction (March 1958), 12:284-303

Davenport, William Henry, ed., Voices in Court; A Treasury
of the Bench, the Bar and the Courtroom. 1958. p. 363-77

Dean, Leonard W., Style and Unity in "Bleak House," Criticism (Summer 1961), 3:206-18

Delespinasse, Doris S., The Significance of Dual Point of
View in "Bleak House," Nineteenth Century Fiction (1968),
23:253-64

Dettelbach, Cynthia, Bird Imagery in "Bleak House," The
Dickensian (Autumn 1963), 59:177-81

Donovan, R. A., Structure and Idea in "Bleak House," ELH
(June 1962), 29:175-201

Dunn, Richard J., Esther's Role in "Bleak House," The
Dickensian (Sept. 1966), 62:163-66

Dyson, A. E., The Inimitable Dickens; A Reading of the Novels.
1970. p. 154-82

Flibbert, Joseph T., "Bleak House" and the Brothers Grimm,
Victorian Newsletter (Fall 1969), #36:1-5

Fredin, Joseph I., Will and Society in "Bleak House," Philological Quarterly (March 1966), 81:95-109

Gill, S. C., Allusion in "Bleak House": A Narrative Device,
Nineteenth Century Fiction (Sept. 1967), 22:145-54

Guerard, Albert J., "Bleak House": Structure and Style,
Southern Review (LSU) (1969), 5:332-49

Lovett, Robert W., Mr. Spectator in "Bleak House," The
Dickensian (1963), 59:124-29

Manheim, Leonard F., Thanatos: The Death Instinct in
Dickens' Later Novels, Psychoanalysis and Psychoanalytic
Review (Winter 1960-61), 47:17-31

Monod, Sylvere, Esther Summerson, Charles Dickens, and
the Reader in "Bleak House," Dickens Studies (1969), 5:5-25

Moth, Susan, The Light/Darkness/Sight Imagery in "Bleak
House," Dickens Studies (1965), 1:76-85

Nadelhaft, Janice, The English Malady, Corrupted Humors and
Krook's Death, Studies in the Novel (Summer 1969), 1:230-39

Partlow, Robert B., Jr., ed., Dickens the Craftsman; Strategies of Presentation. 1970. p. 115-39

Pederson, Winifred J., Jo in "Bleak House," The Dickensian
(Autumn 1964), 60:162-67

Prins, Albert James, The Fabulous Art: Myth, Metaphor and
Moral Vision in Dickens' "Bleak House," Dissertation Abstracts (1964), 25:1896

Rathburn, Robert C. and Martin Steinman, eds., From Jane
Austen to Joseph Conrad; Essays Collected in Memory of
James T. Hillhouse. 1958. p. 92-105

Rosso, Martha, Dickens and Esther, The Dickensian (May
1969), 65:90-94

Roulet, Ann, A Comparative Study of "Nicholas Nickleby" and
"Bleak House," The Dickensian (Spring 1964), 60:117-24

Sørensen, Kund, Subjective Narration in "Bleak House," English Studies (Dec. 1959), 40:431-39

Steig, Michael, The Iconography of the Hidden Face, Dickens
Studies (1968), 4:19-22

Stokes, E., "Bleak House" and "Scarlet Letter," AUMLA (Nov.
1969), #32:177-89

Weinstein, Philip M., Structure and Collapse: A Study of
"Bleak House," Dickens Studies (1968), 4:4-18

Wiley, Elizabeth, Four Strange Cases, The Dickensian (May
1962), 58:120-25

Wilkinson, Ann Y., "Bleak House": From Faraday to Judgment
Day, ELH (1967), 34:225-47

Zabel, Morton Dauwen, ed., Craft and Character; Texts, Methods and Vocation in Modern Fiction. 1957. p. 15-49

David Copperfield, 1849-50

Andersen, Sally S., Dickens and the Problem of Maturity: "Dombey and Son," "David Copperfield," "Bleak House," "Great Expectations," and "Our Mutual Friend," Dissertation Abstracts (1968), 28:3135A

Beebe, Maurice, Ivory Towers and Sacred Founts; The Artist as Hero in Fiction from Goethe to Joyce. 1964. p. 65-113

Bell, Vereen M., The Emotional Matrix of "David Copperfield," Studies in English Literature, 1500-1900 (1968), 8:633-49

Collins, P. A. W., The Middlesex Magistrate in "David Copperfield," Notes and Queries (March 1961), 8:86-91

Collins, Phillip, "David Copperfield" and East Anglia, The Dickensian (1965), 61:46-51

Coolidge, Archibald C., Dickens and Latitudinarian Christianity, The Dickensian (Winter 1963), 59:57-60

Dunn, Richard J., "David Copperfield": All Dickens Is There, English Journal (1965), 54:789-94

Dyson, A. E., The Inimitable Dickens; A Reading of the Novels. 1970. p. 119-53

Eoff, Sherman Hinkle, The Modern Spanish Novel; Comparative Essays Examining the Philosophical Impact of Science on Fiction. 1961. p. 21-50

Gard, Roger, David Copperfield, Essays in Criticism (July 1965), 15:313-25

Goldfarb, Russell M., Sexual Repression and Victorian Literature. 1970. p. 122-26

Hardy, Barbara, The Change of Heart in Dickens' Novels, Victorian Studies (Sept. 1961), 5:49-67

Hardy, Barbara, The Moral Art of Dickens. 1970. p. 122-38

Harris, Wendell V., Of Time and the Novel, Bucknell Review (1968), 16:114-29

Hornback, Bert G., Frustration and Resolution in "David Copperfield," Studies in English Literature, 1500-1900 (1969) 8:651-67

Kelly, Jean McClure, The Modern Tones of Charles Dickens, The Dickensian (Autumn 1961), 57:160-65

Kettle, Arnold, Thoughts on "David Copperfield," Review of English Studies (1961), 2:64-74

Kincaid, James Russell, A Critical Study of "David Copperfield," Dissertation Abstracts (1966), 27:478A

Kincaid, James Russell, The Darkness of "David Copperfield,"
Dickens Studies (1965), 1:65–75

Kincaid, James Russell, Dickens' Subversive Humor: "David
Copperfield," Nineteenth Century Fiction (March 1968), 22:
313–29

Kincaid, James Russell, The Structure of "David Copperfield,"
Dickens Studies (1966), 2:74–95

Kincaid, James Russell, Symbol and Subversion in "David
Copperfield," Studies in the Novel (1969), 1:196–206

Marshall, William H., The Image of Steerforth and the Structure of "David Copperfield," Tennessee Studies in Literature
(1960), 5:57–65

Maugham, William Somerset, Art of Fiction; An Introduction
to Ten Novels and Their Authors. 1955. p. 135–61

Monod, Sylvère, James Steerforth ou le Problème du mal
dans "David Copperfield," Annales de l'Université de Paris
(1967), 37:166–76

Pearce, Roy Harvey, ed., Experience in the Novel; Selected
Papers from the English Institute. 1968. p. 21–48

Schilling, Bernard Nicholas, The Comic Spirit: Boccaccio to
Thomas Mann. 1965. p. 98–144

Schweitzer, Joan, "David Copperfield" and Ernest Pontifex,
The Dickensian (1967), 63:42–45

Skottowe, P. F., Thomas Talfourd and "David Copperfield,"
The Dickensian (Jan. 1969), 65:25–31

Spilka, Mark, "David Copperfield" as Psychological Fiction,
Critical Quarterly (Winter 1959), 1:292–301

Spilka, Mark, Kafka and Dickens; The Country Sweetheart,
American Imago (Winter 1959), 16:367–78

Stone, Harry, Fairy Tales and Ogres; Dickens' Imagination
and "David Copperfield," Criticism (1964), 6:324–30

Strong, Leonard Alfred Goerge, Personal Remarks. 1953. p.
103–22

Tick, Stanley, The Memorializing of Mr. Dick, Nineteenth
Century Fiction (Sept. 1969), 24:142–53

Vann, J. Don, The Death of Dora Spenlow in "David Copperfield," Victorian Newsletter (Fall 1962), #22:19–20

Wilson, Angus, Charles Dickens: A Haunting, Critical Quarterly (Summer 1960), 2:101–08

Dombey and Son, 1846–48

Andersen, Sally S., Dickens and the Problem of Maturity:
"Dombey and Son," "David Copperfield," "Bleak House,"

"Great Expectations," and "Our Mutual Friend," Dissertation
Abstracts (1968), 28:3135A

Axton, William, "Dombey and Son": From Stereotype to Ar-
chetype, ELH (1964), 31:301–17

Axton, William, Tonal Unity in "Dombey and Son," Modern
Language Association. Publications (1963), 78:341–48

Carlton, William J., A Note on Captain Cuttle, The Dickensian
(1968), 64:152–56

Collins, Philip, "Dombey and Son"—Then and Now, The Dickensian (May 1967), 63:82–94

Coolidge, Archibald C., Dickens and Latitudinarian Christianity, The Dickensian (Winter 1963), 59:57–60

Dyson, A. E., The Inimitable Dickens; A Reading of the
Novels. 1970. p. 96–118

English Association. Essays and Studies, 1951. 1951. p.
70–93

Goldfarb, Russell M., Sexual Repression and Victorian Literature. 1970. p. 119–22

Howard, David, et al, Tradition and Tolerance in Nineteenth
Century Fiction; Critical Essays on Some English and American Novels. 1967. p. 99–140

Leavis, F. R., Dombey and Son, Sewanee Review (Spring 1962),
70:177–201

Mack, Maynard and Ian Gregor, eds., Imagined Worlds; Essays
on Some English Novels and Novelists in Honour of John Butt.
1968. p. 173–82

Phillips, George L., Dickens and the Chimney-Sweepers, The
Dickensian (Winter 1963), 59:28–44

Stone, Harry, Dickens and Leitmotif: Music-Staircase Imagery
in "Dombey and Son," College English (1963), 25:217–20

Stone, Harry, The Novel as Fairy Tale; Dickens' "Dombey and
Son," English Studies (Feb. 1966), 47:1–27

Tillotson, Kathleen May, Novels of the 1840's. 1961. p. 157–99

Williams, Raymond, The English Novel; From Dickens to
Lawrence. 1970. p. 37–47

Wright, Austin, ed., Victorian Literature; Modern Essays in
Criticism. 1961. p. 136–53

Edwin Drood, 1870

Bilham, D. M., "Edwin Drood": To Resolve a Mystery, The
Dickensian (Sept. 1966), 62:181–93

Cohen, Jane R., Dickens' Artists and Artistry in "The Mystery
of Edwin Drood," Dickens Studies (1967), 3:126–45

Coolidge, Archibald C., Dickens' Complex Plots, The Dicken-
sian (Autumn 1961), 57:174–82
Coolidge, Archibald C., Dickens and Latitudinarian Chris-
tianity, The Dickensian (Winter 1963), 59:57–60
Cox, Arthur J., The "Drood" Remains, Dickens Studies (1966),
2:33–44
Cox, Arthur J., The Morals of Edwin Drood, The Dickensian
(Jan. 1962), 58:32–43
Dyson, A. E., Edwin Drood: A Horrible Wonder Apart, Criti-
cal Quarterly (Summer 1969), 11:138–57
Dyson, A. E., The Inimitable Dickens; A Reading of the
Novels. 1970. p. 267–93
Greenhalgh, Mollie, Edwin Drood: The Twilight of a God, The
Dickensian (May 1959), 55:68–75
Manheim, Leonard F., Thanatos: The Death Instinct in
Dickens' Later Novels, Psychoanalysis and Psychoanalytic
Review (Winter 1960–61), 47:17–31
Mitchell, Charles, "Mystery of Edwin Drood": The Interior
and Exterior of Self, ELH (June 1966), 33:228–46
Pritchett, Victor Sawdon, The Living Novel and Later Appre-
ciations. 1964. p. 81–87
Stelzmann, Rainulf, "The Mystery of Edwin Drood": Ein Neuer
Lösungsversuch, Archiv für das Studium der Neueren
Sprachen und Literaturen (1957), 193:285–91
Stone, Harry, Dickens and Interior Monologue, Philological
Quarterly (Jan. 1959), 38:52–65
Winters, Warrington, The Death Hug in Charles Dickens,
Literature and Psychology (Spring 1966), 16:109–15

Great Expectations, 1860–61

Andersen, Sally S., Dickens and the Problem of Maturity:
"Dombey and Son," "David Copperfield," "Bleak House,"
"Great Expectations," and "Our Mutual Friend," Dissertation
Abstracts (1968), 28:3135A
Bell, Vereen M., Parents and Children in "Great Expectations,"
Victorian Newsletter (Spring 1965), #27:21–24
Bodelsen, C. A., Some Notes on Dickens' Symbolism, English
Studies (Dec. 1959), 40:420–31
Charles Dickens, 1812–1870; A Centennial Volume, ed. by
E. W. F. Tomlin. 1969. p. 109–31 and 237–63
Coolidge, Archibald C., Jr., "Great Expectations," the Culmi-
nation of a Developing Art, Mississippi Quarterly (Fall 1961),
14:190–96

Crews, Frederick, ed., Psychoanalysis and Literary Process.
    1970. p. 25-65
Drew, Elizabeth A., The Novel; A Modern Guide to Fifteen
    English Masterpieces. 1963. p. 191-207
Dunn, Richard J., Drummle and Startop; Doubling in "Great
    Expectations," The Dickensian (May 1967), 63:125-27
Dyson, A. E., The Inimitable Dickens; A Reading of the
    Novels. 1970. p. 228-47
Edminson, Mary, The Date of the Action in "Great Expecta-
    tions," Nineteenth Century Fiction (1958), 13:22-35
Fielding, K. J., The Critical Autonomy of "Great Expectations,"
    Review of English Literature (July 1961), 2:75-88
Forker, Charles R., The Language of Hands in "Great Expec-
    tations," Texas Studies in Literature and Language (1961),
    3:280-93
Goldfarb, Russell M., The Menu of "Great Expectations,"
    Victorian Newsletter (Spring 1962), #21:18-19
Gordon, Andrew, Jaggers and the Moral Scheme of "Great
    Expectations," The Dickensian (Jan. 1969), 65:3-11
Gregory, Marshall W., Values and Meaning in "Great Expec-
    tations": The Two Endings Revisited, Essays in Criticism
    (1969), 19:402-09
Hallam, Clifford B., The Structure of "Great Expectations" in
    Respect to Style and Artistry, Dickens Studies (1966), 2:26-32
Hardy, Barbara, Food and Ceremony in "Great Expectations,"
    Essays in Criticism (1963), 13:351-63
Hardy, Barbara, The Moral Art of Dickens. 1970. p. 139-55
Hynes, Joseph A., Image and Symbol in "Great Expectations,"
    ELH (1963), 30:258-92
Kelty, Jean McClure, The Modern Tones of Charles Dickens,
    The Dickensian (Autumn 1961), 57:160-65
Kieft, Ruth M. Vande, Patterns of Communication in "Great
    Expectations," Nineteenth Century Fiction (March 1961), 15:
    325-34
Levine, George, Communication in "Great Expectations," Nine-
    teenth Century Fiction (Sept. 1963), 18:175-81
Levine, M. H., Hand and Hearts in "Great Expectations," Ball
    State University Forum (Autumn 1965), 6:22-24
Lindberg, John, Individual Conscience and Social Injustice in
    "Great Expectations," College English (Nov. 1961), 23:118-22
Marcus, Mordecai, The Pattern of Self-Alienation in "Great
    Expectations," Victorian Newsletter (1964), #26:9-12
Marcus, Philip L., Theme and Suspense in the Plot of "Great

Expectations," Dickens Studies (1966), 2:57–73

Marshall, William H., The Conclusion of "Great Expectations" as the Fulfillment of Myth, Personalist (Summer 1963), 44: 337–47

Meisel, Martin, The Ending of "Great Expectations," Essays in Criticism (July 1965), 15:326–31

Meisel, Martin, Miss Havisham Brought to Book, Modern Language Association. Publications (June 1966), 81:278–85

Monod, Sylvère, "Great Expectations" a Hundred Years After, The Dickensian (Sept. 1960), 56:133–40

Moore, Jack B., Heart and Hands in "Great Expectations," The Dickensian (Jan. 1965), 61:52–56

Moynahan, Julian, The Hero's Guilt; The Case of "Great Expectations," Essays in Criticism (Jan. 1960), 10:60–79

New, William H., The Four Elements in "Great Expectations," Dickens Studies (1967), 3:111–21

Nisbet, Ada, The Autobiographical Matrix of "Great Expectations," Victorian Newsletter (Spring 1959), #15:10–13

Parish, Charles, A Boy Brought Up "by Hand," Nineteenth Century Fiction (Dec. 1962), 17:286–88

Partlow, Robert B., Jr., The Moving I: A Study of the Point of View in "Great Expectations," College English (1961), 23: 122–31

Pearce, Richard A., Stages of the Clown; Perspectives on Modern Fiction from Dostoyevsky to Beckett. 1970. p. 26–46

Raleigh, John Henry, Dickens and the Sense of Time, Nineteenth Century Fiction (Sept. 1958), 13:127–37

Reed, James, Fulfillment of Pip's Expectations, The Dickensian (Jan. 1959), 55:12–18

Reeves, Bruce, Pipes and Pipe-Smoking in "Great Expectations," The Dickensian (1966), 62:174–78

Røstvig, Maren-Sofie, et al, The Hidden Sense and Other Essays. 1963. p. 197–226

Shapiro, Charles, ed., Twelve Original Essays on Great English Novels. 1960. p. 103–24

Stewart, James T., Miss Havisham and Miss Grierson, Furman Studies (Fall 1958), 6:21–23

Stone, Harry, Fire, Hand, and Gate: Dickens' "Great Expectations," Kenyon Review (Autumn 1962), 24:662–91

Sweeney, Patricia R., Mr. Howse, Mr. Thackeray and Mr. Pirrip: The Question of Snobbery in "Great Expectations," The Dickensian (Jan. 1968), 64:55–63

Tetzeli von Rosador, Kurt, Charles Dickens: "Great Expectations": Das Ende eines Ich-Romans, Die Neueren Sprachen (Aug. 1969), 18:399-408

Vasta, Edward, "Great Expectations" and "The Great Gatsby," The Dickensian (Autumn 1964), 60:167-72

Wagenknecht, Edward Charles, Dickens and the Scandal-Mongers; Essays in Criticism. 1965. p. 132-36

Wall, Stephen, Dickens' Plot of Fortune, Review of English Literature (Jan. 1965), 6:56-67

Wentersdorf, Karl P., Mirror-Images in "Great Expectations," Nineteenth Century Fiction (1966), 21:203-24

Wilson, Angus, Charles Dickens: A Haunting, Critical Quarterly (Summer 1960), 2:101-08

Hard Times, 1854

Atkinson, F. G., "Hard Times": Motifs and Meanings, Use of English (Spring 1963), 14:165-69

Berman, Ronald, Human Scale: A Note on "Hard Times," Nineteenth Century Fiction (1967), 22:288-93

Carnall, Geoffrey, Dickens, Mrs. Gaskell and the Preston Strike, Victorian Studies (Sept. 1964), 8:31-48

Collins, Philip, Dickens and Popular Amusements, The Dickensian (Jan. 1965), 61:7-19

Cooperman, Stanley, Dickens and the Secular Blasphemy; Social Criticism in "Hard Times," "Little Dorrit," and "Bleak House," College English (1960), 22:156-60

Crockett, Judith, Theme and Metaphor in "Hard Times," Spectrum (Fall 1962), 6:80-81

Deneau, Daniel P., The Brother-Sister Relationship in "Hard Times," The Dickensian (Autumn 1964), 60:173-77

Downs, Robert Bingham, Molders of the Modern Mind; One Hundred Eleven Books that Shaped Western Civilization. 1961. p. 265-67

Dyson, A. E., "Hard Times": The Robber Fancy, The Dickensian (May 1963), 65:67-79

Dyson, A. E., The Inimitable Dickens; A Reading of the Novels. 1970. p. 183-202

Fielding, K. J., "Hard Times" for the Present, The Dickensian (Sept. 1967), 43:149-52

Goldfarb, Russell M., Sexual Repression and Victorian Literature. 1970. p. 126-29

Hirsch, David H., "Hard Times" and F. R. Leavis, Criticism (1964), 6:1-16

Johnson, Alan P., "Hard Times": "Performance" or "Poetry,"
Dickens Studies (1969), 5:62—80

Lamb, Cedric, Love and Self-Interest in Dickens' Novels,
Paunch (Dec. 1968), #33:32—46

Lodge, David, Language of Fiction; Essays in Criticism and
Verbal Analysis of the English Novel. 1966. p. 144—63

Mack, Maynard, Ian Gregor, eds., Imagined Worlds; Essays
on some English Novels and Novelists in Honour of John
Butt. 1968. p. 183—203

Sonstroem, David, Fettered Fancy in "Hard Times," Modern
Language Association. Publications (1969), 84:520—29

Voss, A. E., A Note on Theme and Structure in "Hard Times,"
Theoria (1964), #23:35—42

Wilson, Angus, Charles Dickens: A Haunting, Critical Quarterly (Summer 1960), 2:101—08

Little Dorrit, 1855—57

Bell, Vereen M., Mrs. General as Victorian England: Dickens'
Image of His Time, Nineteenth Century Fiction (1965), 20:
177—84

Bergler, Edmund, "Little Dorrit" and Dickens' Intuitive Knowledge of Psychic Masochism, American Imago (1957), 14:371—
88

Butt, John, The Topicality of "Little Dorrit," University of
Toronto Quarterly (Oct. 1959), 29:1—10

Coolidge, Archibald, Dickens' Complex Plots, The Dickensian
(Autumn 1961), 57:174—82

Cooperman, Stanley, Dickens and the Secular Blasphemy;
Social Criticism in "Hard Times," "Little Dorrit," and "Bleak
House," College English (Dec. 1960), 22:156—60

Dyson, A. E., The Inimitable Dickens; A Reading of the Novels.
1970. p. 203—11

Gervais, David, The Poetry of "Little Dorrit," Cambridge
Quarterly (1969), 4:38—53

McMaster, R. D., Little Dorrit: Experience and Design,
Queen's Quarterly (Winter 1961), 67:530—38

Meckier, Jerome, Dickens' "Little Dorrit": "Sundry Curious
Vàriations on the Same Tune," Dickens Studies (1967), 3:51—
62

Partlow, Robert B., Jr., ed., Dickens the Craftsman; Strategies of Presentation. 1970. p. 140—64

Pearce, Roy Harvey, ed., Experience in the Novel; Selected
Papers from the English Institute. 1968. p. 107—31

Sherif, Nur, The Victorian Sunday in "Little Dorrit" and
"Thyrza," Cairo Studies in English (1960), p. 155–65
Slater, Michael, ed., Dickens 1970. Centenary Essays. 1970.
p. 125–49
Wain, John, Essays on Literature and Ideas. 1963. p. 219–32
Wall, Stephen, Dickens' Plot of Fortune, Review of English
Literature (Jan. 1965), 6:56–67
Wilde, Alan, Mr. F's Aunt and the Analogical Structure of
"Little Dorrit," Nineteenth Century Fiction (June 1964), 19:
33–44
Wilson, Angus, Charles Dickens; A Haunting, Critical Quar-
terly (Summer 1960), 2:101–08

Martin Chuzzlewit, 1843–44

Coolidge, Archibald, Dickens' Complex Plots, The Dickensian
(Autumn 1961), 57:174–82
Dyson, A. E., The Inimitable Dickens; A Reading of the Novels.
1970. p. 71–95
Dyson, A. E., "Martin Chuzzlewit": Howls the Sublime, Criti-
cal Quarterly (Autumn 1967), 9:234–53
Goldfarb, Russell M., Sexual Repression and Victorian Litera-
ture. 1970. p. 116–19
Hardy, Barbara, The Change of Heart in Dickens' Novels,
Victorian Studies (Sept. 1961), 5:49–67
Hardy, Barbara, The Moral Art of Dickens. 1970. p. 100–21
Phillips, George L., Dickens and the Chimney-Sweepers, The
Dickensian (Winter 1963), 59:28–44
Ridland, J. M., Huck, Pip, and Plot, Nineteenth Century Fiction
(Dec. 1965), 20:286–90
Shain, Charles E., The English Novelists and the Civil War,
American Quarterly (Fall 1962), 14:399–421
Shereikis, Richard J., From Pickwick to Pecksniff: An Analy-
sis of "Martin Chuzzlewit" and Its Significance to Dickens'
Career, Dissertation Abstracts (1969), 29:3588A
Steig, Michael, "Martin Chuzzlewit": Pinch and Pecksniff,
Studies in the Novel (Summer 1969), 1:181–88
Wall, Stephen, Dickens' Plot of Fortune, Review of English
Literature (Jan. 1965), 6:56–67
Whitley, John S., The Two Hells of Martin Chuzzlewit, Papers
of the Michigan Academy of Science, Arts and Letters (1965),
1:585–97

The Mystery of Edwin Drood, SEE Edwin Drood

Nicholas Nickleby, 1838-39

Kelty, Jean McClure, The Modern Tones of Charles Dickens,
    The Dickensian (Autumn 1961), 57:160-65
Reed, John R., Some Indefinable Resemblance: Moral Form
    in Dickens' "Nicholas Nickleby," Papers on Language and
    Literature (1967), 3:134-47
Roulet, Ann, A Comparative Study of "Nicholas Nickleby" and
    "Bleak House," The Dickensian (Spring 1964), 60:117-24
Thompson, Leslie M., Mrs. Nickleby's Monologue: The
    Dichotomy of Pessimism and Optimism in "Nicholas Nickle-
    by," Studies in the Novel (Summer 1969), 1:222-29
Williams, Raymond, The English Novel; From Dickens to
    Lawrence. 1970. p. 50-52
Wing, G. D., A Part to Tear a Cat in, The Dickensian (Jan.
    1968), 64:10-19

Old Curiosity Shop, 1840-41

Dyson, A. E., The Inimitable Dickens; A Reading of the Novels.
    1970. p. 21-46
Dyson, A. E., "The Old Curiosity Shop": Innocence and the
    Grotesque, Critical Quarterly (Summer 1966), 8:111-30
Gibson, John W., "The Old Curiosity Shop": The Critical
    Allegory, The Dickensian (Autumn 1964), 60:178-83
McLean, Robert Simpson, Putting Quilp to Rest, Victorian
    Newsletter (Fall 1968), #34:29-33
Manheim, Leonard F., Thanatos: The Death Instinct in
    Dickens' Later Novels, Psychoanalysis and Psychoanalytic
    Review (Winter 1960-61), 47:17-31
Partlow, Robert B., Jr., ed., Dickens the Craftsman; Strate-
    gies of Presentation. 1970. p. 44-94
Senelick, Laurence, Little Nell and the Prurience of Senti-
    mentality, Dickens Studies (1967), 3:146-59
Steig, Michael, The Central Action of "Old Curiosity Shop" or
    Little Nell Revisited Again, Literature and Psychology
    (Summer 1965), 15:163-70
Winters, Warrington, "The Old Curiosity Shop": A Consumma-
    tion Devoutly to Be Wished, The Dickensian (Sept. 1967), 43:
    176-80

Oliver Twist, 1837-39

Bishop, Jonathan, The Hero-Villain of "Oliver Twist," Victorian
    Newsletter (Spring 1959), #15:14-16

Colby, Robert Alan, Fiction with a Purpose; Major and Minor
    Nineteenth Century Novels. 1967. p. 105–37
Duffy, Joseph M., Jr., Another Version of Pastoral: "Oliver
    Twist," ELH (1968), 35:403–21
English Association, Essays and Studies, 1951. 1951. p. 87–
    105
Eoff, Sherman, "Oliver Twist" and the Spanish Picaresque
    Novel, Studies in Philology (1957), 54:440–47
Fiedler, Leslie Aaron, ed., Art of the Essay. 1958. p. 598–
    603
Frederick, Kenneth C., The Cold, Cold Hearth: Domestic
    Strife in "Oliver Twist," College English (1966), 27:465–70
Gold, Joseph, Dickens' Exemplary Aliens: Bumble the Beadle
    and Fagin the Fence, Mosaic (1968), 2:77–89
Greene, Graham, Collected Essays. 1969. p. 101–10
Kincaid, James P., Laughter and "Oliver Twist," Modern Lan-
    guage Association. Publications (1968), 83:63–70
Lane, Lauriat, Jr., Dickens' Archetypal Jew, Nineteenth
    Century Fiction (June 1958), 13:94–100
McLean, Robert S., Fagin: An Early View of Evil, Lock Haven
    Review (1967), 9:29–36
Marcus, Steven, Who is Fagin?, Commentary (June 1962), 33:
    48–59
Page, Norman, "A Language Fit for Heroes": Speech in "Oliver
    Twist" and "Our Mutual Friend," The Dickensian (May 1969),
    65:100–07
Patten, Robert L., Capitalism and Compassion in "Oliver
    Twist," Studies in the Novel (Summer 1969), 1:207–21
Phillips, George L., Dickens and the Chimney-Sweepers, The
    Dickensian (Winter 1963), 59:28–44
Tartella, Vincent Paul, Charles Dickens' "Oliver Twist":
    Moral Realism and the Uses of Style, Dissertation Abstracts
    (1961), 22:1616–17
Tillotson, Kathleen, Oliver Twist, Essays and Studies by Mem-
    bers of the English Society (1959), 12:87–105
Williamson, Colin, Two Missing Links in "Oliver Twist," Nine-
    teenth Century Fiction (Dec. 1967), 22:225–34
Winters, Warrington, The Death Hug in Charles Dickens, Lit-
    erature and Psychology (Spring 1966), 16:109–15

Our Mutual Friend, 1864–66

Andersen, Sally S., The De-Spiritualization of the Elements in

"Our Mutual Friend," Discourse (1969), 12:423–33

Andersen, Sally S., Dickens and the Problem of Maturity: "Dombey and Son," "David Copperfield," "Bleak House," "Great Expectations," and "Our Mutual Friend," Dissertation Abstracts (1968), 28:3135A

Barnard, Robert, The Choral Symphony: "Our Mutual Friend," Review of English Literature (July 1961), 2:89–99

Collins, Thomas J., Some Mutual Sets of Friends: Moral Monitors in "Emma" and "Our Mutual Friend," The Dickensian (Jan. 1969), 65:32–34

Dunn, Richard J., Dickens and the Tragi-Comic Grotesque, Studies in the Novel (Summer 1969), 1:147–56

Dyson, A. E., The Inimitable Dickens; A Reading of the Novels. 1970. p. 248–66

English Association. Essays and Studies, 1966. 1966. Vol. 19. p. 92–105

Goldfarb, Russell M., Sexual Repression and Victorian Literature. 1970. p. 129–32

Hardy, Barbara, The Change of Heart in Dickens' Novels, Victorian Studies (Sept. 1961), 5:49–67

Hobsbaum, Philip, The Critics and "Our Mutual Friend," Essays in Criticism (July 1963), 13:231–40

Knoepflmacher, U. C., Laughter and Despair; Readings in Ten Novels of the Victorian Age. 1971. p. 137–67

Lamb, Cedric, Love and Self-Interest in Dickens' Novels, Paunch (Dec. 1968), #33:32–46

Lane, Lauriat, Dickens' Archetypal Jew, Modern Language Association. Publications (1958), 73:94–100

Lane, Lauriat, Dickens and the Double, The Dickensian (Jan. 1959), 55:47–55

Lanham, Richard A., "Our Mutual Friend": The Birds of Prey, Victorian Newsletter (Fall 1963), #24:6–12

McMaster, R. D., Birds of Prey: A Study of "Our Mutual Friend," Dalhousie Review (Summer 1960), 40:372–81

Manheim, Leonard F., Thanatos: The Death Instinct in Dickens' Later Novels, Psychoanalysis and Psychoanalytic Review (Winter 1960–61), 47:17–31

Miyoshi, Masao, Resolution of Identity in "Our Mutual Friend," Victorian Newsletter (Fall 1964), #26:5–9

Monod, Sylvère, L'Expression dans "Our Mutual Friend": "Manière" ou "Manièrisme?," Études Anglaises (1957), 10: 37–48

Muir, Kenneth, Image and Structure in "Our Mutual Friend,"

Essays and Studies (1966), 19:92–105

Nelson, Harland S., Dickens' "Our Mutual Friend" and Henry Mayhaw's "London Labour and the London Poor," Nineteenth Century Fiction (1965), 20:207–22

Oppel, Horst, Charles Dickens: "Our Mutual Friend," Die Neueren Sprachen (Oct. 1962), #10:437–54

Oppel, Horst, Der Moderne Englische Roman; Interpretationen. 1965. p. 15–33

Page, Norman, "A Language Fit for Heroes": Speech in "Oliver Twist" and "Our Mutual Friend," The Dickensian (May 1969), 65:100–07

Rérat, A., Le Romanesque dans "L'Ami Commun," Les Langues Modernes (May–June 1958), 52:30–36

Sharp, Sister M. Corona, The Archetypal Feminine: "Our Mutual Friend," University of Kansas City Review (1961), 27:307–11

Sharp, Sister M. Corona, A Study of the Archetypal Feminine: "Our Mutual Friend," University of Kansas City Review (1961), 28:74–80

Shea, F. X., Mr. Venus Observed: The Plot Change in "Our Mutual Friend," Papers in Language and Literature (1968), 4:170–81

Shea, F. X., No Change of Intension in "Our Mutual Friend," The Dickensian (Jan. 1967), 63:37–40

Thompson, Leslie M., The Marks of Pride in "Our Mutual Friend," The Dickensian (Spring 1964), 60:124–28

Wall, Stephen, Dickens' Plot of Fortune, Review of English Literature (Jan. 1965), 6:56–67

Williams, Raymond, The English Novel; From Dickens to Lawrence. 1970. p. 55–57

Pickwick Papers, 1836–37

Auden, Wystan Hugh, The Dyer's Hand and Other Essays. 1962. p. 407–28

Axton, William, Unity and Coherence in "The Pickwick Papers," Studies in English Literature, 1500–1900 (1965), 5:633–76

Bevington, David M., Seasonal Relevance in "The Pickwick Papers," Nineteenth Century Fiction (1961), 16:219–30

Easson, Angus, Imprisonment for Debt in "Pickwick Papers," The Dickensian (May 1968), 64:105–12

Fadiman, Clifton, Party of One; The Selected Writings of Clifton Fadiman. 1955. p. 203–25

Hardy, Barbara, The Moral Art of Dickens. 1970. p. 81–99

Kincaid, Jr. R., Education of Mr. Pickwick, <u>Nineteenth Century Fiction</u> (Sept. 1969), 24:127–41

Patten, Robert L., The Art of "Pickwick's" Interpolated Tales, <u>ELH</u> (1967), 34:349–66

Patten, Robert L., Boz, Phiz, and Pickwick in the Pound, <u>ELH</u> (1969), 36:575–91

Winters, Warrington, The Death Hug in Charles Dickens, <u>Literature and Psychology</u> (Spring 1966), 16:109–15

A Tale of Two Cities, 1859

Dyson, A. E., <u>The Inimitable Dickens; A Reading of the Novels.</u> 1970. p. 212–27

Fleishman, Avrom, <u>The English Historical Novel; Walter Scott to Virginia Woolf.</u> 1971. p. 114–26

Gregory, Michael, Old Bailey Speech in "A Tale of Two Cities," <u>Review of English Literature</u> (April 1965), 6:42–55

Manheim, Leonard, "A Tale of Two Cities": A Study in Psychoanalytic Criticism, <u>English Review</u> (N.Y.) (Spring 1959), p. 13–28

Marshall, William H., The Method of "A Tale of Two Cities," <u>The Dickensian</u> (Autumn 1961), 57:183–89

Partlow, Robert B., Jr., ed., <u>Dickens the Craftsman; Strategies of Presentation.</u> 1970. p. 165–86

Stange, G. Robert, Dickens and the Fiery Past: "A Tale of Two Cities" Reconsidered, <u>English Journal</u> (1957), 44:381–90

Wagenknecht, Edward Charles, <u>Dickens and the Scandalmongers; Essays in Criticism.</u> 1965. p. 121–31

Zabel, Morton Dauwen, ed., <u>Craft and Character; Texts, Methods and Vocation in Modern Fiction.</u> 1957. p. 49–69

BENJAMIN DISRAELI

Coningsby; or, The New Generation, 1844

Greene, D. J., Becky Sharp and Lord Steyne—Thackeray or Disraeli?, <u>Nineteenth Century Fiction</u> (Sept. 1961), 16:157–6

McCabe, Bernard, Disraeli and the "Baronial Principle": Som Versions of Romantic Medievalism, <u>Victorian Newsletter</u> (Fall 1968), #34:7–13

Thackeray, William Makepeace, <u>Contributions to the Morning Chronicle; Now First Reprinted.</u> 1955. p. 39–50

Sybil; or, The Two Nations, 1845

McCabe, Bernard, Disraeli and the "Baronial Principle": Som

Versions of Romantic Medievalism, <u>Victorian Newsletter</u>
(Fall 1968), #34:7–13
Thackeray, William Makepeace, <u>Contributions to the Morning</u>
<u>Chronicle; Now First Reprinted.</u> 1955. p. 77–86

Tancred; or, The New Crusade, 1847

 Dahl, Curtis, Baroni in Disraeli's "Tancred," <u>Notes and</u>
 <u>Queries</u> (1958), 5:152
 Levine, R. A., Disraeli's "Tancred" and the Great Asian
 Mystery, <u>Nineteenth Century Fiction</u> (June 1967), 22:71–85

CHARLES LUTWIDGE DODGSON

SEE

LEWIS CARROLL

ARTHUR CONAN DOYLE

The Sign of the Four, 1889

 Boyd, Andrew, Dr. Watson's Dupe, <u>Encounter</u> (March 1960),
 14:64–66

The Hound of the Baskervilles, 1902

 Kissane, James and John M. Kissane, Sherlock Holmes and the
 Ritual of Reason, <u>Nineteenth Century Fiction</u> (March 1963),
 17:353–62

DAPHNE DU MAURIER

Frenchman's Creek, 1942

 Rountree, Thomas J., "Frenchman's Creek" as a Variation of
 "The Gypsy Laddie," <u>Tennessee Folklore Society Bulletin</u>
 (1959), 25:85–87

LAWRENCE DURRELL

Alexandria Quartet, 1956–60

 Arthos, John, Lawrence Durrell's Gnosticism, <u>Personalist</u>
 (1962), 42:360–73
 Baldanza, Frank, Lawrence Durrell's "Word Continuum,"
 <u>Critique; Studies in Modern Fiction</u> (Spring–Summer 1961),
 4:3–17

Bode, Carl, Durrell's Way to Alexandria, College English (1961), 22:531–38

Bork, Alfred M., Durrell and Relativity, Centennial Review (Spring 1963), 7:191–203

Burns, J. Christopher, Durrell's Heraldic Universe, Modern Fiction Studies (Autumn 1967), 13:375–88

Cate, Curtis, Lawrence Durrell, Atlantic Monthly (Dec. 1961), 208:63–69

Corke, Hilary, Lawrence Durrell, Literary Half-Yearly (Jan. 1961), 2:43–49

Crowder, Richard, Durrell, "Libido" and "Eros," Ball State University Forum (Winter 1962–63), 3:34–39

Decancq, Roland, What Lies Beyond? An Analysis of Darley's "Quest" in Lawrence Durrell's "Alexandria Quartet," Revue des Langues Vivantes (1968), 34:134–50

DeMott, Benjamin, Grading the Emanglons, Hudson Review (1960), 13:457–64

Dobrée, Bonamy, Durrell's Alexandrian Series, Sewanee Review (Winter 1961), 69:61–79

Enright, Dennis Joseph, Alexandrian Nights' Entertainments: Lawrence Durrell's "Quartet," International Literary Annual (1961), 3:30–39

Enright, Dennis Joseph, Conspirators and Poets. 1966. p. 111–20

Eskin, Stanley G., Durrell's Themes in the Alexandria Quartet, Texas Quarterly (Winter 1962), 5:43–60

Friedman, Alan W., Art for Love's Sake; Lawrence Durrell and "The Alexandria Quartet," Dissertation Abstracts (1966), 27:1365A–66A

Glicksburg, Charles I., The Fictional World of Lawrence Durrell, Bucknell Review (March 1963), 11:118–33

Glicksberg, Charles I., The Self in Modern Literature. 1963. p. 89–94

Goldberg, Gerald Jay, The Search for the Artist in Some Recent British Fiction, South Atlantic Quarterly (Summer 1963), 62:387–401

Gossman, Ann, Some Characters in Search of a Mirror, Critique; Studies in Modern Fiction (Spring 1966), 8:79–84

Goulianos, Joan, Lawrence Durrell and Alexandria, Virginia Quarterly Review (1969), 45:664–73

Hagergård, Sture, Om Medvetandets Struktur, Horisont (1966), 13:21–23

Hagopian, John V., The Resolution of the "Alexandria Quartet,"

Critique; Studies in Modern Fiction (Spring 1964), 7:97–106

Hasnard, Jean, Lawrence Durrell; A European Writer, Durham University Journal (March 1968), 60:171–81

Hauge, Ingvar, Lawrence Durrell fram til "Alexandria-Kvartetten," Samtiden (1962), 71:220–26

Hawkins, Joanna Lynn, A Study of the Relationship of Point of View to the Structure of "The Alexandria Quartet," Dissertation Abstracts (1965), 26:3338–39

Highet, Gilbert, The Alexandrian of Lawrence Durrell, Horizon (March 1960), 2:113–18

Howarth, Herbert, A Segment of Durrell's "Quartet," University of Toronto Quarterly (April 1963), 32:282–93

Hutchens, Eleanor H., The Heraldic Universe in "The Alexandria Quartet," College English (Oct. 1962), 24:56–61

Johnson, Ann S., Lawrence Durrell's "Prism-Sightedness": The Structure of "The Alexandria Quartet," Dissertation Abstracts (1968), 29:264A

Katope, Christopher G., Cavafy and Durrell's "The Alexandria Quartet," Comparative Literature (1969), 21:125–38

Kelly, John C., Lawrence Durrell: "The Alexandria Quartet," Studies (Spring 1963), 52:52–68

Kruppa, Joseph E., Durrell's "Alexandria Quartet" and the Implosion of the Modern Consciousness, Modern Fiction Studies (Autumn 1967), 13:401–16

Lebas, Gérard, Lawrence Durrell's "Alexandria Quartet" and the Critics: A Survey of Published Criticism, Caliban (1969), 6:91–114

Lemon, Lee T., "The Alexandria Quartet": Form and Fiction, Wisconsin Studies in Contemporary Literature (Autumn 1963), 4:327–38

Levidova, I., A "Four-Decker" in Stagnant Waters, Anglo-Soviet Journal (Summer 1962), 23:39–41

Levitt, Morton P., Art and Correspondences: Durrell, Miller and the "Alexandria Quartet," Modern Fiction Studies (Autumn 1967), 13:299–318

Littlejohn, David, The Permanence of Durrell, Colorado Quarterly (Summer 1965), 14:63–71

Lombardo, Agostino, Il Quartetto di Alessandria, Terzo Programma (1961), #1:186–92

Lund, Mary Graham, Alexandrian Projection, Antioch Review (Summer 1961), 21:198–204

Lund, Mary Graham, Durrell: Soft Focus on Crime, Prairie Schooner (Winter 1961), 35:339–44

Lund, Mary Graham, Eight Aspects of Melissa, Forum
    (Houston) (Summer 1961), 3:11-14
Manzalaoui, Mahmoud, Curate's Egg: An Alexandrian Opinion
    of Durrell's "Quartet," Études Anglaises (July-Sept.
    1962), 15:248-60
Michot, Paulette, Lawrence Durrell's "Alexandria Quartet,"
    Revue des Langues Vivantes (1960), 26:361-67
Morcos, Mona L., Elements of the Autobiography in "The Alex-
    andria Quartet," Modern Fiction Studies (1967), 13:343-59
Oppel, Horst, ed., Der Moderne Englische Roman: Interpre-
    tationen. 1965. p. 399-416
Proser, Matthew N., Darley's Dilemma: The Problem of
    Structure in Durrell's "Alexandria Quartet," Critique; Studies
    in Modern Fiction (Spring-Summer 1961), 4:18-28
Read, Phyllis J., The Illusion of Personality: Cyclical Time in
    Durrell's "Alexandria Quartet," Modern Fiction Studies
    (Autumn 1967), 13:389-99
Robinson, W. R., Intellect and Imagination in "The Alexandria
    Quartet," Shenandoah (Summer 1967), 18:55-68
Scholes, Robert, Return to Alexandria: Lawrence Durrell and
    Western Narrative Tradition, Virginia Quarterly Review
    (Summer 1964), 40:411-20
Serpieri, Alessandro, Il Quartetto di Alessandro di Lawrence
    Durrell, Il Ponte (1962), 18:48-57
Sertoli, Giuseppe, Lawrence Durrell e il "Quartetto di Ales-
    sandria," English Miscellany (1967), 18:207-56
Servotte, Herman, "The Alexandria Quartet" van Lawrence
    Durrell, Dietsche Warande en Belfort (1963), 108:646-58
Shapiro, Charles, ed., Contemporary British Novelists. 1965.
    p. 16-35
Steiner, George, Language and Silence; Essays on Language,
    Literature and the Inhuman. 1967. p. 280-87
Sutherland, William O. S., ed., Six Contemporary Novels: Six
    Introductory Essays in Modern Fiction. 1963. p. 6-21
Weatherhead, A. K., Romantic Anachronism in "The Alexandria
    Quartet," Modern Fiction Studies (Summer 1964), 10:128-36

Balthazar, 1958

    Bode, Carl, Durrell's Way to Alexandria, College English
        (May 1961), 22:531-38
    Cami, Ben, Lawrence Durrell: Een Paar Notas, De Vlaamse
        Gids (Oct. 1958), 42:635-37
    DeMott, Benjamin, Grading the Emanglons, Hudson Review
        (Autumn 1960), 13:456-64

Flint, R. W., A Major Novelist, Commentary (April 1959), 27:
  353–56
Hamard, Jean-Paul, L'Espace et le Temps dans les Romans
  de Lawrence Durrell, Critique (Paris) (April 1960), 16:387–
  413
Mackworth, Cecily, Lawrence Durrell and the New Romanticism, Twentieth Century (March 1960), 167:203–13
SEE ALSO Alexandria Quartet

Clea, 1960

  Bode, Carl, Durrell's Way to Alexandria, College English
    (May 1961), 22:531–38
  Corke, Hilary, Mr. Durrell and Brother Criticus, Encounter
    (May 1960), 14:65–70
  DeMott, Benjamin, Grading the Emanglons, Hudson Review
    (Autumn 1960), 13:456–64
  Kermode, Frank, Fourth Dimension, Review of English Litera-
    ture (April 1960), 1:73–77
  Mackworth, Cecily, Lawrence Durrell and the New Romanti-
    cism, Twentieth Century (March 1960), 167:203–13
  SEE ALSO Alexandria Quartet

Justine, 1956

  Albérès, R. M., Lawrence Durrell ou le Roman Pentagonal,
    Revue de Paris (Feb. 1965), p. 102–12
  Bode, Carl, Durrell's Way to Alexandria, College English
    (May 1961), 22:531–38
  Cami, Ben, Lawrence Durrell: Een Paar Notas, De Vlaamse
    Gids (Oct. 1958), 42:635–37
  DeMott, Benjamin, Grading the Emanglons, Hudson Review
    (Autumn 1960), 13:456–64
  Flint, R. W., A Major Novelist, Commentary (April 1959), 27:
    353–56
  Hamard, Jean-Paul, L'Espace et le Temps dans les Romans
    de Lawrence Durrell, Critique (Paris) (April 1960), 16:387–
    413
  Mackworth, Cecily, Lawrence Durrell and the New Romanti-
    cism, Twentieth Century (March 1960), 167:203–13
  SEE ALSO Alexandria Quartet

Mountolive, 1958

  Albérès, R. M., Lawrence Durrell ou le Roman Pentagonal,
    Revue de Paris (Feb. 1965), p. 102–12
  Bode, Carl, Durrell's Way to Alexandria, College English
    (May 1961), 22:531–38

DeMott, Benjamin, Grading the Emanglons, Hudson Review
(Autumn 1960), 13:456–64

Flint, R. W., A Major Novelist, Commentary (April 1959), 27:
353–56

Hamard, Jean-Paul, L'Espace et le Temps dans les Romans
de Lawrence Durrell, Critique (Paris) (April 1960), 16:387–
413

Kazin, Alfred, Contemporaries. 1962. p. 188–92

Mackworth, Cecily, Lawrence Durrell and the New Romanticism, Twentieth Century (March 1960), 167:203–13

Mullins, Edward, On "Mountolive," Two Cities (April 15, 1959),
Issue 1

SEE ALSO Alexandria Quartet

MARIA EDGEWORTH

The Absentee, 1809

Altieri, Joanne, Style and Purpose in Maria Edgeworth's
Fiction, Nineteenth Century Fiction (Dec. 1968), 23:265–78

Flanagan, Thomas James Bonner, Irish Novelists, 1800–1850.
1959. p. 80–91

Kooiman-Van Middendorp, Gerarda M., The Hero in the Feminine Novel. 1966. p. 43–48

Castle Rackrent, 1800

Altieri, Joanne, Style and Purpose in Maria Edgeworth's
Fiction, Nineteenth Century Fiction (Dec. 1968), 23:265–78

Flanagan, Thomas James Bonner, Irish Novelists, 1800–1850.
1959. p. 69–79

Hoyt, Charles Alva, ed., Minor British Novelists. 1967. p.
13–31

Newcomer, James, "Castle Rackrent": Its Structure and Its
Irony, Criticism (Nov. 1966), 8:170–79

Newcomer, James, The Disingenuous Thady Quirk, Studies in
Short Fiction (1964), 2:44–50

Ormond, 1817

Flanagan, Thomas James Bonner, Irish Novelists, 1800–1850.
1959. p. 92–106

GEORGE ELIOT

Adam Bede, 1859

Adam, I. W., Restoration Through Feeling in George Eliot's

Fiction: A New Look at Hetty Sorrel, Victorian Newsletter
(Fall 1962), #22:9-12

Auster, Henry, Local Habitations; Regionalism in the Early
Novels of George Eliot. 1970. p. 38-41 and 102-34

Buchen, Irving H., Arthur Donnithorne and "Zeluco": Characterization via Literary Allusion in "Adam Bede," Victorian
Newsletter (Spring 1963), #23:18-19

Burton, Thomas G., Hetty Sorrel: The Forlorn Maiden,
Victorian Newsletter (1966), 30:24-26

Carroll, David, ed., George Eliot: The Critical Heritage.
1971. p. 71-108

Colby, Robert A., Miss Evans, Miss Mulock, and Hetty Sorrel,
English Language Notes (1965), 2:206-11

Deneau, Daniel P., Inconsistencies and Inaccuracies in "Adam
Bede," Nineteenth Century Fiction (June 1959), 14:71-75

Foakes, R. A., "Adam Bede" Reconsidered, English (London)
(Summer 1959), 12:173-76

Hardy, Barbara, ed., Critical Essays on George Eliot. 1970.
p. 19-41

Harvey, W. J., The Treatment of Time in "Adam Bede," Anglia
(1957), 75:373-84

Jones, R. T., George Eliot. 1970. p. 6-18

Jones, W. Gareth, George Eliot's "Adam Bede" and Tolstoy's
Conception of "Anna Karenina," Modern Language Review
(July 1966), 61:473-81

Knoepflmacher, V. C., George Eliot, Feuerbach, and the Question of Criticism, Victorian Studies (March 1964), 7:306-09

Knoepflmacher, U. C., The Post-Romantic Imagination: "Adam
Bede," Wordsworth and Milton, ELH (1967), 34:518-40

Kooiman-Van Middendorp, Gerarda M., The Hero in the Feminine Novel. 1966. p. 96-123

Milner, Ian, The Structure of Values in "Adam Bede," Philologica Pragensia (1966), 9:281-91

Ryals, Clyde DeL., The Thorn Imagery in "Adam Bede,"
Victorian Newsletter (Fall 1962), #22:12-13

Sprague, Rosemary, George Eliot; A Biography. 1968. p.
150-64

Stevenson, Lionel, 1859: Year of Fulfillment, Centennial Review (Fall 1959), 3:337-56

Thale, Jerome, "Adam Bede": Arthur Donnithorne and Zeluco,
Modern Language Notes (April 1955), 70:263-65

Thale, Jerome, Novels of George Eliot. 1959. p. 14-35

Williams, Raymond, The English Novel; From Dickens to
Lawrence. 1970. p. 24-26

Daniel Deronda, 1876

Adam, Ian, Character and Destiny in George Eliot's Fiction,
Nineteenth Century Fiction (Sept. 1965), 20:127-44

Beaty, Jerome, "Daniel Deronda" and the Question of Unity in
Fiction, Victorian Newsletter (Spring 1959), #15:16-20

Beeton, D. R., George Eliot's Greatest and Poorest Novel:
An Appraisal of "Daniel Deronda," English Studies in Africa
(Sept. 1965), 8:8-27

Carroll, David, ed., George Eliot: The Critical Heritage.
1971. p. 360-447

Carroll, David, An Image of Disenchantment in the Novels of
George Eliot, Review of English Studies (1960), 11:29-41

Carroll, David, "Mansfield Park" and "David Deronda" and
Ordination, Modern Philology (Feb. 1965), 62:217-26

Carroll, David, The Unity of "Daniel Deronda," Essays in
Criticism (1959), 9:369-80

Deneau, Daniel Pierre, From "Amos Barton" to "Daniel
Deronda": Studies in the Imagery of George Eliot's Fiction,
Dissertation Abstracts (1959), 20:1783

Fisch, Harold, Daniel Deronda or Gwendolen Harleth?, Nineteenth Century Fiction (March 1965), 19:345-56

Hardy, Barbara, ed., Critical Essays on George Eliot. 1970.
p. 133-50

Hester, Erwin, George Eliot's Use of Historical Events in
"Daniel Deronda," English Language Notes (1966), 4:115-18

Jones, R. T., George Eliot. 1970. p. 97-116

Kriefall, Luther H., A Victorian Apocalypse: A Study of
George Eliot's "Daniel Deronda" and Its Relation to David S.
Strauss' "Das Leben Jesu," Dissertation Abstracts (1967),
28:234A

Knoepflmacher, Ulrich Camillus, "Daniel Deronda" and William
Shakespeare, Victorian Newsletter (Spring 1961), #19:27-28

Knoepflmacher, Ulrich Camillus, Religious Humanism and the
Victorian Novel; George Eliot, Walter Pater, and Samuel
Butler. 1965. p. 116-48

Kooiman-Van Middendorp, Gerarda M., The Hero in the Feminine Novel. 1966. p. 96-123

Leavis, F. R., George Eliot's Zionist Novel, Commentary
(Oct. 1960), 30:317-25

Lerner, Laurence, The Education of Gwendolen Harleth, Critical Quarterly (Winter 1965), 7:355-64

Marquand, David, The Invisible Power, New Society (Sept. 11,
1969), p. 403

Pinney, Thomas, The Authority of the Past in George Eliot's
   Novels, Nineteenth Century Fiction (Sept. 1966), 21:131-48
Preyer, Robert, Beyond the Literal Imagination: Vision and
   Unreality in "Daniel Deronda," Victorian Studies (Sept. 1960),
   4:33-54
Robinson, Carole, The Severe Angel: A Study of "Daniel
   Deronda," ELH (1964), 31:278-300
Rothstein, Eric and Thomas K. Dunseath, Literary Mono-
   graphs, I. 1967. p. 203-43 and 315-18
Sprague, Rosemary, George Eliot; A Biography. 1968. p.
   286-302
Steinhoff, William R., The Metaphorical Texture of "Daniel
   Deronda," Books Abroad (1961), 35:220-24
Swann, Brian, Eyes in the Mirror; Imagery and Symbolism in
   "Daniel Deronda," Nineteenth Century Fiction (March 1969),
   23:434-45
Thale, Jerome, "Daniel Deronda": The Darkened World, Mod-
   ern Fiction Studies (1957), 3:119-26
Thale, Jerome, Novels of George Eliot. 1959. p. 121-36
Williams, Raymond, The English Novel: From Dickens to
   Lawrence. 1970. p. 86-88

Felix Holt, Radical, 1866

Adam, Ian, Character and Destiny in George Eliot's Fiction,
   Nineteenth Century Fiction (Sept. 1965), 20:127-44
Allott, Miriam, George Eliot in the 1860's, Victorian Studies
   (Dec. 1961), 5:93-108
Carroll, David R., Felix Holt: Society as Protagonist, Nine-
   teenth Century Fiction (1962), 17:237-52
Carroll, David, ed., George Eliot: The Critical Heritage.
   1971. p. 251-85
Hardy, Barbara, ed., Critical Essays on George Eliot. 1970.
   p. 99-115
Harper, Howard M., Jr. and Charles Edge, eds., The Classic
   British Novel. 1972. p. 103-21
Jones, R. T., George Eliot. 1970. p. 43-56
Kooiman-Van Middendorp, Gerarda M., The Hero in the Femi-
   nine Novel. 1966. p. 96-123
Myers, W. F. T., Politics and Personality in "Felix Holt,"
   Renaissance and Modern Studies (1966), 10:5-33
Sambrook, A. J., The Natural Historian of Our Social Classes,
   English (Summer 1962), 14:130-34
Sprague, Rosemary, George Eliot; A Biography. 1968. p. 230-41

Thale, Jerome, Novels of George Eliot. 1959. p. 87–105
Thomson, Fred C., "Felix Holt" as Classic Tragedy, Nine-
  teenth Century Fiction (June 1961), 16:47–58
Thomson, Fred C., The Genesis of "Felix Holt," Modern Lan-
  guage Association. Publications (Dec. 1959), 74:576–84
Thomson, Fred C., The Legal Plot in "Felix Holt," Studies in
  English Literature, 1500–1900 (Autumn 1967), 7:691–704
Wolff, Michael, The Uses of Context: Aspects of the 1860's,
  Victorian Studies (Supp. 1965), 9:47–63

Middlemarch, 1871–72

Allott, Miriam, George Eliot in the 1860's, Victorian Studies
  (Dec. 1961), 5:93–108
Auster, Henry, Local Habitations; Regionalism in the Early
  Novels of George Eliot. 1970. p. 55–62
Bedient, Calvin, "Middlemarch": Touching Down, Hudson Re-
  view (1969), 22:70–84
Beaty, Jerome, The Forgotten Past of Will Ladislaw, Nine-
  teenth Century Fiction (1958), 13:159–63
Beaty, Jerome, History by Indirection: The Era of Reform in
  "Middlemarch," Victorian Studies (Dec. 1957), 1:173–79
Carroll, David, ed., George Eliot: The Critical Heritage.
  1971. p. 286–359
Carroll, David, An Image of Disenchantment in the Novels of
  George Eliot, Review of English Studies (1960), 11:29–41
Carroll, David, Unity Through Analogy: An Interpretation of
  "Middlemarch," Victorian Studies (1959), 2:305–16
Collits, T. J., "Middlemarch" and Moral Stupidity, Melbourne
  Critical Review (1967), #10:88–98
Damm, Robert F., Sainthood and Dorothea Brooke, Victorian
  Newsletter (Sept. 1969), #35:18–22
Duerksen, Roland A., Shelley in "Middlemarch," Keats-Shelley
  Journal (Winter 1965), 14:23–31
Feltes, N. N., George Eliot and the Unified Sensibility, Modern
  Language Association. Publications (1964), 79:130–36
Ferguson, Suzanne C., Mme. Laure and Operative Irony in
  "Middlemarch": A Structural Analogy, Studies in English
  Literature, 1500–1900 (Autumn 1963), 3:509–16
Fernando, Lloyd, George Eliot, Feminism, and Dorothea
  Blake, Review of English Literature (Jan. 1963), 4:76–90
Ford, Boris, The Pelican Guide to English Literature. Vol. 6.
  1958. p. 274–93
Goldfarb, Russell M., Caleb Garth of "Middlemarch," Victorian

Newsletter (1964), #26:14-19

Greenberg, Robert A., The Heritage of Will Ladislaw, _Nineteenth Century Fiction_ (March 1961), 15:355-58

Griffin, Robert P., Image and Intent: Some Observations on Style in "Middlemarch," _Ball State University Forum_ (1969), 10:60-63

Hagan, John, "Middlemarch": Narrative Unity in the Story of Dorothea Brooke, _Nineteenth Century Fiction_ (June 1961), 16:17-31

Hardy, Barbara, ed., _Critical Essays on George Eliot._ 1970. p. 116-32

Hastings, Robert, Dorothea Brooke: The Struggle for Existence in "Middlemarch," _Thoth_ (Spring 1963), 4:61-66

Hornback, Bert G., The Organization of "Middlemarch," _Papers on Language and Literature_ (Spring 1966), 2:169-75

Isaacs, Neil D., "Middlemarch": Crescendo of Obligatory Drama, _Nineteenth Century Fiction_ (June 1963), 18:21-34

Jones, R. T., _George Eliot._ 1970. p. 57-96

Kenney, Edwin J., Jr., George Eliot's Presence in "Middlemarch," _Dissertation Abstracts_ (1968), 29:1570A

Kermode, Frank, Lawrence and the Apocalyptic Types, _Critical Quarterly_ (1968), 10:14-38

Knoepflmacher, U. C., _Laughter and Despair: Readings in Ten Novels of the Victorian Age._ 1971. p. 168-201

Kohl, Norbert, George Eliot, "Middlemarch": "Prelude"—Eine Interpretation, _Deutsche Vierteljahrsschrift für Liturwissenschaft und Geistesgeschichte_ (May 1968), 42:182-201

Lerner, Laurence, "The Cool Gaze and the Warm Heart," _Listener_ (1960), 64:518-19

Luecke, Sister Jane Marie, Ladislaw and the "Middlemarch" Vision, _Nineteenth Century Fiction_ (June 1964), 19:55-64

Lyons, Richard S., The Method of "Middlemarch," _Nineteenth Century Fiction_ (June 1966), 21:35-47

Lyons, Richard Smilie, A Study of "Middlemarch," _Dissertation Abstracts_ (1961), 21:2276-77

Monod, Sylvère, George Eliot et les Personnages de "Middlemarch," _Études Anglaises_ (Oct.-Dec. 1959), 12:306-14

Pinney, Thomas, Another Note on the Forgotten Past of Will Ladislaw, _Nineteenth Century Fiction_ (June 1962), 17:69-73

Pinney, Thomas, The Authority of the Past in George Eliot's Novels, _Nineteenth Century Fiction_ (Sept. 1966), 21:131-48

Pritchett, V. S., The Pains of Others, _New Statesman_ (Nov. 12, 1965), p. 737-38

Rathburn, Robert C. and Martin Steinman, eds., From Jane
  Austen to Joseph Conrad; Essays Collected in Memory of
  James T. Hillhouse. 1958. p. 194–207
Riemer, A. P., Ariadne and Cleopatra: The Treatment of
  Dorothea in "Middlemarch," Southern Review (Australia)
  (1966), 2:50–58
Shapiro, Charles, ed., Twelve Original Essays on Great En-
  glish Novels. 1960. p. 125–52
Slatoff, Walter J., With Respect to Readers; Dimensions of
  Literary Response. 1970. p. 79–82
Sprague, Rosemary, George Eliot: A Biography. 1968. p.
  266–81
Thale, Jerome, Novels of George Eliot. 1959. p. 106–20
Tillyard, Eustace Mandeville Wetenhall, Epic Strain in the
  English Novel. 1958. p. 168–86
Tomlinson, T. B., "Middlemarch" and Modern Society, Mel-
  bourne Critical Review (1963), #6:44–55
Troost, Betty Todd, English Wit: George Eliot in "Scenes of
  Clerical Life" and "Middlemarch," Mankoto State College
  Studies (Dec. 1968), 3:19–26
Willey, Frederick, Appearance and Reality in "Middlemarch,"
  Southern Review (LSU) (1969), 5:419–35
Williams, Raymond, The English Novel: From Dickens to
  Lawrence. 1970. p. 87–94

The Mill on the Floss, 1860

  Auster, Harry, Local Habitations; Regionalism in the Early
    Novels of George Eliot. 1970. p. 136–74
  Bellringer, A. W., Education in "The Mill on the Floss," Re-
    view of English Literature (July 1966), 7:52–61
  Blondel, Jacques, Morale, Psychologie, Destinée dan "Le
    Moulin sur la Floss," Les Langues Modernes (1965), 59:
    342–48
  Carroll, David, ed., George Eliot: The Critical Heritage.
    1971. p. 109–67
  Carroll, David, An Image of Disenchantment in the Novels of
    George Eliot, Review of English Studies (1960), 11:29–41
  Colby, Robert Alan, Fiction with a Purpose; Major and Minor
    Nineteenth Century Novels. 1967. p. 213–55
  Drew, Elizabeth A., The Novel; A Modern Guide to Fifteen
    English Masterpieces. 1963. p. 127–40
  Hardy, Barbara, ed., Critical Essays on George Eliot. 1970.
    p. 42–58

Jones, R. T., George Eliot. 1970. p. 19–30

Knoepflmacher, U. C., Laughter and Despair: Readings in
Ten Novels of the Victorian Age. 1971. p. 109–36

Lee, R. H., The Unity of "The Mill on the Floss," English
Studies in Africa (March 1964), 7:34–53

Levine, George, Intelligence as Deception: "The Mill on the
Floss," Modern Language Association. Publications (1965),
80:402–09

Mack, Maynard and Ian Gregor, eds., Imagined Worlds:
Essays on Some English Novels and Novelists in Honour of
John Butt. 1968. p. 77–92

Osgerby, J. R., Eliot's "Mill on the Floss," Use of English
(Autumn 1965), 17:18–24

Paris, Bernard J., The Inner Conflicts of Maggie Tulliver: A
Horneyan Analysis, Centennial Review (1969), 13:166–99

Pinney, Thomas, The Authority of the Past in George Eliot's
Novels, Nineteenth Century Fiction (Sept. 1966), 21:131–48

Rubin, L., River Imagery as a Means of Foreshadowing in
"The Mill on the Floss," Modern Language Notes (Jan. 1956),
71:18–22

Smith, David J., The Arrested Heart: Familial Love and
Psychic Conflict in Five Mid-Victorian Novels, Dissertation
Abstracts (Dec. 1966), 26:1839A

Smith, David, Incest Patterns in Two Victorian Novels, Literature and Psychology (Summer 1965), 15:135–62

Sprague, Rosemary, George Eliot: A Biography. 1968. p.
174–85

Thale, Jerome, Image and Theme: "The Mill on the Floss,"
University of Kansas City Review (1957), 23:227–34

Thale, Jerome, Novels of George Eliot. 1959. p. 36–57

Williams, Raymond, The English Novel: From Dickens to
Lawrence. 1970. p. 75–77

Romola, 1863

Allott, Mirian, George Eliot in the 1860's, Victorian Studies
(Dec. 1961), 5:93–108

Carroll, David, ed., George Eliot: The Critical Heritage.
1971. p. 195–251

Carroll, David, An Image of Disenchantment in the Novels of
George Eliot, Review of English Studies (1960), 11:29–41

Dalaura, David J., "Romola" and the Origin on the Paterian
View of Life, Nineteenth Century Fiction (Dec. 1966), 21:
225–33

Fleishman, Avrom, The English Historical Novel; Walter
    Scott to Virginia Woolf. 1971. p. 155—63
Hardy, Barbara, ed., Critical Essays on George Eliot. 1970.
    p. 78—98
Huzzard, John A., The Treatment of Florence and Florentine
    Characters in George Eliot's "Romola," Italica (1957), 34:
    158—65
Kooiman-Van Middendorp, Gerarda M., The Hero in the
    Feminine Novel. 1966. p. 96—123
Peterson, Virgil A., "Romola": A Victorian Quest for Values,
    West Virginia University Philological Papers (1967), 16:
    49—62
Pinney, Thomas, The Authority of the Past in George Eliot's
    Novels, Nineteenth Century Fiction (Sept. 1966), 21:131—48
Poston, Lawrence, III, "Romola" and Thomas Trollope's
    "Filippo Strozzi," Victorian Newsletter (1964), #25:20—22
Poston, Lawrence, III, Setting and Theme in "Romola," Nine-
    teenth Century Fiction (March 1966), 20:355—66
Robinson, Carole, "Romola": A Reading of the Novel, Victo-
    rian Studies (Sept. 1962), 6:29—42
Sambrook, A. J., The Natural Historian of Our Social Classes,
    English (Summer 1962), 14:130—34
Sprague, Rosemary, George Eliot: A Biography. 1968. p.
    202—22
Thale, Jerome, The Novels of George Eliot. 1959. p. 70—86

Silas Marner, 1861

Adam, Ian, Character and Destiny in George Eliot's Fiction,
    Nineteenth Century Fiction (Sept. 1965), 20:127—43
Auster, Harry, Local Habitations; Regionalism in the Early
    Novels of George Eliot. 1970. p. 185—188 and 195—205
Carroll, David, ed., George Eliot: The Critical Heritage.
    1971. p. 168—94
Hardy, Barbara, ed., Critical Essays on George Eliot. 1970.
    p. 59—77
Jones, R. T., George Eliot. 1970. p. 31—42
Milner, Ian, Structure and Quality in "Silas Marner," Studies
    in English Literature, 1500—1900 (Autumn 1966), 6:717—29
Rothstein, Eric and Thomas K. Dunseath, Literary Mono-
    graphs, I. 1967. p. 167—200 and 312—14
Sambrook, A. J., The Natural Historian of Our Social Classes,
    English (Summer 1962), 14:130—34
Sprague, Rosemary, George Eliot: A Biography. 1968. p. 196—
    200

Thale, Jerome, George Eliot's Fable for Her Times, College
    English (1958), 19:141–46
Thale, Jerome, Novels of George Eliot. 1959. p. 58–69
Thomson, Fred C., The Theme of Alienation in "Silas Marner,"
    Nineteenth Century Fiction (June 1965), 20:69–84

A. E. ELLIS (pseud)

The Rack, 1959

Pritchett, V. S., The Rack, New Statesman (Nov. 22, 1958),
    56:729–30

MARY ANN EVANS

SEE

GEORGE ELIOT

HENRY FIELDING

Amelia, 1751

Baker, Sheridan, Fieldings's "Amelia" and the Materials of
    Romance, Philological Quarterly (April 1962), 41:437–49
Bloch, Tuvia, The Prosecution of the Maidservant in "Amelia,"
    English Language Notes (1969), 6:269–71
Coolidge, John S., Fielding and "Conservation of Character,"
    Modern Philology (May 1960), 57:245–59
Erzgräber, Willi, Das Menschenbild in Henry Fieldings
    Roman "Amelia," Die Neueren Sprachen (1957), p. 105–16
Johnson, E. D. H., "Vanity Fair" and "Amelia": Thackeray in
    the Perspective of the Eighteenth Century, Modern Philology
    (Nov. 1961), 59:100–13
Kaul, A. N., The Action of English Comedy; Studies in the
    Encounter of Abstraction and Experience from Shakespeare
    to Shaw. 1970. p. 188–92
Le Page, Peter L., Prison and the Dark Beauty of Amelia,
    Criticism (Fall 1967), 9:337–54
Longmire, Samuel E., The Narrative Structure of Fielding's
    "Amelia," Dissertation Abstracts (1969), 29:3103A–04A
Nathan, Sabine, The Anticipation of Nineteenth Century Ideo-
    logical Trends in Fielding's "Amelia," Zeitschrift für
    Anglistik und Amerikanistik (1958), 6:382–409
Price, Martin, To the Palace of Wisdom; Studies in Order and
    Energy from Dryden to Blake. 1964. p. 285–311

Sherbo, Arthur, The Time-Scheme in "Amelia," Boston University Studies in English (1960), 4:223–28

Tichý, Aleš, Remarks on the Flow of Time in the Novels of Henry Fielding, BRNO Studies in English (1959), 2:55–75

Thomas, D. S., Fortune and the Passions in Fielding's "Amelia," Modern Language Review (April 1965), 50:176–87

Wendt, Allan, The Naked Virtue of "Amelia," ELH (1960), 27: 131–48

Winterowd, Walter Ross, The Poles of Discourse: A Study of Eighteenth Century Rhetoric in "Amelia" and "Clarissa," Dissertation Abstracts (1965), 26:360–61

Wolff, Cynthia M., Fielding's "Amelia": Private Virtue and Public Good, Texas Studies in Language and Literature (1968), 10:37–55

The History of the Adventures of Joseph Andrews and of his Friend, Mr. Abraham Adams, Written in Invitation of the Manner of Cervantes, SEE Joseph Andrews

The History of Tom Jones, A Foundling, SEE Tom Jones

Jonathan Wild, 1743

Evans, David L., The Theme of Liberty in "Jonathan Wild, Papers in Language and Literature (1967), 3:302–13

Farrell, William J., The Mock-Heroic Form in "Jonathan Wild," Modern Philology (Feb. 1966), 63:216–26

Hatfield, G. W., Puffs and Pollitricks: "Jonathan Wild" and the Political Corruption of Language, Philological Quarterly (April 1967), 46:248–67

Hopkins, Robert H., Language and Comic Play in Fielding's "Jonathan Wild," Criticism (Summer 1966), 8:213–28

Kishler, Thomas C., Heartfree's Function in "Jonathan Wild," Satire Newsletter (Spring 1964), 1:32–34

Pinkus, Philip, Satire and St. George, Queen's Quarterly (Spring 1963), 70:30–49

Preston, John, The Ironic Mode: A Comparison of "Jonathan Wild" and "The Beggar's Opera," Essays in Criticism (July 1966), 16:268–80

Rinehart, Hollis, "Jonathan Wild" and the Cant Dictionary, Philological Quarterly (April 1969), 48:220–25

Shea, Bernard, Machiavelli and Field's "Jonathan Wild," Modern Language Association. Publications (1957), 72:55–73

Smith, Raymond, The Ironic Structure of Fielding's "Jonathan Wild," Ball State University Forum (Autumn 1965), 6:3–9

Smith, Robert A., The "Great Man" Motif in "Jonathan Wild" and "The Beggar's Opear," College Language Association Journal (1959), 2:183-84

Wendt, Allan, The Moral Allegory of "Jonathan Wild," ELH (Dec. 1957), 24:306-20

Joseph Andrews, 1742

Battestin, Martin C., Fielding's Changing Politics and Joseph Andrews, Philological Quarterly (Jan. 1960), 39:39-55

Battestin, Martin C., Fielding's "Joseph Andrews": Studies Towards a Critical and Textual Edition, Dissertation Abstracts (1959), 19:2080

Battestin, Martin C., Lord Hervey's Role in "Joseph Andrews," Philological Quarterly (April 1963), 42:226-41

Brooks, D., Interpolated Tales of Joseph Andrews Again, Modern Philology (Feb. 1968), 65:208-13

Brooks, Douglas, "Joseph Andrews" and "Pamela," Essays in Criticism (1969), 19:348-51

Brooks, Douglas, Richardson's "Pamela" and Fielding's "Joseph Andrews," Essays in Criticism (April 1967), 17: 158-68

Conti, Paola Corlaiacomo, Natura e Civiltà in Henry Fielding, English Miscellany (1968), 19:105-32

Enck, John Jacob, Elizabeth T. Porter and Alvin Whitley, eds., The Comic in Theory and Practice. 1960. p. 100-01

Fowler, Alastair, ed., Silent Poetry; Essays in Numerological Analysis. 1970. p. 234-60

Freedman, William A., Joseph Andrews; Clothing and the Concretization of Character, Discourse (Summer 1961), 304-10

Goldberg, Homer, Comic Prose Epic or Comic Romance: The Argument of the Preface to "Joseph Andrews," Philological Quarterly (1964), 43:193-215

Goldberg, Homer, The Interpolated Stories in "Jonathan Andrews" or "The History of the World in General" Satirically Revised, Modern Philology (May 1966), 63:295-310

Haslinger, Adolph, Die Funktion des Stadt-Land-Themas in Henry Fieldings "Tom Jones" und "Joseph Andrews," Die Neueren Sprachen (March 1965), 14:101-09

Jacobson, William Spencer, The Rhetorical Structure of Fielding's Epic "Joseph Andrews," Dissertation Abstracts (1966), 27:1057A-58A

Kaul, A. N., The Action of English Comedy; Studies in the Encounter of Abstraction and Experience from Shakespeare to Shaw. 1970. p. 166-74

MacAndrew, M. Elizabeth, Fielding's Use of Names in "Joseph Andrews," Names (1968), 16:362-70

McCullen, J. T., Fielding's Beau Didapper, English Language Notes (1964), 2:98-100

Oda, Minoru, "Joseph Andrews" as a Literary Experiment, Memoirs of Osaka Kyoiku University (1968), 17:69-80

Olsen, Flemming, Notes on the Structure of "Joseph Andrews," English Studies (1969), 50:340-51

Reid, Benjamin Lawrence, The Long Boy and Others; Wherein Will be Found a Gathering of Essays, Written to Divert and Entertain, and at the Same Time to Instruct, Concerning Several Distinguished Gentlemen of Divers Occupations and Wit; Newly Imprinted for Scholarly Inspection. 1969. p. 52-77

Reid, Benjamin Lawrence, Utmost Merriment, Strictest Decency: "Joseph Andrews," Sewanee Review (Autumn 1967), 75:559-84

Schilling, Bernard Nicholas, The Comic Spirit: Boccaccio to Thomas Mann. 1965. p. 43-97

Shapiro, Charles, ed., Twelve Original Essays on Great English Novels. 1960. p. 23-41

Spector, Robert Donald, ed., Essays on the Eighteenth Century Novel. 1965. p. 78-91

Taylor, Dick, Jr., Joseph as Hero of "Joseph Andrews," Tulane Studies in English (1957), 7:91-109

Tichý, Aleš, Remarks on the Flow of Time in the Novels of Henry Fielding, BRNO Studies in English (1959), 2:55-75

Virginia University Bibliographic Society. Studies in Bibliography; Papers of the Bibliographic Society of the University of Virginia. 1963. Vol. 16, p. 81-117

Wright, Andrew, "Joseph Andrews": Mask and Feast, Essays in Criticism (July 1963), 13:209-21

The Life of Mr. Jonathan Wild, SEE Jonathan Wild

Tom Jones, 1749

Alter, Robert, Rogue's Progress; Studies in the Picaresque Novel. 1964. p. 80-105

Battestin, Martin C., Fielding's Definition of Wisdom: Some Functions of Ambiguity and Emblem in "Tom Jones," ELH (June 1968), 35:188-217

Battestin, Martin C., Tom Jones and "His Egyptian Majesty": Fielding's Parable of Government, Modern Language Association. Publications (1967), 82:68-77

Bliss, Michael, Fielding's Bill of Fare in "Tom Jones," ELH (Spring 1963), 30:236-43

Böckmann, Paul, ed., Stil-Und Formprobleme in der Literatur. 1959. p. 238-43

Bort, Barry D., Incest Theme in "Tom Jones," American Notes and Queries (Feb. 1965), 3:83-84

Cazenave, Michel, A Propos de "Tom Jones," Novelle Revue Française (Nov. 1964), 12:891-94

Combs, William W., The Return to Paradise Hall: An Essay on "Tom Jones," South Atlantic Quarterly (1967), 67:419-36

Coolidge, John S., Fielding and "Conservation of Character," Modern Philology (May 1960), 57:245-59

DeBruyn, John, Tom Jones and Arthur Pendennis, Lit (Spring 1966), #7:81-88

Drew, Elizabeth A., The Novel: A Modern Guide to Fifteen English Masterpieces. 1963. p. 59-74

Dyson, Anthony Edward, The Crazy Fabric; Essays in Irony. 1965. p. 14-32

Edwards, P. D., Education and Nature in "Tom Jones" and "The Ordeal of Richard Feverel," Modern Language Review (Jan. 1968), 63:23-32

Empson, William, Tom Jones, Kenyon Review (Spring 1958), 20:217-49

Enright, D. J., Peeping at Tom, New Statesman (June 10, 1966), 71:846-47

Feil, J. P., Fielding's Character of Mrs. Whitefield, Philological Quarterly (Oct. 1960), 39:508-10

Ferguson, Oliver W., Partridge's Vile Encomium: Fielding and Honest Billy Mills, Philological Quarterly (Jan. 1964), 43:73-78

Goldknopf, David, The Failure of Plot in "Tom Jones," Criticism (1969), 11:262-74

Harper, Howard M., Jr. and Charles Edge, eds., The Classic British Novel. 1972. p. 3-21

Haslinger, Adolph, Die Funktion des Stadt-Land-Themas in Henry Fieldings "Tom Jones" und "Joseph Andrews," Die Neueren Sprachen (March 1965), 14:101-09

Hatfield, Glenn W., The Serpent and the Dove: Fielding's Irony and the Prudence Theme of "Tom Jones," Modern Philology (Autumn 1967), 65:17-32

Hutchens, Eleanor N., Prudence in "Tom Jones": A Study of Connotative Irony, Philological Quarterly (Oct. 1960), 39:496-507

Hutchens, Eleanor N., Verbal Irony in "Tom Jones," Modern
  Language Association. Publications (March 1962), 72:46–50
Johnson, Maurice, Device of Sophia's Muff in "Tom Jones,"
  Modern Language Notes (Dec. 1959), 74:685–90
Kaul, A. N., The Action of English Comedy; Studies in the
  Encounter of Abstraction and Experience from Shakespeare
  to Shaw. 1970. p. 151–57, 174–88
Lavin, Henry St. C., Rhetoric and Realism in "Tom Jones,"
  University Review (Oct. 1965), 32:19–25
Lutwick, Leonard, Mixed and Uniform Prose Styles in the
  Novel, Journal of Aesthetics and Art Criticism (March 1960),
  18:350–57
Lynch, James J., Structural Techniques in "Tom Jones," Zeit-
  schrift für Anglistik und Amerikanistik (1959), 7:5–16
Mack, Maynard and Ian Gregor, ed., Imagined Worlds; Essays
  on some English Novels and Novelists in Honour of John Butt.
  1968. p. 91–110
McKillop, Elan D., Some Recent Reviews of "Tom Jones," Col-
  lege English (Oct. 1959), 21:17–22
Mandel, Jerome, The Man of the Hill and Mrs. Fitzpatrick:
  Character and Narrative Technique in "Tom Jones," Papers
  in Language and Literature (1969), 5:26–38
Maugham, William Somerset, Art of Fiction; An Introduction
  to Ten Novels and Their Authors. 1955. p. 33–54
Milburn, Daniel Judson, The Age of Wit, 1650–1750. 1966. p.
  77–119
Miller, Henry Knight, Some Functions of Rhetoric in "Tom
  Jones," Philological Quarterly (June 1966), 45:209–35
Murray, P. B., Summer, Winter, Spring, Autumn in "Tom
  Jones," Modern Language Notes (April 1961), 76:324–26
Nassar, Eugene Paul, The Rape of Cinderella: Essays in
  Literary Continuity. 1970. p. 71–84
Pierce, Robert B., Moral Education in the Novel of the 1750's,
  Philological Quarterly (Jan. 1965), 44:73–87
Powers, Lyall H., "Tom Jones" and Jacob de la Vallée, Papers
  of the Michigan Academy of Science, Arts, and Letters (1961),
  47:659–67
Preston, John, Plot as Irony: The Reader's Role in "Tom
  Jones," ELH (Sept. 1968), 35:365–80
Preston, John, "Tom Jones" and "The Pursuit of True Judg-
  ment," ELH (Sept. 1966), 33:315–26
Price, John Valdimir, Sex and the Foundling Boy; The Prob-
  lem in "Tom Jones," Review of English Literature (Oct.

1967), 8:42-52

Price, Martin, To the Palace of Wisdom; Studies in Order and Energy from Dryden to Blake. 1964. p. 285-311

Rawson, C. J., Professor Empson's "Tom Jones," Notes and Queries (Nov. 1959), 6:400-04

Rexroth, Kenneth, Classics Revisited. 1968. p. 212-17

Schneider, Daniel J., Sources of Comic Pleasure in "Tom Jones," Connecticut Review (Oct. 1967), 1:51-65

Schonhorn, Manuel, Fielding's Digressive-Parodic Artistry: "Tom Jones" and the Man on the Hill, Texas Studies in Language and Literature (1968), 10:207-14

Spector, Robert Donald, ed., Essays on the Eighteenth Century Novel. 1965. p. 92-130

Tichý, Aleš, Remarks on the Flow of Time in the Novels of Henry Fielding, BRNO Studies in English (1959), 2:55-75

FORD MADOX FORD

The Fifth Queen; And How She Came to Court, 1906

Fleishman, Avrom, The English Historical Novel; Walter Scott to Virginia Woolf. 1971. p. 209-11

The Good Soldier, 1915

Andreach, Robert J., Ford's "The Good Soldier": The Quest for Permanence and Stability, Tennessee Studies in Literature (1965), 10:81-92

Baernstein, Jo-Ann, Image, Identity, and Insight in "The Good Soldier," Critique; Studies in Modern Fiction (Jan. 1967), 9:19-42

Barnes, Daniel R., Ford and the "Slaughtered Saints": A New Reading of "The Good Soldier," Modern Fiction Studies (Summer 1968), 14:157-70

Bender, Todd K., The Sad Tale of Dowell: Ford Madox Ford's "The Good Soldier," Criticism (Fall 1962), 4:353-68

Bort, Barry D., "The Good Soldier": Comedy or Tragedy?, Twentieth Century Literature (Jan. 1967), 12:194-202

Braybrooke, Neville, Fiction's Long Shadow: "The Good Soldier," Contemporary Review (Nov. 1966), 209:261-64

Cox, James Trammell, The Finest French Novel in the English Language, Modern Fiction Studies (Spring 1963), 9:79-93

Cox, James Trammell, Ford's "Passion for Provence," ELH (Dec. 1961), 28:383-98

Goldring, Douglas, South Lodge: Reminiscences of Violet
    Hunt, Ford Madox Ford, and "The English Review" Circle.
    1943. p. 116–22
Gordon, Ambrose, Jr., At the Edge of Silence: "The Good
    Soldier" as "War Novel," Modern Fiction Studies (Sept.
    1963), 9:67–78
Hafley, James, The Moral Structure of "The Good Soldier,"
    Modern Fiction Studies (Summer 1959), 5:121–28
Hanzo, T. A., Downward to Darkness, Sewanee Review
    (Autumn 1966), 74:832–55
Huntley, H. Robert, The Alien Protagonist: Ford Madox Ford.
    1970. p. 167–84
Hynes, Samuel, The Epistemology of "The Good Soldier,"
    Sewanee Review (Spring 1961), 69:225–35
Isaacs, Neil D., Ford Madox Ford and the Tietjens Fulfillment,
    Lock Haven Bulletin (1959), 1:58–65
Isaacs, Neil D., The Narrator of "The Good Soldier," English
    Literature in Transition (1880–1920) (1963), 6:14–15
Johnson, Ann S., Narrative Form in "The Good Soldier,"
    Critique; Studies in Modern Fiction (1969), 11:70–80
Lehan, Richard, Ford Madox Ford and the Absurd: "The Good
    Soldier," Texas Studies in Literature and Language (1963),
    5:219–31
Lid, R. W., Ford's "Good Soldier": A Triumph of Narrative,
    First Person (Fall 1960), 1:45–56
Lid, R. W., On the Time-Scheme of "The Good Soldier," En-
    glish Literature in Transition (1880–1920) (1961), 4:9–10
Lid, R. W., Ford Madox Ford, Flaubert, and the English Novel,
    Spectrum (Spring–Summer 1962), 6:10–19
Loeb, Harold, Ford Madox Ford's "The Good Soldier," Carleton
    Miscellany (Spring 1965), 6:27–41
McCaughey, G. S., The Mocking Bird and the Tomcat; An Ex-
    amination of Ford Madox Ford's "The Good Soldier," Humani-
    ties Association Bulletin (Spring 1965), 16:49–58
McFate, Patricia and Bruce Golden, "The Good Soldier": A
    Tragedy of Self-Deception, Modern Fiction Studies (Spring
    1963), 9:50–60
Mais, Stuart P., Why We Should Read. 1921. p. 126–38
Meixner, John A., The Saddest Story, Kenyon Review (Spring
    1960), 22:234–64
Moser, Thomas, Towards "The Good Soldier": Discovery of a
    Sexual Theme, Daedalus (Spring 1963), 92:312–25
Mosher, Harold F., Jr., Wayne Booth and the Failure of Rheto-
    ric in "The Good Soldier," Caliban (1969), 6:49–52

Pritchett, V. S., Fordie, New Statesman and Nation (June 22, 1962), p. 906-07

Ray, Robert J., Style in "The Good Soldier," Modern Fiction Studies (Spring 1963), 9:61-66

Schorer, Mark, ed., Modern British Fiction. 1961. p. 160-75

Weisenfarth, Joseph, Criticism and the Semiosis of "The Good Soldier," Modern Fiction Studies (Spring 1963), 9:39-49

Wiley, Paul, Novelist of Three Worlds; Ford Madox Ford. 1962. p. 172-203

Ladies Whose Bright Eyes, 1911

Cassell, Richard A., The Two Sorrells of Ford Madox Ford, Modern Philology (Nov. 1961), 59:114-21

Huntley, H. Robert, The Alien Protagonist: Ford Madox Ford. 1970. p. 142-48

The Last Post, 1928

Kashner, Rita J., Tietjens' Education: Ford Madox Ford's Tetralogy, Critical Quarterly (Summer 1966), 8:150-63

Mr. Fleight, 1913

Huntley, H. Robert, The Alien Protagonist; Ford Madox Ford. 1970. p. 151-56

Parade's End, 1924-28

Allen, Walter, The English Novel; A Short Critical History. 1954. p. 317-19

Arnold, Aerol, Why Structure in Fiction: A Note to Social Scientists, American Quarterly (Fall 1958), 10:325-37

Auden, Wystan Hugh, Il Fait Payer, Mid-Century (Feb. 1961), #22:3-10

Bergonzi, Bernard, Heroes' Twilight; A Study of the Literature of the Great War. 1966. p. 171-97

Brown, Francis, ed., Highlights of Modern Literature. 1954. p. 113-18

Delbaere-Garant, J., "Who Shall Inherit England?": A Comparison Between "Howard's End," "Parade's End," and "Unconditional Surrender," English Studies (1969), 50:101-05

Firebaugh, Joseph J., Tietjens and the Tradition, Pacific Spectator (Winter 1952), 6:23-32

Gordon, Ambrose, Jr., A Diamond of Pattern: The War of Ford Madox Ford, Sewanee Review (Summer 1962), 70:464-83

Gordon, Ambrose, Jr., "Parade's End": Where War Was Fairy Tale, Texas Studies in Literature and Language (Spring 1963), 5:25-41

Grainger, J. H., A Presentment of Englishry, Contemporary Review (1968), 213:151-56

Griffith, Marlene, A Double Reading of "Parade's End," Modern Fiction Studies (Spring 1963), 9:25-38

Isaacs, Neil D., Ford Madox Ford and the Tietjens Fulfillment, Lock Haven Bulletin (1959), 1:58-65

Kenner, Hugh, Gnomon; Essays on Contemporary Literature. 1958. p. 144-61

Kashner, Rita J., Tietjens' Education: Ford Madox Ford's Tetralogy, Critical Quarterly (Summer 1966), 8:150-63

Lid, R. W., Return to Yesterday, Jubilee (March 1962), 9: 37-40

McCormick, John, Catastrophe and Imagination: An Interpretation of the Recent English and American Novel. 1957. p. 217-21

Meixner, John A., Ford Madox Ford's Novels: A Critical Study. 1962. p. 196-256

Schorer, Mark, ed., Modern British Fiction. 1961. p. 143-59

Seiden, Melvin, The Living Dead—VI: Ford Madox Ford and His Tetralogy, London Magazine (Aug. 1959), 6:45-55

Seiden, Melvin, Persecution and Paranoia in "Parade's End," Criticism (Summer 1966), 8:246-62

Walter, E. V., The Political Sense of Ford Madox Ford, New Republic (March 26, 1956), 134:17-19

Wiley, Paul, Novelist of Three Worlds: Ford Madox Ford. 1962. p. 212-47

Williams, William Carlos, Selected Essays. 1954. p. 315-23

Young, Kenneth, Ford Madox Ford. 1956. p. 28-35

EDWARD MORGAN FORSTER

Howard's End, 1910

Allen, Walter, Reassessments—"Howard's End," New Statesman and Nation (March 19, 1955), 49:407-08

Austin, Don, The Problem of Continuity in Three Novels of E. M. Forster, Modern Fiction Studies (Autumn 1961), 7:217-28

Bentley, Eric, ed., The Importance of Scrutiny. 1948. p. 301-04

Berland, Alwyn, James and Forster: The Morality of Class, Cambridge Journal (Feb. 1953), 6:259-80

Bradbury, Malcolm, E. M. Forster's "Howard's End," Critical Quarterly (Autumn 1962), 4:229-41

Brower, Reuben A., Beyond E. M. F.: Part 1—The Earth, Foreground (Spring-Summer 1946), 1:164-74

Brown, E. K., E. M. Forster and the Contemplative Novel, University of Toronto Quarterly (April 1934), 3:349-61

Brown, E. K., Rhythm in the Novel. 1950. p. 46-55

Bullett, Gerald, Modern English Fiction. 1926. p. 71-77

Burra, Peter, The Novels of E. M. Forster, Nineteenth Century and After (Nov. 1934), 116:581-94

Churchill, Thomas, Place and Personality in "Howard's End," Critique; Studies in Modern Fiction, (Spring-Summer 1962), 5:61-73

Crews, Frederick C., E. M. Forster: The Limitations of Mythology, Comparative Literature (Spring 1960), 12:97-112

Delbaere-Garant, J., "Who Shall Inherit England?": A Comparison Between "Howard's End," "Parade's End," and "Unconditional Surrender," English Studies (1969), 50:101-105

Doughty, Howard M., The Novels of E. M. Forster, Bookman (Oct. 1932), 75:542-49

Dobrée, Bonamy, Modern Prose Style. 1934. p. 35-38

Eagleton, Terry, Exiles and Émigrés; Studies in Modern Literature. 1970. p. 38-40

Gindin, James, Harvest of a Quiet Eye; The Novel of Compassion. 1971. p. 157-59

Godfrey, Denis, E. M. Forster's Other Kingdom. 1968. p. 106-51

Green, R., Mssrs. Wilcox and Kurtz; Hollow Men, Twentieth Century Literature (Jan. 1969), 14:231-39

Hall, James, Forster's Family Reunions, ELH (March 1958), 25:60-78

Hall, James, The Tragic Comedians; Seven Modern British Novelists. 1963. p. 11-30

Hannah, Donald, The Limitations of Liberalism in E. M. Forster's Work, English Miscellany (1962), 13:165-78

Hoare, Dorothy M., Some Studies in the Modern Novel. 1938. p. 88-90

Hoffman, Frederick J., "Howard's End" and the Bogey of Progress, Modern Fiction Studies (Autumn 1961), 7:243-57

Holt, Lee E., E. M. Forster and Samuel Butler, Modern Language Association. Publications (Sept. 1946), 61:804-19

Hoy, Cyrus, Forster's Metaphysical Novel, Modern Language Association. Publications (March 1960), 75:126-36

Jacobson, Dan, Forster's Cave, New Statesman (Oct. 14, 1966), p. 560

Kaiser, Rudolf, E. M. Forster: Gedankliche Analyse seines
    Romans "Howard's End" im Rahmen des Gesamtwerkes, Die
    Neueren Sprachen (Aug. 1962), #8:341-63
Karl, Frederick R. and Marvin Magalaner, A Reader's Guide
    to Great Twentieth Century English Novels. 1959. p. 103-24
Koljević, Svetozar, E. M. Forster: Sceptic as Novelist, Mad
    River Review (Fall-Winter 1965), 1:3-15
Langbaum, Robert, The Modern Spirit: Essays on the Conti-
    nuity of Nineteenth and Twentieth Century Literature. 1970.
    p. 136-39
Lovett, Robert M. and Helen S. Hughes, The History of the
    Novel in England. 1932. p. 417-19
McConkey, James, The Novels of E. M. Forster. 1957. p.
    74-80
Macdonald, Alastair, Class-Consciousness in E. M. Forster,
    University of Kansas City Review (Spring 1961), 27:235-40
McDowell, Frederick P. W., "The Mild Intellectual Light":
    Idea and Theme in "Howard's End," Modern Language Asso-
    ciation. Publications (Sept. 1959), 74:453-63
Mais, S. P. B., Why We Should Read. 1921. p. 152-56
Maskell, Duke, Style and Symbolism in "Howard's End,"
    Essays in Criticism (July 1969), 19:292-308
Missey, James, The Connected and the Unconnected in "How-
    ard's End," Wisconsin Studies in Literature (1969), #6:72-89
Moseley, Edwin M., A New Correlative for "Howard's End":
    Demeter and Persephone, Lock Haven Bulletin (1961), 1:1-6
Müllenbrock, Heinz-Joachim, Gesellschaftliche Thematik in
    E. M. Forsters Roman "Howard's End," Anglia (1969), 87:
    367-91
O'Connor, William Van, ed., Forms of Modern Fiction. 1948.
    p. 161-74
Oliver, Harold J., The Art of E. M. Forster. 1960. p. 39-56
Schorer, Mark, ed., Modern British Fiction. 1961. p. 176-94
Swinnerton, Frank, The Georgian Scene. 1934. p. 395-98
Thomson, George H., Theme and Symbol in "Howard's End,"
    Modern Fiction Studies (Autumn 1961), 7:229-42
Westburg, Barry R., Forster's Fifth Symphony: Another As-
    pect of "Howard's End," Modern Fiction Studies (Winter
    1964-65), 10:359-65

The Longest Journey, 1907

Austin, Don, The Problem of Continuity in Three Novels of E.
    M. Forster, Modern Fiction Studies (Autumn 1961), 7:217-28

Bentley, Eric, ed., The Importance of Scrutiny. 1948. p.
298–301
Brower, Reuben A., Beyond E. M. Forster: Part 1—The
Earth, Foreground (Spring–Summer 1946), 1:164–74
Crews, Frederick C., E. M. Forster: The Limitations of
Mythology, Comparative Literature (Spring 1960), 12:97–112
Crews, Frederick C., "The Longest Journey" and the Perils of
Humanism, ELH (1959), 26:575–96
Gindin, James, Harvest of a Quiet Eye; The Novel of Compas-
sion. 1971. p. 175–77
Godfrey, Denis, E. M. Forster's Other Kingdom. 1968. p.
44–67
Hall, James, Forster's Family Reunions, ELH (1958), 25:
60–78
Hoare, Dorothy M., Some Studies in the Modern Novel. 1938.
p. 74–85
Holt, Lee E., E. M. Forster and Samuel Butler, Modern Lan-
guage Association. Publications (Sept. 1946), 61:807–10
McConkey, James, The Novels of E. M. Forster. 1957. p.
64–69 and 107–17
McDowell, Frederick P. W., Forster's Many-Faceted Uni-
verse: Idea and Paradox in "The Longest Journey," Critique;
Studies in Modern Fiction (Fall–Winter 1960–61), 4:41–62
Magnus, John, Ritual Aspects of E. M. Forster's "The Longest
Journey," Modern Fiction Studies (Summer 1967), 13:195–210
Oliver, Harold J., The Art of E. M. Forster. 1960. p. 22–38
Raleigh, John Henry, Victorian Morals of the Modern Novel,
Partisan Review (Spring 1958), 25:241–64
Schorer, Mark, ed., Modern British Fiction. 1961. p. 176–94
Thomson, George H., Symbolism in E. M. Forster's Earlier
Fiction, Criticism (1961), 3:304–20

A Passage to India, 1924

Austin, Edgar A., Rites of Passage in "A Passage to India,"
Orient/West (1964), 9:64–72
Bell, Vereen M., Comic Seriousness in "A Passage to India,"
South Atlantic Quarterly (Summer 1967), 66:606–17
Bentley, Eric, ed., The Importance of Scrutiny. 1948. p.
304–07
Boyle, Ted E., Adela Quested's Delusion: The Failure of
Rationalism in "Passage to India," College English (March
1965), 26:478–80
Brander, Lawrence, E. M. Forster and India, Review of En-

glish Literature (Oct. 1962), 3:76–84

Brooks, Gilbert Benjamin, Crescent and Green; A Miscellany of Writings on Pakistan. 1955. p. 120–30

Brown, E. K., E. M. Forster and the Contemplative Novel, University of Toronto Quarterly (April 1934), 3:349–61

Burke, Kenneth, Language as Symbolic Action; Essays on Life, Literature and Method. 1966. p. 223–39

Cecil, David, Poets and Storytellers. 1949. p. 184–90

Charques, R. D., Contemporary Literature and Social Revolution. 1933. p. 122–24

Chaudhuri, Nirad C., Passage from India, Encounter (June 1954), 2:19–24

Clubb, Roger L., "A Passage to India": The Meaning of the Marabar Caves, CLA Journal (March 1963), 6:184–93

Cooperman, Stanley, The Imperial Posture and the Shrine of Darkness: Kipling's "The Naulahka" and E. M. Forster's "A Passage to India," English Literature in Transition (1880–1920) (1963), 6:9–13

Crews, Frederick C., E. M. Forster: The Limitations of Mythology, Comparative Literature (Spring 1960), 12:97–112

Dauner, Louise, What Happened in the Cave? Reflections on "A Passage to India," Modern Fiction Studies (Autumn 1961), 7:258–70

Decap, Roger, Un Roman Pascalien: "A Passage to India" di E. M. Forster, Caliban (1968), 5:103–28

Dobrée, Bonamy, The Lamp and the Lute; Studies in Six Modern Authors. 1929. p. 82–84

D'Souga, Frank and Jagdish Shivpuri, eds., Siddha III. 1968. p. 55–86

Evans, B. Ifor, English Literature Between the Wars. 1949. p. 36–38

Friedman, Alan, The Turn of the Novel. 1966. p. 106–29

Fussell, Paul, Jr., E. M. Forster's Mrs. Moore: Some Suggestions, Philological Quarterly (Oct. 1953), 32:388–95

Garnett, David, E. M. Forster and John Galsworthy, Review of English Literature (Leeds) (Jan. 1964), 5:7–18

Gilomen, W., Fantasy and Prophecy in E. M. Forster's Work, English Studies (Amsterdam) (Aug. 1946), 27:97–112

Godfrey, Denis, E. M. Forster's Other Kingdom. 1968. p. 152–204

Gould, Gerald, The English Novel Today. 1924. p. 184–89

Gowda, H. H. Anniah, E. M. Forster's India, Literary Half-Yearly (Jan. 1963), 4:45–52

Gransden, K. W., E. M. Forster at 80, Encounter (Dec. 1958),
    11:77-81

Hale, Nancy, A Passage to Relationship, Antioch Review
    (Spring 1960), 20:19-30

Hall, James, Forster's Family Reunions, ELH (March 1958),
    25:60-78

Hamill, Elizabeth, These Modern Writers. 1946. p. 137-44

Hannah, Donald, The Limitations of Liberalism in E. M.
    Forster's Work, English Miscellany (1962), 13:165-78

Hickley, Dennis, Ou-Boum and Verbum, Downside Review
    (Spring 1954), 72:172-80

Hoare, Dorothy M., Some Studies in the Modern Novel. 1938.
    p. 90-95

Hoggart, Richard, The Unsuspected Audience, New Statesman
    and Nation (Sept. 6, 1958), 56:308-10

Hollingsworth, Keith, "A Passage to India": The Echoes in the
    Marabar Caves, Criticism (Summer 1962), 4:210-24

Holt, Lee, E., E. M. Forster and Samuel Butler, Modern Lan-
    guage Association. Publications (Sept. 1946), 61:804-19

Horowitz, Ellin, The Communal Ritual and the Dying God in
    E. M. Forster's "A Passage to India," Criticism (1964), 6:
    70-88

Hunt, John D., Muddle and Mystery in "A Passage to India,"
    ELH (Dec. 1966), 33:497-517

Jacobson, Dan, Forster's Cave, New Statesman (Oct. 14, 1966),
    p. 560

Johnson, E. H., The Intelligence of E. M. Forster, Personalist
    (Jan. 1954), 35:50-58

Karl, Frederick R. and Marvin Magalaner, A Reader's Guide
    to Great Twentieth Century English Novels. 1959. p. 103-24

Keir, W. A. S., "A Passage to India" Reconsidered, Cambridge
    Journal (April 1952), 5:426-35

Kermode, John Frank, Puzzles and Epiphanies; Essays and
    Reviews 1958-1961 (1962), p. 79-85

Kilner, G., Some Questions of Interpretation in "A Passage to
    India," Use of English (Summer 1965), 16:302-07

Koljević, Svetozar, E. M. Forster: Sceptic as Novelist, Mad
    River Review (Fall-Winter 1965), 1:3-15

Langbaum, Robert, The Modern Spirit; Essays on the Conti-
    nuity of Nineteenth and Twentieth Century Literature. 1970.
    p. 141-46

Leach, Elsie, Forster's "A Passage to India," Explicator
    (Nov. 1954), 13:Item 13

Levine, June P., E. M. Forster's "A Passage to India": Creation and Criticism, Dissertation Abstracts (1968), 28: 3189A-90A

McConkey, James, The Novels of E. M. Forster. 1957. p. 80-93 and 132-60

McDonald, Walter R., Forster's "Passage to India," Explicator (March 1967), 25:Item 54

McLuhan, H. M., Kipling and Forster, Sewanee Review (Summer 1944), 52:332-42

Martin, John S., Mrs. Moore and the Marabar Caves: A Mythological Reading, Modern Fiction Studies (Winter 1965-66), 11:429-33

Moran, Ronald, "Come, Come," "Boum, Boum": "Easy" Rhythm in E. M. Forster's "A Passage to India," Ball State University Forum (1968), 9:3-9

Nirenberg, Edwin, The Withered Priestess: Mrs. Moore's Incomplete Passage to India, Modern Language Quarterly (1964), 25:198-204

O'Connor, William Van, ed., Forms of Modern Fiction. 1948. p. 169-71

Oliver, Harold J., The Art of E. M. Forster. 1960. p. 57-81

Oppel, Horst, ed., Der Moderne Englische Roman: Interpretationen. 1965. p. 135-59

Pedersen, Glenn, Forster's Symbolic Form, Kenyon Review (Spring 1959), 21:231-49

Rahman, Kalimur, Race-Relations in "A Passage to India," Venture (March 1961), 2:56-69

Raina, M. L., Imagery in "A Passage to India": A Further Note, English Literature in Transition (1880-1920) (1967), 10:8-9

Raina, M. L., Traditional Symbolism and Forster's "Passage to India," Notes and Queries (Nov. 1966), 13:416-17

Savage, D. S., The Withered Branch: Studies in the Modern Novel. 1950. p. 67-69

Schorer, Mark, ed., Modern British Fiction. 1961. p. 210-24

Shahane, V. A., Forster's "A Passage to India," Explicator (Dec. 1967), 26:Item 36

Shahane, V. A., Symbolism in E. M. Forster's "A Passage to India": Temple, English Studies (Dec. 1963), 44:423-31

Shalvi, Alice and A. A. Mendilov, eds., Studies in English Language and Literature. 1966. p. 258-79

Shapiro, Charles, ed., Twelve Original Essays on Great English Novels. 1960. p. 253-75

Shonfield, Andrew, The Politics of Forster's India, Encounter (Jan. 1968), 30:62—68

Shusterman, David, The Curious Case of Professor Godbole: "A Passage to India" Re-Examined, Modern Language Association. Publications (1961), 76:426—35

Singh, Bhupal, A Survey of Anglo-Indian Fiction. 1934. p. 221—33

Singh, St. Nihal, Indians and Anglo-Indians: As Portrayed to Britons by British Novelists, Modern Review (Sept. 1924), 36:251—56

Spencer, Michael, Hinduism in E. M. Forster's "A Passage to India," Journal of Asian Studies (Feb. 1968), 27:281—95

Thomas, Roy and Howard Erskine-Hill, "A Passage to India": Two Points of View, Anglo-Welsh Review (Summer 1965), 15:44—50

Thomson, George H., A Note on the Snake Imagery of "A Passage to India," English Literature in Transition (1880—1920), (1966), 9:108—110

Thomson, George H., Thematic Symbol in "A Passage to India," Twentieth Century Literature (July 1961), 7:51—63

Tindall, William York, The Literary Symbol. 1955. p. 142—44 and 189—90

Verschoyle, Derek, ed., The English Novelists. 1936. p. 273—75

Wallace, A. Doyle and Woodburn O. Ross, eds., Studies in Honor of John Wilcox, by Members of the English Department, Wayne State University. 1958. p. 227—37

Warren, Austin, Rage for Order: Essays in Criticism. 1948. p. 134—39

White, Margaret B., An Experiment in Criticism, Dissertation Abstracts (1968), 29:1521A

Zabel, Morton Dauwen, Craft and Character in Modern Fiction. 1957. p. 239—44

Zwerdling, Alex, The Novels of E. M. Forster, Twentieth Century Literature (Jan. 1957), 2:171—81

A Room with a View, 1908

Austin, Don, The Problem of Continuity in Three Novels of E. M. Forster, Modern Fiction Studies (Autumn 1961), 7:217—28

Fletcher, Ian, ed., Romantic Mythologies. 1967. p. 271—97

Friedman, Alan, The Turn of the Novel. 1966. p. 106—29

Gindin, James, Harvest of a Quiet Eye; The Novel of Compassion. 1971. p. 169—71

Godfrey, Denis, E. M. Forster's Other Kingdom. 1968. p. 68–107

Hale, James, Forster's Family Reunions, ELH (1958), 25: 60–78

Hoare, Dorothy M., Some Studies in the Modern Novel. 1938. p. 72–74

Holt, Lee E., E. M. Forster and Samuel Butler, Modern Language Association. Publications (Sept. 1946), 61:804–19

Liddell, Robert, A Treatise on the Novel. 1947. p. 64–68

Lucas, John, Wagner and Forster: "Parsifal" and "A Room with a View," ELH (March 1966), 33:92–117

McConkey, James, The Novels of E. M. Forster. 1957. p. 54–61 and 97–101

Oliver, Harold, The Art of E. M. Forster. 1960. p. 22–38

Where Angels Fear to Tread, 1905

Bentley, Phyllis, The Novels of E. M. Forster, English Journal (April 1948), 37:163–70

Gindin, James, Harvest of a Quiet Eye; The Novel of Compassion. 1971. p. 164–67

Godfrey, Denis, E. M. Forster's Other Kingdom. 1968. p. 20–43

Hall, James, Forster's Family Reunions, ELH (1958), 25:60–78

Hoare, Dorothy M., Some Studies in the Modern Novel. 1938. p. 78–82

Karl, Frederick R. and Marvin Magalaner, A Reader's Guide to Great Twentieth Century English Novels. 1959. p. 103–24

McConkey, James, The Novels of E. M. Forster. 1957. p. 61–64 and 97–107

Oliver, Harold, The Art of E. M. Forster. 1960. p. 22–38

Warren, Austin, Rage for Order: Essays in Criticism. 1948. p. 127–29

Wilde, Alan, The Aesthetic View of Life: "Where Angels Fear to Tread," Modern Fiction Studies (Autumn 1961), 7:207–16

Zabel, Morton Dauwen, Craft and Character in Modern Fiction. 1957. p. 230–36

JOHN GALSWORTHY

Forsyte Saga, 1906

Aiken, Conrad Potter, Reviewer's ABC; Collected Criticism of Conrad Aiken, from 1916 to the Present. 1958. p. 213–17

Chicherin, A., A Reconsideration of Opinions about "The Forsyte Saga," Voprosi Literaturi (Jan. 1958), #1:152-66

Hamilton, Robert, The Forsyte Saga, Quarterly Review (Oct.
1966), 30:431-41

Lambert, J. W., The Galsworthy Saga, Horizon (Autumn
1968), 10:106-11

Stevens, Earl Eugene, A Study of the Structure of John Galsworthy's "The Forsyte Saga," Dissertation Abstracts (1963),
24:2489

Van Egmond, Peter, Naming Technique in John Galsworthy's
"The Forsyte Saga," Names (1968), 16:371-79

Wilson, A., Galsworthy's "Forsyte Saga," New Statesman
(March 3, 1956), 51:187

In Chancery, SEE Forsyte Saga

Indian Summer of a Forsyte, SEE Forsyte Saga

Man of Property, 1904

Bergonzi, Bernard, Properties, Spectator (Feb. 15, 1963),
#7025:201

Pallette, Drew B., Young Galsworthy; The Forging of a Satirist,
Modern Philology (Feb. 1959), 56:178-86
SEE ALSO Forsyte Saga

The Silver Spoon, SEE Forsyte Saga

Swan Song, SEE Forsyte Saga

To Let, SEE Forsyte Saga

The White Monkey, SEE Forsyte Saga

ELIZABETH GASKELL

Cranford, 1853

Dodsworth, Martin, Women Without Men at Cranford, Essays
in Criticism (April 1963), 13:132-45

Ganz, Margaret, Elizabeth Gaskell; the Artist in Conflict.
1969. p. 141-54

Hoyt, Charles Alva, ed., Minor British Novelists. 1967. p.
98-108

Short, Clarice, Studies in Gentleness, Western Humanities
Review (1957), 11:387-93

Tarratt, Margaret, "Cranford" and the Strict Code of Gentility,

Essays in Criticism (April 1968), 18:152–63

Wolfe, P. A., Structure and Movement in "Cranford," *Nine-teenth Century Fiction* (Sept. 1968), 23:161–76

Wright, Edgar, Mrs. Gaskell and the World of "Cranford," *Review of English Literature* (Leeds) (Jan. 1965), 6:68–79

Mary Barton, 1848

Ganz, Margaret, *Elizabeth Gaskell: The Artist in Conflict.* 1969. p. 49–77

Handley, Graham, Mrs. Gaskell's Reading: Some Notes on Echoes and Epigraphs in "Mary Barton," *Durham University Journal* (1967), 28:131–38

Hoyt, Charles Alva, ed., *Minor British Novelists.* 1967. p. 98–108

Kooiman-Van Middendorp, Gerarda M., *The Hero in the Feminine Novel.* 1966. p. 82–95

Tillotson, Kathleen Mary, *Novels of the 1840's.* 1961. p. 202–23

North and South, 1855

Bowen, Elizabeth, *Seven Winters; Memories of a Dublin Child-hood.* 1962. p. 139–47

Chapple, J. A. V., "North and South": A Reassessment, *Essays in Criticism* (Oct. 1967), 17:461–72 and (Oct. 1968), 18:461–70

Ganz, Margaret, *Elizabeth Gaskell; The Artist in Conflict.* 1969. p. 78–105

Kooiman-Van Middendorp. Gerarda M., *The Hero in the Femi-nine Novel.* 1966. p. 82–95

Schneewind, Jerome B., Moral Problems and Moral Philosophy in the Victorian Period, *Victorian Studies* (Supp. 1965), 9: 29–46

Ruth, 1853

Ganz, Margaret, *Elizabeth Gaskell; The Artist in Conflict.* 1969. p. 105–31

Sylvia's Lovers, 1863

Ganz, Margaret, *Elizabeth Gaskell: The Artist in Conflict.* 1969. p. 230–52

Kooiman-Van Middendorp, Gerarda M., *The Hero in the Femi-nine Novel.* 1966. p. 82–95

Wives and Daughters, 1864–66

Ganz, Margaret, Elizabeth Gaskell: The Artist in Conflict. 1969. p. 161–81

GEORGE GISSING

Born In Exile, 1892

Rathburn, Robert and Martin Steinman, eds., From Jane Austen to Joseph Conrad; Essays Collected in Memory of James T. Hillhouse. 1958. p. 246–56

Crown of Life, 1899

Coustillas, Pierre, Gissing's Feminine Portraiture, English Literature in Transition (1880–1920) (1963), 6:130–41

Demos, 1886

Goode, John, Gissing, Morris, and English Socialism, Victorian Studies (Dec. 1968), 12:201–26

Goode, John, Gissing's "Demos," Victorian Studies (June 1969), 12:431–40

Kocmanová, Jessie, The Revolt of the Workers in the Novels of Gissing, James and Conrad, BRNO Studies in English (1959), 1:119–39

Lelchuk, Alan, "Demos": The Ordeal of the Two Gissings, Victorian Studies (March 1969), 12:357–74

Sporn, Paul, Gissing's "Demos": Late Victorian Values and the Displacement of Conjugal Love, Studies in the Novel (Fall 1969), 1:334–46

In the Year of Jubilee, 1894

Coustillas, Pierre, Gissing's Feminine Portraiture, English Literature in Transition (1880–1920) (1963), 6:130–41

Selig, Robert L., A Sad Heart at the Late-Victorian Culture Market: George Gissing's "In the Year of the Jubilee," Studies in English Literature, 1500–1900 (Autumn 1969), 9:703–20

The Nether World, 1889

Kocmanová, Jessie, The Revolt of the Workers in the Novels of Gissing, James and Conrad, BRNO Studies in English (1959), 1:119–39

New Grub Street, 1891

> Bergonzi, Bernard, The Novelist as Hero, The Twentieth
> Century (Nov. 1958), 164:444—55
> Pritchett, Victor Sawdon, The Living Novel and Later Appre-
> ciations. 1964. p. 154—60
> Saagpakk, Paul F., Psychological Elements in British Novels
> from 1890—1930, Dissertation Abstracts (Sept. 1966), 27:782A

The Old Women, 1893

> Chialant, Maria T., "The Old Women" di George Gissing, e il
> Movimento Femminista, Annali Istituto Universitario
> (Naples) (1967), 10:155—87

The Private Papers of Henry Rycroft, 1903

> Cope, Jackson I., Definition as Structure in Gissing's "Rycroft
> Papers," Modern Fiction Studies (1957), 3:127—40
> Koike, Shigeru, Gissing in Japan, Bulletin of the New York
> Public Library (Nov. 1963), 67:565—73

Thyrza, 1887

> Kocmanová, Jessie, The Revolt of the Workers in the Novels
> of Gissing, James and Conrad, BRNO Studies in English
> (1959), 1:119—39
> Sherif, Nur, The Victorian Sunday in "Little Dorrit" and
> "Thyrza," Cairo Studies in English (1960), p. 155—65

Veranilda, 1904

> Coustillas, Pierre, The Stormy Publication of Gissing's
> "Veranilda," Bulletin of the New York Public Library (1968),
> 72:588—610

Workers in the Dawn, 1880

> Coustillas, Pierre, Gissing's Feminine Portraiture, English
> Literature in Transition (1880—1920) (1963), 6:130—41

WILLIAM GODWIN

Caleb Williams, 1794

> Cruttwell, P., On "Caleb Williams," Hudson Review (Spring
> 1958), 11:87—95
> Duerksen, R. A., "Caleb Williams," Political Justice and
> "Billy Budd," American Literature (Nov. 1966), 38:372—76

Dumas, Donald G., William Godwin's "Caleb Williams": Doctrine into Art, Dissertation Abstracts (1969), 29:4453A–54A

Faulkner, Peter, William Godwin's Humanistic Novel, Humanist (Feb. 1968), 83:55–57

Gross, Harvey, The Pursuer and the Pursued: A Study of "Caleb Williams," Texas Studies in Literature and Language (Autumn 1959), 1:401–11

Hunt, Leigh, Leigh Hunt's Literary Criticism. 1956. p. 372–75

Marshall, William H., "Caleb Williams" and "The Cenci," Notes and Queries (July 1960) 7:260–63

Rothstein, Eric, Allusion and Analogy in the Romance of "Caleb Williams," University of Toronto Quarterly (1967), 37:18–30

Storch, Rudolf F., Metaphors of Private Guilt and Social Rebellion in Godwin's "Caleb Williams," ELH (1967), 34:188–207

Woodcock, George, William Godwin, University Libertarian (April 1957), #3:4–6

Cloudesley, 1830

Sherburn, George, Gissing's Later Novels, Studies in Romanticism (Winter 1962), 1:65–82

Deloraine, 1833

Sherburn, George, Gissing's Later Novels, Studies in Romanticism (Winter 1962), 1:65–82

Fleetwood; or, The New Man of Feeling, 1805

Sherburn, George, Gissing's Later Novels, Studies in Romanticism (Winter 1962), 1:65–82

Imogen; A Pastoral Romance, 1784

England, Martha Winburn, Further Discussion of Godwin's "Imogen": Felix Culpa, Bulletin of the New York Public Library (1963), 67:115–18

Marken, Jack W., Godwin's "Imogen" Rediscovered, Bulletin of the New York Public Library (1963), 67:7–16

Pollin, Burton R., Primitivism in "Imogen," Bulletin of the New York Public Library (March 1963), 47:186–90

Primer, Irwin, Further Discussions of Godwin's "Imogen": Some Inplications or Irony, Bulletin of the New York Public Library (April 1963), 47:257–60

Mandeville, A Tale of the Seventeenth Century, 1817

> Lingner, Erika, et al, Essays in Honour of William Gallacher.
> 1966. p. 111–17
> Sherburn, George, Gissing's Later Novels, Studies in Roman-
> ticism (Winter 1962), 1:65–82

St. Leon: A Tale of the Sixteenth Century, 1799

> Sherburn, George, Gissing's Later Novels, Studies in Roman-
> ticism (Winter 1962), 1:65–82

WILLIAM GERALD GOLDING

Free Fall, 1959

> Babb, Howard S., The Novels of William Golding. 1970. p.
> 96–132
> Boyle, Ted E., The Denial of the Spirit: An Explication of
> William Golding's "Free Fall," Wascana Review (1966), 1:
> 3–10
> Broes, Arthur T., The Two Worlds of William Golding, Car-
> negie Series in English (1963), 7:1–14
> Gallagher, Michael P., The Human Image in William Golding,
> Studies (1965), 54:197–216
> Gindin, James, "Gimmick" and Metaphor in the Novels of
> William Golding, Modern Fiction Studies (1960), 6:145–52
> Goldberg, Gerald Jay, The Search for the Artist in Some
> Recent British Fiction, South Atlantic Quarterly (Summer
> 1963), 62:387–401
> Gregor, Ian and Mark Kinkead-Weekes, The Strange Case of
> Mr. Golding and His Critics, Twentieth Century (Feb. 1960),
> 167:115–25
> Harris, Wendell V., Golding's "Free Fall," Explicator (May
> 1965), 23:Item 76
> MacShane, Frank, The Novels of William Golding, Dalhousie
> Review (Summer 1962), 42:171–83
> Mitchell, Juliet, Concepts and Technique in William Golding,
> New Left Review (May–June 1962), #15:63–71
> Pendry, E. D., William Golding and "Mankind's Essential Ill-
> ness," Moderna Sprak (1961), 55:1–7
> Wain, John, Lord of the Agonies, Aspect (April 1963), #3:56–67
> Walker, Marshall, William Golding: From Paradigm to Pyra-
> mid, Studies in Literary Imagination (Oct. 1969), 2:67–82
> Walters, Margaret, Two Fabulists: Golding and Camus, Mel-

bourne Critical Review (1961), 4:18-29

The Inheritors, 1955

Ali, Nasood, Amjad, "The Inheritors": An Experiment in Technique, Venture (April 1969), 5:123-30

Babb, Howard S., The Novels of William Golding. 1970. p. 36-63

Bufkin, E. C., The Ironic Art of William Golding's "The Inheritors," Texas Studies in Literature and Language (1968), 9:567-78

Davenport, Guy, Jungles of the Imagination, National Review (Oct. 9, 1962), 13:273-74

Duncan, Kirby L., William Golding and Vardis Fisher: A Study in Parallels and Extensions, College English (Dec. 1965), 27:232-35

Freedman, Ralph, The New Realism: The Fancy of William Golding, Perspective (1958), 10:118-28

Gallagher, Michael P., The Human Image in William Golding, Studies (1965), 54:197-216

Gindin, James, "Gimmick" and Metaphor in the Novels of William Golding, Modern Fiction Studies (1960), 6:145-52

Green, Peter, The World of William Golding, Review of English Literature (April 1960), 1:62-72

Josipovici, Gabriel, The World and the Book; A Study of Modern Fiction. 1971. p. 238-43

MacShane, Frank, The Novels of William Golding, Dalhousie Review (Summer 1962), 42:171-83

Mitchell, Juliet, Concepts and Technique in William Golding, New Left Review (May-June 1962), #15:63-71

Sternlicht, Sanford, Songs of Innocence and Songs of Experience in "Lord of the Flies" and "The Inheritors," Midwest Quarterly (1968), 9:383-90

Thomson, George H., The Real World of William Golding, Alphabet (Nov. 1964), 9:26-33

Walter, Margaret, Two Fabulists: Golding and Camus, Melbourne Critical Review (1961), 4:18-29

Lord of the Flies, 1954

Babb, Howard S., The Novels of William Golding. 1970. p. 6-34

Baker, James R., Why It's No Go: A Study of William Golding's "Lord of the Flies," Arizona Quarterly (Winter 1963), 19:293-305

Biles, Jack I., Piggy: Apologia Pro Vita Sua, Studies in Literary Imagination (Oct. 1968), 1:83–109

Braybrooke, Neville, Two William Golding Novels: Two Aspects of His Work, Queen's Quarterly (Spring 1969), 76:92–100

Bufkin, E. C., "Lord of the Flies": An Analysis, Georgia Review (Spring 1965), 19:40–57

Cohn, Alan M., The Berengaria Allusion in "Lord of the Flies," Notes and Queries (Nov. 1966), 13:419–20

Cockren, Thomas Marcellus, Is Golding Calvinistic?, America (July 16, 1963), 109:18–20

Cox, C. B., Lord of the Flies, Critical Quarterly (Summer 1960), 2:112–17

Egan, John M., Golding's View of Man, America (Jan. 26, 1963) 108:140–41

Freedman, Ralph, The New Realism: The Fancy of William Golding, Perspective (1958), 10:118–28

Gaskin, J. C. A., Beelzebub, Hibbert Journal (Winter 1967–68), 66:58–61

Gindin, James, "Gimmick" and Metaphor in the Novels of William Golding, Modern Fiction Studies (1960), 6:145–52

Golding, William Gerald, ed., The Hot Gates and Other Occasional Pieces. 1966. p. 85–101

Gordon, Robert C., Classical Themes in "Lord of the Flies," Modern Fiction Studies (Winter 1965–66), 11:424–27

Grande, Luke M., The Appeal of Golding, Commonweal (Dec. 7, 1962), 77:457–59

Green, Peter, The World of William Golding, Review of English Literature (April 1960), 1:62–72

Gulbin, Suzanne, Parallels and Contrasts in "Lord of the Flies" and "Animal Farm," English Journal (1966), 55:86–88

Herndl, George C., Golding and Salinger: A Clear Choice, Wiseman Review (Winter 1964–65), #502:309–22

Kearns, Frances E., Salinger and Golding: Conflict on the Campus, America (Jan. 26, 1963), 108:136–39

Kvam, Ragnar, William Golding, Vinduet (Autumn 1959), 13:292–98

Lederer, Richard H., Student Reactions to "Lord of the Flies," English Journal (1964), 53:575–79

Leed, Jacob, Golding's "Lord of the Flies," Explicator (Sept. 1965), 24:Item 8

Levitt, Leon, Trust the Tale: A Second Reading of "Lord of the Flies," English Journal (April 1969), 58:521–22

MacLure, Millar, Allegories of Innocence, Dalhousie Review (Summer 1960), 40:145-56

MacShane, Frank, The Novels of William Golding, Dalhousie Review (Summer 1962), 42:171-83

Manheim, Leonard Falk and Eleanor B. Manheim, eds., Hidden Patterns; Studies in Psychoanalytic Literary Criticism. 1966. p. 259-74

Michel-Michot, Paulette, The Myth of Innocence, Revue des Langues Vivantes (1962), 28:510-20

Mitchell, Charles, "Lord of the Flies" and the Escape from Freedom, Arizona Quarterly (Spring 1966), 22:27-40

Mitchell, Juliet, Concepts and Technique in William Golding, New Left Review (May-June 1962), #15:63-71

Niemeyer, Carl, The Coral Island Revisited, College English (Jan. 1961), 22:241-45

O'Hara, J. D., Mute Choirboys and Angelic Pigs: The Fable in "Lord of the Flies," Texas Studies in Literature and Language (1966), 7:411-20

Oldsey, Bern and Stanley Weintraub, "Lord of the Flies": Beelzebub Revisited, College English (Nov. 1963), 25:90-99

Oliphant, Robert, Public Voices and Wise Guys, Virginia Quarterly Review (Autumn 1961), 37:522-37

Oppel, Horst, ed., Der Moderne Englische Roman: Interpretationen. 1965. p. 328-43

Page, Norman, Lord of the Flies, Use of English (Autumn 1964), 16:44-45 and 57

Pira, Gisela, Die Macht des Bösen in Goldings Roman "Lord of the Flies," Die Neueren Sprachen (Feb. 1969), 18:67-73

Pritchett, V. S., God's Folly, New Statesman (April 10, 1964), p. 562-63

Richter, Irmgard, Betrachtungen zu William Goldings "Lord of the Flies," Die Neueren Sprachen (July 1965), 14:332-36

Rosenberg, Bruce A., Lord of the Fire-Flies, Centennial Review (1967), 11:128-39

Rosenfield, Claire, "Men of Smaller Growth": A Psychological Analysis of William Golding's "Lord of the Flies," Literature and Psychology (Autumn 1961), 11:93-101

Schroth, Raymond A., Lord of the Flies, America (Feb. 18, 1967), 116:254

Sternlicht, Sanford, Songs of Innocence and Songs of Experience in "Lord of the Flies" and "The Inheritors," Midwest Quarterly (July 1968), 9:383-90

Talon, Henri, Irony in "Lord of the Flies," Essays in Criticism (July 1968), 18:296−309

Taylor, Harry H., The Case Against William Golding's Simon-Piggy, Contemporary Review (Sept. 1966), 209:155−60

Thomson, George H., The Real World of William Golding, Alphabet (Nov. 1964), 9:26−33

Townsend, R. C., "Lord of the Flies": Fool's Gold?, Journal of General Education (July 1964), 16:153−60

Veidemanis, Gladys, "Lord of the Flies" in the Classroom—No Passing Fad, English Journal (1964), 53:569−74

Walters, Margaret, Two Fabulists: Golding and Camus, Melbourne Critical Review (1961), 4:18−29

Warner, Oliver, Mr. Golding and Marryat's "Little Savage," Review of English Literature (1964), 5:51−55

Watson, Kenneth, A Reading of "Lord of the Flies," English (Spring 1964), 15:2−7

Whitbread, Thomas Bacon, ed., Seven Contemporary Authors; Essays on Cozzens, Miller, West, Golding, Heller, Albee, and Powers. 1966. p. 73−95

Pincher Martin, 1956

Babb, Howard S., The Novels of William Golding. 1970. p. 64−94

Biles, Jack I. and Carl R. Kropf, The Cleft Rock of Conversion: "Robinson Crusoe" and "Pincher Martin," Studies in the Literary Imagination (1969), 2:17−43

Braybrooke, Neville, The Return of "Pincher Martin," Commonweal (Oct. 25, 1968), 89:115−18

Braybrooke, Neville, Two William Golding Novels: Two Aspects of His Work, Queen's Quarterly (Spring 1969), 76:92−100

Bufkin, E. C., William Golding's Morality Play, Studies in Literary Imagination (Oct. 1969), 2:5−16

Cox, C. B., William Golding's "Pincher Martin," Listener (March 12, 1964), 71:430−31

Freedman, Ralph, The New Realism: The Fancy of William Golding, Perspective (1958), 10:118−28

Gallagher, Michael P., The Human Image in William Golding, Studies (1965), 54:197−216

Gindin, James, "Gimmick" and Metaphor in the Novels of William Golding, Modern Fiction Studies (1960), 6:145−52

Green, Peter, The World of William Golding, Essays by Divers Hands (1963), 32:37−57

Josipovici, Gabriel, The World and the Book; A Study of Modern Fiction. 1971. p. 243−46

LaChance, Paul R., "Pincher Martin": The Essential Dilemma of Modern Man, Cithara (May 1969), 8:55−60

MacShane, Frank, The Novels of William Golding, Dalhousie Review (Summer 1962), 42:171−83

Mitchell, Juliet, Concepts and Technique in William Golding, New Left Review (May−June 1962), #15:63−71

Pritchett, V. S., God's Folly, New Statesman (April 10, 1964), p. 562−63

Quinn, Michael, An Unheroic Hero: William Golding's "Pincher Martin," Critical Quarterly (Autumn 1962), 4:247−56

Sasso, Laurence J., Jr., A Note on the Dwarf in "Pincher Martin," Massachusettes Studies in English (Spring 1968), 1: 66−68

Whitbread, Thomas Bacon, ed., Seven Contemporary Authors: Essays on Cozzens, Miller, West, Golding, Heller, Albee, and Powers. 1966. p. 73−95

The Pyramid, 1967

Babb, Howard S., The Novels of William Golding. 1970. p. 168−96

Dick, Bernard F., "The Pyramid": Mr. Golding's "New" Novel, Studies in Literary Imagination (Oct. 1969), 2:83−95

Henry, Avril, William Golding: "The Pyramid," Southern Review (Australia) (1968), 3:5−31

T. L. S., Essays and Reviews from the Times Literary Supplement, 1967−68. Vol. 6. 1968−69. p. 109−12

Walker, Marshall, William Golding from Paradigm to Pyramid, Studies in Literary Imagination (Oct. 1969), 2:67−82

The Spire, 1964

Anderson, David, The Tragic Protest; A Christian Study of Some Modern Literature. 1970. p. 165−79

Babb, Howard S., The Novels of William Golding. 1970. p. 134−65

Crompton, D. W., The Spire, Critical Quarterly (Spring 1967), 9:63−79

Dick, Bernard F. and Raymond J. Porter, Jocelin and Oedipus, Cithara (Nov. 1966), 6:43−48

Furbank, P. N., Golding's "Spire," Encounter (May 1964), 22: 59−61

Gallagher, Michael P., The Human Image in William Golding, Studies (1965), 54:197−216

Hyman, Stanley Edgar, Standards; A Chronicle of Books for
Our Time. 1966. p. 219-23

Josipovici, Gabriel, The World and the Book; A Study of Modern Fiction. 1971. p. 247-51

Kort, Wesley, The Groundless Glory of Golding's "The Spire,"
Renascence (1968), 20:75-78

Lodge, David, William Golding, Spectator (April 10, 1964),
#7085:489-90

Pritchett, V. S., God's Folly, New Statesman (April 10, 1964),
p. 562-63

Roper, Derek, Allegory and Novel in Golding's "The Spire,"
Wisconsin Studies in Contemporary Literature (Winter 1967),
8:19-30

Skilton, David, Golding's "The Spire," Studies in Literary
Imagination (Oct. 1969), 2:45-56

Steiner, George, Language and Silence; Essays on Language,
Literature and the Inhuman. 1967. p. 288-94

Sternlicht, Sanford, The Sin of Pride in Golding's "The Spire,"
Minnesota Review (1965), 5:59-60

Sullivan, Walter, The Long Chronicle of Guilt: William Golding's "The Spire," Hollins Critic (June 1964), 1:1-12

Sutherland, Raymond Carter, Medieval Elements in "The Spire,"
Studies in Literary Imagination (Oct. 1969), 2:57-65

T. L. S., Essays and Reviews from The Times Literary Supplement, 1964-65. Vol. 3. 1965-66. p. 35-41

Temple, E. R. A., William Golding's "The Spire": A Critique,
Renascence (1968), 20:171-73

Walker, Marshall, William Golding from Paradigm to Pyramid,
Studies in Literary Imagination (Oct. 1969), 2:67-82

OLIVER GOLDSMITH

The Vicar of Wakefield, 1766

Adelstein, Michael E., Duality of Theme in "The Vicar of Wakefield," College English (Feb. 1961), 22:315-21

Adelstein, Michael E., "The Vicar of Wakefield": Its Relationship to the Eighteenth Century Novel, Dissertation Abstracts
(1958), 19:1376

Dahl, Curtis, Patterns of Disguise in "The Vicar of Wakefield,"
ELH (June 1958), 25:90-104

Golden, Morris, The Family-Wanderer Theme in Goldsmith,
ELH (1958), 25:181-93

Golden, Morris, Image Frequency and the Split in "The Vicar of Wakefield," Bulletin of the New York Public Library (Sept. 1959), 63:473−77

Jaarsman, Richard J., Satiric Intent in "The Vicar of Wakefield," Studies in Short Fiction (Summer 1968), 5:331−41

McDonald, Daniel, "The Vicar of Wakefield": A Paradox, College Language Association Journal (1966), 10:23−33

Orwell, George, Collected Essays, Journalism, and Letters of George Orwell, ed. Sonia Orwell, Vol. 3. 1968. p. 268−73

Peterson, Patricia C., Comic Unity in Oliver Goldsmith's "The Vicar of Wakefield," Dissertation Abstracts (1968), 29:1877A

Pritchett, V. S., Oliver Goldsmith, New Statesman (March 25, 1966), p. 427−28

Steeves, Harrison Ross, Before Jane Austen; The Shaping of the English Novel in the Eighteenth Century. 1965. p. 193−203

Sutherland, William O. S., The Art of the Satirist; Essays on the Satire of Augustan England. 1965. p. 84−91

HENRY GREEN

Back, 1946

Phelps, Robert, The Vision of Henry Green, Hudson Review (1952−53), 5:614−21

Shapiro, Stephen A., Henry Green's "Back": The Presence of the Past, Critique; Studies of Modern Fiction (Spring 1964), 7:87−96

Concluding, 1948

Hall, James, The Fiction of Henry James: Paradoxes of Pleasure and Pain, Kenyon Review (1957), 19:76−88

Hall, James, The Tragic Comedians; Seven Modern British Novelists. 1963. p. 66−81

Phelps, Robert, The Vision of Henry Green, Hudson Review (1952−53), 5:614−21

Weatherhead, A. Kingsley, Structure and Texture in Henry Green's Latest Novels, Accent (Spring 1959), 19:111−22

Doting, 1952

Phelps, Robert, The Vision of Henry Green, Hudson Review (1952−53), 5:614−21

Weatherhead, A. Kingsley, Structure and Texture in Henry
  Green's Latest Novels, <u>Accent</u> (Spring 1959), 19:111–22

Loving, 1945

Churchill, Thomas, "Loving": A Comic Novel, <u>Critique</u>
  (Spring–Summer 1961), 4:29–38
Davidson, Barbara, The World of "Loving," <u>Wisconsin Studies</u>
  <u>in Contemporary Literature</u> (Winter 1961), 2:65–78
Hall, James, <u>The Tragic Comedians; Seven Modern British</u>
  <u>Novelists.</u> 1963. p. 66–81
Johnson, Bruce M., "Loving": A Study of Henry Green, <u>Dis-</u>
  <u>sertation Abstracts</u> (1959), 20:2292
Labor, Earle, Henry Green's Web of Loving, <u>Critique; Studies</u>
  <u>in Modern Fiction</u> (Fall–Winter 1960–61), 4:29–40
Phelps, Robert, The Vision of Henry Green, <u>Hudson Review</u>
  (1952–53), 5:614–20

Nothing, 1950

Phelps, Robert, The Vision of Henry Green, <u>Hudson Review</u>
  (1952–53), 5:614–21
Weatherhead, A. Kingsley, Structure and Texture in Henry
  Green's Latest Novels, <u>Accent</u> (Spring 1959), 19:111–22

Party-Going, 1939

Johnson, Bruce, Henry Green's Comic Symbolism, <u>Ball State</u>
  <u>University Forum</u> (Autumn 1965), 6:29–35
Phelps, Robert, The Vision of Henry Green, <u>Hudson Review</u>
  (1952–53), 5:614–20

GRAHAM GREENE

Brighton Rock, 1938

Consolo, Dominick P., Music as Motif: The Unity of "Brighton
  Rock," <u>Renascence</u> (Fall 1962), 15:12–20
Eagleton, Terry, <u>Exiles and Emigrés; Studies in Modern Lit-</u>
  <u>erature.</u> 1970. p. 131–35
Eishiskina, N., Graham Greene's Novels, <u>Voprosi Literaturi</u>
  (June 1961), #6:149–69
Evans, Robert O., ed., <u>Graham Greene: Some Critical Con-</u>
  <u>siderations.</u> 1963. p. 151–68
Friedman, Melvin J., ed., <u>The Vision Obscured; Perception of</u>
  <u>Some Twentieth Century Catholic Novelists.</u> 1970. p. 109–20
Kellogg, Gene, <u>The Vital Tradition; The Catholic Novel in a</u>

Period of Convergence. 1970. p. 117–22

Lewis, R. W., The Fiction of Graham Greene; Between the Horror and the Glory, Kenyon Review (1957), 19:56–75

McCall, Dan, "Brighton Rock": The Price of Order, English Language Notes (June 1966), 3:290–94

Marian, Sister, Graham Greene's People: Being and Becoming, Renascence (Autumn 1965), 18:16–22

Mooney, Harry J., Jr. and Thomas F. Staley, eds., The Shapeless God; Essays on Modern Fiction. 1968. p. 42–45

Ruotolo, L. P., "Brighton Rock's" Absurd Heroine, Modern Language Quarterly (Dec. 1964), 25:425–33

Smith, A. J. M., Graham Greene's Theological Thrillers, Queen's Quarterly (Spring 1961), 68:15–33

Wilshere, A. D., Conflict and Conciliation in Graham Greene, Essays and Studies (1966), 19:122–37

A Burnt-Out Case, 1961

Anisimov, I., Graham Greene's Novels, Inostrannaya Literatura (Oct. 1964), #10:221–26

Dooley, D. J., "A Burnt-Out Case" Reconsidered, Wiseman Review (Summer 1963), #496:168–78

Dooley, D. J., The Suspension of Disbelief: Greene's "A Burnt-Out Case," Dalhousie Review (1963), 43:343–52

Eagleton, Terry, Exiles and Emigrés; Studies in Modern Literature. 1970. p. 121–25

Eishiskina, N., Graham Greene's Novels, Voprosi Literaturi (June 1961), #6:149–69

Engelborghs, M., Graham Greene's "A Burnt-Out Case," Kultuurleven (Oct. 1961), 28:610–15

Hess, M. Whitcomb, Graham Greene's Travesty on "The Ring and the Book," Catholic World (Oct. 1961), 195:37–42

Kermode, Frank, Mr. Greene's Eggs and Crosses, College English (April 1961), 16:69–75

Kermode, Frank, Puzzles and Epiphanies; Essays and Reviews, 1958–1961. 1962. p. 176–87

Marian, Sister, Graham Greene's People; Being and Becoming, Renascence (Autumn 1965), 18:16–22

Noxon, James, Kierkegaard's Stages and "A Burnt-Out Case," Review of English Literature (Jan. 1962), 3:90–101

O'Connell, Donat, Our Men in Africa, Spectator (Jan. 20, 1961), #6917:80

Poole, Roger, "Those Sad Arguments": Two Novels of Graham Greene, Renaissance and Modern Studies (Spring 1968), 1:66–68

Sackville-West, Edward, Time-Bomb, Month (March 1961), 25:175–78

Servotte, Herman, Bedenkingen Bij "A Burnt-Out Case": Graham Greene's Jongste Roman, Dietsche Warande en Belfort (1961), 106:371–75

Simon, John K., Off the "Voie Royale": The Failure of Greene's "A Burnt-Out Case," Symposium (1964), 18:163–69

Smith, Francis J., The Anatomy of "A Burnt-Out Case," America (Sept. 9, 1961), 105:711–12

Stratford, Philip, Chalk and Cheese; A Comparative Study of "A Kiss for the Leper" and "A Burnt-Out Case," University of Toronto Quarterly (Oct. 1963), 33:200–18

Weyergans, Franz, "La Saison des Pluies" de Graham Greene, Revue Nouvelle (April 1961), 33:417–20

The Comedians, 1966

Allen, Walter, The Comedians, London Magazine (March 1966), 5:73–80

Barker, Paul, The Masks of Graham Greene: "The Comedians," New Society (Jan. 27, 1966), p. 29

Davenport, John, The Last Albigensian, Spectator (Jan. 28, 1966), #7179:110–11

DeVitis, A. A., Greene's "The Comedians": Hollower Men, Renascence (Spring 1966), 18:129–36

Gilman, Richard, Up from Hell with Graham Greene, New Republic (Jan. 29, 1966), 154:25–29

Lindman-Stafford, Kerstin, En Sorts Komedi, Horisont (1966), 13:27–30

Lodge, David, Graham Greene's Comedians, Commonweal (Feb. 25, 1966), 83:604–06

Mooney, Harry J., Jr., and Thomas F. Staley, eds., The Shapeless God, Essays on Modern Fiction. 1968. p. 57–65

The Confidential Agent, 1939

Eishiskina, N., Graham Greene's Novels, Voprosi Literaturi (June 1961), #6:149–69

Lewis, R. W., The Fiction of Graham Greene: Between the Horror and the Glory, Kenyon Review (1957), 19:56–75

The End of the Affair, 1951

Braybrooke, Neville, Graham Greene—The Double Man: An Approach to His Novel "The End of the Affair," Queen's Quarterly (Spring 1970), 77:29–39

Eagleton, Terry, Exiles and Emigrés; Studies in Modern Lit-
  erature. 1970. p. 19-21
Gardiner, Harold Charles, In All Conscience; Reflections on
  Books and Culture. 1959. p. 96-102
Hortman, Wilhelm, Graham Greene: The Burnt-Out Catholic,
  Twentieth Century Literature (July 1964), 10:64-76
Ivaschova, Valentina, Legende und Wahrheit über Graham
  Greene, Zeitschrift für Anglistik und Amerikanistik (1962),
  10:229-58
Lodge, David, The Use of Key-Words in the Novels of Graham
  Greene—Love, Hate, and "The End of the Affair," Blackfriars
  (Nov. 1961), 42:468-74
Mooney, Harry J., Jr., and Thomas F. Staley, eds., The Shape-
  less God; Essays on Modern Fiction. 1968. p. 51-57
Reinhardt, Kurt Frank, The Theological Novel of Modern
  Europe; An Analysis of Masterpieces by Eight Authors. 1969.
  p. 170-202
Smith, A. J. M., Graham Greene's Theological Thrillers,
  Queen's Quarterly (Spring 1961), 68:15-33
West, Anthony, Principles and Persuasions; The Literary
  Essays of Anthony West. 1957. p. 195-200

A Gun for Sale, 1936

Allott, Kenneth and Miriam Farris, The Art of Graham Greene.
  1951. p. 100-17
Lewis, R. W., The Fiction of Graham Greene: Between the
  Horror and the Glory, Kenyon Review (1957), 19:56-75
Traversi, Derek, Graham Greene, Twentieth Century (1951),
  149:231-40 and 319-28

The Heart of the Matter, 1948

Anisimov, I., Graham Greene's Novels, Inostrannaya Litera-
  tura (Oct. 1964), #10:221-26
Barratt, Harold, Adultery as Betrayal in Graham Greene,
  Dalhousie Review (Autumn 1965), 45:324-32
DeVitis, A. A., The Church and Major Scobie, Renascence
  (1958), 10:115-20
Eagleton, Terry, Exiles and Emigrés; Studies in Modern Lit-
  erature. 1970. p. 109-12
Eishiskina, N., Graham Greene's Novels, Voprosi Literaturi
  (June 1961), #6:149-69
Evans, Robert O., ed., Graham Greene: Some Critical Con-
  siderations. 1963. p. 169-80

Friedman, Melvin J., ed., The Vision Obscured; Perception
of Some Twentieth Century Catholic Novelists. 1970. p.
120-28

Jouve, Raymond, La Damnation de Scobie?, Etudes (Nov.
1949), 243:164-77

Kellogg, Gene, The Vital Tradition; The Catholic Novel in a
Period of Convergence. 1970. p. 127-30

Lewis, R. W. B., The Trilogy of Graham Greene, Modern
Fiction Studies (Autumn 1957), 3:195-215

Maekawa Shunichi Kyoju Kanreki Kinev-Ronbunshu. 1968. p.
25-37

Marković, Vida E., The Changing Face; Disintegration of Personality in the Twentieth Century British Novel, 1900-1950.
1970. p. 82-96

Mooney, Harry J., Jr., and Thomas F. Staley, eds., The Shapeless God; Essays on Modern Fiction. 1968. p. 48-51

Mueller, William Randolph, Prophetic Voice in Modern Fiction.
1959. p. 136-57

Orwell, George, The Collected Essays, Journalism, and Letters of George Orwell, ed. by Sonia Orwell and Ian Angus.
Vol. 4. 1968. p. 439-46

Reinhardt, Kurt Frank, The Theological Novel of Modern
Europe; An Analysis of Masterpieces of Eight Authors.
1969. p. 170-202

Smith, A. J. M., Graham Greene's Theological Thrillers,
Queen's Quarterly (Spring 1961), 68:15-33

Wichert, Robert A., The Quality of Graham Greene's Mercy,
College English (Nov. 1963), 25:99-103

Wilshire, A. D., Conflict and Conciliation in Graham Greene,
Essays and Studies (1966), 19:122-37

Our Man in Havana, 1958

Eishiskina, N., Graham Greene's Novels, Voprosi Literaturi
(June 1961), #6:149-69

Engelborghs, M., De Nieuwe Roman van Graham Greene,
Kultuurleven (Feb. 1959), 26:119-22

Kazin, Alfred, Contemporaries. 1962. p. 158-61

Lanina, T., Paradoxes of Graham Greene, Inostrannaya Literatura (March 1959), #3:188-96

The Power and the Glory, 1940

Davies, Horton, A Mirror of the Ministry in Modern Novels.
1959. p. 81-110

Eagleton, Terry, Exiles and Emigrés; Studies in Modern Literature. 1970. p. 112–15 and 116–18

Eishiskina, N., Graham Greene's Novels, Voprosi Literaturi
(June 1961), #6:149–69

Evans, Robert O., ed., Graham Greene; Some Critical Considerations. 1963. p. 181–87

Grob, Alan, "The Power and the Glory": Graham Greene's
Argument from Design, Criticism (Winter 1969), 11:1–30

Haber, Herbert R., The Two Worlds of Graham Greene, Modern Fiction Studies, (Autumn 1957), 3:256–68

Harmer, Ruth Mulvey, Greene World of Mexico: The Birth of
a Novelist, Renascence (Summer 1963), 15:171–82

Hoggart, Richard, Speaking to Each Other; Essays. Vol. 2.
1970. p. 40–55

Kellogg, Gene, The Vital Tradition; The Catholic Novel in a
Period of Convergence. 1970. p. 123–25

Lewis, R. W. B., The Trilogy of Graham Greene, Modern
Fiction Studies (Autumn 1957), 3:195–215

McDonnell, Lawrence V., The Priest-Hero in the Modern
Novel, Catholic World (Feb. 1963), 196:306–11

Marie-Celeste, Sister, Georges Bernanos et Graham Greene,
Revue des Lettres Modernes (1965), 127–29:43–70

Michener, Richard L., Apocalyptic Mexico: "The Plumed
Serpent" and "The Power and the Glory," University Review
(June 1968), 34:313–16

Mooney, Harry J., Jr. and Thomas F. Staley, eds., The
Shapeless God; Essays on Modern Fiction. 1968. p. 45–48

Oppel, Horst, ed., Der Moderne Englische Roman: Interpretationen. 1965. p. 245–61

Parc, Robert du, Saint ou Mandit? Le Pretre dans "La Puis-
sance et la Gloire," Etudes (March 1949), 240:368–81

Patten, Karl, The Structure of "The Power and the Glory,"
Modern Fiction Studies (Autumn 1957), 3:225–34

Reinhardt, Kurt Frank, The Theological Novel of Modern
Europe; An Analysis of Masterpieces of Eight Authors.
1969. p. 170–202

Smith, A. J. M., Graham Greene's Theological Thrillers,
Queen's Quarterly (Spring 1961), 68:15–33

White, W. D., "The Power and the Glory": An Apology to the
Church, University of Portland Review (Spring 1969), 21:
14–22

Wichert, Robert A., The Quality of Graham Greene's Mercy,
College English (Nov. 1963), 25:99–103

Wilshire, A. D., Conflict and Conciliation in Graham Greene, Essays and Studies (1966), 19:122−37

The Quiet American, 1955

Anisimov, I., Graham Greene's Novels, Inostrannaya Literatura (Oct. 1964), #10:221−26

Duffy, Joseph M., Jr., The Lost World of Graham Greene, Thought (Summer 1958), 33:229−47

Eagleton, Terry, Exiles and Emigrés; Studies in Modern Literature. 1970. p. 125−28

Eishiskina, N., Graham Greene's Novels, Voprosi Literaturi (June 1961), #6:149−69

Evans, Robert O., Existentialism in Greene's "The Quiet American," Modern Fiction Studies (Autumn 1957), 3:241−48

Evans, Robert O., ed., Graham Greene: Some Critical Considerations. 1963. p. 188−206

Hughes, R. E., "The Quiet American": The Case Reopened, Renascence (1959), 12:41−42

Lanina, T., Paradoxes of Graham Greene, Inostrannays Literatura (March 1959), #3:188−96

Lewis, R. W. B., The Fiction of Graham Greene: Between the Horror and the Glory, Kenyon Review (1957), 19:56−75

Poole, Roger, "Those Sad Arguments": Two Novels of Graham Greene, Renaissance and Modern Studies (Spring 1968), 1: 66−68

Rudman, Harry W., Clough and Graham Greene's "The Quiet American," Victorian Newsletter (1961), #19:14−15

This Gun for Hire, SEE A Gun for Sale

HENRY RIDER HAGGARD

Allan Quatermain, 1887

Atwood, Margaret, Superwoman Drawn and Quartered: The Early Forms of "She," Alphabet (July 1965), #10:65−82

Cetywayo and His White Neighbors, 1882

Cohen, Morton, Rider Haggard; His Life and His Works. 1960. p. 67−70 and 72−77

Dawn, 1884

Atwood, Margaret, Superwoman Drawn and Quartered: The Early Forms of "She," Alphabet (July 1965), #10:65−82

King Solomon's Mines, 1885

> Atwood, Margaret, Superwoman Drawn and Quartered: The
> Early Forms of "She," Alphabet (July 1965), #10:65-82
> Cohen, Morton, Rider Haggard; His Life and His Works. 1960.
> p. 115-18 and 231-37
> Pritchett, V. S., Rider Haggard, New Statesman and Nation
> (Aug. 27, 1960), p. 277-78

She, 1887

> Atwood, Margaret, Superwoman Drawn and Quartered: The
> Early Forms of "She," Alphabet (July 1965), #10:65-82
> Bowen, Elizabeth, Seven Winters; Memories of a Dublin Child-
> hood. 1962. p. 228-37
> Cohen, Morton, Rider Haggard; His Life and His Works. 1960.
> p. 181-84
> Pritchett, V. S., Rider Haggard, New Statesman and Nation
> (Aug. 27, 1960), p. 277-78

The Witch's Head, 1885

> Atwood, Margaret, Superwoman Drawn and Quartered: The
> Early Forms of "She," Alphabet (July 1965), #10:65-82

THOMAS HARDY

Desperate Remedies, 1871

> Bailey, J. O., Hardy's Visions of the Self, Studies in Philology
> (Jan. 1959), 56:74-101
> Carpenter, Richard C., Hardy's "Gurgoyles," Modern Fiction
> Studies (1960), 6:223-32
> Chew, Samuel C., Thomas Hardy: Poet and Novelist. 1928.
> p. 21-24
> Cox, R. G., ed., Thomas Hardy; The Critical Heritage. 1970.
> p. 1-8
> Hardy, Evelyn, Thomas Hardy; A Critical Biography. 1954.
> p. 97-107
> Hornback, Bert G., The Metaphor of Chance; Vision and Tech-
> nique in the Works of Thomas Hardy. 1971. p. 41-46
> Jones, Lawrence O., "Desperate Remedies" and the Victorian
> Sensation Novel, Nineteenth Century Fiction (June 1965), 20:
> 35-50
> Lea, Hermann, Thomas Hardy's Wessex. 1913. p. 233-39
> Millgate, Michael, Thomas Hardy; His Career as a Novelist.

1971. p. 29-35

Smith, Curtis C., Natural Settings and Natural Characters in Hardy's "Desperate Remedies" and "A Pair of Blue Eyes," Thoth (Spring 1967), 8:84-97

Webster, Harvey Curtis, On a Darkling Plain: The Art and Thought of Thomas Hardy. 1947. p. 93-98

Far from the Madding Crowd, 1874

Abercrombie, Lascelles, Thomas Hardy; A Critical Study. 1912. p. 97-128

Andersen, Carol Reed, Time, Space and Perspective in Thomas Hardy, Nineteenth Century Fiction (Dec. 1954), 9: 206-08

Bailey, J. O., Hardy's Mephistotelian Visitants, Modern Language Association. Publications (Dec. 1946), 61:1147-50

Babb, H., Setting and Theme in "Far from the Madding Crowd," ELH (June 1963), 30:147-61

Baker, Ernest A., The History of the English Novel. Vol. 9. 1938. p. 32-36

Brooks, Jean R., Thomas Hardy; The Poetic Structure. 1971. p. 158-76

Carpenter, Richard C., Hardy's "Gurgoyles," Modern Fiction Studies (Autumn 1960), 6:223-32

Carpenter, Richard C., The Mirror and the Sword; Imagery in "Far from the Madding Crowd," Nineteenth Century Fiction (March 1964), 18:331-45

Chapman, Frank, Far from the Madding Crowd, The Use of English (Autumn 1959), 11:12-15

Cox, R. G., ed., Thomas Hardy; The Critical Heritage. 1970. p. 19-45

Drew, Elizabeth A., The Novel; A Modern Guide to Fifteen English Masterpieces. 1963. p. 141-55

Friedman, Alan, The Turn of the Novel. 1966. p. 38-74

Gindin, James, Harvest of a Quiet Eye; The Novel of Compassion. 1971. p. 90-95

Hardy, Florence Emily, The Early Life of Thomas Hardy, 1840-1891. 1928. p. 125-36

Hornback, Bert G., The Metaphor of Chance; Vision and Technique in the Works of Thomas Hardy. 1971. p. 51-56

Hyde, William J., Hardy's View of Realism; A Key to the Rustic Characters, Victorian Studies (1958-59), 2:45-59

James, Henry, Literary Reviews and Essays; On American, English and French Literature. 1957. p. 291-97

Lea, Hermann, Thomas Hardy's Wessex. 1913. p. 32–44
Liddell, Robert, Some Principles of Fiction. 1953. p. 73–75
Lynd, Robert, Books and Writers. 1952. p. 178–82
McDowall, Arthur, Thomas Hardy: A Critical Study. 1931.
  p. 65–68
Maekawa Shunichi Kyōju Kanreki Kinen-Ronbunshū. 1968. p.
  129–40
Miller, J. Hillis, Thomas Hardy; Distance and Desire. 1970.
  p. 57–70
Millgate, Michael, Thomas Hardy; His Career as a Novelist.
  1971. p. 79–95
Moore, John Robert, Two Notes on Thomas Hardy, Nineteenth
  Century Fiction (Sept. 1950), 5:159–63
Rutland, W. R., Thomas Hardy; A Study of His Writings and
  Their Background. 1938. p. 167–75
Sampson, E. C., Telling Time by the Stars in "Far from the
  Madding Crowd," Notes and Queries (Feb. 1967), 14:63–64
Schweik, Robert C., The Early Development of Hardy's "Far
  from the Madding Crowd," Texas Studies in Literature and
  Language (1967), 9:415–28
Scott, James F., Spectacle and Symbol in Thomas Hardy's
  Fiction, Philological Quarterly (Oct. 1965), 44:527–44
Smart, Alastair, Pictorial Imagery in the Novels of Thomas
  Hardy, Review of English Studies (1961), 12:262–80
Weber, Carl J., Hardy of Wessex; His Life and Literary
  Career. 1940. p. 60–66

The Hand of Ethelberta, 1876

Beach, Joseph Warren, The Technique of Thomas Hardy.
  1922. p. 110–13
Ellis, Havelock, From Marlowe to Shaw: The Studies, 1876–
  1936, in English Literature of Havelock Ellis. 1950. p.
  245–58
Hardy, Florence Emily, The Early Life of Thomas Hardy,
  1840–1891. 1928. p. 135–37 and 141–43
Hornback, Bert G., The Metaphor of Chance; Vision and Tech-
  nique in the Works of Thomas Hardy. 1971. p. 56–59
Lea, Hermann, Thomas Hardy's Wessex. 1913. p. 240–50
Millgate, Michael, Thomas Hardy; His Career as a Novelist.
  1971. p. 105–16
Short, Clarice, In Defense of "Ethelberta," Nineteenth Century
  Fiction (June 1958), 13:48–57

Jude the Obscure, 1895

Alexander, B. J., Thomas Hardy's "Jude the Obscure"; A Rejection of Traditional Christianity's "Good" God Theory, Southern Quarterly (Oct. 1964), 3:74-82

Allen, Walter, The English Novel. 1954. p. 243-46

Bailey, J. O., Hardy's visions of the Self, Studies in Philology (Jan. 1959), 56:74-101

Baker, Ernest A., The History of the English Novel. Vol. 9. 1938. p. 75-80

Bellman, Samuel I., How "New" a Woman Was Hardy's Sue Bridehead?, Colby Library Quarterly (Aug. 1956), 4:137-39

Braybrooke, Patrick, Thomas Hardy and His Philosophy. 1924. p. 84-95

Brooks, Jean R., Thomas Hardy; The Poetic Structure. 1971. p. 254-75

Brown, Douglas, Thomas Hardy. 1954. p. 98-100

Bull, Philip, Thomas Hardy and Social Change, Southern Review (Australia) (1969), 3:199-213

Clifford, Emma, The Child: The Circus: and "Jude the Obscure," Cambridge Journal (June 1954), 7:531-46

Conacher, W. M., "Jude the Obscure": A Study, Queen's Quarterly (Autumn 1928), 35:529-40

Cox, R. G., ed., Thomas Hardy: The Critical Heritage. 1970. p. 249-315

Dawson, E. W., Two "Flat" Characters in "Jude the Obscure," Lock Haven Review (1964), #6:36-44

Ellis, Havelock, From Marlowe to Shaw: The Studies, 1876-1936, in English Literature of Havelock Ellis. 1950. p. 274-84

Emmett, V. J., Jr., Marriage in Hardy's Later Novels, Midwest Quarterly (1968-69), 10:331-48

Fleissner, Robert F., The Name of Jude, Victorian Newsletter (Spring 1965), 27:24-26

Freeman, John, The Moderns: Essays in Literary Criticism. 1916. p. 123-26

Friedman, Alan, The Turn of the Novel. 1966. p. 38-74

Gindin, James, Harvest of a Quiet Eye; The Novel of Compassion. 1971. p. 91-100

Gordon, Walter K., Father Time's Suicide Note in "Jude the Obscure," Nineteenth Century Fiction (Dec. 1967), 22:298-300

Hardy, Evelyn, Thomas Hardy; A Critical Biography. 1954. p. 242-55

Hardy, Florence Emily, The Later Years of Thomas Hardy, 1892-1928. 1930. p. 37-44

Harper, Howard M., Jr. and Charles Edge, eds., The Classic British Novel. 1972. p. 143-65

Heilman, Robert B., Hardy's Sue Bridehead, Nineteenth Century Fiction (March 1966), 20:307-23

Hellstrom, Ward, Hardy's Use of Setting and "Jude the Obscure," Victorian Newsletter (Spring 1964), #25:11-13

Hellstrom, Ward, "Jude the Obscure" as Pagan Self-Assertion, Victorian Newsletter (Spring 1966), #29:26-27

Hellstrom, Ward, A Study of "Jude the Obscure," Dissertation Abstracts (1962), 22:3645

Hommage à Paul Dottin. Caliban #3. Special Issue. 1966. p. 185-214

Hoopes, Kathleen R., Illusion and Reality in "Jude the Obscure," Nineteenth Century Fiction (1957), 12:154-57

Hornback, Bert G., The Metaphor of Chance; Vision and Technique in the Works of Thomas Hardy. 1971. p. 126-39

Horne, Lewis B., Fawley's Quests: A Reading of "Jude the Obscure," Tennessee Studies in Literature (1964), 9:117-27

Howe, Irving, Hardy as a "Modern Novelist," New Republic (June 26, 1965), 152:19-22

Howells, William Dean, Criticism and Fiction and Other Essays. 1959. p. 148-53

Hyde, William J., Hardy's Response to the Critics of "Jude," Victorian Newsletter (Spring 1961), #19:1-5

Hyde, William J., Theoretic and Practical Unconventionality in "Jude the Obscure," Nineteenth Century Fiction (Sept. 1965), 20:155-64

Knoepflmacher, U. C., Laughter and Despair; Readings in Ten Novels of the Victorian Age. 1971. p. 202-39

Lawrence, David H., Phoenix; The Posthumous Papers of D. H. Lawrence. 1936. p. 488-510

Lawyer, W. R., Thomas Hardy's "Jude the Obscure," Paunch (Feb. 1967), #28:6-54

Lea, Hermann, Thomas Hardy's Wessex. 1913. p. 45-66

McDowall, Arthur, Thomas Hardy; A Critical Study. 1931. p. 83-88

McDowell, Frederick P. W., Hardy's "Seemings or Personal Impressions": The Symbolical Use of Image and Contrast in

"Jude the Obscure," Modern Fiction Studies (Autumn 1960), 6:233–50

McDowell, Frederick P. W., In Defense of Arabella: A Note on "Jude the Obscure," English Language Notes (June 1964), 1:274–80

Mack, Maynard and Ian Gregor, eds., Imagined Worlds: Essays on Some English Novels and Novelists in Honour of John Butts. 1968. p. 237–56

Miller, J. Hillis, Thomas Hardy; Distance and Desire. 1970. p. 165–67 and 234–36

Millgate, Michael, Thomas Hardy; His Career as a Novelist. 1971. p. 317–35

Mizener, Arthur, The Sense of Life in the Modern Novel. 1964. p. 55–77

Montgomery, Marion, The Pursuit of the Worthy: Thomas Hardy's Greekness in "Jude the Obscure," Denver Quarterly (Winter 1967), 1:29–43

Muller, Herbert J., Modern Fiction. 1937. p. 151–58

Paterson, John, The Genesis of "Jude the Obscure," Studies in Philology (Jan. 1960), 57:87–98

Pritchett, V. S., In My Good Books. 1942. p. 99–106

Rutland, W. R., Thomas Hardy; A Study of His Writings and Their Background. 1938. p. 239–57

Saagpakk, Paul F., Psychological Elements in British Novels from 1890–1930, Dissertation Abstracts (Sept. 1966), 27:782A

Schorer, Mark, ed., Modern British Fiction. 1961. p. 45–64

Schutte, William and others, Six Novelists, Carnegie Studies in English (1959), 5:41–52

Scott, James F., Spectacle and Symbol in Thomas Hardy's Fiction, Philological Quarterly (Oct. 1965), 44:527–44

Slack, Robert C., The Text of Hardy's "Jude the Obscure," Nineteenth Century Fiction (1957), 11:261–75

Smart, Alastair, Pictorial Imagery in the Novels of Thomas Hardy, Review of English Studies (1961), 12:262–80

Taube, Myron, "The Atmosphere . . . from Cyprus": Hardy's Development of Theme in "Jude the Obscure," Victorian Newsletter (Fall 1967), #32:16–18

Tomlinson, Mary, Jude the Obscure, South Atlantic Quarterly (Oct. 1924), 23:235–46

Weatherby, Hal L., Jude the Victorian, Southern Humanities Review (Summer 1967), 1:158–69

Weber, Carl J., Hardy of Wessex; His Life and Career. 1940. p. 141–53

Weber, Carl J., Jude from Obscurity via Notoriety to Fame,
  Colby Library Quarterly (Jan. 1946), 1:209-15
Yevish, Irving A., The Attack on "Jude the Obscure": A Re-
  appraisal Some Seventy Years After, Journal of General
  Education (Jan. 1967), 18:239-48

A Laodicean, 1881

Bailey, J. O., Hardy's "Mephistophelian Visitants," Modern
  Language Association. Publications (Dec. 1946), 61:1155-60
Bailey, J. O., Hardy's Visions of the Self, Studies in Philology
  (Jan. 1959), 56:74-101
Beach, Joseph Warren, The Technique of Thomas Hardy.
  1922. p. 117-21
Drake, Robert Y., Jr., "A Laodicean": A Note on a Minor
  Novel, Philological Quarterly (1961), 40:602-06
Grimsditch, Herbert B., Character and Environment in the
  Novels of Thomas Hardy. 1925. p. 36-38 and 102-05
Guerard, Albert J., Thomas Hardy; The Novels and Stories.
  1949. p. 53-55
Hardy, Evelyn, Thomas Hardy; A Critical Biography. 1954.
  p. 177-82
Lea, Hermann, Thomas Hardy's Wessex. 1913. p. 251-56
Millgate, Michael, Thomas Hardy; His Career as a Novelist.
  1971. p. 165-73
Webster, Harvey Curtis, On a Darkling Plain; The Art and
  Thought of Thomas Hardy. 1947. p. 141-43

The Mayor of Casterbridge, 1886

Abercrombie, Lascelles, Thomas Hardy; A Critical Study.
  1912. p. 97-128
Bailey, J. O., Hardy's "Mephistophelian Visitants," Modern
  Language Association. Publications (1946), 61:1161-64
Bailey, J. O., Hardy's Visions of the Self, Studies in.Philology
  (Jan. 1959), 56:74-101
Baker, James R., Thematic Ambiguity in "The Mayor of
  Casterbridge," Twentieth Century Literature (April 1955),
  1:13-16
Beckman, Richard, A Character Typology for Hardy's Novels,
  ELH (1963), 30:70-87
Brogan, Howard O., "Visible Essences"in "The Mayor of Cast-
  erbridge," ELH (Dec. 1950), 17:307-23
Brogan, Howard O., Science and Narrative Structure in Austen,
  Hardy and Woolf, Nineteenth Century Fiction (March 1957),

11:276-87

Brooks, Jean R., Thomas Hardy; The Poetic Structure. 1971.
p. 196-215

Chew, Samuel C., Thomas Hardy; Poet and Novelist. 1928.
p. 46-51

Cooley, John R., The Importance of Things Past; An Archetypal Reading of "The Mayor of Casterbridge," Massachusetts Studies in English (1967), 1:17-21

Cox, R. G., ed., Thomas Hardy; The Critical Heritage. 1970.
p. 133-40

Davidson, Donald, Still Rebels, Still Yankees, and Other Essays. 1957. p. 62-83

Emmett, V. J., Jr., Marriage in Hardy's Later Novels, Midwest Quarterly (1968-69), 10:331-48

Faurot, Ruth M., The Halo Over Lucetta Templeman, English
Literature in Transition (1880-1920) (1968), 11:81-85

Friedman, Norman, Criticism and the Novel; Hardy, Hemingway, Crane, Woolf, and Conrad, Antioch Review (Fall 1958),
18:343-70

Gindin, James, Harvest of a Quiet Eye; The Novel of Compassion. 1971. p. 79-83

Gregor, Ian, What Kind of Fiction did Hardy Write?, Essays
in Criticism (1966), 16:290-308

Hardy, Evelyn, Thomas Hardy; A Critical Biography. 1954.
p. 194-207

Heilman, Robert B., Hardy's "Mayor": Notes on Style, Nineteenth Century Fiction (March 1964), 18:307-29

Heilman, Robert B., Hardy's "Mayor" and the Problem of
Intention, Criticism (1963), 5:199-213

Hornback, Bert G., The Metaphor of Chance; Vision and Technique in the Works of Thomas Hardy. 1971. p. 83-108

Karl, Frederick R., An Age of Fiction; The Nineteenth Century
British Novel. 1965. p. 295-322

Karl, Frederick R., "The Mayor of Casterbridge": A New
Fiction Defined, Modern Fiction Studies (Autumn 1960), 6:
195-213

Kiely, Robert, Vision and Viewpoint in "The Mayor of Casterbridge," Nineteenth Century Fiction (Sept. 1968), 23:189-200

Kovácsi, Gábor and Ross Pudaloff, Either Rage or Submit:
The Human Body in "Casterbridge," Paunch (Dec. 1967),
#30:48-66

Lea, Hermann, Thomas Hardy's Wessex. 1913. p. 83-106

Mack, Maynard and Ian Gregor, eds., Imagined Worlds; Es-

says on Some English Novels and Novelists in Honour of
John Butt. 1968. p. 225-36

McCuller, J. T., Jr., Henchard's Sale of Susan in "The Mayor
of Casterbridge," English Language Notes (1965), 2:217-18

Miller, J. Hillis, Thomas Hardy; Distance and Desire. 1970.
p. 147-50 and 234-36

Millgate, Michael, Thomas Hardy; His Career as a Novelist.
1971. p. 221-34

Moore, John Robert, Two Notes on Thomas Hardy, Nineteenth
Century Fiction (Sept. 1950), 5:159-63

O'Dea, Raymond, The "Haunting Shade" that Accompanies the
Virtuous Elizabeth-Jane in "The Mayor of Casterbridge,"
Victorian Newsletter (Spring 1967), #31:33-36

Paterson, John, Hardy, Faulkner and the Prosaics of Tragedy,
Anglia (1960), 78:156-75

Paterson, John, "The Mayor of Casterbridge" as Tragedy,
Victorian Studies (Dec. 1959), 3:151-72

Peterson, Audrey C., Point of View in Thomas Hardy's "The
Mayor of Casterbridge" and "Tess of the d'Urbervilles,"
Dissertation Abstracts (1967), 28:240A-241A

Riesner, Dieter and Helmut Gneuss, eds., Festschrift für
Walter Hübner. 1964. p. 267-326

Rutland, W. R., Thomas Hardy; A Study of His Writings and
Their Background. 1938. p. 197-211

Schorer, Mark, ed., Modern British Fiction. 1961. p. 10-29

Schweik, Robert C., Character and Fate in Hardy's "The Mayor
of Casterbridge," Nineteenth Century Fiction (Dec. 1966), 21:
249-62

Scott, James F., Spectacle and Symbol in Thomas Hardy's
Fiction, Philological Quarterly (Oct. 1965), 44:527-44

Templeman, William D., Hardy's Wife-Selling Incident and a
Letter by Warren Hastings, Huntington Library Quarterly
(Feb. 1955), 18:183-87

Weber, Carl J., Hardy of Wessex; His Life and Literary
Career. 1940. p. 99-107

Weber, Carl J., Restoration of Hardy's Starved Goldfinch in
"The Mayor of Casterbridge," Modern Language Association.
Publications (June 1940), 55:617-19

Weber, Carl J. and F. B. Pinion, "The Mayor of Casterbridge":
An Anglo-American Dialogue, Library Chronicle of the University of Texas (1967), 8:3-12

West, Ray B., Jr. and R. W. Stallman, The Art of Modern
Fiction. 1949. p. 594-605

A Pair of Blue Eyes, 1876

Bailey, J. O., Hardy's "Imbedded Fossil," Studies in Philology
   (July 1945), 42:663−74
Blunden, Edmund, Thomas Hardy. 1942. p. 189−201
Braybrooke, Patrick, Thomas Hardy and His Philosophy.
   1928. p. 13−23
Cox, R. G., ed., Thomas Hardy; The Critical Heritage. 1970.
   p. 15−18
Hardy, Evelyn, Thomas Hardy; A Critical Biography. 1954.
   p. 128−32
Hardy, Florence, The Early Life of Thomas Hardy, 1840−
   1891. 1928. p. 96−98 and 118−26
Hornback, Bert G., The Metaphor of Chance; Vision and Tech-
   nique in the Works of Thomas Hardy. 1971. p. 46−51
Lea, Hermann, Thomas Hardy's Wessex. 1913. p. 165−83
Millgate, Michael, Thomas Hardy; His Career as a Novelist.
   1971. p. 66−76
Smith, Curtis C., Natural Settings and Natural Characters in
   Hardy's "Desperate Remedies" and "A Pair of Blue Eyes,"
   Thoth (Spring 1967), 8:84−97

The Return of the Native, 1878

Abercrombie, Lascelles, Thomas Hardy; A Critical Study.
   1912. p. 97−128
Andersen, Carol Reed, Time, Space, and Perspective in
   Thomas Hardy, Nineteenth Century Fiction (Dec. 1954), 9:
   192−208
Anderson, Marcia Lee, Hardy's Debt to Webster in "The Re-
   turn of the Native," Modern Language Notes (Nov. 1939), 54:
   497−501
Bailey, J. O., Hardy's "Mephistophelian Visitants," Modern
   Language Association. Publications (Dec. 1946), 61:1146−84
Bailey, J. O., Hardy's Visions of the Self, Studies in Philology
   (Jan. 1959), 56:74−101
Bailey, J. O., Temperment as Motive in "The Return of the
   Native," English Fiction in Transition (1880−1920) (1962),
   5:21−29
Baker, Ernest A., The History of the English Novel. Vol. 9.
   1938. p. 36−43
Beach, Joseph Warren, Bowdlerized Versions of Hardy, Mod-
   ern Language Association. Publications (Dec. 1921), 36:
   632−43

Brooks, Jean R., Thomas Hardy; The Poetic Structure. 1971. p. 177-95

Bull, Philip, Thomas Hardy and Social Change, Southern Review (Australia) (1969), 3:199-213

Chew, Samuel C., Thomas Hardy: Poet and Novelist. 1928. p. 39-42

Coates, William Ames, Thomasin and the Reddleman, University of Ceylon Review (April 1961), 19:61-67

Cox, R. G., ed., Thomas Hardy; The Critical Heritage. 1970. p. 46-59

Crompton, Louis, The Sunburnt God: Ritual and Tragic Myth in "The Return of the Native," Boston University Studies in English (Winter 1961), 4:229-40

Deen, Leonard W., Heroism and Pathos in Hardy's "Return of the Native," Nineteenth Century Fiction (Dec. 1960), 15:207-19

Emmett, V. J., Jr., Marriage in Hardy's Later Novels, Midwest Quarterly (1968-69), 10:331-48

Fernando, Lloyd, Thomas Hardy's Rhetoric of Painting, Review of English Literature (Oct. 1965), 6:62-73

Goldberg, M. A., Hardy's Double-Visioned Universe, Essays in Criticism (Oct. 1957), 7:374-82

Gregor, Ian, What Kind of Fiction Did Hardy Write?, Essays in Criticism (1966), 16:290-308

Greshoff, C. J., A Note on "The Return of the Native," Standpunte (1964), 18:33-41

Hardy, Evelyn, Thomas Hardy; A Critical Biography. 1954. p. 159-68

Hornback, Bert G., The Metaphor of Chance; Vision and Technique in the Works of Thomas Hardy. 1971. p. 15-40

Hunt, Kellogg W., "Lord Jim" and "The Return of the Native": A Contrast, English Journal (Oct. 1960), 49:447-56

Jaffe, Adrian H. and Herbert Weisinger, eds., The Laureate Fraternity; An Introduction to Literature. 1960. p. 264-67

Johnson, S. F., Hardy and Burke's "Sublime," English Institute Essays (1958), p. 55-86

Korninger, Siegfried, ed., Studies in English Language and Literature; Presented to Professor Dr. Karl Brunner on the Occasion of His 70th Birthday. 1958. p. 58-73

Lawrence, David H., Phoenix; The Posthumous Papers of D. H. Lawrence. 1936. p. 413-21

Lea, Hermann, Thomas Hardy's Wessex. 1913. p. 67-82

McCann, Eleanor, Blind Will or Blind Hero: Philosophy and

Myth in Hardy's "Return of the Native," Criticism (Spring
1961), 3:140–57

McDowall, Arthur, Thomas Hardy; A Critical Study. 1931.
p. 68–71 and 153–55

Miller, J. Hillis, Thomas Hardy; Distance and Desire. 1970.
p. 87–92 and 159–61

Millgate, Michael, Thomas Hardy; His Career as a Novelist.
1971. p. 130–44

Paterson, John, The "Poetics" of "The Return of the Native,"
Modern Fiction Studies (Autumn 1960), 6:214–22

Paterson, John, "The Return of the Native" as Antichristian
Document, Nineteenth Century Fiction (Sept. 1959), 14:111–27

Pinck, Joan B., The Reception of Thomas Hardy's "The Return
of the Native," Harvard Library Bulletin (1969), 17:291–308

Rutland, W. R., Thomas Hardy; A Study of His Writings and
Their Background. 1938. p. 177–88

Schweik, Robert C., Theme, Character and Perspective in
Hardy's "The Return of the Native," Philological Quarterly
(Oct. 1962), 41:757–67

Scott, James F., Spectacle and Symbol in Thomas Hardy's
Fiction, Philological Quarterly (Oct. 1965), 44:527–44

Scott, Nathan, Jr., The Literary Imagination and the Victorian
Crisis of Faith; The Example of Thomas Hardy, Journal of
Religion (1960), 40:267–81

Shapiro, Charles, ed., Twelve Original Essays on Great English Novels. 1960. p. 153–73

Smart, Alastair, Pictorial Imagery in the Novels of Thomas
Hardy, Review of English Studies (1961), 12:262–80

Stallman, Robert Wooster, The Houses that James Built, and
Other Literary Studies. 1961. p. 53–63

Vandiver, Edward P., Jr., "The Return of the Native" and
Shakespeare, Furman Studies (Nov. 1964), 12:11–15

Vickery, John B., ed., Myth and Literature; Contemporary
Theory and Practice. 1966. p. 289–97

Weber, Carl J., Hardy of Wessex; His Life and Career. 1940.
p. 70–77

Weber, Carl J., Hardy's Grim Note in "The Return of the
Native," Papers of the Bibliographical Society of America
(1942), 36:37–45

Wheeler, Otis B., Four Versions of "The Return of the Native,"
Nineteenth Century Fiction (June 1959), 14:27–44

Williams, Raymond, The English Novel; From Dickens to
Lawrence. 1970. p. 102–06

Yoshikawa, Michio, On "The Return of the Native," Essays (Dec. 1962), #15:2-14

Tess of the D'Urbervilles, 1891

Andersen, Carol Reed, Time, Space and Perspective in Thomas Hardy, Nineteenth Century Fiction (Dec. 1954), 9: 192-208

Bailey, J. O., Hardy's Visions of the Self, Studies in Philology (Jan. 1959), 56:74-101

Baker, Ernest A., The History of the English Novel. Vol. 9. 1938. p. 68-75

Brick, Allan, Paradise and Consciousness in Hardy's "Tess," Nineteenth Century Fiction (Sept. 1962), 17:115-34

Brooks, Jean R., Thomas Hardy; The Poetic Structure. 1971. p. 233-53

Carpenter, Richard C., Hardy's "Gurgoyles," Modern Fiction Studies (1960), 6:223-32

Cary, Joyce, Art and Reality; Ways of the Creative Process. 1958. p. 168-72

Child, Harold H., Essays and Reflections. 1948. p. 64-72

Cox, R. G., ed., Thomas Hardy; The Critical Heritage. 1970. p. 178-221

Davis, W. Eugene, "Tess of the D'Urbervilles": Some Ambiguities about a Pure Woman, Nineteenth Century Fiction (March 1968), 22:397-401

Efron, Arthur, The Tale, the Teller and Sexuality in "Tess of the D'Urbervilles," Paunch (Feb. 1967), #28:55-80

Elsbree, Langdon, "Tess" and the Local Cerelia, Philological Quarterly (Oct. 1961), 11:606-13

Emmett, V. J., Jr., Marriage in Hardy's Later Novels, Midwest Quarterly (1968-69), 10:331-48

Fleishman, Avrom, The English Historical Novel; Walter Scott to Virginia Woolf. 1971. p. 189-97

Freeman, John, The Moderns; Essays in Literary Criticism. 1916. p. 117-23

Friedman, Alan, The Turn of the Novel. 1966. p. 38-74

Gindin, James, Harvest of a Quiet Eye; The Novel of Compassion. 1971. p. 91-98

Gose, Elliott B., Jr., Psychic Evolution: Darwinism and Initiation in "Tess of the D'Urbervilles," Nineteenth Century Fiction (1963), 18:261-72

Griffith, Philip Malone, The Image of the Trapped Animal in Hardy's "Tess of the D'Urbervilles," Tulane Studies in English (1963), 13:85–94

Grimsditch, Herbert B., Character and Environment in the Novels of Thomas Hardy. 1925. p. 30–34, 100–02, 116–20, 141–44, and 150–54

Hardy, Evelyn, Thomas Hardy; A Critical Biography. 1954. p. 226–41

Hardy, Florence Emily, The Early Life of Thomas Hardy, 1840–1891. 1928. p. 289–91

Hardy, Florence Emily, The Later Years of Thomas Hardy, 1892–1928. 1930. p. 3–8

Hazen, James F., The Tragedy of Tess Durbeyfield, Texas Studies in Literature and Language (1969), 11:779–94

Herman, William R., Hardy's "Tess of the D'Urbervilles," Explicator (Dec. 1959), 18:Item 16

Holloway, John, The Charted Mirror; Literary and Critical Essays. 1960. p. 108–17

Hornback, Bert G., The Metaphor of Chance; Vision and Technique in the Works of Thomas Hardy. 1971. p. 109–25

Kirk, Rudolf and C. F. Main, eds., Essays in Literary History Presented to J. Milton French. 1960. p. 197–216

Lang, Varley, Crabbe and "Tess of the D'Urbervilles," Modern Language Notes (May 1938), 53:369–70

Lawrence, Dan H., Henry James and Stevenson Discuss "Vile" Tess, Colby Library Quarterly (May 1953), 3:164–68

Lawrence, David H., Phoenix; The Posthumous Papers of D. H. Lawrence. 1936. p. 482–88

Lea, Hermann, Thomas Hardy's Wessex. 1913. p. 3–31

Lodge, David, Language of Fiction; Essays in Criticism and Verbal Analysis of the English Novel. 1966. p. 164–88

McDowall, Arthur, Thomas Hardy; A Critical Study. 1931. p. 79–84

Marshall, George O., Jr., Hardy's "Tess" and Ellen Glasgow's "Barren Ground," Texas Studies in Literature and Language (Winter 1960), 1:517–21

Miller, J. Hillis, Thomas Hardy; Distance and Desire. 1970. p. 79–82, 102–05, and 234–36

Millgate, Michael, Thomas Hardy; His Career as a Novelist. 1971. p. 263–80

Mordell, Albert, ed., Notorious Literary Attacks. 1926. p. 221–31

O'Grady, Walter, On Plot in Modern Fiction; Hardy, James and Conrad, Modern Fiction Studies (Summer 1965), 11:107–15

Marshall, William H., Motivation in "Tess of the D'Urbervilles," Revue des Langues Vivantes (1963), 29:224–31

Oppel, Horst, ed., Der Moderne Englische Roman; Interpretationen. 1965. p. 34–48

Osgerby, J. R., Thomas Hardy's "Tess of the D'Urbervilles," Use of English (Winter 1962), 14:109–15

Paris, B. J., Confusion of Many Standards: Conflicting Value Systems in "Tess of the D'Urbervilles," Nineteenth Century Fiction (June 1969), 24:57–79

Peterson, Audrey C., Point of View in Thomas Hardy's "The Mayor of Casterbridge" and "Tess of the D'Urbervilles," Dissertation Abstracts (1967), 28:240A–241A

Pittfield, Robert L., In the Footsteps of Tess D'Urberville, General Magazine and Historical Chronicle (July 1930), p. 497–507

Rathburn, Robert C. and Martin Steinman, Jr., eds., From Jane Austen to Joseph Conrad; Essays Collected in Memory of James T. Hillhouse. 1958. p. 237–39 and 242–45

Richard, Hugo M., Hardy's "Tess of the D'Urbervilles," Explicator (April 1956), 14:Item 42

Rutland, W. R., Thomas Hardy; A Study of His Writings and Their Background. 1938. p. 221–39

Schorer, Mark, ed., Modern British Fiction. 1961. p. 30–44

Schweik, Robert C., Moral Perspective in "Tess of the D'Urbervilles," College English (1962), 24:14–18

Selna, Barbara, Hardy's "Tess of the D'Urbervilles," Explicator (Feb. 1962), 20:Item 47

Sheppard, John T., Music at Belmont and Other Essays and Addresses. 1951. p. 163–78

Smart, Alastair, Pictorial Imagery in the Novels of Thomas Hardy, Review of English Studies (1961), 12:262–80

Tanner, Tony, Colour and Movement in Hardy's "Tess of the D'Urbervilles," Critical Quarterly (Autumn 1968), 10:219–39

Van Dyke, Henry, The Man Behind the Book; Essays in Understanding. 1929. p. 283–305

Verschoyle, Derek, ed., The English Novelists. 1936. p. 236–39

Weber, Carl J., Care and Carelessness in Hardy, Modern Language Notes (Jan. 1935), 50:41–43

Weber, Carl J., Hardy of Wessex; His Life and Career. 1940. p. 116–33

Weber, Carl J., Tess Since "Forty-One," Colby Library Quarterly (May 1954), 3:232–34

Williams, Raymond, The English Novel from Dickens to
Lawrence. 1970. p. 107–13

Wing, George, Tess and the Romantic Milkmaid, Review of
English Literature (Leeds) (Jan. 1962), 3:22–30

The Trumpet-Major, 1880

Beach, Joseph Warren, The Technique of Thomas Hardy.
1922. p. 113–17

Brown, Douglas, Thomas Hardy. 1954. p. 112–15

Cox, R. G., ed., Thomas Hardy; The Critical Heritage. 1970.
p. 71–77

Freeman, John, The Moderns; Essays in Literary Criticism.
1916. p. 104–110

Lea, Hermann, Thomas Hardy's Wessex. 1913. p. 184–93

McDowall, Arthur, Thomas Hardy; A Critical Study. 1931. p.
93–95

Weber, Carl J., A Connecticut Yankee in King Alfred's Country, The Colophon (Spring 1936), n.s.1:525–35

Weber, Carl J., A Ghost from a Barber Shop, New Colophon
(1948), 1:185–89

Two on a Tower, 1882

Beach, Joseph Warren, The Technique of Thomas Hardy.
1922. p. 121–24

Cox, R. G., ed., Thomas Hardy; The Critical Heritage. 1970.
p. 97–100

Lea, Hermann, Thomas Hardy's Wessex. 1913. p. 194–200

McDowall, Arthur, Thomas Hardy; A Critical Study. 1931.
p. 97–100

Millgate, Michael, Thomas Hardy; His Career as a Novelist.
1971. p. 183–93

Rutland, W. R., Thomas Hardy; A Study of His Writings and
Their Background. 1938. p. 192–96

Weber, Carl J., The Manuscript of Hardy's "Two on a Tower,"
Papers of the Bibliographic Society of America (1946), 40:
1–21

Under the Greenwood Tree, 1872

Bailey, J. O., Hardy's Mephistotelian Visitants, Modern Language Association. Publications (Dec. 1946), 61:1146–47

Brown, Douglas, Thomas Hardy. 1954. p. 45–48

Cox, R. G., ed., Thomas Hardy; The Critical Heritage. 1970.
p. 9–14

Danby, John, Under the Greenwood Tree, Critical Quarterly
(Spring 1959), 1:5-13
Gindin, James, Harvest of a Quiet Eye; The Novel of Compas-
sion. 1971. p. 91-93
Hardy, Florence Emily, The Early Life of Thomas Hardy,
1840-1891. 1928. p. 120-22
Lea, Hermann, Thomas Hardy's Wessex. 1913. p. 118-28
McDowall, Arthur, Thomas Hardy; A Critical Study. 1931. p.
91-93
Pritchett, V. S., In My Good Books. 1942. p. 99-106
Weber, Carl J., Hardy of Wessex; His Life and Career. 1940.
p. 52-54
Webster, Harvey Curtis, On a Darkling Plain; The Art and
Thought of Thomas Hardy. 1947. p. 98-100

The Well Beloved, 1897

Bailey, J. O., Hardy's Visions of the Self, Studies in Philology
(Jan. 1959), 56:74-101
Bartlett, Phyllis, "Seraph of Heaven": A Shelleyean Dream in
Hardy's Fiction, Modern Language Association. Publications
(Sept. 1955), 70:624-35
Beach, Joseph Warren, The Technique of Thomas Hardy.
1922. p. 127-33
Braybrooke, Patrick, Thomas Hardy and His Philosophy.
1928. p. 76-83
Brown, E. K., Rhythm in the Novel. 1950. p. 13-16
Cox, R. G., ed., Thomas Hardy; The Critical Heritage. 1970.
p. 316-18
Gerber, Helmut E., Hardy's "The Well Beloved" as a Comment
on the Well Despised, English Language Notes (Sept. 1963),
1:48-53
Hardy, Florence Emily, The Later Years of Thomas Hardy,
1892-1928. 1930. p. 59-61
Hornback, Bert G., The Metaphor of Chance; Vision and Tech-
nique in the Works of Thomas Hardy. 1971. p. 72-77
Lea, Hermann, Thomas Hardy's Wessex. 1913. p. 201-11
Miller, Milton L., Nostalgia: A Psychoanalytic Study of
Marcel Proust. 1956. p. 116-21
Millgate, Michael, Thomas Hardy; His Career as a Novelist.
1971. p. 293-307
Webster, Harvey Curtis, On a Darkling Plain; The Art and
Thought of Thomas Hardy. 1947. p. 180-83

Woodlanders, 1887

Abercrombie, Lascelles, Thomas Hardy; A Critical Study.
    1912. p. 97–128
Bailey, J. O., Hardy's Mephistotelian Visitants, Modern Lan-
    guage Association. Publications (Dec. 1946), 61:1164–69
Beach, Joseph Warren, The Technique of Thomas Hardy.
    1922. p. 158–76
Brooks, Jean R., Thomas Hardy; The Poetic Structure. 1971.
    p. 216–32
Brown, Douglas, Thomas Hardy. 1954. p. 70–89
Collie, M. J., Social Security in Literary Criticism, Essays
    in Criticism (April 1959), 9:151–58
Drake, Robert Y., Jr., "The Woodlanders" as Traditional
    Pastoral, Modern Fiction Studies (Autumn 1960), 6:251–57
Edgar, Pelham, The Art of the Novel. 1933. p. 164–71
Fayen, George S., Jr., Hardy's "The Woodlanders": Inward-
    ness and Memory, Studies in English Literature, 1500–1900
    (Autumn 1961), 1:81–100
Gindin, James, Harvest of a Quiet Eye; The Novel of Compas-
    sion. 1971. p. 98–101
Grimsditch, Herbert B., Character and Environment in the
    Novels of Thomas Hardy. 1925. p. 63–68
Hardy, Evelyn, Thomas Hardy; A Critical Biography. 1954.
    p. 208–15
Hardy, Florence Emily, The Early Life of Thomas Hardy,
    1840–1891. 1928. p. 242–44
Hornback, Bert G., The Metaphor of Chance; Vision and Tech-
    nique in the Works of Thomas Hardy. 1971. p. 69–72
Lea, Hermann, Thomas Hardy's Wessex. 1913. p. 107–17
McDowall, Arthur, Thomas Hardy; A Critical Study. 1931. p.
    75–79
Matchett, William H., "The Woodlanders"; or, Realism in
    Sheep's Clothing, Nineteenth Century Fiction (March 1955),
    9:241–61
Meibergen, C. R., The Woodlanders, Englische Studien (Oct.
    1917), 51:226–47
Shine, Hill, ed., Booker Memorial Studies. 1950. p. 133–53
Weber, Carl J., Hardy of Wessex; His Life and Career. 1940.
    p. 108–14
Weber, Carl J., Hardy and "The Woodlanders," Review of
    English Studies (July 1939), 15:215–22

Weber, Carl J., Hardy's Song in "The Woodlanders," ELH
(Nov. 1935), 2:242-45

Webster, Harvey Curtis, On a Darkling Plain; The Art and
Thought of Thomas Hardy. 1947. p. 166-73

JAN DE HARTOG

The Inspector, 1960

Cargas, Harry J., The Twentieth Century's Aeschylus of the
Sea, Classical Bulletin (March 1969), 45:71-72

ANTHONY HOPE HAWKINS

SEE

ANTHONY HOPE

ANTHONY HOPE

A Man of Mark, 1890

Barr, Donald, I've Been Reading; Anthony Hope and Edgar
Wallace, as a Matter of Fact, Columbia University Forum
(Winter 1960), 3:38-41

Prisoner of Zenda, 1894

Barr, Donald, I've Been Reading; Anthony Hope and Edgar
Wallace, as a Matter of Fact, Columbia University Forum
(Winter 1960), 3:38-41

Muggeridge, Malcolm, A Knight's Tale, New Statesman and
Nation (May 18, 1962), p. 721-22

WILLIAM HENRY HUDSON

The Purple Land, 1885

Barges, J. L., Other Inquisitions, 1937-1952. 1964. p. 141-45

FORD MADOX HUEFFER

SEE

FORD MADOX FORD

RICHARD ARTHUR WARREN HUGHES

The Fox in the Attic, 1961

    Bosano, J., Richard Hughes, Études Anglaises (1963), 16:
262-269

A High Wind in Jamaica, 1929

    Henighan, T. J., Nature and Convention in "A High Wind in
Jamaica," Critique; Studies in Modern Fiction (1967), 9:5-18
Tranter, H. L., Set Books: "High Wind in Jamaica," Use of
English (Autumn 1962), 14:36-41
Woodward, Daniel H., The Delphic Voice; Richard Hughes' "A
High Wind in Jamaica," Papers in Language and Literature
(1967), 3:57-74

THOMAS HUGHES

Tom Brown's School Days, 1857

    Allsop, K., Coupon for Instant Tradition; On "Tom Brown's
School Days," Encounter (Nov. 1965), 25:60-63
Winn, William E., "Tom Brown's School Days" and the Development of Muscular Christianity, Church History (March
1960), 29:64-73

ALDOUS HUXLEY

After Many a Summer Dies the Swan, 1939

    Holmes, Charles M., Aldous Huxley and the Way to Reality.
1970. p. 120-28
Nagarajan, S., Religion in Three Recent Novels of Aldous
Huxley, Modern Fiction Studies (Summer 1959), 5:153-65

Antic Hay, 1923

    Enrath, Clyde, Mysticism in Two of Aldous Huxley's Early
Novels, Twentieth Century Literature (1960), 6:123-32
Holmes, Charles M., Aldous Huxley and the Way to Reality.
1970. p. 25-33
Karl, Frederick R. and M. Magalaner, A Reader's Guide to
Great Twentieth Century English Novels. 1959. p. 257-84
Montgomery, Marion, Aldous Huxley's Uncomparable Man in
"Antic Hay," Discourse (Oct. 1960), 3:227-32

Brave New World, 1932

Clareson, Thomas D., The Classics: Aldous Huxley's "Brave New World," Extrapolation (1961), 11:33–40

Coleman, D. C., Bernard Shaw and "Brave New World," Shaw Review (1967), 10:6–8

Enroth, Clyde, Mysticism in Two of Aldous Huxley's Early Novels, Twentieth Century Literature (1960), 6:123–32

Firchow, P. E., Satire of Huxley's "Brave New World," Modern Fiction Studies (Winter 1966–67), 12:451–60

Grushow, Ira, "Brave New World" and "The Tempest," College English (1962), 24:42–45

Hoffman, Charles G., The Changes in Huxley's Approach to the Novel of Ideas, Personalist (Winter 1961), 42:85–90

Holmes, Charles M., Aldous Huxley and the Way to Reality. 1970. p. 82–89

Holmes, Charels M., Aldous Huxley's Struggle with Art, Western Humanities Review (Spring 1961), 15:149–56

Howe, Irving, The Fiction of Anti-Utopia, New Mexico Quarterly (April 23, 1962), 146:13–16

Jones, William M., The Iago of "Brave New World," Western Humanities Review (1961), 15:275–78

Karl, Frederick R. and M. Magalaner, A Reader's Guide to Great Twentieth Century English Novels. 1959. p. 257–84

Kessler, Martin, Power and the Perfect State; A Study in Disillusionment as Reflected in Orwell's "Nineteen Eighty-Four" and Huxley's "Brave New World," Political Science Quarterly (Dec. 1957), 72:565–77

Leeper, Geoffrey, The Happy Utopias of Aldous Huxley and H. G. Wells, Meanjin (1965), 24:120–24

Oppel, Horst, ed., Der Moderne Englische Roman; Interpretationen. 1965. p. 201–21

Pendexter, Hugh III, Huxley's "Brave New World," Explicator (1962), 20:Item 58

The Perennial Prophet, London Times Literary Supplement (Feb. 27, 1959), p. 105

Pinkus, Philip, Satire and St. George, Queen's Quarterly (Spring 1963), 70:30–49

Thomas, W. K., "Brave New World" and the Houyhnhnms, Revue de l'Université d'Ottawa (1967), 37:688–96

Wilson, Robert H., Versions of "Brave New World," Library Chronicle of the University of Texas (1968), 8:28–41

Crome Yellow, 1922

Dommergues, André, Aldous Huxley: Une Oeuvre de Jeunesse:
"Crome Yellow," Études Anglaises (1968), 21:1–18
Farmer, David, A Note on the Text of Huxley's "Crome Yel-
low," Papers of the Bibliographical Society of America
(1969), 63:131–33
Holmes, Charles M., Aldous Huxley and the Way to Reality.
1970. p. 21–26
Holmes, Charles M., Aldous Huxley's Struggle with Art, West-
ern Humanities Review (Spring 1961), 15:149–56
Karl, Frederick R. and M. Magalaner, A Reader's Guide to
Great Twentieth Century English Novels. 1959. p. 257–84

Eyeless in Gaza, 1936

Holmes, Charles M., Aldous Huxley and the Way to Reality.
1970. p. 97–109
Karl, Frederick R. and M. Magalaner, A Reader's Guide to
Great Twentieth Century English Novels. 1959. p. 257–84
Sponberg, Florence L., Huxley's Perennial Preoccupation.
Mankato State College Studies (Dec. 1968), 3:1–18

The Genius and the Goddess, 1955

Nagarajan, S., Religion in Three Recent Novels of Aldous
Huxley, Modern Fiction Studies (Summer 1959), 5:153–65

Island, 1962

Leeper, Geoffrey, The Happy Utopias of Aldous Huxley and H.
G. Wells, Meanjin (1963), 24:120–24
McMichael, Charles T., Aldous Huxley's "Island": The Final
Vision, Studies in the Literary Imagination (1968), 1:73–82
Sponberg, Florence L., Huxley's Perennial Preoccupation,
Mankato State College Studies (Dec. 1968), 3:1–18
Stewart, D. H., Aldous Huxley's "Island," Queen's Quarterly
(1963), 70:326–35
Watt, Donald J., Vision and Symbol in Aldous Huxley's
"Island," Twentieth Century Literature (1968), 14:149–60

Point Counter Point, 1928

Baldanza, Frank, "Point Counter Point": Aldous Huxley on the
Human Figure, South Atlantic Quarterly (1958), 58:248–57
Holmes, Charles M., Aldous Huxley and the Way to Reality.
1970. p. 53–71

Karl, Frederick R. and M. Magalaner, A Reader's Guide to
Great Twentieth Century English Novels. 1959. p. 257-84
O'Brien, Justin, The French Literary Horizon. 1967. p.
103-08
Thompson, Leslie M., A Lawrence-Huxley Parallel: "Women
in Love" and "Point Counter Point," Notes and Queries (Feb.
1968), 15:58-59
Watson, David S., "Point Counter Point"; The Modern Satiric
Novel a Genre? Satire Newsletter (1969), 6:31-35

Those Barren Leaves, 1925

Holmes, Charles M., Aldous Huxley and the Way to Reality.
1970. p. 53-64

Time Must Have a Stop, 1944

Nagarajan, S., Religon in Three Recent Novels of Aldous
Huxley, Modern Fiction Studies (Summer 1959), 5:153-65
Sponberg, Florence L., Huxley's Perennial Preoccupation.
Mankato State College Studies (Dec. 1968), 3:1-18

PAMELA HANSFORD JOHNSON

The Unspeakable Skipton, 1959

A Corvo of Our Day, London Times Literary Supplement
(Jan. 9, 1959), p. 18

SAMUEL JOHNSON

Rasselas, 1759

Al Aoun, Dina Abdul-Hamid, Some Remarks on a Second Read-
ing of "Rasselas," Cairo Studies in English: Bicentenary
Essays on "Rasselas," a Supp. (Supp. 1959), p. 15-20
Allen, John M., "Rasselas" and "The Vanity of Human Wishes,"
Criticism (1961), 3:295-303
Baker, Sheridan, "Rasselas": Psychological Irony and Ro-
mance, Philological Quarterly (1966), 45:249-61
Barnett, George L., "Rasselas" and "The Vicar of Wakefield,"
Notes and Queries (1957), 4:302-305
Bernard, F. V., The Hermit of Paris and the Astronomer in
"Rasselas," Journal of English and Germanic Philology
(1968), 67:272-78

Camden, C., ed., Restoration and Eighteenth Century Literature. 1963. p. 125–42

Casini, Paolo, "Rasselas" o il mito della Feliciti, L'Approdo (1960), 6:37–45

Clifford, James L., Some Remarks on "Candide" and "Rasselas," Cairo Studies in English: Bicentenary Essays on "Rasselas," a Supp. (Supp. 1959), p. 7–14

Eddy, Donald D., The Publication Date of the First Edition of "Rasselas," Notes and Queries (1962), 9:21–22

Fisher, Marvin, The Pattern of Conservatism in Johnson's "Rasselas" and Hawthorne's "Tales," Journal of the History of Ideas (1958), 19:173–96

Gabrieli, Vittorio, ed., Friendship's Garland: Essays Presented to Mario Praz on his Seventieth Birthday. Vol. 1. 1966. p. 243–70

Goodyear, Louis E., "Rasselas" Journey from Amhara to Cairo Viewed from Arabia, Cairo Studies in English; Bicentenary Essays on "Rasselas," a Supp. (Supp. 1959), p. 21–29

Jones, E., Artistic Form of "Rasselas," Review of English Studies (Nov. 1967), 18:387–401

Joost, Nicholas, Whispers of Fancy; or, The Meaning of "Rasselas," Modern Age (1957), 1:166–73

Kenney, William, Johnson's "Rasselas" after Two Centuries, Boston University Studies in English (1957), 111:88–96

Kenney, William "Rasselas" and the Theme of Diversification, Philological Quarterly (1959), 38:84–89

Kolb, Gwin J., The "Paradise" in Abyssinia and the "Happy Valley" in "Rasselas," Modern Philology (1958), 56:10–16

Kolb, Gwin J., "Rasselas": Purchase Price, Proprietors and Printings, Studies in Bibliography; Papers of the Bibliographical Society of the University of Virginia (1962), 15: 256–59

Leyburn, Ellen Douglass, No Romantic Absurdities or Incredible Fictions: The Relation of Johnson's "Rasselas" to Lobo's "Voyage to Abyssinia," Modern Language Association. Publications (Dec. 1955), 70:1059–67

Leyburn, Ellen Douglass, Two Allegorical Treatments of Man: "Rasselas" and "La Pesta," Criticism (1962), 4:197–209

Link, Frederick M., "Rasselas" and the Quest for Happiness, Boston University Studies in English (1957), 3:121–23

Lockhart, Donald M., The Fourth Son of the Mighty Emperor: The Ethiopian Background of Johnson's "Rasselas," Modern Language Association. Publications (1963), 68:516–28

Lombardo, Agostino, The Importance of Imlac, Cairo Studies in English: Bicentenary Essays on "Rasselas," a Supp. (Supp. 1959), p. 31–49

Mack, Maynard and Ian Gregor, eds., Imagined Worlds; Essays on Some English Novels and Novelists in Honour of John Butt. 1968. p. 111–36

Mahmoud, Fatma Moussa, "Rasselas" and "Vathek," Cairo Studies in English: Bicentenary Essays on "Rasselas," a Supp. (Supp. 1959), p. 51–57

Manzalaoui, Mahmoud, Rasselas and some Medieval Ancillaries, Cairo Studies in English: Bicentenary Essays on "Rasselas," a Supp. (Supp. 1959), p. 59–73

Moore, John Robert, "Rasselas" in Retrospect, Cairo Studies in English: Bicentenary Essays on "Rasselas," a Supp. (Supp. 1959), p. 81–84

Preston, T. R., Biblical Context of Johnson's "Rasselas," Modern Language Association. Publications (March 1969), 84:274–81

Rawson, C. J., The Continuation of "Rasselas," Cairo Studies in English: Bicentenary Essays on "Rasselas," a Supp. (Supp. 1959), p. 85–95

Reed, Kenneth T., "This Tasteless Tranquility": A Freudian Note on Johnson's "Rasselas," Literature and Psychology (1969), 19:61–62

Sherburn, George, "Rasselas" Returns—To What?, Philological Quarterly (1959), 38:383–84

Steeves, Harrison Ross, Before Jane Austen; The Shaping of the English Novel in the Eighteenth Century. 1965. p. 226–42

Suderman, Elmer F., "Candide," "Rasselas" and Optimism, Iowa English Yearbook (1966), 11:37–43

Sutherland, W. O. S., The Art of the Satirist. 1965. p. 92–104

Tillotson, Geoffrey, Time in "Rasselas," Cairo Studies in English: Bicentenary Essays on "Rasselas," a Supp. (Supp. 1959), p. 97–103

Wahba, Maydi, A Note on the Manner of Concluding in "Rasselas," Cairo Studies in English: Bicentenary Essays on "Rasselas," a Supp. (Supp. 1959), p. 105–10

Weitzman, Arthur J., More Light on "Rasselas": The Background of the Egyptian Episodes, Philological Quarterly (Jan. 1969), 48:42–58

West, Paul, "Rasselas": The Humanist as Stoic, English (Summer 1961), 13:181–85

JAMES JOYCE

Finnegan's Wake, 1939

Adams, Robert Martin, The Bent Knife Blade: Joyce in the
1960's, Partisan Review (Fall 1962), 29:507–18

Adams, Robert Martin, James Joyce; Common Sense and
Beyond. 1967. p. 172–213

Arnold, Armin, James Joyce. 1963. p. 55–86

Asenjo, F. G., The General Problem of Sentence Structure;
An Analysis Prompted by the Loss of Subject in "Finnegan's
Wake," Centennial Review of Arts and Science (Fall 1964),
8:398–408

Atherton, J. S., A Few More Looks at the Wake, James Joyce
Quarterly (Spring 1965), 2:142–49

Atherton, J. S., James Joyce and "Finnegan's Wake," Manchester Review (1961), 9:97–108

Atherton, J. S., Joyce's "Finegan's Wake," Explicator (May
1953), 11:Item 52

Atherton, J. S., To Give Down the Banks and Hark from the
Tomb!, James Joyce Quarterly (Winter 1967), 4:75–83

Aubert, Jacques, A Moment of Impropriety, Wake Newsletter
(June 1964), 1:1–4

Aubert, Jacques, Notes on the French Element in "Finnegan's
Wake," James Joyce Quarterly (1968), 5:110–24

Baker, James R., James Joyce; Affirmation after Exile, Modern Language Quarterly (1957), 18:275–81

Bates, Ronald, The Feast Is a Flyday, James Joyce Quarterly
(Spring 1965), 2:174–87

Beechhold, Henry F., Finn MacCool and "Finnegan's Wake,"
James Joyce Quarterly (1958), 2:3–12

Beechhold, Henry F., Joyce's "Finnegan's Wake," Explicator
(Jan. 1961), 19:Item 27

Begnal, Michael H., The Fables of "Finnegan's Wake," James
Joyce Quarterly (1969), 6:357–67

Begnal, Michael H., The Narrator of "Finnegan's Wake, Eire-
Ireland (Autumn 1969), 4:38–49

Begnal, Michael H., The Prankquean in "Finnegan's Wake,"
James Joyce Quarterly (1964), 2:33–41

Benstock, Bernard, Americana in "Finnegan's Wake," Bucknell Review (1964), 12:64–81

Benstock, Bernard, Every Telling Has a Taling; A Reading of
the Narrative of "Finnegan's Wake," Modern Fiction Studies
(Spring 1969), 15:3–25

Benstock, Bernard, The Final Apostacy; James Joyce and
    "Finnegan's Wake," ELH (1961), 28:417-37
Benstock, Bernard, A "Finnegan's Wake" Address Book,
    James Joyce Quarterly (1965), 2:195-203
Benstock, Bernard, The Gastronome's "Finnegan's Wake,"
    James Joyce Quarterly (Spring 1965), 2:188-94
Benstock, Bernard, Joyce's "Finnegan's Wake," Explicator
    (June 1957), 15:Item 59
Benstock, Bernard, L. Boom as Dreamer in "Finnegan's
    Wake," Modern Language Association. Publications (March
    1967), 82:91-97
Benstock, Bernard, Mick and Nick in "Finnegan's Wake," Ball
    State University Forum (1965), 6:25-28
Benstock, Bernard, Persian in "Finnegan's Wake," Philologi-
    cal Quarterly (Jan. 1965), 44:100-09
Benstock, Bernard, A "Portrait of the Artist" in "Finnegan's
    Wake," Bucknell Review (1961), 4:257-71
Benstock, Bernard, The Quiddity of Shem and the Whatness of
    Shaun, James Joyce Review (Fall 1963), 1:26-33
Benstock, Bernard, The Reel "Finnegan's Wake," New Orleans
    Review (Fall 1968), 1:60-64
Bierman, Robert, The Dreamer and the Dream in "Finnegan's
    Wake," Renascence (Summer 1959), 11:197-200
Bierman, Robert, "Ulysses" and "Finnegan's Wake": The
    Explicit, the Implicit and the Tertium Quid, Renascence
    (1958), 11:14-19
Bierman, Robert, "White and Pink Elephants": "Finnegan's
    Wake" and the Tradition of Unintelligibility, Modern Fiction
    Studies (1958), 4:62-70
Bird, Stephen B., Some American Notes to "Finnegan's Wake,"
    Wake Newsletter (Dec. 1966), 3:119-24
Bogan, Louise, Selected Criticism. 1955. p. 142-53
Bonheim, Helmut, The Father in "Finnegan's Wake," Studia
    Neophilologica (1959), 31:182-90
Bonheim, Helmut, God and the Gods in "Finnegan's Wake,"
    Studia Neophilologica (1962), 34:294-314
Bonheim, Helmut, Tory in "Finnegan's Wake," Notes and
    Queries (1961), 8:349-50
Broes, Arthur T., The Bible in "Finnegan's Wake," Wake
    Newsletter (1965), n.s.2:3-11 and 3:102-05
Broes, Arthur T., More People at the Wake, Wake Newsletter
    (Dec. 1966), 3:125-28 and (Feb. 1967), 4:25-30
Burgess, Anthony, Re Joyce. 1965. p. 177-272

Burgum, Edwin Berry, The Novel and the World's Dilemma.
    1947. p. 109–19
Byrne, Patrick, Joyce's Dream Book Took Seventeen Years
    to Write, Irish Digest (July 1964), 81:73–76
Carlson, Marvin, Henrik Ibsen and "Finnegan's Wake," Com-
    parative Literature (Spring 1960), 12:133–41
Christiani, Donnia, H. C. Earwicker the Ostman, James Joyce
    Quarterly (Spring 1965), 2:150–57
Cohn, Alan M., Rosenbach Copinger and Sylvia Beach in
    "Finnegan's Wake," Modern Language Association. Publica-
    tions (June 1962), 77:342–44
Coleman, Elliott, Heliotropical Noughttime: Light and Color
    in "Finnegan's Wake," Texas Quarterly (1961), 4:162–77
Collins, Ben L., Joyce's "Haveth Childers Everywhere,"
    Explicator (Dec. 1951), 10:Item 21
Colum, Padraic, Notes on "Finnegan's Wake," Yale Review
    (March 1941), 30:640–45
Cook, Albert, The Dark Voyage and the Golden Mean: A
    Philosophy of Comedy. 1949. p. 155–60
Cope, Jackson I., From Egyptian Rubbish Heaps to "Finnegan's
    Wake," James Joyce Quarterly (1966), 3:166–70
Daiches, David, The Novel and the Modern World. 1964. p.
    113–37
DeCampos, Augusto, Un Lance de "Des" do "Grande Sertao,"
    Revista do Livre (Dec. 1959), 4:9–28
DuBouchet, Andre, ed., Lire "Finnegan's Wake?," Nouvelle
    Revue Française (Dec. 1957), 10:1054–64
Eco, Umberto, Diario Minimo. 1963. p. 109–25
Eco, Umberto, Le Poetiche di Joyce: Dalla Summa al
    "Finnegan's Wake." 1966. p. 113–63
Ellmann, R., "Ulysses" and the "Odyssey," English Studies
    (Oct. 1962), 43:423–26
Epstein, E. L., Interpreting "Finnegan's Wake": A Half-Way
    House, James Joyce Quarterly (1966), 3:252–71
Fáj, Attila, Probable Byzantine and Hungarian Models of
    "Ulysses" and "Finnegan's Wake," Arcadia (1968), 3:48–72
Flora, Francesco, Di un Saggio sull' "Ulysses" di Joyce,
    Letterature Moderne (1961), 11:149–78
Fowlie, W., Love in Literature. 1965. p. 80–127
Frye, Northrop, Fables of Identity. 1963. p. 256–64
Frye, Northrop, Quest and Cycle in "Finnegan's Wake," James
    Joyce Review (1957), 1:39–47
Giedion-Welcker, Carola, Die Funktion der Sprache in der

Heutigen Dichtung, Transition (Feb. 1933), 22:90–100

Gillet, Louis, A Propos de "Finnegan's Wake," Babel (1940), 1:101–13

Gillet, Louis, Joyce's Testament: "Finnegan's Wake," Quarterly Review of Literature (Winter 1944), 1:87–99

Glasheen, Adaline, Out of My Census, Analyst (June 1959), 17:1–73

Glasheen, Adaline, Part of what Thunder said in "Finnegan's Wake," Analyst (Nov. 1964), 23:1–29

Glasheen, Adaline, The Strange Cold Fowl in "Finnegan's Wake," Spectrum (Fall 1960), 4:38–64

Goldberg, S. L., James Joyce. 1962. p. 103–15

Golding, Louis, James Joyce. 1933. p. 142–56

Goldman, Arnold, James Joyce. 1968. p. 73–102

Graham, Philip L., Japlatin, with my Younkle's Owlseller, Wake Newsletter (Sept. 1962), 5:1–2

Graham, Philip L. and Philip B. Sullivan and G. F. Richter, Mind Your Hats Goan in! Notes on the Museyroom Episode of "Finnegan's Wake," Analyst (July 1962), 21:1–21 and (Oct. 1962), 22:1–24

Gysen, Rene, Links en Rechts, Komma (1966), 2:57–63

Halper, Nathan, Joyce and Eliot; A Tale of Shem and Shaun, Nation (May 31, 1965), 200:590–95

Halper, Nathan, Twelve O'Clock in "Finnegan's Wake," James Joyce Review (1957), 1:3–18

Hart, Clive, The Elephant in the Belly: Eregesis of "Finnegan's Wake," Wake Newsletter (May 1963), 13:1–8

Hart, Clive, His Good Smetterling of Entymology, Wake Newsletter (Feb. 1967), 4:14–24

Hart, Clive, The Hound and the Type-Bed: Further Notes on the Text of "Finnegan's Wake," Wake Newsletter (Aug. 1966), 3:77–84

Hart, Clive, Joyce's "Finnegan's Wake," Explicator (June 1959), 17:Item 63

Hart, Clive, Notes on the Text of "Finnegan's Wake," Journal of English and Germanic Philology (April 1960), 59:229–39

Hart, Clive, Shem's Bodily Get-Up: A Note on Some Unused Theology, James Joyce Quarterly (Fall 1965), 3:66–68

Hayman, David, Dramatic Motion in "Finnegan's Wake," Texas Studies in English (1958), 37:155–76

Hayman, David, From "Finnegan's Wake": A Sentence in Progress, Modern Language Association. Publications (March 1958), 73:136–54

Hayman, David, Joyce et Mallarme. 1956. p. 121–81

Hayman, David, Pound at the Wake of the Uses of a Contemporary, James Joyce Quarterly (Spring 1965), 2:204–16

Henrici, Waldtraud B., Anspielungen auf Ibsens Dramen in "Finnegans Wake," Orbis Litterarium (1968), 23:127–60

Henseler, Donna L., "Harpsdichord," the Formal Principle of HCE, ALP, and the Cad, James Joyce Quarterly (Fall 1968), 6:53–68

Hodgart, Matthew and Mabel Worthington, Song in the Work of James Joyce. 1959. p. 24–58 and 85–171

Hornik, Marcel P., A Page in "Finnegan's Wake" Explained, Modern Language Notes (1960), 75:123–26

Jarrell, Mackie L., Swiftiana in "Finnegan's Wake," ELH (1969), 26:271–94

Jenkins, William D., From a Hugglebeddy Faun, James Joyce Quarterly (Fall 1968), 6:89–91

Jenkins, William D., Tales of a Bayside Inn, Wake Newsletter (April 1966), 3:20–24

Johnston, Denis, Clarify Begins at: The Non-Information of "Finnegan's Wake," Massachusettes Review (1964), 5:357–64

Jolas, Eugene, Elucidation du Monomythe de James Joyce, Critique (July 1948), 4:579–95

Jolas, Eugene, Paul Elliott and Robert Sace, First Aid to the Enemy, Transition (Dec. 1927), 9:161–76

Jolas, Eugene, The Revolution of the Word, Modern Quarterly (Fall 1929), 5:273–92

Jones, C. A., "Finnegan's Wake" and Its Detractors, Graffiti (Sept.–Dec. 1941), 1:5–11

Kelleher, John V., Notes on "Finnegan's Wake," Analyst (April 1957), 12:9–15 and (March 1958), 15:9–13

Kenner, Hugh, Dublin's Joyce. 1956. p. 265–370

Kiralis, Karl, Joyce and Blake; A Basic Source for "Finnegan's Wake," Modern Fiction Studies (1958), 4:329–34

Knuth, Leo, Some Notes on Malay Elements in "Finnegan's Wake," Wake Newsletter (Aug. 1968), 5:51–63

Kopper, Edward A., Jr., Joyce's "Finnegan's Wake," Explicator (1964), 22:Item 34

Kopper, Edward A., Jr., Saint Patrick in "Finnegan's Wake," Wake Newsletter (1967), 4:85–93

Kopper, Edward A., Jr., Some Additional Christian Allusions in "Wake," Analyst (1965), 24:5–24

Laidlaw, R. P., More Huck Finn in "Finnegan's Wake," Wake Newsletter (Dec. 1968), 5:83–87

Levin, Harry, James Joyce; A Critical Introduction. 1941. p. 139-205

Levin, Harry, Contexts of Criticism. 1957. p. 269-86

Levin, Harry, New Directions in Prose and Poetry. 1939. p. 253-87

Levitt, Morton P., Shalt Be Accurst? The Martyr in James Joyce, James Joyce Quarterly (Summer 1968), 5:285-96

Litz, Walton, Art of James Joyce; Method and Design in "Ulysses" and "Finnegan's Wake." 1961. p. 76-128

Litz, Walton, James Joyce. 1966. p. 99-111

MacCarvill, Eileen, Les Années de Formation de James Joyce à Dublin, Archives des Lettres Modernes (1958), 12:1-31

McHugh, Roger, James Joyce's Synge-Song, Envoy (Nov. 1950), 3:12-17

Magalaner, Marvin, ed., A James Joyce Miscellany. 1959. p. 195-207 and 209-223

Majault, Joseph, James Joyce. 1963. p. 85-93

Mason, Eudo C., Exzentrische Bahnen; Studien zum Dichter-bewusstsein der Neuzeit. 1963. p. 284-92

Mercier, Vivian, The Irish Comic Tradition. 1962. p. 226-36

Miller, Norbert, ed., Romananfänge; Versuch zu einer Poetik des Romans. 1965. p. 317-43

Misra, B. P., Joyce's Use of Indian Philosophy in "Finnegan's Wake," Indian Journal of English Studies (1960), 1:70-78

Mitchell, Breen, The Newer Alchemy; Lord Rutherford and "Finnegan's Wake," Wake Newsletter (1966), 3:96-102

Maholy-Nagy, L., Vision in Motion. 1947. p. 344-51

Morse, J. Mitchell, Burrus, Caseous and Nicholas of Cusa, Modern Language Notes (April 1960), 75:326-34

Morse, J. Mitchell, Charles Nodier and "Finnegan's Wake," Comparative Literature Studies (June 1968), 5:195-201

Morse, J. Mitchell, The Disobedient Artist; Joyce and Loyola, Modern Language Association. Publications (1957), 72: 1018-35

Morse, J. Mitchell, HCE's Chaste Ecstasy, Yale Review (Spring 1967), 56:397-405

Morse, J. Mitchell, The Sympathetic Alien; James Joyce and Catholicism. 1959. p. 38-67

Moseley, Virginia, Joyce and the Bible. 1967. p. 144-50

Moseley, Virginia, Ramasbatham, Wake Newsletter (June 1965), 2:10-15

Noon, William T., Joyce and Aquinas. 1957. p. 126-60

Noon, William T., Roll Away the Reel World; "Finnegan's

Wake" after Twenty-Five Years, America (Oct. 31, 1964),
111:517-20
Nuñez, Estuardo, James Joyce y Victor Llona, Revista Perua-
na de Cultura (June 1966), #7-8:221-28
O'Brien, Darcy, Joyce and Sexuality, Twentieth Century Lit-
erature (Nov. 1969), #2:32-38
O'Brien, Darcy, The Twins that Tick Homo Vulgaris: A Study
of Shem and Shaun, Modern Fiction Studies (Summer 1966),
12:183-99
O'Hehir, Brendan, O'Cannochar, O Conchobhair, Conchobhar,
Wake Newsletter (August 1967), 4:67-72
Paris, Jean, Finnegan's Wake, Tel Quel (1967), 30:58-66
Pelorson, Georges, "Finnegan's Wake" de James Joyce ou les
Livres de l'Homme, Revue de Paris (Sept. 1939), 1:227-35
Peter, John, Joyce and the Novel, Kenyon Review (Autumn
1956), 18:619-32
Petijean, Armand M., James Joyce et l'Absorption du Monde
par les Langage, Cahiers, du Sud (Oct. 1934), 11:607-23
Petijean, Armand M., Joyce and Mythology: Mythology and
Joyce, Transition (July 1935), #23:133-42
Petijean, Armand M., Signification de Joyce, Études Anglaises
(Sept. 1937), 1:405-17
Pinguentini, Gianni, James Joyce in Italia. 1963. p. 276-313
Polsky, Ned, Joyce's "Finnegan's Wake," Explicator (Dec.
1950), 9:Item 24
Powys, John Cowper, Finnegan's Wake, La Nouvelle Revue
(Feb. 1968), #182:273-89
Rodewald, Clark, A Note on the Names in "Finnegan's Wake,"
English Language Notes (1965), 2:292-93
Ryf, Robert S., A New Approach to Joyce; A Portrait of the
Artist as a Guidebook. 1962. p. 98-105
Sage, Robert, Etc, Transition (Fall 1928), 14:171-76
Salemson, Harold J., James Joyce and the New World, Modern
Quarterly (Fall 1929), 5:294-312
Schlauch, Margaret, The Language of James Joyce, Science
and Society (Fall 1939), 3:482-97
Schorer, Mark, ed., Modern British Fiction. 1961. p. 358-75
Sedelow, Walter A., Jr., Joyce's "Finnegan's Wake," Explica-
tor (Feb. 1955), 13:Item 27
Semmler, Clement, For the Uncanny Man; Essays Mainly
Literary. 1963. p. 93-108 and 121-26
Senn, Fritz, Every Kleitty of a Scoldermeid; Sexual-Political
Analogies, Wake Newsletter (June 1962), #3:1-7

Senn, Fritz, Ossianic Echoes, Wake Newsletter (April 1966),
    3:25-36
Senn, Fritz, Reading in Progress; Words and Letters in
    "Finnegan's Wake," Leuvense Bijdragen (1968), 57:2-18
Senn, Fritz, Some Conjectures About Homosexuality in "Fin-
    negan's Wake," Wake Newsletter (Oct. 1969), 6:70-72
Senn, Fritz, The Tellings of the Taling, James Joyce Quarterly
    (Spring 1967), 4:229-33
Sherwood, John C., Joyce and the Empire; Some Thoughts on
    "Finnegan's Wake," Studies in the Novel (1969), 1:357-63
Spender, Stephen, The Struggle of the Modern. 1963. p. 189-
    206
Spielberg, Peter, Addenda: More Food for the Gastronomes:
    "Finnegan's Wake," James Joyce Quarterly (1966), 3:297-98
Staley, Thomas F., ed., James Joyce Today. 1966. p. 135-65
Stanford, Donald E., ed., Nine Essays in Modern Literature.
    1965. p. 3-35
Stephens, James, James, Seumas and Jacques; Unpublished
    Writings of James Stephens. 1964. p. 160-62
Stewart, J. I. M., James Joyce. 1957. p. 32-37
Stewart, J. I. M., Eight Modern Writers. 1963. p. 465-83
Strong, L. A. G., James Joyce and Vocal Music, Essays and
    Studies by Members of the English Association (1945), 31:
    95-106
Taplin, Walter, James Joyce Wrote English, The Critic (Spring
    1947), 1:11-16
Tello, Jaime, Un Experimento Joyceano, Revista Naccional de
    Cultura (Sept. -Dec. 1961), 29:61-79
Thompson, W. I., Language of "Finnegan's Wake," Sewanee
    Review (Jan. 1964), 72:78-90
Troy, William, William Troy; Selected Essays. 1967. p. 94-
    109
Tyler, Hamilton, Finnegan's Epic, Circle (1946), #7-8:14-26
Tysdahl, B. J., Joyce and Ibsen; A Study in Literary Influence.
    1968. p. 123-210
Tysdahl, B. J., A Norse Hundred Lettered Name in "Finnegan's
    Wake," Orbis Litterarum (1964), 19:232-33
Ussher, Hermut, Three Great Irishmen: Shaw, Yeats and
    Joyce. 1953. p. 115-18 and 139-50
Vickery, J. B., ed., Myth and Literature. 1966. p. 201-212
Visser, G. J., James Joyce's Prose and Welsh Cynghanedd,
    Neophilologus (Oct. 1963), 47:305-19
Wagner, Geoffrey, Wyndham Lewis and James Joyce: A Study

in Controversy, <u>South Atlantic Quarterly</u> (Jan. 1957), 56:57–66

Werckmeister, O. K., Das Book of Kells in "Finnegans Wake," <u>Neue Rundschau</u> (1966), 67:44–63

Wilder, Thornton, Giordano Bruno's Last Meal in "Finnegan's Wake," <u>Hudson Review</u> (1963), 16:74–79

Wilson, Robert Anton, Joyce and Tao, <u>James Joyce Review</u> (1959), 3:8–16

Worthington, Mabel P., Another Classical Allusion in "Finnegan's Wake," <u>Wake Newsletter</u> (1967), 4:38

Worthington, Mabel P., Nursery Rhymes in "Finnegan's Wake," <u>American Folklore</u> (Jan. 1957), 70:37–48

Zettersten, Arne, Graphs and Symbols in "Finnegan's Wake," <u>English Studies</u> (1969), 50:516–24

A Portrait of the Artist as a Young Man, 1916

Abernathy, F. E., Stephen's Passage Through the Wilderness, <u>New Orleans Review</u> (Winter 1969), 1:162–65

Adams, Robert Martin, <u>James Joyce; Common Sense and Beyond</u>. 1967. p. 91–116

Anderson, Chester G., The Text of James Joyce's "A Portrait of the Artist as a Young Man," <u>Neuphilologische Mitteilungen</u> (1964), 65:160–200

Anderson, Margaret, ed., <u>The Little Review Anthology</u>. 1953. p. 129–31

Andreach, Robert J., <u>Studies in Structure; The Stages of the Spiritual Life in Four Modern Authors</u>. 1964. p. 40–71

Aspell, Joseph, Fire Symbolism in "A Portrait of the Artist as a Young Man," <u>University of Dayton Review</u> (1968–69), 5:29–39

August, Eugene R., Father Arnall's Use of Scripture in "A Portrait," <u>James Joyce Quarterly</u> (1967), 4:275–79

Bates, Ronald, The Correspondence of Birds to Things of the Intellect, <u>James Joyce Quarterly</u> (Summer 1965), 2:281–90

Beckson, Karl, Stephen Dedalus and the Emblematic Cosmos, <u>James Joyce Quarterly</u> (Fall 1968), 6:95–96

Beebe, Maurice, <u>Ivory Towers and Sacred Founts</u>. 1964. p. 260–95

Berger, Hélène, L'Avant-Portrait ou la Bifurcation d'Une Vocation, <u>Tel Quel</u> (Summer 1965), #22:69–76

Berger, Hélène, Portrait de sa Femme par l'Artiste, <u>Lettres Nouvelles</u> (March–April 1966), p. 41–67

Bernhardt-Kabisch, E., Joyce's "A Portrait of the Artist as a

Young Man," Explicator (1960), 18:Item 24

Biderson, Ellis, Joyce Without Fear, English Journal (Feb. 1968), 57:200−02

Booth, Wayne, The Rhetoric of Fiction. 1961. p. 324−36

Boyd, Elizabeth J., James Joyce's Hell-Fire Sermons, Modern Language Notes (Nov. 1960), 75:561−71

Browne, R. B., W. J. Roscelli and R. J. Loftus, eds., The Celtic Cross. 1964. p. 11−21

Burgess, Anthony, Re Joyce. 1965. p. 50−69

Burke, Kenneth, Three Definitions, Kenyon Review (Spring 1951), 5:181−86

Burrows, John, A Sketch of Joyce's "Portrait," Balcony, The Sydney Review (Spring 1965), #3:23−29

Carothers, Robert L., The Hand and Eye in Joyce's "Portrait," Serif (March 1967), 4:17−29

Connolly, Thomas E., Kinesis and Stasis: Structural Rhythm in Joyce's "Portrait," University Review (Dublin) (1966), 3: 21−30

Crews, Frederick C., ed., Psychoanalysis and Literary Process. 1970. p. 118−62

Daiches, David, The Novel and the Modern World. 1960. p. 83−97

Desnoes, Edmundo, La Mirada de Joyce, Edita (Havana) (Oct. 1964), 1:1−4

Dibble, Brian, A Brunonian Reading of Joyce's "Portrait of the Artist," James Joyce Quarterly (1967), 4:280−85

Drew, Elizabeth A., The Novel; A Modern Guide to Fifteen English Masterpieces. 1963. p. 245−61

Dundes, Alan, Re: Joyce—No In at the Womb, Modern Fiction Studies (1962), 8:137−47

Egri, Peter, The Function of Dreams and Visions in "A Portrait" and "Death in Venice," James Joyce Quarterly (1968), 5:86−102

Ellmann, Richard, ed., Edwardian and Late Victorian; English Institute Essays, 1959. 1960. p. 188−210

Fenichel, Robert R., A Portrait of the Artist as a Young Orphan: Aspects of Paternity in "A Portrait of the Artist as a Young Man" and "Ulysses," Literature and Psychology (Spring 1959), 19:19−22

Feshbach, Sidney, A Slow and Dark Birth: A Study of the Organization of "A Portrait of the Artist as a Young Man," James Joyce Quarterly (1967), 4:289−300

Geckle, George J., Stephen Dedalus and W. B. Yeats: The

Making of the Villanelle, Modern Fiction Studies (Spring
1969), 15:87-96
Gerard, Albert, Le Dédale de James Joyce, Revue Nouvelle
(1958), 27:493-501
Gillie, Christopher, Character in English Literature. 1965.
p. 177-202
Goldberg, S. L., Joyce and the Artist's Fingernails, Review of
English Literature (April 1961), 2:59-73
Goldman, Arnold, The Joyce Paradox; Form and Freedom in
His Fiction. 1966. p. 22-73
Goldman, Arnold. James Joyce. 1968. p. 4-6 and 11-29
Gorman, Herbert, James Joyce; His First Forty Years. 1924.
p. 65-100
Grayson, Thomas W., James Joyce and Stephen Dedalus; The
Theory of Aesthetics, James Joyce Quarterly (Summer 1967),
4:310-19
Hanlon, James, Reality in James Joyce's "A Portrait of the
Artist as a Young Man," Shippensburg State College Review
(Oct. 1968), p. 31-34
Harper, Howard M., Jr. and Charles Edge, eds., The Classic
British Novel. 1972. p. 183-201
Hayman, David, "A Portrait of the Artist as a Young Man" and
L'Education Sentimentale; The Structural Affinities, Orbis
Litterarum (1964), 19:161-75
Kain, Richard M. and Robert E. Scholes, eds., The First Ver-
sion of Joyce's "Portrait," Yale Review (1960), 49:355-69
Karl, Frederick R. and M. Magalaner, A Reader's Guide to
the Great Twentieth Century English Novels. 1959. p. 208-
53
Kaye, Julian B., Who Is Betty Byrne?, Modern Language Notes
(Feb. 1956), 71:93-95
Kelly, Edward H., Joyce's "A Portrait of the Artist as a Young
Man," Explicator (1969), 27:Item 32
Kenner, Hugh, Dublin's Joyce. 1956. p. 109-57
Kenner, Hugh, Joyce's "Portrait": A Reconsideration, Univer-
sity of Windsor Review (1965), 1:1-15
Lemon, L. T., "Portrait of the Artist as a Young Man": Motif
as Motivation and Structure, Modern Fiction Studies (Winter
1966-67), 12:439-50
Levitt, Morton P., Shalt be Accurst? The Martyr in James
Joyce, James Joyce Quarterly (Summer 1968), 5:285-96
Lind, Ilse Dusoir, "The Way of All Flesh" and "A Portrait of
the Artist as a Young Man": A Comparison, Victorian News-

letter (Spring 1956), #9:7-10

Litz, Walton, James Joyce. 1966. p. 60-72

Magalaner, Marvin, ed., A James Joyce Miscellany. 1957. p. 26-30

Magalaner, Marvin, ed., A James Joyce Miscellany. 2nd Series 1959. p. 67-77 and 79-91

Magalaner, Marvin, Reflections on "A Portrait of the Artist," James Joyce Quarterly (1967), 4:343-46

Manso, Peter, The Metaphoric Style of Joyce'" "Portrait," Modern Fiction Studies (1967), 13:221-36

Marković, Vida E., The Changing Face; Disintegration of Personality in the Twentieth Century British Novel, 1900-1950. 1970. p. 38-53

Mayoux, Jean Jacques, Joyce et ses Personnages, Revue de Paris (Feb. 1965), p. 39-53

Misra, B. P., Indian Inspiration of James Joyce. n.d. p. 29-32

Morse, J. Mitchell, The Disobedient Artist; Joyce and Loyola, Modern Language Association. Publications (1957), 72:1018-35

Moseley, Virginia, Joyce and the Bible. 1967. p. 31-44

Mueller, William Randolph, The Prophetic Voice in Modern Fiction. 1959. p. 27-55

Naganowski, Egon, Telemach w Labiryncie Swiata; o Twórczosci James Joyce 'a. 1962. p. 62-77

Naremore, James, Style as Meaning in "A Portrait of the Artist," James Joyce Quarterly (1967), 4:331-42

Noon, William T., James Joyce and Aquinas. 1957. p. 18-59

Noon, William T., Three Young Men in Rebellion, Thought (Winter 1963), 38:560-77

O'Brien, Darcy, The Twins that Tick Homo Vulgaris: A Study of Shem and Shaun, Modern Fiction Studies (Summer 1966), 12:183-99

O'Connor, Frank, The Mirror in the Roadway; A Study of the Modern Novel. 1956. p. 301-08

Oppel, Horst., ed., Der Moderne Englische Roman: Interpretationen. 1965. p. 78-114

Pascal, Roy, The Autobiographical Novel and the Autobiography, Essays in Criticism (April 1959), 9:134-50

Pearce, Donald R., "My Dead King!" The Dinner Quarrel in Joyce's "Portrait of the Artist," Modern Language Notes (April 1951), 66:249-51

Poss, Stanley H., "A Portrait of the Artist" as Beginner, University of Kansas City Review (1960), 26:189-96

Poss, Stanley, "A Portrait of the Artist as Hard-Boiled Messiah, Modern Language Quarterly (March 1966), 27:68-79

Poss, Stanley, Stephen's Words, Joyce's Attitude, Research Studies (1960), 28:156-61

Ranald, Margaret Loftus, Stephen Dedalus' Vocation and the Irony of Religious Ritual, James Joyce Quarterly (Winter 1965), 2:97-102

Redford, Grant H., The Role of Structure in Joyce's "Portrait," Modern Fiction Studies (Spring 1958), 4:21-30

Scholes, Robert, Stephen Dedalus, Poet or Esthete?, Modern Language Association. Publications (1964), 79:484-89

Schorer, Mark, ed., Modern British Fiction. 1961. p. 322-35

Sharpless, F. Parvin, Irony in Joyce's "Portrait": The Stasis of Pity, James Joyce Quarterly (1967), 4:320-30

Slatoff, Walter J., With Respect to Readers; Dimensions of Literary Response. 1970. p. 116-18

Sole, J. L., Structure in Joyce's "A Portrait," Serif (1968), 5:9-13

Staley, Thomas F., ed., James Joyce Today. 1966. p. 54-82

Stewart, J. I. M., James Joyce. 1957. p. 15-22

Stewart, J. I. M., Eight Modern Masters. 1963. p. 442-50

Thrane, James R., Joyce's Sermon on Hell; Its Source and Backgrounds, Modern Philology (Feb. 1960), 57:172-98

Tysdahl, B. J., Joyce and Ibsen; A Study in Literary Influence. 1968. p. 59-86

Unterecker, John, ed., Approaches to the Twentieth Century Novel. 1965. p. 9-50

Van Laan, Thomas F., The Meditative Structure of Joyce's "Portrait," James Joyce Quarterly (1964), 1:3-13

Wasson, Richard, Stephen Dedalus and the Imagery of Sight; A Psychological Approach, Literature and Psychology (Fall 1965), 15:195-209

Will, Frederic, ed., Heredities; Seven Essays on the Modern Experience of the Classical. 1964. p. 31-54

Woodward, A. G., Technique and Feeling in James Joyce's "A Portrait of the Artist as a Young Man," English Studies in Africa (1961), 4:39-53

Stephen Hero—A Part of the First Draft of "A Portrait of the Artist as a Young Man," 1944

Connolly, Thomas, "Stephen Hero" Revisited, James Joyce Review (1959), 3:40-46

Curran, Constantine, James Joyce Remembered. 1968. p.

51-58 and 77-82

Burgess, Anthony, Re Joyce. 1965. p. 48-50

Forster, Jean-Paul, Joyce, "Stephen Hero," et Stephen
Dedalus, Etudes de Lettres (July-Sept. 1966), 9:149-64

Givens, Seon, ed., James Joyce: Two Decades of Criticism.
1948. p. 190-97

Goldman, Arnold, The Joyce Paradox; Form and Freedom in
His Fiction. 1966. p. 120-25

Guidi, Augusto, Il Primo Joyce. 1954. p. 41-56

Hennig, John, "Stephen Hero" and "Wilhelm Meister": A Study
of Parallels, German Life and Letters (Oct. 1951), 5:22-29

Morse, J. Mitchell, The Disobedient Artist: Joyce and Loyola,
Modern Language Association. Publications (1957), 72:
1018-35

Naganowski, Egon, Telemach w Labiryncie Swiata o Twórczosci James Joyce 'a. 1962. p. 59-62

Prescott, Joseph, Exploring James Joyce. 1964. p. 17-28

Prescott, Joseph, "Stephen Hero" van James Joyce, De
Vlaamse Gids (Oct. 1964), 48:663-73

Ryf, Robert S., A New Approach to Joyce: "A Portrait of the
Artist" as a Guidebook. 1962. p. 42-58

Stern, Richard G., Proust and Joyce Underway: "Jean San-
teuil" and "Stephen Hero," Kenyon Review (Summer 1956),
18:486-96

Stewart, J. I. M., Eight Modern Writers. 1963. p. 438-47

Ulysses, 1922

Adams, Robert Martin, James Joyce; Common Sense and Beyond. 1967. p. 117-71

Ahearn, Edward J., Religious Values in Joyce's "Ulysses,"
Christian Scholar (Summer 1961), 44:139-45

Aldington, Richard, Literary Studies and Reviews. 1924. p.
192-207

Alexander, Sidney, Bloomsday in Italy, The Reporter (April
13, 1961), 24:38-42

Anderson, Margaret, ed., The Little Review Anthology. 1953.
p. 297-311

Arnold, Armin, James Joyce. 1963. p. 35-54

Bajarlia, Juan Jacobo, Literature de Vanguardia—Del
"Ulysses" de Joyce y las Escuelas Poeticas. 1946. p. 13-57

Baker, James R., James Joyce: Affirmation after Exile, Modern Language Quarterly (1957), 18:275-81

Bass, Richard K., Joyce's "Ulysses," Explicator (1966), 24:

Item 55

Bauerle, Ruth, A Sober Drunken Speech: Stephen's Parodies in "The Oxen of the Sun," James Joyce Quarterly (Fall 1967), 5:40–46

Beebe, Maurice, Ivory Towers and Sacred Founts. 1964. p. 260–95

Bennett, John Z., Unposted Letter; Joyce's Leopold Bloom, Bucknell Review (March 1966), 14:1–13

Benstock, Bernard, Arthur Griffith in "Ulysses": The Explosion of a Myth, English Language Notes (1966), 4:123–28

Berger, Alfred Paul, James Joyce, Adman, James Joyce Quarterly (Fall 1965), 3:25–33

Berger, Hélène, Stephen, Hamlet, Will: Joyce par delà Shakespeare, Études Anglaises (Oct.–Dec. 1964), 17:571–85

Blackmur, Richard Palmer, Eleven Essays in the European Novel. 1964. p. 27–47

Blackmur, Richard Palmer, A Primer of Ignorance. 1967. p. 59–80

Blodgett, Harriet, Joyce's Time Mind in "Ulysses": A New Emphasis, James Joyce Quarterly (1967), 5:22–29

Borel, Jacques, Petite Introduction à l'Ulysse' de Joyce, Temps Modernes (1968), 23:1291–1307

Boyle, Robert, "Ulysses" as Frustrated Sonata Form, James Joyce Quarterly (1965), 2:247–54

Briand, Paul L., Jr., The Catholic Mass in James Joyce's "Ulysses," James Joyce Quarterly (1968), 5:312–22

Bryer, Jackson R., Joyce, "Ulysses," and the Little Review, South Atlantic Quarterly (Spring 1967), 66:148–64

Burgess, Anthony, Re Joyce. 1965. p. 70–176

Burgess, Anthony, The Reticence of "Ulysses," Spectator (June 7, 1969), p. 748

Cambon, Glauco, La Traduzione Italiana d "Ulisses," Veltro (Rome) (1962), 6:579–96

Castronovo, David, Touching the Much Vexed Questions of Stimulants: Drinkers and Drinking in James Joyce's "Ulysses," November Review (Fall 1966), #3:20–45

Church, Margaret, Joyce's "Ulysses," Explicator (June 1961), 19:Item 66

Clarke, John, Joyce and Blakean Vision, Criticism (Spring 1963), 5:173–80

Cohn, A. M., Douglas Hyde in "Ulysses," English Studies (Aug. 1962), 43:255–56

Coleman, Elliott, A Note on Joyce and Jung, James Joyce

Quarterly (Fall 1963), 1:11–16

Cope, Jackson I., Rhythmic Gesture: Image and Aesthetic in Joyce's "Ulysses," ELH (March 1962), 29:67–89

Crews, Frederick C., ed., Psychoanalysis and Literary Process. 1970. p. 118–62

Cronin, Anthony, A Question of Modernity. 1966. p. 58–96

Curtius, Ernest Robert, Technique and Thematic Development in James Joyce, Transition (June 1929), #16–17:310–25

D'Agostino, Nemi, "Ulisse" o la Ricerca della Condizione Umana, Belfagor (Jan. 1961), 16:96–102

Daiches, David, The Novel and the Modern World. 1960. p. 83–97, 98–112, and 113–37

Dalton, Jack P., "Ulysses" X 2: A New Conversion Table, James Joyce Quarterly (1964), 1:52–55

Davenport, W. H., ed., Voices in Court. 1958. p. 218–23

Davidson, Donald, Decorum in the Novel, Modern Age (Winter 1964–65), 9:34–48

Day, R. A., Joyce's Waste Land and Eliot's Unknown God, Literary Monographs (1971), 4:137–206

Decker, Heinz, Der Innere Monolog: Zur Analyse des "Ulysses," Akzente (April 1961), 8:99–125

The Dial, A Dial Miscellany. 1963. p. 97–103 and 113–16

Dibble, Brian, Vico, Bruno and Stephen Dedalus in Dalkey: An Analysis of the Nestor Episode of James Joyce's "Ulysses," Barat Review (Jan. 1966), 1:40–48

Downs, R. B., First Freedom. 1960. p. 83–89

Duncan, Joseph E., The Modality of the Audible in Joyce's "Ulysses," Modern Language Association. Publications (1957), 62:286–95

Dundes, Alan, Re: Joyce—No In at the Womb, Modern Fiction Studies (1962), 8:137–47

Durzak, Manfred, Hermann Broch und James Joyce, Deutsche Vierteljahrschrift und Geistesgeschichte (1966), 40:391–433

East, S. T., ed., Law in American Society. 1964. p. 70–73

Eco, Umbero, Le Poetiche di Joyce: Dalla Summa al "Finnegan's Wake," 1966. p. 59–111

Ellenbogen, Eileen, Leopold Bloom— Jew, Changing World (Winter 1947–48), #3:79–86

Ellmann, Richard, James Joyce's "Ulysses," Inventorio (1962), 17:22–23

Ellmann, Richard, "Ulysses" and the "Odyssey," English Studies (1962), 43:423–26

Empson, William, The Theme of "Ulysses," Twentieth Century

Studies (Nov. 1969), 1:39−40

Epstein, Edmund L., Cruxes in "Ulysses": Notes Toward an
  Edition and Annotation, _James Joyce Review_ (1957), 1:25−36

Fáj, Attila, Probable Byzantine and Hungarian Models of
  "Ulysses" and "Finnegan's Wake," _Arcadia_ (1968), 3:48−72

Feeney, William J., Ulysses and the Phoenix Park Murder,
  James Joyce Quarterly (1964), 1:56−58

Fehr, Bernhard, James Joyce's "Ulysses," _Englische Studien_
  (1925−26), 60:180−205

Feibleman, James K., _In Praise of Comedy_. 1939. p. 230−36

Fenichel, Robert R., A Portrait of the Artist as a Young
  Orphan: Aspects of Paternity in "A Portrait of the Artist as
  a Young Man" and "Ulysses," _Literature and Psychology_
  (Spring 1959), 19:19−22

Frye, Northrop, ed., _Sound and Poetry_. 1956. p. 16−54

Fisher, Franklin, James Joyce and the Misfortunes of Mr.
  Bloom, _Spectrum_ (Winter 1966), 8:76−83

Ford, Ford Madox, "Ulysses" and the Handling of Indecencies,
  English Review (Dec. 1922), 35:538−48

Frank, Joseph, _The Widening Gyre_. 1963. p. 14−19

Galloway, David D., Moses−Bloom−Herzog: Bellow's
  Everyman, _Southern Review_ (B.R.) (Jan. 1966), 2:61−76

Gerard, Martin, Is Your Novel Really Necessary?, _X, A
  Quarterly Review_ (Nov. 1959), 1:46−52

Gibson, George H., The Odyssey of Leopold Bloom's Bar of
  Soap, _Furman Studies_ (May 1966), 13:15−19

Gilbert, Stuart, "Ulysses" par James Joyce, _Nouvelle Revue
  Française_ (April 1, 1929), 32:567−79

Gill, Richard, The "Corporal Works of Mercy" as a Moral
  Pattern in Joyce's "Ulysses," _Twentieth Century Literature_
  (April 1963), 9:17−21

Gindin, James, _Harvest of a Quiet Eye; The Novel of Compas-
  sion_. 1971. p. 222−36

Goldberg, S. L., Art and Freedom; The Aesthetic of "Ulysses,"
  ELH (1957), 24:44−64

Goldberg, S. L., _James Joyce_. 1962. p. 69−102

Goldman, Arnold, _James Joyce_. 1968. p. 30−72

Goldman, Arnold, _The Joyce Paradox; Form and Freedom in
  His Fiction_. 1966. p. 76−167

Goldman, Arnold, Some Proposed Emendations in the Text of
  Joyce's "Ulysses," _Notes and Queries_ (1963), 10:148−50

González, Manuel Pedro, El "Ulises" Cuarenta Años Despúes,
  Cuadernos Americanos (May−June 1963), 128:210−27

Gorman, Herbert, James Joyce; His First Forty Years. 1924.
    p. 116-29
Gross, Harvey, From Barabas to Bloom; Notes on the Figure
    of the Jew, Western Humanities Review (Spring 1957), 11:
    149-56
Grossvogel, David I., Limits of the Novel. 1968. p. 256-99
Hall, Vernon, Jr., Joyce's "Ulysses," Explicator (Dec. 1951),
    10:Item 22
Hamalian, Leo, The "Gift of Guilt" in "Ulysses," Renascence
    (Fall 1966), 19:21-29
Handler, Philip, The Case for Edouard Dujardin, Romanic
    Review (Oct. 1965), 56:194-202
Hardy, Barbara, Form as End and Means in "Ulysses," Orbis
    Litterarum (1964), 19:194-200
Hartt, Julian N., The Lost Image of Man. 1963. p. 18-30
Hayman, David, Forms of Folly in Joyce; A Study of Clowning
    in "Ulysses," ELH (June 1967), 34:260-83
Hayman, David, Joyce et Mallarme. 1956. p. 76-117
Heppenstall, Rayner, The Fourfold Tradition. 1961. p. 132-59
Herring, Phillip F., The Bedsteadfastness of Molly Bloom,
    Modern Fiction Studies (Spring 1969), 15:49-61
Hesse, Eva, ed., New Approaches to Ezra Pound; A Coordinated
    Investigation of Pound's Poetry and Ideas. 1969. p. 125-44
Hodgart, Matthew and Mabel Worthington, Song in the Work of
    James Joyce. 1959. p. 62-84
Isaacs, Neil D., The Autoerotic Metaphor in Joyce, Sterne,
    Lawrence, Stevens, and Whitman, Literature and Psychology
    (Spring 1965), 15:92-106
Jenkins, William D., It Seems There Were Two Irishmen . . . ,
    Modern Fiction Studies (Spring 1969), 15:63-71
Josephson, Matthew, One Thousand One Nights in a Barroom,
    Or the Irish Odysseus, Broom (Sept. 1922), 3:146-50
Kaplan, Harold J., The Passive Voice; An Approach to Modern
    Fiction. 1966. p. 43-91
Karl, Frederick R. and M. Magalaner, A Reader's Guide to
    Great Twentieth Century English Novels. 1959. p. 208-53
Kelly, H. A., Consciousness in the Monologues of "Ulysses,"
    Modern Language Quarterly (March 1963), 24:3-12
Kenner, Hugh, Dublin's Joyce. 1956. p. 19-26 and 158-262
Kenner, Hugh, Flaubert, Joyce and Beckett. 1962. p. 30-66
Killeen, J. F., James Joyce's Roman Prototype, Comparative
    Literature (Summer 1957), 9:192-203
Killham, John, Ineluctable Modality in Joyce's "Ulysses,"

University of Toronto Quarterly (1965), 34:269-289
Klein, A. M., A Shout in the Streets, New Directions (1951),
13:327-45
Knight, G. W., Neglected Powers. 1971. p. 142-55
Korg, Jacob, Possible Source of the Circe Chapter of
"Ulysses," Modern Language Notes (Feb. 1956), 71:96-98
Koljevic, Svetozar, Igra Svesti i Postojanja u Dzojsovom
"Ulisu," Izraz (1966), 10:429-43
Kuehn, Robert E., Mr. Bloom and Mr. Joyce: A Note on
"Heroism" in "Ulysses," Wisconsin Studies in Contemporary
Literature (1963), 4:209-15
Kulemeyer, G., Studien zur Psychologie im Neuen Englische
Roman. 1933. p. 16-34
Lennan, T., The Happy Hunting Ground, University of Toronto
Quarterly (April 1960), 29:386-96
Leventhal, A. J., The Jew Errant, Dubliner (Spring 1963), 2:
11-24
Littmann, Mark E. and Charles A. Schweighauser, Astronomi-
cal Allusions and Their Meaning and Purpose in "Ulysses,"
James Joyce Quarterly (1965), 2:238-246
Litz, Walton, Early Vestiges of Joyce's "Ulysses," Modern
Language Association. Publications (March 1956), 71:51-60
Litz, Walton, Joyce's Notes for the Last Episodes of "Ulysses,"
Modern Fiction Studies (1958), 4:3-20
Litz, Walton, The Last Adventure of Ulysses, Princeton Uni-
versity Library Chronicle (1967), 28:63-75
Lorch, Thomas M., The Relationship Between "Ulysses" and
"The Waste Land," Texas Studies in Literature and Language
(1964), 6:123-33
Lutwick, Leonard, Mixed and Uniform Prose Styles in the
Novel, Journal of Aesthetics and Art Criticism (March 1960),
18:350-57
Mack, Maynard and Ian Gregor, eds., Imagined Worlds; Es-
says on Some English Novels and Novelists in Honour of
John Butt. 1968. p. 419-39
McNelly, Willis, E., Liturgical Deviations in "Ulysses," James
Joyce Quarterly (1965), 2:291-98
Macias, Raul, "Ulises": Mito y Realidad, Union (Havana)
(Jan.-April 1963), 2:101-10
Magalaner, Marvin, ed., A James Joyce Miscellany. 1959. p.
15-66, 79-91, 133-38, and 139-49
Majault, Joseph, James Joyce. 1963. p. 72-84

Manheim, Leonard F. and E. R. Manheim, eds., Hidden Patterns. 1966. p. 192−219

Mercanton, Jacques, Poètes de l'Univers. 1947. p. 13−56

Mickelson, Anne, Joyce's "Ulysses," Explicator (March 1968), 26:Item 58

Miller, Joseph Hillis, ed., Aspects of Narrative; Selected Papers from the English Institute. 1971. p. 1−45

Miller-Budnitskaya, R., James Joyce's "Ulysses," Dialectics (1938), #5:6−26

Milner, Ian, The Heroic and the Mock-Heroic in James Joyce's "Ulysses," Philologica Pragensia (1959), 2:37−45

Montgomery, Niall, Joyeux Quicum Ulysse, Envoy (May 1951), 5:31−43

More, Paul Elmer, On Being Human. 1936. p. 74−96

Morse, J. Mitchell, The Disobedient Artist: Joyce and Loyola, Modern Language Association. Publications (1957), 72:1018−35

Morse, J. M., Mr. Joyce and Shakespeare, Englische Studien (1930), 65:367−81

Morse, Josiah Mitchell, More Early Vestiges of "Ulysses," Modern Language Association. Publications (Dec. 1956), 71:1173

Moseley, Virginia, Joyce and the Bible. 1967. p. 57−143

Moseley, Virginia, The Martha-Mary Theme in "Ulysses," Midwest Quarterly (Winter 1963), 4:165−78

Moss, Judith P., Elijah Ben Bloom: A Note on Joyce's "Ulysses," Massachusettes Studies in English (1969), 2:19−21

Muir, Edwin, The Structure of the Novel. 1928. p. 126−33

Nassar, Eugene Paul, The Rape of Cinderella. 1970. p. 59−70

Noon, William T., Joyce and Aquinas. 1957. p. 86−125

O'Brien, Darcy, The Conscience of James Joyce. 1967. p. 94−217

O'Brien, Darcy, Joyce and Sexuality, Twentieth Century Literature (Nov. 1969), #2:32−38

O'Brien, Darcy, The Twins that Tick Homo Vulgaris: A Study of Shem and Shaun, Modern Fiction Studies (Summer 1966), 12:183−99

O'Hehir, Brendan, An Unnoticed Textual Crux in "Ulysses," James Joyce Quarterly (1968), 5:296−98

Peake, Charles, "Ulysses" and Some Modern Criticisms, Literary Half-Yearly (Jan. 1961), 2:26−40

Peradotto, John J., Liturgical Pattern in "Ulysses," Modern

Language Notes (April 1960), 75:321–26

Perspectives in Literary Symbolism; ed. by Joseph Strelka. 1968. p. 199–213

Pinguentini, Gianni, James Joyce in Italia. 1963. p. 240–75

Plebe, Armando, L"Ulisse" di Joyce e l'Estetica dell'Arte al Quadrato, Giornale Critico Filosofia Italiana (April–June 1962), 41:219–37

Poss, Stanley, "Ulysses" and the Comedy of the Immobilized Act, ELH (1957), 24:65–83

Prescott, Joseph, The Characterization of Leopold Bloom, Literature and Psychology (Winter 1959), 9:3–4

Prescott, Joseph, Mosenthal's "Deborah" and Joyce's "Ulysses," Modern Language Notes (May 1952), 67:334–36

Prescott, Joseph, Notes on Joyce's "Ulysses," Modern Language Quarterly (June 1952), 13:149–62

Raleigh, John Henry, Who Was M'Intosh?, James Joyce Review (1959), 3:59–62

Reilly, J. P., Aesthetics as a Way of Life: A Study of James Joyce, Fresco (Fall 1959), 10:37–47

Rosenberg, Kurt, James Joyce; Ein Wanderer ins Reich des Unbewussten, Geist und Zeit (1959), #4:114–27

Rothstein, Eric and Thomas K. Dunseath, Literary Monographs, I. 1967. p. 247–98 and 319–20

Russell, H. K., The Incarnation in "Ulysses," Modern Fiction Studies (Spring 1958), 4:53–61

Ryf, Robert S., A New Approach to Joyce: "A Portrait of the Artist as a Young Man" as a Guidebook. 1962. p. 77–97

Salus, Peter H., Joyce's "Ulysses," Explicator (1965), 23: Item 67

Schaarschmidt, G., Interior Monologue and Soviet Literary Criticism, Canadian Slavonic Papers (1966), 8:143–53

Scheurle, William, Joyce's "Ulysses," Explicator (1962), 20: Item 70

Schneider, Daniel, Technique of Cognition in Modern Fiction, Journal of Aesthetics and Art Criticism (Spring 1968), 26: 317–28

Schorer, Mark, ed., Modern British Fiction. 1961. p. 336–57

Schwegel, Douglas M., Joyce's "Ulysses," Explicator (1969), 27:Item 49

Senn, Fritz, Seven Against Uly, James Joyce Quarterly (Spring 1967), 4:170–93

Shapiro, Leo, The "Zion" Motif in Joyce's "Ulysses," Jewish Frontier (Sept. 1946), 13:14–17

Shapiro, Stephen, Leopold Bloom and Gulley Jimson: The
Economics of Survival, Twentieth Century Literature (April
1964), 10:3−11

Sharpe, Garold, The Philosophy of James Joyce, Modern Fiction Studies (Summer 1963), 9:120−26

Silverstein, Norman, Bruno's Particles of Reminiscence,
James Joyce Quarterly (Summer 1965), 2:271−80

Simon, Irène, Formes du Roman Anglais de Dickens à Joyce.
1949. p. 388−437

Slabey, Robert M., Faulkner's "Mosquitoes" and Joyce's
"Ulysses," Revue des Langues Vivantes (1962), 28:435−37

Smith, Grover, Jr., The Cryptogram in Joyce's "Ulysses": A
Misprint, Modern Language Association. Publications
(1958), 73:446−47

Soupault, Philippe, Souvenirs de James Joyce. 1945. p. 35−56

Spencer, John, A Note on the "Steady Monologuy of the Interi-
ors," Review of English Literature (April 1965), 6:32−41

Sprinchorn, Evert, "Ulysses" in England: Some British Joyce-
ana, James Joyce Quarterly (1966), 3:223−24

Staley, T. F. and B. Benstock, eds., Approaches to Ulysses;
Ten Essays. 1970. p. 157−78, 179−87, and 199−285

Staley, Thomas F., ed., James Joyce Today; Essays on the
Major Works; Commemorating the Twenty-fifth Anniversary
of His Death. 1966. p. 83−95

Stanford, W. B., The Mysticism that Pleased Him, Envoy (May
1951), 5:62−69

Stanford, W. B., The Ulysses Theme; A Study in the Adaptability of a Traditional Hero. 1954. p. 211−24

Stanzel, Franz, Die Typischen Erzahlsituationen im Roman.
1955. p. 122−44

Stavron, C. N., Gulliver's Voyage to the Land of Dubliners,
South Atlantic Quarterly (Autumn 1960), 59:490−99

Stavron, C. N., Mr. Bloom and Nikos' Odysseus, South Atlantic
Quarterly (Winter 1963), 62:107−118

Stavron, C. N., The Love Songs of Jonathan Swift, George
Bernard Shaw, and James A. A. Joyce, Midwest Quarterly
(Winter 1965), 6:135−62

Steinberg, Erwin R., A Book with Molly in It, James Joyce
Review (Spring−Summer 1958), 2:55−62

Steinberg, Erwin R., Introducing the Stream-of-Consciousness
Technique in "Ulysses," Style (1968), 2:49−58

Steinberg, Erwin R., "Lestrygonians," a Pale "Proteus?,"
Modern Fiction Studies (Spring 1969), 15:73−83

Stephens, James, James, Seumas and Jacques; Unpublished
   Writings of James Stephens. 1964. p. 156–59
Stern, Frederick C., Pyrrhus, Fenians and Bloom, James
   Joyce Quarterly (Spring 1968), 5:211–28
Stewart, J. I. M., Eight Modern Masters. 1963. p. 451–65
Stewart, J. I. M., James Joyce. 1957. p. 23–32
Strelka, Joseph, ed., Perspectives in Literary Symbolism.
   1968. p. 199–213
Sühnel, Rudolf, Die Literarischen Voraussetzungen von Joyces
   "Ulysses," Germanisch-Romanische Monatsschrift (1962),
   12:202–211
Sultan, Stanley, Joyce's Irish Politics, Massachusetts Review
   (1961), 2:549–56
Sultan, Stanley, An Old Irish Model for "Ulysses," James
   Joyce Quarterly (1968), 5:103–09
Sultan, Stanley, The Sirens at the Ormond Bar: Ulysses,
   University of Kansas City Review (1959), 26:83–92
Summerhayes, Don, Joyce's "Ulysses" and Whitman's "Self":
   A Query, Wisconsin Studies in Contemporary Literature
   (1963), 4:216–24
Tillyard, E. M. W., Epic Strain in the English Novel. 1958.
   p. 187–96
Tompkins, Phillip K., James Joyce and the Enthymeme; The
   Seventh Episode of "Ulysses," James Joyce Quarterly (1968),
   5:199–205
Toor, David, Joyce's "Ulysses," Explicator (1966), 24:Item 65
Tracy, Robert, Leopold Bloom Fourfold; A Hungarian-Hebraic-
   Hellenic-Hibernian Hero, Massachusetts Review (Spring–
   Summer 1965), 6:523–38
Troy, William, William Troy; Selected Essays. 1957. p. 89–
   93
Tysdahl, B. J., Joyce and Ibsen; A Study in Literary Influence.
   1968. p. 103–22
Ussher, Arland, Three Great Irishmen: Shaw, Yeats and
   Joyce. 1953. p. 120–32
Van Caspel, P. P. J., The Theme of the Red Carnation in
   James Joyce's "Ulysses," Neophilologus (July 1954), 38:
   189–98
Vogel, Jane, The Consubstantial Family of Stephen Dedalus,
   James Joyce Quarterly (Winter 1965), 2:109–31
Wasson, Richard, Stephen Dedalus and the Imagery of Sight:
   A Psychological Approach, Literature and Psychology (Fall
   1965), 15:195–209

Watson, Edward A., A Stoom-Bloom Scientific Objectivity
Versus Romantic Subjectivity in the Ithica Episode of Joyce's
"Ulysses," University of Windsor Review (1966), 2:11-25

Weber, L. Sherwood, et al, From Homer to Joyce; A Study
Guide to Thirty-Six Great Books. 1959. p. 262-75

Whaley, H. R., Role of the Blind Piano Tuner in Joyce's
"Ulysses," Modern Fiction Studies (Winter 1970-71), 16:
531-35

Whitaker, Thomas R., The Drinkers and History; Rabelais,
Balzac and Joyce, Comparative Literature (Spring 1959), 11:
157-64

White, John, "Ulysses": The Metaphysical Foundations and
Grand Design, Modern Fiction Studies (Spring 1969), 15:27-
35

Will, Frederic, ed., Hereditas; Seven Essays on the Modern
Experience of the Classical. 1964. p. 31-54

Worthington, Mabel P., Joyce's "Ulysses," Explicator (Jan.
1963), 21:Item 37

Wykes, David, The Odyssey in "Ulysses," Texas Studies in
Literature and Language (1968), 10:301-16

Zabel, Morton Dauwen, ed., Literary Opinion in America.
1962. p. 183-206

Zipf, George K., The Repetition of Words, Time-Perspective
and Semantic Balance, Journal of General Psychology (Jan.
1945), 32:127-48

JOSEPH KELL

SEE

ANTHONY BURGESS

CHARLES KINGSLEY

Two Years Ago, 1857

Waller, John O., Charles Kingsley and the American Civil
War, Studies in Philology (July 1963), 60:554-68

Westward Ho!, 1855

Eliot, George (Pseud.), Essays, 1963, p. 123-36

RUDYARD KIPLING

Kim, 1901

Carrington, Charles, Elliot Gilbert on "Kim," Kipling Journal
   (Sept. 1967), 34:7-8
Cohen, Morton N., "Kim" at an American College, Kipling
   Journal (June 1968), 35:10-12
Gilbert, Elliot L., Carrington on Gilbert on "Kim," Kipling
   Journal (March 1968), 35:15-17
Gilbert, Elliot L., "Kim"—Novel or Propaganda?, Kipling
   Journal (June 1967), 34:8-11
Jefferson, D. W., ed., The Morality of Art; Essays Presented
   to G. Wilson Knight by His Colleagues and Friends. 1969.
   p. 210-21
Munro, John, Kipling's "Kim" and Co-Existence, English Lit-
   erature in Transition (1880-1920) (1964), 7:222-27
Raskin, Jonah, The Mythology of Imperialism. 1971. p. 99-
   125
Rowse, Alfred Leslie, The English Spirit; Essays in Litera-
   ture and History. 1967. p. 229-45
Rutherford, Andrew, ed., Kipling's Mind and Art; Selected
   Critical Essays. 1964. p. 197-234
Welzel, Helga, Kim, Kipling Journal (Sept. 1967), 34:17-21
   and (Dec. 1967), 34:15-19

The Light that Failed, 1890

Miller, Betty Bergson, Kipling's First Novel, Cornhill (Spring
   1956), 168:405-12
Peterson, William S., "The Light that Failed": Kipling's Version of Decadence, English Literature in Transition (1880-
   1920) (1966), 9:153-55
Rutherford, Andrew, ed., Kipling's Mind and Art; Selected
   Critical Essays. 1964. p. 197-234
Solomon, Eric, "The Light that Failed" as a War Novel, English Literature in Transition (1880-1920) (1962), 5:30-34

The Naulahka, 1892

Cooperman, Stanley, The Imperial Posture and the Shrine of
   Darkness: Kipling's "The Naulahka" and E. M. Forster's "A
   Passage to India," English Literature in Transition (1880-
   1920) (1963), 6:9-13

TEODOR JOZEF KONRAD KORZENIOWSKI

SEE

JOSEPH CONRAD

DAVID HERBERT LAWRENCE

Aaron's Rod, 1922

Barry, Sandra, Singularity of Two; The Plurality of One,
Paunch (April 1966), #26:34-39

Canby, Henry Seidel, Definitions: Essays in Contemporary
Criticism. 1924. p. 117-20

Cunliffe, J. W., English Literature in the Twentieth Century.
1933. p. 219-22

Draper, R. P., ed., D. H. Lawrence; The Critical Heritage.
1970. p. 177-83

Freeman, Mary, D. H. Lawrence; A Basic Study of His Ideas.
1955. p. 121-26

Gindin, James, Harvest of a Quiet Eye; The Novel of Compassion. 1971. p. 205-07

Hogan, Robert, The Amorous Whale; A Study in the Symbolism
of D. H. Lawrence, Modern Fiction Studies (Spring 1959), 5:
39-46

Leavis, F. R., D. H. Lawrence; Novelist. 1956. p. 23-39

Murry, John Middleton, Son of Woman: The Story of D. H.
Lawrence. 1931. p. 180-204

Stoll, John E., The Novels of D. H. Lawrence. 1971. p. 198-
222

Tiverton, Father William, D. H. Lawrence and Human Existence. 1951. p. 46-50

Vivas, Eliseo, The Two Lawrences, Bucknell Review (March
1958), 7:113-32

Yudhishtar, Conflict in the Novels of D. H. Lawrence. 1969.
p. 210-32

Kangaroo, 1923

Alldritt, Keith, The Visual Imagination of D. H. Lawrence.
1971. p. 223-26

Alexander, John, D. H. Lawrence's "Kangaroo": Fantasy, Fact
or Fiction?, Meanjin Quarterly (1965), 24:179-97

Atkinson, Curtis, Was There Fact in D. H. Lawrence's "Kanga-

roo?," Meanjin Quarterly (1965), 24:358−59
Bentley, Eric, A Century of Hero Worship. 1944. p. 234−39
Freeman, Mary, D. H. Lawrence; A Basic Study of His Ideas.
  1955. p. 158−76
Draper, R. P., Authority and the Individual: A Study of D. H.
  Lawrence's "Kangaroo," Critical Quarterly (Autumn 1959),
  1:208−15
Draper, R. P., ed., D. H. Lawrence; The Critical Heritage.
  1970. p. 214−23
Gurko, Leo, "Kangaroo": D. H. Lawrence in Transit, Modern
  Fiction Studies (1965), 10:349−58
Hogan, Robert, The Amorous Whale; A Study in the Symbolism
  of D. H. Lawrence, Modern Fiction Studies (Spring 1959), 5:
  39−46
Leavis, F. R., D. H. Lawrence; Novelist. 1956. p. 39−44
McCormick, John, Catastrophe and Imagination; A Re-Inter-
  pretation of the Recent English and American Novel. 1957.
  p. 244−48
Murry, John Middleton, Son of Woman; The Story of D. H.
  Lawrence. 1931. p. 218−39
Stoll, John E., The Novels of D. H. Lawrence. 1971. p. 198−
  222
Tiverton, Father William, D. H. Lawrence and Human Exis-
  tence. 1951. p. 59−66
West, Anthony, D. H. Lawrence. 1950. p. 124−27
Yudhishtar. Conflict in the Novels of D. H. Lawrence. 1969.
  p. 232−50

Lady Chatterley's Lover, 1928

Appleman, Philip, D. H. Lawrence and the Intrusive Knock,
  Modern Fiction Studies (Winter 1957−58), 3:328−32
Balakian, Nona, The Prophetic Vogue of the Anti-Heroine,
  Southwest Review (Spring 1962), 47:134−41
Bedford, Sybille, The Last Trial of Lady Chatterley, Esquire
  (1961), 55:132−55
Bedient, Calvin, The Radicalism of "Lady Chatterley's Lover,'
  Hudson Review (1966), 19:407−16
Brophy, Brigid, Don't Never Forget; Collected Views and Re-
  Reviews. 1967. p. 101−05
Burns, Wayne, "Lady Chatterley's Lover": A Pilgrim's Prog-
  ress for Our Time, Paunch (1966), #26:16−33
Cavitch, David, Solipsism and Death in D. H. Lawrence's Late
  Works, Massachusetts Review (Summer 1966), 7:495−508

Daleski, H. M., The Duality of Lawrence, Modern Fiction
 Studies (Spring 1959), 5:3-18

Donald, D. R., The First and Final Versions of "Lady Chatterley's Lover," Theoria (1964), #22:85-97

Draper, R. P., ed., D. H. Lawrence; The Critical Heritage.
 1970. p. 278-97

Eagleton, Terry, Exiles and Émigrés; Studies in Modern Literature. 1970. p. 214-16

Ehrstine, John W., The Dialectic in D. H. Lawrence, Research
 Studies (1965), 83:11-26

Encounter, Encounters; An Anthology from the First Ten
 Years of "Encounter" Magazine. 1963. p. 277-90

Freeman, Mary, D. H. Lawrence; A Basic Study of His Ideas.
 1955. p. 215-23

Fuller, Edmund, Books with Men Behind Them. 1962. p. 16-
 35

Hall, Stuart, "Lady Chatterley's Lover": The Novel and Its
 Relationship to Lawrence's Work, New Left Review (Nov.-
 Dec. 1960), #6:32-35

Harding, D. W., Lawrence's Evils, Spectator (Nov. 11, 1960),
 #6907:735-36

Harkin, M., For the Public Good; A Summary of the "Lady
 Chatterley's Lover" Controversy, Manchester Review (1960),
 9:91-93

Hewitt, Cecil Ralph, After Lady Chatterley, New Statesman
 (Nov. 12, 1960), 60:730+

Hewitt, Cecil Ralph, Lady Chatterley's Triumph, New Statesman (Nov. 5, 1960), 60:682

Hinz, Evelyn J., D. H. Lawrence's Clothes Metaphor, D. H.
 Lawrence Review (Summer 1968), 1:87-113

Hochman, Baruch, Another Ego; The Changing View of Self
 and Society in the Work of D. H. Lawrence. 1970. p. 221-28

McCurdy, Harold Crier, Literature and Personality; Analysis
 of the Novels of D. H. Lawrence, Character and Personality
 (1940), 8:191-97

Kauffman, Stanley, "Lady Chatterley" at Last, Meanjin (Dec.
 1959), 18:450-55

Kazin, Alfred, Contemporaries. 1962. p. 105-13

Kazin, Alfred, Lady Chatterley in America, Atlantic (July
 1959), 204:33-36

Kinkead-Weekes, M., Eros and Metaphor; Sexual Relationships
 in the Fiction of D. H. Lawrence, Twentieth Century Studies
 (Nov. 1969), 1:3-19

Klein, Robert C., I, Thou, and You in Three Lawrencian Relationships, Paunch (April 1968), #31:52−70

Knight, G. Wilson, Lawrence, Joyce and Powys, Essays in
Criticism (Oct. 1961), 11:403−17

Knoepflmacher, U. C., The Rival Ladies; Mrs. Ward's "Lady
Connie" and Lawrence's "Lady Chatterley's Lover," Victorian Studies (Dec. 1960), 4:141−58

Lauter, Paul, Lady Chatterley with Love and Money, New
Leader (Sept. 21, 1959), 42:23−24

McIntosh, Angus and Michael A. K. Halliday, Patterns of Language; Papers in General, Descriptive and Applied Linguistics. 1967. p. 151−64

McHenry, G. B., Carrying On, Melbourne Critical Review
(1967), #10:46−62

McLennan, Hugh, The Defense of Lady Chatterley, Canadian
Literature (1960), #6:18−23

Maldonado Denis, Manuel, Sobre la Lectura de "Lady Chatterley's Lover," Torre (Jan.−March 1962), 10:159−71

Mandel, Oscar, Ignorance and Privacy, American Scholar
(1960), 29:509−19

Moore, Harry T., The Life and Works of D. H. Lawrence.
1951. p. 258−69

Moore, Harry T., ed., A D. H. Lawrence Miscellany. 1959.
p. 262−64

Moynahan, Julian, "Lady Chatterley's Lover": The Deed of
Life, ELH (1959), 26:66−90

Murry, John Middleton, Son of Woman; The Story of D. H.
Lawrence. 1931. p. 339−49

Murry, John Middleton, Reminiscences of D. H. Lawrence.
1933. p. 269−76

Nin, Anais, D. H. Lawrence; An Unprofessional Study. 1932.
p. 141−46

Peter, John, The Bottom of the Well, Essays in Criticism
(1962), 12:226−27

Peter, John, Lady Chatterley Again, Essays in Criticism
(1962), 12:445−47

Porter, Katherine A., A Wreath for the Gamekeeper,
Encounter (Feb. 1960), 14:69−77

Read, Herbert, On D. H. Lawrence, Twentieth Century (June
1959), 165:556−66

Rudikoff, Sonya, D. H. Lawrence and Our Life Today: Re-
reading "Lady Chatterley's Lover," Commentary (1959),
28:408−13

Schorer, Mark, ed., Modern British Fiction. 1961. p. 285–
307

Schorer, Mark, On "Lady Chatterley's Lover," Evergreen
Review (1957), 1:149–78

Schorer, Mark, The World We Imagine; Selected Essays.
1968. p. 122–46

Sheerin, John B., Sane Censorship and Lady Chatterley,
Catholic World (1959), 189:412–16

Stoll, John E., The Novels of D. H. Lawrence. 1971. p. 223–
50

Strickland, G., First "Lady Chatterley's Lover," Encounter
(Jan. 1971), 36:44–52

Thody, Philip, "Lady Chatterley's Lover": A Pyrrhic Victory,
Threshold (1961–62), 5:36–49

Tiverton, Father William, D. H. Lawrence and Human Existence. 1951. p. 77–89

Tudsbery, M. T., Lady Chatterley's Lover, Notes and Queries
(1961), 8:149

Way, Brian, Sex and Language, New Left Review (Sept.–Oct.
1964), #27:66–80

Weiss, Daniel, D. H. Lawrence's Great Circle; From "Sons
and Lovers" to "Lady Chatterley," Psychoanalytic Review
(Fall 1963), 50:112–38

Welch, Colin, Black Magic, White Lies, Encounter (Feb. 1961),
16:75–79

Welch, Colin and E. L. Mascall, Chatterley and the Law, Encounter (1961), 16:85

Welker, Robert H., Advocate of Eros; Notes on D. H. Lawrence, American Scholar (Spring 1961), 30:191–202

West, Rebecca, et al, "Chatterley," the Witnesses, and the
Law, Encounter (March 1961), 16:52–56

Williams, Raymond, The English Novel; From Dickens to
Lawrence. 1970. p. 182–84

Williams, Raymond, Modern Tragedy. 1966. p. 121–38

Yudhishtar, Conflict in the Novels of D. H. Lawrence. 1969.
p. 266–87 and 298–301

Lost Girl, 1920

Freeman, Mary, D. H. Lawrence; A Basic Study of His Ideas.
1955. p. 117–20

Gurko, Leo, "The Lost Girl": D. H. Lawrence Is a "Dickens
of the Midlands," Modern Language Association. Publications (1963), 78:601–05

Hough, Graham, The Dark Sun; A Study of D. H. Lawrence.
1957. p. 90-95
Murry, John Middleton, Son of Woman; The Story of D. H.
Lawrence. 1931. p. 125-33
Murry, John Middleton, Reminiscences of D. H. Lawrence.
1933. p. 214-18
Rees, Richard, Brave Men; A Study of D. H. Lawrence and
Simone Weil. 1958. p. 73-88
Yudhishtar, Conflict in the Novels of D. H. Lawrence. 1969.
p. 200-10

The Plumed Serpent, 1926

Alldritt, Keith, The Visual Imagination of D. H. Lawrence.
1971. p. 227-32
Cowan, James C., The Symbolic Structure of "The Plumed
Serpent," Tulane Studies in English (1965), 14:75-96
Daleski, H. M., The Duality of Lawrence, Modern Fiction
Studies (Spring 1959), 5:3-18
Draper, R. P., ed., D. H. Lawrence; The Critical Heritage.
1970. p. 263-71
Freeman, Mary, D. H. Lawrence; A Basic Study of His Ideas.
1955. p. 177-88
Gindin, James, Harvest of a Quiet Eye; The Novel of Com-
passion. 1971. p. 217-21
Leavis, F. R., D. H. Lawrence; Novelist. 1956. p. 67-73
Michener, Richard L., Apocalyptic Mexico; "The Plumed
Serpent" and "The Power and the Glory," University Review
(1968), 34:313-16
Moore, Harry Thornton, ed., A D. H. Lawrence Miscellany.
1959. p. 239-61
Murry, John Middleton, Son of Woman; The Story of D. H.
Lawrence. 1931. p. 282-302
Porter, Katherine Anne, The Collected Essays and Occasional
Writings of Katherine Anne Porter. 1970. p. 421-25
Requardt, Egon, D. H. Lawrence; Solipsist oder Prophet einer
neuen Gemeinschaft?, Die Neueren Sprachen (Nov. 1963),
#11:506-15
Spilka, Mark, The Love Ethic of D. H. Lawrence. 1955. p.
205-19
Stoll, John E., The Novels of D. H. Lawrence. 1971. p. 198-
222
Tedlock, E. W., Jr., D. H. Lawrence's Annotations of Ouspen-
sky's "Tertium Organum," Texas Studies in Literature and

Language (Summer 1960), 2:206-18
Vaskeel, H. J., D. H. Lawrence; Social Theorist and Mystic,
Visvabharati Quarterly (Summer 1960), 26:24-44
Waters, Frank, Quetzalcoatl Versus D. H. Lawrence's
"Plumed Serpent," Western American Literature (1968), 3:
103-13
West, Anthony, D. H. Lawrence. 1950. p. 127-31
Yudhishtar, Conflict in the Novels of D. H. Lawrence. 1969.
p. 250-66

The Rainbow, 1915

Alldritt, Keith, The Visual Imagination of D. H. Lawrence.
1971. p. 54-69 and 73-136
Clements, A. L., The Quest for the Self; D. H. Lawrence's
"The Rainbow," Thoth (Spring 1962), 3:90-100
Cross, Barbara, Lawrence and the Unbroken Circle, Per-
spective (Summer 1959), 11:81-89
Daleski, H. M., The Duality of Lawrence, Modern Fiction
Studies (Spring 1959), 5:3-18
Draper, R. P., ed., D. H. Lawrence; The Critical Heritage.
1970. p. 84-109
Eagleton, Terry, Exiles and Émigrés; Studies in Modern
Literature. 1970. p. 200-08
Ehrstine, John W., The Dialectic in D. H. Lawrence, Re-
search Studies (1965), 83:11-26
Freeman, Mary, D. H. Lawrence; A Basic Study of His Ideas.
1955. p. 36-48
Friedman, Alan, The Turn of the Novel. 1966. p. 130-78
Gindin, James, Harvest of a Quiet Eye; The Novel of Com-
passion. 1971. p. 207-12
Goldberg, S. L., "The Rainbow": "Fiddle-Bow and Sand,"
Essays in Criticism (1961), 11:418-434
Hochman, Baruch, Another Ego; The Changing View of Self
and Society in the Work of D. H. Lawrence. 1970. p. 35-44
Idema, James M., The Hawk and the Plover: The Polarity of
Life in the Jungle Aviary of D. H. Lawrence's Mind in "Sons
and Lovers" and "The Rainbow," Forum (Houston) (1961), 3:
11-14
Karl, Frederick R. and M. Magalaner, A Reader's Guide to
Great Twentieth Century English Novels. 1959. p. 154-204
Kingsmill, Hugh, The Life of D. H. Lawrence. 1938. p. 74-80
Kinkead-Weekes, M., Eros and Metaphor; Sexual Relation-
ships in the Fiction of D. H. Lawrence, Twentieth Century

Studies (Nov. 1969), 1:3–19

Klein, Robert C., I, Thou and You in Three Lawrencian Relationships, Paunch (April 1968), #31:52–70

Kuo, Carol Haseley, Lawrence's "The Rainbow," Explicator
(1961), 19:Item 70

Mari, Haruhide, Lawrence's Imagistic Development in "The
Rainbow" and "Women in Love," ELH (1964), 3:460–81

Marković, Vida E., The Changing Face; Disintegration of
Personality in the Twentieth Century British Novel, 1900–
1950. p. 19–37

Moore, Harry T., ed., A D. H. Lawrence Miscellany. 1959.
p. 56–82

Mudrick, Marvin, The Originality of "The Rainbow," Spectrum
(Winter 1959), 3:3–28

Murry, John Middleton, Son of Woman; The Story of D. H.
Lawrence. 1931. p. 59–75

Nin, Anais, D. H. Lawrence; An Unprofessional Study. 1932.
p. 14–19 and 26–28

Sager, Keith, The Genesis of "The Rainbow" and "Women in
Love," D. H. Lawrence Review (1968), 1:179–99

Sale, Roger, The Narrative Technique of "The Rainbow,"
Modern Fiction Studies (Spring 1959), 5:29–38

Schneider, Daniel, Techniques of Cognition in Modern Fiction,
Journal of Aesthetics and Art Criticism (Spring 1968), 26:
317–28

Schorer, Mark, ed., Modern British Fiction. 1961. p. 244–66

Stoll, John E., The Novels of D. H. Lawrence. 1971. p. 106–
50.

Stroupe, John S., D. H. Lawrence's Portrait of Ben Franklin
in "The Rainbow," Iowa English Yearbook (1966), #11:64–68

Tiverton, Father William, D. H. Lawrence and Human Existence. 1951. p. 19–28

Wasson, Richard, Comedy and History in "The Rainbow,"
Modern Fiction Studies (1967), 13:465–77

Yudhishtar, Conflict in the Novels of D. H. Lawrence. 1969.
p. 113–57

Sons and Lovers, 1913

Alldritt, Keith, The Visual Imagination of D. H. Lawrence.
1971. p. 16–42

Appleman, Philip, D. H. Lawrence and the Intrusive Knock,
Modern Fiction Studies (Winter 1957–58), 3:328–32

Beebe, Maurice, Ivory Towers and Sacred Founts; The Artist

as Hero in Fiction from Goethe to Joyce. 1964. p. 65–113

Beebe, Maurice, Lawrence's Sacred Fount: The Artist Theme of "Sons and Lovers," Texas Studies in Literature and Language (1962), 4:539–52

Bramley, J. A., D. H. Lawrence's Sternest Critic, Hibbert Journal (1965), 63:109–11

Daleski, H. M., The Duality of Lawrence, Modern Fiction Studies (Spring 1959), 5:3–18

Draper, R. P., D. H. Lawrence on Mother-Love, Essays in Criticism (July 1958), 8:285–89

Draper, R. P., ed., D. H. Lawrence; The Critical Heritage. 1970. p. 58–80

Eagleton, Terry, Exiles and Émigrés; Studies in Modern Literature. 1970. p. 192–200

Ehrstine, John W., The Dialectic in D. H. Lawrence, Research Studies (1965), 83:11–26

Freeman, Mary, D. H. Lawrence; A Basic Study of His Ideas. 1955. p. 9–19

Gindin, James, Harvest of a Quiet Eye; The Novel of Compassion. 1971. p. 206–10

Gregory, Horace, D. H. Lawrence; Pilgrim of the Apocalypse. 1957. p. 17–28

Hinz, Evelyn J., D. H. Lawrence's Clothes Metaphor, D. H. Lawrence Review (Summer 1968), 1:87–113

Idema, James M., The Hawk and the Plover: "The Polarity of Life" in the "Jungle Aviary" of D. H. Lawrence's Mind in "Sons and Lovers" and "The Rainbow," Forum (Houston) (1961), 3:11–14

Jeffries, C., Metaphor in "Sons and Lovers," The Personalist (June 1948), 29:287–92

Karl, Frederick R. and M. Magalaner, A Reader's Guide to Great Twentieth Century English Novels. 1959. p. 154–204

Kazin, Alfred, Sons, Lovers and Mothers, Partisan Review (Summer 1962), 29:373–85

Kinkead-Weekes, M., Eros and Metaphor; Sexual Relationships in the Fiction of D. H. Lawrence, Twentieth Century Studies (Nov. 1969), 1:3–19

Kittner, Alfred Booth, "Sons and Lovers"; A Freudian Appreciation, Psychoanalytic Review (1916), 3:295–317

Klein, Robert C., I, Thou, and You in Three Lawrencian Relationships, Paunch (April 1968), #31:52–70

Leaver, Florence B., The Man-Nature Relationship of D. H. Lawrence's Novels, University of Kansas City Review (Summer 1953), 19:241−44

Littlewood, J. C. F., Son and Lover, Cambridge Quarterly
(Autumn−Winter 1969−70), 4:323−61

Moore, Harry T., The Intelligent Heart: The Story of D. H.
Lawrence. 1954. p. 35−46

Muller, Herbert J., Modern Fiction; A Study of Values. 1937.
p. 269−72

Murry, John Middleton, Son of Woman; The Story of D. H.
Lawrence. 1931. p. 5−22

New, William H., Character as Symbol: Annie's Role in "Sons
and Lovers," D. H. Lawrence Review (1968), 1:31−43

O'Connor, Frank, The Mirror in the Roadway; A Study of the
Modern Novel. 1956. p. 270−79

Pascal, Roy, The Autobiographical Novel and the Autobiography, Essays in Criticism (April 1959), 9:134−50

Pritchett, Victor Sawdon, The Living Novel and Later Appreciations. 1964. p. 182−89

Reddick, Bryan, "Sons and Lovers": The Omniscient Narrator,
Thoth (1966), 7:68−75

Requardt, Egon, David Herbert Lawrence's "Sons and Lovers,"
Die Neueren Sprachen (1961), #5:230−34

Rossman, Charles, The Gospel According to D. H. Lawrence:
Religion in "Sons and Lovers," D. H. Lawrence Review
(Spring 1970), 3:31−41

Saagpakk, Paul F., Psychological Elements in British Novels
from 1890−1930, Dissertation Abstracts (Sept. 1966), 27:782A

Schorer, Mark, ed., Modern British Fiction. 1961. p. 225−43

Smith, Grover, Jr., The Doll-Burners: D. H. Lawrence and
Louisa Alcott, Modern Language Quarterly (March 1958), 19:
28−32

Stoll, John E., The Novels of D. H. Lawrence. 1971. p. 62−
105

Tomlinson, T. B., Lawrence and Modern Life: "Sons and
Lovers," and "Women in Love," Critical Review (Melbourne)
(1965), #8:3−18

Vaskeel, H. J., D. H. Lawrence: Social Theorist and Mystic,
Visvabharati Quarterly (Summer 1960), 26:24−44

Vredenburgh, Joseph L., Further Contributions to a Study of
the Incest Object, American Imago (Fall 1959), 16:263−68

Weiss, Daniel, D. H. Lawrence's Great Circle: From "Sons
and Lovers" to "Lady Chatterley," Psychoanalytic Review
(Fall 1963), 50:112−38

Wickham, Anna, The Spirit of the Lawrence Women, Texas

Quarterly (Autumn 1966), 9:31–50
Williams, Raymond, The English Novel; From Dickens to
Lawrence. 1970. p. 173–76
Woolf, Virginia, Collected Essays. 1967. p. 352–55
Yudhishtar, Conflict in the Novels of D. H. Lawrence. 1969.
p. 82–113

The Trespasser, 1912

Appleman, Philip, D. H. Lawrence and the Intrusive Knock,
Modern Fiction Studies (Winter 1957–58), 3:328–32
Freeman, Mary, D. H. Lawrence; A Basic Study of His Ideas.
1955. p. 30–35
Moore, Harry T., The Life and Works of D. H. Lawrence.
1951. p. 82–88
Stoll, John E., The Novels of D. H. Lawrence. 1971. p. 42–61

The White Peacock, 1911

Alldritt, Keith, The Visual Imagination of D. H. Lawrence.
1971. p. 4–15
Fahey, William, Lawrence's "White Peacock," Explicator
(Dec. 1958), 17:Item 17
Freeman, Mary, D. H. Lawrence; A Basic Study of His Ideas.
1955. p. 20–29
McCurdy, Harold Grier, Literature and Personality; Analysis
of the Novels of D. H. Lawrence, Character and Personality
(1940), 8:182–90
Murry, John Middleton, Son of Woman; The Story of D. H.
Lawrence. 1931. p. 22–30
Osgerby, J. R., Set Books; D. H. Lawrence's "The White Pea-
cock," Use of English (Summer 1962), 13:256–61
Stanford, Raney, Thomas Hardy and Lawrence's "The White
Peacock," Modern Fiction Studies (Spring 1959), 5:19–28
Stoll, John E., The Novels of D. H. Lawrence. 1971. p. 16–41
West, Anthony, D. H. Lawrence. 1950. p. 106–11

Women in Love, 1920

Alldritt, Keith, The Visual Imagination of D. H. Lawrence.
1971. p. 139–41, 159–61, and 162–218
Barrière, Française, "Women in Love" ou le Roman de l'An-
tagonisme, Les Langues Modernes (1969), 63:293–303
Beker, Miroslav, "The Crown," "The Reality of Peace" and
"Women in Love," D. H. Lawrence Review (1969), 2:254–64
Bickerton, Derek, The Language of "Women in Love," Review

of English Literature (Leeds) (1967), 8:56–67

Branda, Eldon S., Textual Changes in "Women in Love," Texas
Studies in Literature and Language (1964), 6:306–21

Chamberlain, Robert L., Pussum, Minette and the Africo-
Nordic Symbol in Lawrence's "Women in Love," Modern
Language Association. Publications (1963), 78:407–16

Collins, Joseph, The Doctor Looks at Literature. 1923. p.
276–84

Draper, R. P., ed., D. H. Lawrence; The Critical Heritage.
1970. p. 157–72

Drew, Elizabeth A., The Novel; A Modern Guide to Fifteen
English Masterpieces. 1963. p. 208–23

Eagleton, Terry, Exiles and Émigrés; Studies in Modern Literature. 1970. p. 208–14

Ehrstine, John W., The Dialectic in D. H. Lawrence, Research
Studies (1965), 83:11–26

Erlich, Richard D., Catastrophism and Coition: Universal and
Individual Development in "Women in Love," Texas Studies
in Literature and Language (1967), 9:117–28

Ford, George H., An Introductory Note to D. H. Lawrence's
Prologue to "Women in Love," Texas Quarterly (1963), 6:
92–97

Ford, George H., The Wedding Chapter of D. H. Lawrence's
"Women in Love," Texas Studies in Literature and Language
(1964), 6:134–47

Freeman, Mary, D. H. Lawrence; A Basic Study of His Ideas.
1955. p. 59–69

Friedman, Alan, The Turn of the Novel. 1966. p. 130–78

Gindin, James, Harvest of a Quiet Eye; The Novel of Compassion. 1971. p. 210–19

Hall, William F., The Image of the Wolf in Chapter Thirty of
D. H. Lawrence's "Women in Love," D. H. Lawrence Review
(1969), 2:272–74

Harper, Howard M., Jr., and Charles Edge, eds., The Classic
British Novel. 1972. p. 202–19

Hinz, Evelyn J., D. H. Lawrence's Clothes Metaphor, D. H.
Lawrence Review (Summer 1968), 1:87–113

Hochman, Baruch, Another Ego; The Changing View of Self
and Society in the Work of D. H. Lawrence. 1970. p. 36–44
and 142–46

Karl, Frederick R. and M. Magalaner, eds., A Reader's Guide
to Great Twentieth Century English Novels. 1959. p. 154–
204

Kermode, Frank, Lawrence and the Apocalyptic Types, Criti-
cal Quarterly (1968), 10:14-38
Kinkead-Weekes, M., Eros and Metaphor; Sexual Relation-
ships in the Fiction of D. H. Lawrence, Twentieth Century
Studies (Nov. 1969), 1:3-19
Knight, G. Wilson, Lawrence, Joyce and Powys, Essays in
Criticism (Oct. 1961), 11:403-17
Krieger, Murray, The Tragic Vision; Variations on a Theme
in Literary Interpretation. 1960. p. 22-49
Langman, F. H., Women in Love, Essays in Criticism (1967),
17:183-206
Martin, W. R., Freedom Together in D. H. Lawrence's
"Women in Love," English Studies in Africa (1965), 8:111-20
Moody, H. L. B., African Sculpture Symbols in a Novel by D.
H. Lawrence, Ibadan (1969), 26:73-77
Moore, Harry T., ed., A D. H. Lawrence Miscellany. 1959.
p. 83-102
Murry, John Middleton, Son of Woman, The Story of D. H.
Lawrence. 1931. p. 218-27
Newman, Paul B., The Natural Aristocrat in Letters, Univer-
sity Review (Oct. 1964), 31:23-31
Nin, Anais, D. H. Lawrence; An Unprofessional Study. 1932.
p. 97-112
Ort, Daniel, Lawrence's "Women in Love," Explicator (1969),
27:Item 38
Pirenet, C., La Structure Symbolique de "Women in Love,"
Études Anglaises (1969), 22:137-51
Potter, Stephen, D. H. Lawrence; A First Study. 1930. p.
60-70
Schorer, Mark, ed., Modern British Fiction. 1961. p. 267-84
Schorer, Mark, ed., The World We Imagine; Selected Essays.
1968. p. 107-21
Seligmann, Herbert J., D. H. Lawrence; An American Inter-
pretation. 1924. p. 8-15
Sepčič, Visnja, Notes on the Structure of "Women in Love,"
Studia Romanica et Anglica Zagrabiensia (1966), #21-22:
289-304
Smailes, T. A., The Mythical Bases of "Women in Love,"
D. H. Lawrence Review (1968), 1:129-36
Stewart, Bruce, Where There's Muck There's Polytheism;
"Women in Love," Month (Feb. 1970), 1:117-19
Stoll, John E., The Novels of D. H. Lawrence. 1971. p.
151-97

Thompson, Leslie M., A Lawrence-Huxley Parallel; "Women in Love" and "Point Counter Point," Notes and Queries (Feb. 1968), 15:58-59

Tiverton, Father William, D. H. Lawrence and Human Existence. 1951. p. 28-37

Tomlinson, T. B., Lawrence and Modern Life: "Sons and Lovers" and "Women in Love," Critical Review (Melbourne) (1965), #8:3-18

Unterecker, John, ed., Approaches to the Twentieth Century Novel. 1965. p. 51-78

Vakeel, H. J., D. H. Lawrence; Social Theorist and Mystic, Visvabharati Quarterly (Summer 1960), 26:24-44

Vivas, Eliseo, The Substance of "Women in Love," Sewanee Review (Autumn 1958), 66:588-632

Vivas, Eliseo, The Two Lawrences, Bucknell Review (March 1958), 7:113-32

Williams, Raymond, The English Novel; From Dickens to Lawrence. 1970. p. 179-83

Williams, Raymond, Modern Tragedy. 1966. p. 121-38

Yudhishtar, Conflict in the Novels of D. H. Lawrence. 1969. p. 160-200

DORIS LESSING

Children of Violence, 1952-65

McDowell, Frederick P. W., The Fiction of Doris Lessing; An Interim View, Arizona Quarterly (Winter 1965), 21:315-45

The Golden Notebook, 1962

McDowell, Frederick P. W., The Fiction of Doris Lessing; An Interim View, Arizona Quarterly (Winter 1965), 21:315-45

The Grass Is Singing, 1950

McDowell, Frederick P. W., The Fiction of Doris Lessing; An Interim View, Arizona Quarterly (Winter 1965), 21:317-21

In Pursuit of the English, 1960

McDowell, Frederick P. W., The Fiction of Doris Lessing; An Interim View, Arizona Quarterly (Winter 1965), 21:327-30

Landlocked, SEE Children of Violence

A Proper Marriage, SEE Children of Violence

Retreat to Innocence, 1956

McDowell, Frederick P. W., The Fiction of Doris Lessing; An Interim View, Arizona Quarterly (Winter 1965), 21:318-24

A Ripple from the Storm, SEE Children of Violence

CLIVE STAPLES LEWIS

Out of the Silent Planet, 1938

Hillegas, Mark R., ed., Shadows of Imagination; The Fantasies of C. S. Lewis, J. R. R. Tolkien, and Charles Williams. 1969. p. 41-58

Phelan, John M., Men and Morals in Space, America (Oct. 9, 1965), 113:405-07

Spacks, Patricia Meyer, The Myth-Maker's Dilemma: Three Novels by C. S. Lewis, Discourse (Oct. 1959), 2:234-43

Urang, Gunnar, Shadows of Heaven; Religion and Fantasy in the Writing of C. S. Lewis, Charles Williams and J. R. R. Tolkien. 1971. p. 5-50

Perelandra, 1943

Phelan, John M., Men and Morals in Space, America (Oct. 9, 1965), 113:405-07

Spacks, Patricia Meyer, The Myth-Maker's Dilemma: Three Novels by C. S. Lewis, Discourse (Oct. 1959), 2:234-43

Urang, Gunnar, Shadows of Heaven; Religion and Fantasy in the Writing of C. S. Lewis, Charles Williams and J. R. R. Tolkien. 1971. p. 5-50

That Hideous Strength, 1945

Phelan, John M., Men and Morals in Space, America (Oct. 9, 1965), 113:405-07

Spacks, Patricia Meyer, The Myth-Maker's Dilemma: Three Novels by C. S. Lewis, Discourse (Oct. 1959), 2:234-43

Urang, Gunnar, Shadows of Heaven; Religion and Fantasy in the Writing of C. S. Lewis, Charles Williams and J. R. R. Tolkien. 1971. p. 5-50

MATTHEW GREGORY LEWIS

The Monk, 1795

Anderson, H., Manuscript of M. G. Lewis's "The Monk"; Some

Preliminary Notes, Bibliographical Society of America,
Papers (July 1968), 62:427–34

Harper, Howard M., Jr., and Charles Edge, eds., The Classic
British Novel. 1972. p. 36–50

Steeves, Harrison Ross, Before Jane Austen; The Shaping of
the English Novel in the Eighteenth Century. 1965. p. 243–
71

EDWARD GEORGE EARLE LYTTON BULWER-LYTTON,
FIRST BARON LYTTON

SEE

EDWARD GEORGE EARLE BULWER-LYTTON

MALCOLM LOWRY

Under the Volcano, 1947

Barnes, Jim, The Myth of Sisyphus in "Under the Volcano,"
Prairie Schooner (1968), 42:341–48

Berl, Emmanuel, Hommage à Malcolm Lowry, Prevues (Jan.
1963), #143:64–66

Birney, Earle, Against the Spell of Death, Prairie Schooner
(Winter 1963–64), 37:328–33

Day, Douglas, Of Tragic Joy, Prairie Schooner (Winter 1963–
64), 37:354–62

Doyen, Victor, Elements Towards a Spatial Reading of Malcolm Lowry's "Under the Volcano," English Studies (1969),
50:65–74

Edmonds, Dale, "Under the Volcano": A Reading of the
"Immediate Level," Tulane Studies in English (1968), 16:
63–105

Enright, D. J., Malcolm Lowry, New Statesman (Jan. 27,
1967), p. 117–18

Fouchet, Max-Pol, No se Puede . . . , Canadian Literature
(Spring 1961), #8:25–28

French, Warren, ed., The Forties: Fiction, Poetry, Drama.
1969. p. 217–26

Gass, W. H., Fiction and the Figures of Life. 1971. p. 55–76

Heilman, Robert B., The Possessed Artist and the Ailing
Soul, Canadian Literature (Spring 1961), #8:7–16

Hirschman, Jack, Kabbala/Lowry, etc., Prairie Schooner
(Winter 1963–64), 37:347–53

Kilgallin, Anthony R., Faust and "Under the Volcano," Canadian Literature (Autumn 1965), #26:43–54

Kirk, Downie, More than Music; Glimpses of Malcolm Lowry,
 Canadian Literature (Spring 1961), 8:31-38
Kostelantez, R., ed., On Contemporary Literature; An An-
 thology of Critical Essays on the Major Movements and
 Writers of Contemporary Literature. 1964. p. 419-21
McConnell, William, Recollections of Malcolm Lowry,
 Canadian Literature (Autumn 1960), #6:24-31
Mack, Maynard and Ian Gregor, eds., Imagined Worlds; Es-
 says on Some English Novels and Novelists in Honour of
 John Butt. 1968. p. 323-41
Markson, David, Myth in "Under the Volcano," Prairie
 Schooner (Winter 1963-64), 37:339-46
Nimmo, D. C., Lowry's Hell, Notes and Queries (1969), 16:265
Tuohy, Frank, Day of a Dead Man, Spectator (Aug. 25, 1961),
 #6948:262
Woodcock, George, Malcolm Lowry's "Under the Volcano,"
 Modern Fiction Studies (1958), 4:151-56

THOMAS MALORY

Le Morte D'Arthur, 1485

Angelescu, Victor, The Relationship of Gareth and Gawain in
 Malory's "Morte D'Arthur," Notes and Queries (1961), 8:8-9
Barnard, Ellsworth, ed., Edwin Arlington Robinson; Cente-
 nary Essays. 1969. p. 88-105
Davis, Gilbert R., Malory's Tale of Sir Lancelot and the
 Question of Unity in the "Morte D'Arthur," Papers of the
 Michigan Academy of Science, Arts and Letters (1964), 49:
 523-30
Dillon, Bert, Formal and Informal Pronouns of Address in
 Malory's "Le Morte D'Arthur," Annuale Mediaevale (1969),
 10:94-103
DiPasquale, Pasquale, Jr., Malory's Guinevere; Epic Queen,
 Romance Heroine and Tragic Mistress, Bucknell Review
 (May 1968), 16:86-102
Dundes, Alan, The Father, the Son and the Holy Grail, Liter-
 ature and Psychology (Autumn 1962), 12:101-12
Hampsten, Elizabeth, A Reading of Sir Thomas Malory's
 "Morte D'Arthur," North Dakota Quarterly (1967), 35:29-37
Hyman, Stanley Edgar, Standards; A Chronicle of Books for
 Our Time. 1966. p. 143-47
Loomis, Roger Sherman, Studies in Medieval Literature; A
 Memorial Collection of Essays. 1970. p. 59-71
Lumiansky, R. M., Arthur's Final Companions in Malory's

"Morte D'Arthur," Tulane Studies in English (1961), 11:5–19

Lumiansky, R. M., Tristram's First Interviews with Mark in
Malory's "Morte D'Arthur," Modern Language Notes (Nov.
1955), 70:476–78

Mellizo, Felipe, Arturo y "Le Morte," Cuadernos Hispanoamericanos (1969), 229:78–100

Moorman, Charles, Internal Chronology in Malory's "Morte
D'Arthur," Journal of English and Germanic Philology (April
1961), 60:240–49

Moorman, Charles, Lot and Pellinore: The Failure of Loyalty in
Malory's "Morte D'Arthur," Medieval Studies (1963), 25:83–92

Morgan, Henry Grady, The Role of Morgan le Fay in Malory's
"Morte D'Arthur," Southern Quarterly (1964), 2:150–68

Olstead, Myra, Morgan le Fay in Malory's "Morte D'Arthur,"
Bulletin Bibliographique de la Société Internationale
Arthurienne (1967), 19:128–38

Rexroth, Kenneth, Classics Revisited. 1968. p. 164–68

Rexroth, Kenneth, Le Morte D'Arthur, Saturday Review (June
12, 1965), 48:19

Rumble, Thomas Clark, First Explicit in Malory's "Morte
D'Arthur," Modern Language Notes (Dec. 1956), 71:564–66

Rumble, Thomas Clark, Malory's Balin and the Question of
Unity in the "Morte D'Arthur," Speculum (1966), 41:68–85

Schueler, D. G., Tristram Section of Malory's "Morte
D'Arthur," Studies in Philology (Jan. 1968), 65:51–66

Tucker, P. E., Source for the Healing of Sir Urry in the
"Morte D'Arthur," Modern Language Review (Oct. 1955),
50:490–92

Williams, Charles, Image of the City and Other Essays. 1958.
p. 186–94

Wilson, Robert H., The Prose Lancelot in Malory, Texas University. Department of English. Studies in English (1953),
32:1–13

FREDERICK MARRYAT

Mr. Midshipman Easy, 1836

Schuhmann, Kuno, Phrenologie und Ideelogie: Frederick
Marryats "Mr. Midshipman Easy," Die Neueren Sprachen
(1964), 13:567–73

CHARLES ROBERT MATURIN

Melmoth the Wanderer, 1820

Dawson, Leven M., "Melmoth the Wanderer": Paradox and the

Gothic Novel, Studies in English Literature, 1500-1900
(1968), 8:621-32

WILLIAM SOMERSET MAUGHAM

Cakes and Ale, 1930

Brown, Allen B., Substance and Shadow; The Original of the
Characters in "Cakes and Ale," Michigan Academy of Sci-
ence, Arts and Letters. Papers (1960), 45:439-46
West, Anthony, Principles and Persuasions; The Literary
Essays of Anthony West. 1957. p. 155-63

Of Human Bondage, 1915

Davies, Horton, A Mirror of the Ministry in Modern Novels.
1959. p. 113-36
Maugham, W. Somerset, Selected Prefaces and Introductions
of W. Somerset Maugham. 1963. p. 36-39

GEORGE MEREDITH

The Amazing Marriage, 1895

Beer, Gillian, "The Amazing Marriage": A Study in Con-
traries, Review of English Literature (1966), 7:92-105
Beer, Gillian, Meredith; A Change of Masks; A Study of the
Novels. 1970. p. 168-81
Kruppa, Joseph E., Meredith's Late Novels: Suggestions for
a Critical Approach, Nineteenth Century Fiction (Dec. 1964),
19:271-86

The Adventures of Harry Richmond, 1871

Hardy, Barbara, "A Way to Your Hearts Through Fire and
Water": The Structure and Imagery in "Harry Richmond,"
Essays in Criticism (April 1960), 10:163-80
Hergenhan, L. T., Meredith's Attempts to Win Popularity:
Contemporary Reactions, Studies in English Literature,
1500-1900 (Autumn 1964), 4:637-51
Pritchett, Victor Sawdon, The Living Novel and Later Appre-
ciations. 1964. p. 109-21

Beauchamp's Career, 1875

Beer, Gillian, Meredith; A Change of Masks; A Study of the
Novels. 1970. p. 70-107
Karl, Frederick R., "Beauchamp's Career": An English
Ordeal, Nineteenth Century Fiction (Sept. 1961), 16:117-31

Bartlett, Phyllis, The Novels of George Meredith, Review of
English Literature (1962), 3:31-46

Diana of the Crossways, 1885

Beer, Gillian, Meredith; A Change of Masks; A Study of the
Novels. 1970. p. 140-67
Gindin, James, Harvest of a Quiet Eye; The Novel of Com-
passion. 1971. p. 63-76
Kerpneck, Harvey, George Meredith, Sunworshipper and
Diana's Redworth, Nineteenth Century Fiction (June 1963),
18:77-82
Measures, Joyce, Comic Perspectives: Meredith's Clara
Middleton and Diana Warwick as Egoists, Wisconsin Studies
in Literature (1968), #5:30-40

The Egoist, 1879-90

Arinstein, L., Two Letters Concerning the Early Russian
Translation of "The Egoist," Notes and Queries (Jan. 1970),
17:34-36
Beer, Gillian, Meredith; A Change of Masks; A Study of the
Novels. 1970. p. 122-37
Buchen, Irving H., The Egoists in "The Egoist": The Sensu-
alists and the Ascetics, Nineteenth Century Fiction (1964),
19:255-69
Buchen, Irving H., Science, Society and Individuality, Univer-
sity Review (1964), 30:185-92
Gindin, James, Harvest of a Quiet Eye; The Novel of Com-
passion. 1971. p. 58-61, 63-70, and 74-76
Haley, Bruce E., Richard Feverel and Willoughby Patterne;
The Athlete as Egoist, Bucknell Review (Dec. 1968), 16:
107-25
Measures, Joyce, Comic Perspectives: Meredith's Clara
Middleton and Diana Warwick as Egoists, Wisconsin Studies
in Literature (1968), #5:30-40
Schwarz, Daniel R., The Porcelain Pattern Leitmotif in
Meredith's "The Egoist," Victorian Newsletter (1968), 33:
26-28
Stone, Donald David, Novelists in a Changing World; Meredith,
James and the Transformation of English Fiction in the
1880's. 1972. p. 116-37
Sundell, M. G., Functions of Flitch in "The Egoist," Nineteenth
Century Fiction (Sept. 1969), 24:227-35
Watt, Ian Pierre, ed., The Victorian Novel; Modern Essays in

Criticism. 1971. p. 324-36
Wilkenfeld, R. B., Hands Around: Image and Theme in "The
Egoist," ELH (Sept. 1967), 34:367-79

Evan Harrington, 1861

Herzenhan, L. T., Meredith's Use of Revision; A Consideration of the Revisions of "Richard Feverel" and "Evan Harrington," Modern Language Review (Oct. 1964), 59:539-44

Lord Ormont and His Aminta, 1894

Kruppa, Joseph E., Meredith's Late Novels; Suggestions for a
Critical Approach, Nineteenth Century Fiction (Dec. 1964),
19:271-86

One of Our Conquerors, 1891

Beer, Gillian, Meredith; A Change of Masks; A Study of the
Novels. 1970. p. 184-86
Kruppa, Joseph E., Meredith's Late Novels; Suggestions for a
Critical Approach, Nineteenth Century Fiction (Dec. 1964),
19:271-86
Rathburn, Robert C. and Martin Steinmann, Jr., eds., From
Jane Austen to Joseph Conrad: Essays Collected in Memory
of James T. Hillhouse. 1958. p. 222-33
Thomson, Fred C., Symbolic Characterization in "One of Our
Conquerors," Victorian Newsletter (Fall 1964), #26:12-14

The Ordeal of Richard Feverel, SEE Richard Feverel

Rhonda Fleming, 1865

Hergenhan, L. T., Meredith's Attempts to Win Popularity:
Contemporary Reactions, Studies in English Literature,
1500-1900 (Autumn 1964), 4:637-51

Richard Feverel, 1859

Anderson, Warren D. and Thomas D. Clareson, eds., Victorian
Essays; A Symposium; Essays on Occasion of the Centennial
of the College of Wooster in Honor of Emeritus Professor
Waldo H. Dunn. 1967. p. 87-106
Bartlett, Phyllis, The Novels of George Meredith, Review of
English Literature (1962), 3:31-46
Buchen, Irving H., The Importance of the Minor Characters in
"The Ordeal of Richard Feverel," Boston University Studies
in English (Autumn 1961), 5:154-66

Buchen, Irving H., "The Ordeal of Richard Feverel": Science Versus Nature, ELH (1962), 29:47-66

Edwards, P. D., Education and Nature in "Tom Jones" and "The Ordeal of Richard Feverel," Modern Language Review (Jan. 1968), 63:23-32

Edwards, P. D., Goldengrove Unleaving: A Reading of "Richard Feverel," Balcony (Sydney) (1966), #4:38-43

Gindin, James, Harvest of a Quiet Eye; The Novel of Compassion. 1971. p. 64-75

Goldfarb, Russell Marshall, Sexual Repression and Victorian Literature. 1970. p. 158-77

Grabar, T. H., Scientific Education and "Richard Feverel," Victorian Studies (Dec. 1970), 14:129-41

Haley, Bruce E., "Richard Feverel" and Willoughby Patterne: The Athlete as Egoist, Bucknell Review (1968), 16: 107-25

Hergenhan, L. T., Meredith's Use of Revision: A Consideration of the Revisions of "Richard Feverel" and "Evan Harrington," Modern Language Review (Oct. 1964), 59:539-44

Knoepflmacher, U. C., Laughter and Despair; Readings in Ten Novels of the Victorian Age. 1971. p. 109-36

Morris, J. W., Inherent Principles of Order in "Richard Feverel," Modern Language Association. Publications (Sept. 1963), 78:333-40

Poston, Lawrence, III, Dramatic Reference and Structure in "The Ordeal of Richard Feverel," Studies in English Literature, 1500-1900 (1966), 6:743-52

Stevenson, Lionel, 1859: Year of Fulfillment, Centennial Review (Fall 1959), 3:337-56

Stone, Donald David, Novelists in a Changing World; Meredith, James and the Transformation of English Fiction in the 1880's. 1972. p. 100-06

Talon, Henri A., Le Comique, Le Tragique et le Romanesque dans "The Ordeal of Richard Feverel," Études Anglaises (1964), 17:241-61

Williams, I. M., The Organic Structure of "The Ordeal of Richard Feverel," Review of English Studies (Feb. 1967), 18:16-29

Wright, Austin, ed., Victorian Literature; Modern Essays in Criticism. 1961. p. 213-24

Sandra Belloni, 1889

Stone, Donald David, Novelists in a Changing World, Meredith,

James and the Transformation of English Fiction in the
1880's. 1972. p. 106-08
Watson, Robert W., George Meredith's "Sandra Belloni": The
"Philosopher" on the Sentimentalists, ELH (Dec. 1957), 24:
321-35

The Tragic Comedians, 1880

Ardenne, S. R. T. O. d', "Troilus and Criseyde" and "The
Tragiç Comedians," English Studies (Feb. 1963), 44:12-19
Beer, Gillian, Meredith; A Change of Masks; A Study of the
Novels. 1970. p. 137-39
Beer, Gillian, Meredith's Idea of Comedy: 1876-1880, Nine-
teenth Century Fiction (Sept. 1965), 20:165-76
Stone, Donald David, Novelists in a Changing World; Meredith,
James and the Transformation of English Fiction in the
1880's. 1972. p. 137-43

Vittoria, 1867

Hergenhan, L. T., Meredith's Attempts to Win Popularity:
Contemporary Reactions, Studies in English Literature,
1500-1900 (Autumn 1964), 4:637-51

BRIAN MOORE

An Answer from Limbo, 1961

Ricks, Christopher, The Simple Excellence of Brian Moore,
New Statesman (Feb. 18, 1966), p. 227-28

The Emperor of Ice Cream, 1965

Dahlie, H., Brien Moore's Broader Vision: "The Emperor of
Ice Cream," Critique; Studies in Modern Fiction (1967), 9:
43-55
Foster, John Wilson, Crisis and Ritual in Brian Moore's Bel-
fast Novels, Eire-Ireland (Autumn 1968), 3:66-74
Ricks, Christopher, The Simple Excellence of Brian Moore,
New Statesman (Feb. 18, 1966), p. 227-28

The Feast of Lupercal, 1957

Foster, John Wilson, Crisis and Ritual in Brian Moore's Belfast Novels, Eire-Ireland (Autumn 1968), 3:66-74
Ludwig, Jack, Brian Moore: Ireland's Loss, Canada's Novelist, Critique; Studies in Modern Fiction (Spring-Summer
1962), 5:5-14

Ludwig, Jack, Exile from the Emerald Isle, Nation (March 15, 1965), 200:287–88

Ludwig, Jack, Mirror for Moore, Canadian Literature (Winter 1961), #7:18–23

The Lovely Passion of Judith Hearne, 1956

Foster, John Wilson, Crisis and Ritual in Brian Moore's Belfast Novels, Eire-Ireland (Autumn 1968), 3:66–74

Ludwig, Jack, Brian Moore: Ireland's Loss, Canada's Novelist, Critique; Studies in Modern Fiction (Spring–Summer 1962), 5:5–14

Ludwig, Jack, Exile from the Emerald Isle, Nation (March 15, 1965), 200:287–88

Ludwig, Jack, Mirror for Moore, Canadian Literature (Winter 1961), #7:18–23

Ricks, Christopher, The Simple Excellence of Brian Moore, New Statesman (Feb. 18, 1966), p. 227–28

The Luck of Ginger Coffey, 1960

Ludwig, Jack, Brian Moore: Ireland's Loss, Canada's Novelist, Critique; Studies in Modern Fiction (Spring–Summer 1962), 5:5–14

Ludwig, Jack, Mirror for Moore, Canadian Literature (Winter 1961), #7:18–23

GEORGE MOORE

Esther Waters, 1894

Bartlett, Lynn C., Maggie: A New Source for "Esther Waters," English Literature in Transition (1880–1920) (1966), 9:18–20

Jernigan, Jay, Forgotten Serial Version of George Moore's "Esther Waters," Nineteenth Century Fiction (June 1968), 23:99–103

Ohmann, C., George Moore's "Esther Waters," Nineteenth Century Fiction (Sept. 1970), 25:174–87

Watson, Sara Ruth, George Moore and the Dolmetsches, English Literature in Transition (1880–1920) (1963), 6:65–75

A Mummer's Wife, 1885

Heywood, C., Flaubert, Miss Braddon, and George Moore,

Comparative Literature (Spring 1960), 12:151-58

Sister Teresa, 1901

Brown, Calvin S., Balzac as a Source of George Moore's
"Sister Teresa," Comparative Literature (1959), 11:
124-30

IRIS MURDOCH

The Bell, 1958

Bowen, Elizabeth, Sensuality in a Secluded World, Saturday
Review (Oct. 25, 1958), 41:28
Byatt, A. S., Degrees of Freedom; The Novels of Iris Mur-
doch. 1965. p. 73-104
Clayre, Alasdair, Common Cause; A Garden in the Clearing,
Times Literary Supplement (Aug. 7, 1959), p. 30-31
Fraser, G. S., Iris Murdoch; The Solidity of the Normal,
International Literary Annual (1959), 2:37-54
Gerard, Albert, Lettres Anglaises; Iris Murdoch, Revue
Nouvelle (June 1964), 39:633-40
Hall, J., The Lunatic Giant in the Drawing Room. 1968. p.
190-99
Hoffman, Frederick J., Iris Murdoch; The Reality of Persons,
Critique; Studies in Modern Fiction (Spring 1964), 7:48-57
Howe, Irving, Realities and Fiction, Partisan Review (Winter
1959), 26:132-33
Jones, Dorothy, Love and Morality in Iris Murdoch's "The
Bell," Meanjin Quarterly (1967), 26:85-90
Kaehele, S. and H. German, Discovery of Reality in Iris
Murdoch's "The Bell," Modern Language Association. Pub-
lications (Dec. 1967), 82:554-63
McCarthy, Margot, Dualities in "The Bell," Contemporary
Review (Dec. 1968), 213:313-17
McGinnis, Robert M., Murdoch's "The Bell," Explicator
(1969), 28:Item 1
Meidner, Olga McDonald, The Progress of Iris Murdoch,
English Studies in Africa (March 1961), 4:17-38
O'Connor, William Van, Iris Murdoch, the Formal and the

Contingent, Critique; Studies in Modern Fiction (Winter–
Spring 1960), 3:34–46

Pearson, Gabriel, Iris Murdoch and the Romantic Novel, New
Left Review (Jan.–April 1962), #13–14:137–45

Raymond, John, The Unclassifiable Image, New Statesman and
Nation (Nov. 15, 1958), 56:697–98

Schrickx, W., Recente Engelse Romankunst: Iris Murdoch,
Die Vlaamse Gids (August 1962), 46:516–32

Shapiro, Charles, ed., Contemporary British Novelists. 1965.
p. 69–72

Souvage, Jacques, The Novels of Iris Murdoch, Studia Germanica Gandensia (1962), 4:244–47

Souvage, Jacques, Symbol as Narrative Device; An Interpretation of Iris Murdoch's "The Bell," English Studies (April
1962), 43:81–96

Wall, Stephen, The Bell in "The Bell," Essays in Criticism
(1963), 13:265–73

Whiteside, George, The Novels of Iris Murdoch, Critique;
Studies in Modern Fiction (Spring 1964), 7:27–47

Wolfe, Peter, The Disciplined Heart: Iris Murdoch and Her
Novels. 1966. p. 113–38

Bruno's Dream, 1968

Hall, William F., "Bruno's Dream": Technique and Meaning
in the Novels of Iris Murdoch, Modern Fiction Studies
(Autumn 1969), 15:429–43

Kaye, H., Delight and Instruction, New Republic (Feb. 8,
1969), 160:19–20

Thomson, P. W., Iris Murdoch's Honest Puppetry—The Characters of "Bruno's Dream," Critical Quarterly (Autumn
1969), 11:277–83

Tube, Henry, Women's Rites, The Spectator (Jan. 17, 1969),
222:79–80

The Flight from the Enchanter, 1956

Byatt, A. S., Degrees of Freedom; The Novels of Iris Murdoch. 1965. p. 40–60

Felheim, Marvin, Symbolic Characterization in the Novels of
Iris Murdoch, Texas Studies in Literature and Language
(Summer 1960), 2:189–97

German, Howard, Allusions in the Early Novels of Iris Murdoch, Modern Fiction Studies (Autumn 1969), 15:361–77

Hoffman, Frederick J., Iris Murdoch; The Reality of Persons,

Critique; Studies in Modern Fiction (Spring 1964), 7:48-57

Maes-Jelinek, Hena, A House for Free Characters; The Novels of Iris Murdoch, Revue des Langues Vivantes (1963), 39:45-69

Meidner, Olga McDonald, Reviewer's Bane; A Study of Iris Murdoch's "The Flight from the Enchanter," Essays in Criticism (Oct. 1961), 11:435-47

O'Connor, William Van, Iris Murdoch; The Formal and the Contingent, Critique; Studies in Modern Fiction (Winter-Spring 1960), 3:34-46

O'Sullivan, Kevin, Iris Murdoch and the Image of Liberal Man, Yale Literary Magazine (1962), 131:27-36

Schrickx, W., Recente Engelse Romankunst: Iris Murdoch, Die Vlaamse Gids (August 1962), 46:516-32

Shapiro, Charles, ed., Contemporary British Novelists. 1965. p. 65-67

Souvage, Jacques, The Novels of Iris Murdoch, Studia Germanica Gandensia (1962), 4:225-52

Souvage, Jacques, Theme and Structure in Iris Murdoch's "The Flight from the Enchanter," Spieghel Historiael van de Bond van Gentske Germanisten (June 1961), 3:73-88

Whiteside, George, The Novels of Iris Murdoch, Critique; Studies in Modern Fiction (Spring 1964), 7:27-47

Wolfe, Peter, The Disciplined Heart; Iris Murdoch and Her Novels. 1966. p. 68-88

Italian Girl, 1964

Furbank, P. N., Gowned Mortality, Encounter (Nov. 1964), 23:88-90

Halio, Jay L., A Sense of the Present, Southern Review (B.R.) (Autumn 1966), 2:952

Hoffman, Frederick J., The Miracle of Contingency; The Novels of Iris Murdoch, Shenandoah (Autumn 1965), 17:49-56

Kriegel, Leonard, A Surrender of Symbols, Nation (Nov. 9, 1964), 199:339

Pagones, Dorrie, Wanton Waifs and a Roman Woman, Saturday Review (Sept. 19, 1964), 47:48-49

Shapiro, Charles, ed., Contemporary British Novelists. 1965. p. 76-78

Tracy, Honor, Misgivings about Miss Murdoch, New Republic (Oct. 10, 1964), 151:21-22

Tucker, Martin, More Iris Murdoch, Commonweal (Oct. 30, 1964), 81:173-74

Wolfe, Peter, The Disciplined Heart: Iris Murdoch and Her
Novels. 1966. p. 203-08

The Nice and the Good, 1968

Baldanza, Frank, The Nice and the Good, Modern Fiction
Studies (Autumn 1969), 15:417-28
Byatt, A. S., Kiss and Make Up, New Statesman (Jan. 29,
1968), 75:113
Hicks, Granville, Love Runs Rampant, Saturday Review (Jan.
6, 1968), 51:27-28
Taubman, Robert, Not Caring, The Listener (Feb. 1, 1968),
79:148
T. L. S., Essays and Reviews from The Times Literary Sup-
plement, 1967-68. 1969. p. 58-61

The Red and the Green, 1965

Berthoff, Warner, Fortunes of the Novel; Muriel Spark and
Iris Murdoch, Massachusetts Review (Spring 1967), 8:301-32
Bradbury, Malcolm, The Romantic Miss Murdoch, The Spec-
tator (Sept. 3, 1965), 214:293
Halio, Jay L., A Sense of the Present, Southern Review (B.R.)
(Autumn 1966), 2:952
Hicks, Granville, Easter Monday Insights, Saturday Review
(Oct. 30, 1965), 48:41-42
Kemp, Peter, The Fight against Fantasy; Iris Murdoch's
"The Red and the Green," Modern Fiction Studies (Autumn
1969), 15:403-15
Sheed, Wilfred, The Morning After; Selected Essays and Re-
views. 1971. p. 296-98
Sullivan, Richard, Millicent the Magnificent, Critic (Dec.
1965-Jan. 1966), 24:63
T. L. S., Essays and Reviews from The Times Literary Sup-
plement, 1965. 1966. Vol. 4. p. 40-41
Tucker, Martin, The Odd Fish in Murdoch's Kettle, New Re-
public (Feb. 5, 1966), 154:26-28

The Sandcastle, 1957

Byatt, A. S., Degrees of Freedom; The Novels of Iris Mur-
doch. 1965. p. 61-72
Felheim, Marvin, Symbolic Characterization in the Novels of
Iris Murdoch, Texas Studies in Literature and Language
(Summer 1960), 2:189-97
Fraser, G. S., Iris Murdoch: The Solidity of the Normal,

International Literary Annual (1959), 2:37-54
German, Howard, Allusions in the Early Novels of Iris Murdoch, Modern Fiction Studies (Autumn 1969), 15:361-77
Gray, James, Lost Enchantment, Saturday Review (May 18, 1957), 40:41
Hall, James, The Lunatic Giant in the Drawing Room. 1968. p. 186-90
Hoffman, Frederick J., Iris Murdoch; The Reality of Persons, Critique; Studies in Modern Fiction (Spring 1964), 7:48-57
Maes-Jelinek, Hena, A House for Free Characters; The Novels of Iris Murdoch, Revue des Langues Vivantes (1963), 39:45-69
O'Connor, William Van, Iris Murdoch: The Formal and the Contingent, Critique; Studies in Modern Fiction (Winter-Summer 1960), 3:34-46
O'Sullivan, Kevin, Iris Murdoch and the Image of Liberal Man, Yale Literary Magazine (1962), 131:27-36
Schrickx, W., Recente Engelse Romankunst: Iris Murdoch, Die Vlaamse Gids (August 1962), 46:516-32
Sisk, John P., A Sea Change, Commonweal (May 31, 1957), 66:236-37
Souvage, Jacques, The Novels of Iris Murdoch, Studia Germanica Gandensia (1962), 4:241-44
Taylor, Griffin, What Does It Profit a Man . . . ?, Sewanee Review (1958), 66:137-41
Tracy, Honor, Passion in the Groves of Academe, New Republic (June 10, 1957), 136:17
Whiteside, George, The Novels of Iris Murdoch, Critique; Studies in Modern Fiction (Spring 1964), 7:27-47
Wolfe, Peter, The Disciplined Heart; Iris Murdoch and Her Novels. 1966. p. 89-112

The Severed Head, 1961

Bryden, Ronald, Phenomenon, Spectator (June 16, 1961), 206:885
Byatt, A. S., Degrees of Freedom; The Novels of Iris Murdoch. 1965. p. 105-21
Cosman, Max, Priapean Japes, Commonweal (June 9, 1961), 74:286-87
Duchene, Anne, Funny Appalling, The Guardian (June 16, 1961), p. 6
German, Howard, Allusions in the Early Novels of Iris Murdoch, Modern Fiction Studies (Autumn 1969), 15:373-77

Gregor, Ian, Towards a Christian Literary Criticism, The
     Month (1965), 33:239–49
Hall, James, The Lunatic Giant in the Drawing Room. 1968.
     p. 199–200
Hoffman, Frederick J., Iris Murdoch; The Reality of Persons,
     Critique; Studies in Modern Fiction (Spring 1964), 7:48–57
Jacobson, Dan, Farce, Totem and Taboo, New Statesman
     (June 16, 1961), 61:956–57
Kenney, Alice P., The Mythic History of "A Severed Head,"
     Modern Fiction Studies (Autumn 1969), 15:387–401
Maes-Jelinek, Hena, A House for Free Characters; The
     Novels of Iris Murdoch, Revue des Langues Vivantes (1963),
     39:59–62
Miner, Earl, Iris Murdoch: The Uses of Love, Nation (June
     2, 1962), 194:498–99
Moody, Philippa, In the Lavatory of the Athenaeum—Post War
     English Novels, Melbourne Critical Review (1963), 6:83–92
O'Connor, William Van, Iris Murdoch: "A Severed Head,"
     Critique; Studies in Modern Fiction (1962), 5:74–77
O'Connor, William Van, The New University Wits and the End
     of Modernism. 1963. p. 70–74
Pearson, Gabriel, Iris Murdoch and the Romantic Novel, New
     Left Review (Jan.–April 1962), #13–14:137–45
Souvage, Jacques, The Novels of Iris Murdoch, Studia Ger-
     manica Gandensia (1962), 4:225–52
Whiteside, George, The Novels of Iris Murdoch, Critique;
     Studies in Modern Fiction (Spring 1964), 7:27–47
Wolfe, Peter, The Disciplined Heart; Iris Murdoch and Her
     Novels. 1966. p. 139–60

The Time of the Angels, 1966

Eimerl, Sarel, Choreography of Despair, Reporter (Nov. 3,
     1966), 35:45–46
Hicks, Granville, Rector of a Dead God, Saturday Review (Oct.
     29, 1966), 49:25–26
Taubman, Robert, Uncles' War, New Statesman (Sept. 16,
     1966), 72:401–02
T. L. S., Essays and Reviews from The Times Literary Sup-
     plement, 1966. 1967. Vol. 5. p. 33–36

Under the Net, 1954

Batchelor, Billie, Revision in Iris Murdoch's "Under the Net,"
     Books at Iowa (1968), 8:30–36

Bradbury, Malcolm, Iris Murdoch's "Under the Net," Critical
    Quarterly (Spring 1962), 4:47–54
Byatt, A. S., Degrees of Freedom; The Novels of Iris Mur-
    doch. 1965. p. 14–39
Dick, Bernard F., The Novels of Iris Murdoch; A Formula
    for Enchantment, Bucknell Review (May 1966), 14:66–81
Fraser, G. S., Iris Murdoch; The Solidity of the Normal,
    International Literary Annual (1959), 2:37–54
Fries, Udo, Iris Murdoch; "Under the Net." Ein Beitrage zur
    Erzähltechnik im Ich-Roman, Die Neueren Sprachen (Sept.
    1969), 18:449–59
German, Howard, Allusions in the Early Novels of Iris Mur-
    doch, Modern Fiction Studies (Autumn 1969), 15:361–64
Goldberg, Gerald Jay, The Search for the Artist in Some
    Recent British Fiction, South Atlantic Quarterly (Summer
    1963), 62:387–401
Hall, J., The Lunatic Giant in the Drawing Room. 1968. p.
    183–86
Hoffman, Frederick J., Iris Murdoch; The Reality of Persons,
    Critique; Studies in Modern Fiction (Spring 1964), 7:48–57
Holzhaven, Jean, A Palpable Romantic, Commonweal (June 4,
    1954), 60:228
Maes-Jelinek, Hena, A House for Free Characters; The
    Novels of Iris Murdoch, Revue des Langues Vivantes (1963),
    39:45–50
Meidner, Olga McDonald, The Progress of Iris Murdoch,
    English Studies in Africa (March 1961), 4:17–38
O'Connor, William Van, Iris Murdoch; The Formal and the
    Contingent, Critique; Studies in Modern Fiction (Winter–
    Spring 1960), 3:34–46
Porter, Raymond J., "Leitmotif" in Iris Murdoch's "Under the
    Net," Modern Fiction Studies (Autumn 1969), 15:379–85
Schrickx, W., Recente Engelse Romankunst: Iris Murdoch,
    Die Vlaamse Gids (Aug. 1962), 46:516–32
Souvage, Jacques, The Novels of Iris Murdoch, Studia Ger-
    manica Gandensia (1962), 4:225–52
Souvage, Jacques, The Unresolved Tension; An Interpretation
    of Iris Murdoch's "Under the Net," Revue des Langues
    Vivantes (1960), 26:420–29
Webster, Harvey Curtis, Grasp of Absurdity, Saturday Review
    (July 3, 1954), 37:15
Whiteside, George, The Novels of Iris Murdoch, Critique;
    Studies in Modern Fiction (Spring 1964), 7:27–47

Widmann, R. L., Murdoch's "Under the Net": Theory and
Practice of Fiction, Critique; Studies in Modern Fiction
(1968), 10:5-16
Wolfe, Peter, The Disciplined Heart: Iris Murdoch and Her
Novels. 1966. p. 46-67

The Unicorn, 1963

Barrett, William, English Opposites, Atlantic Monthly (June
1963), 211:131-32
Bradbury, Malcolm, Under the Symbol, The Spectator (Sept.
6, 1963), 210-295
Byatt, A. S., Degrees of Freedom; The Novels of Iris Mur-
doch. 1965. p. 146-80
Cook, Eleanor, Mythical Beasts, Canadian Forum (August
1963), 43:113-14
Grigson, Geoffrey, Entre les Tombes, New Statesman (Sept.
13, 1963), 66:321-22
Hall, James, The Lunatic Giant in the Drawing Room. 1968.
p. 206-11
Hebblethwaite, Peter, Out Hunting Unicorns, Month (Oct.
1963), 30:224-28
Hoffman, Frederick J., Iris Murdoch; The Reality of Persons,
Critique; Studies in Modern Fiction (Spring 1964), 7:42-57
Scholes, Robert, The Fabulators. 1967. p. 106-32
Tucker, Martin, Love and Freedom; Golden and Hard Words,
Commonweal (June 21, 1963), 78:357-58
Whitehorn, Katharine, Three Women, Encounter (Dec. 1963),
21:78-82
Whiteside, George, The Novels of Iris Murdoch, Critique;
Studies in Modern Fiction (Spring 1964), 7:27-47
Wolfe, Peter, The Disciplined Heart: Iris Murdoch and Her
Novels. 1966. p. 183-202

An Unofficial Rose, 1962

Barrett, William, Rose with Thorns, Atlantic Monthly (June
1962), 209:108-09
Byatt, A. S., Degrees of Freedom; The Novels of Iris Mur-
doch. 1965. p. 122-45
Hall, James, The Lunatic Giant in the Drawing Room. 1968.
p. 200-06
Hicks, Granville, The Operations of Love, Saturday Review
(May 19, 1962), 45:32
Hoffman, Frederick J., Iris Murdoch; The Reality of Persons,

Critique; Studies in Modern Fiction (Spring 1964), 7:48-57
McDowell, F. P. W., "The Devious Involutions of Human Char-
acter and Emotions": Reflections on Some Recent British
Novels, Wisconsin Studies in Contemporary Literature
(Autumn 1963), 4:353-59
Maes-Jelinek, Hena, A House for Free Characters; The
Novels of Iris Murdoch, Revue des Langues Vivantes (1963),
39:62-66
Miller, Vincent, Unofficial Roses, National Review (Sept. 11,
1962), 13:194-96
Miner, Earl, Iris Murdoch; The Uses of Love, Nation (June 2,
1962), 194:498-99
Taubman, Robert, L'Année Dernière at Dugeness, New States-
man (June 8, 1962), 63:836
Whiteside, George, The Novels of Iris Murdoch, Critique;
Studies in Modern Fiction (Spring 1964), 7:27-47
Wolfe, Peter, The Disciplined Heart; Iris Murdoch and Her
Novels. 1966. p. 161-82

GEORGE ORWELL

Animal Farm, 1945

Colquitt, Betsey Feagan, Orwell; Traditionalist in Wonderland,
Discourse (Autumn 1965), 8:370-83
Cook, Richard, Rudyard Kipling and George Orwell, Modern
Fiction Studies (Summer 1961), 7:125-35
Gulbin, Suzanne, Parallels and Contrasts in "Lord of the Flies"
and "Animal Farm," English Journal (1966), 55:86-90
Harward, Timothy Blake, ed., European Patterns; Contempo-
rary Patterns in European Writing. 1967. p. 44-48
Hoggart, Richard, Speaking to Each Other; Essays. 1970.
Vol. 2. p. 106-10
Lee, Robert E., Orwell's Fiction. 1969. p. 105-27
O'Donnell, Donat, Orwell Looks at the World, New Statesman
and Nation (May 26, 1961), 61:837-38
Oxley, B. T., George Orwell. 1969. p. 75-82
Pinkus, Philip, Satire and St. George, Queen's Quarterly
(Spring 1963), 70:30-49

Burmese Days, 1934

Eagleton, Terry, Exiles and Émigrés; Studies in Modern Literature. 1970. p. 77-87
Lee, Robert E., Orwell's Fiction. 1969. p. 1-22

Lee, Robert E., Symbol and Structure in "Burmese Days": A
Revaluation, Texas Studies in Literature and Language
(1969), 11:819-35
Oxley, B. T., George Orwell. 1969. p. 85-92

A Clergyman's Daughter, 1935

Eagleton, Terry, Exiles and Émigrés; Studies in Modern Lit-
erature. 1970. p. 87-92
Lee, Robert E., Orwell's Fiction. 1969. p. 23-47
Oxley, B. T., George Orwell. 1969. p. 92-98

Coming Up for Air, 1939

Eagleton, Terry, Exiles and Émigrés; Studies in Modern Lit-
erature. 1970. p. 100-03
Lee, Robert E., Orwell's Fiction. 1969. p. 83-104
Oxley, B. T., George Orwell. 1969. p. 105-12
West, Anthony, Principles and Persuasions; Literary Essays
of Anthony West. 1957. p. 164-76

Homage to Catalonia, 1938

Edrich, Emanuel, Naiveté and Simplicity in Orwell's Writing:
"Homage to Catalonia," University of Kansas City Review
(June 1961), 27:289-97
Lee, Robert E., Orwell's Fiction. 1969. p. 66-82
Thompson, Frank H., Jr., Orwell's Image of the Man of Good
Will, College English (Jan. 1961), 22:235-40
Trilling, Lionel, Opposing Self; Nine Essays in Criticism.
1955. p. 151-72

Keep the Aspidistra Flying, 1936

Eagleton, Terry, Exiles and Émigrés; Studies in Modern Lit-
erature. 1970. p. 92-100
Fyvel, T. R., George Orwell and Eric Blair; Glimpses of a
Dual Life, Encounter (July 1959), 13:60-65
Lee, Robert E., Orwell's Fiction. 1969. p. 48-65
Oxley, B. T., George Orwell. 1969. p. 98-105
West, Anthony, Principles and Persuasions; Literary Essays
of Anthony West. 1957. p. 164-76

1984, 1949

Barr, Alan, The Paradise Behind "1984," English Miscellany
(1968), 19:197-203
Colquitt, Betsey Feagan, Orwell; Traditionalist in Wonderland,

Discourse (Autumn 1965), 8:370-83

Connors, J., "Do It to Julia": Thoughts on Orwell's "1984," Modern Fiction Studies (Winter 1970-71), 16:463-73

Deutscher, Isaac, Russia in Transition and Other Essays. 1957. p. 230-45

Dyson, A. E., The Crazy Fabric; Essays in Irony. 1965. p. 197-219

Elsbree, Langdon, The Structured Nightmare of "1984," Twentieth Century Literature (Oct. 1959), 5:135-41

Harris, Harold J., Orwell's Essays and "1984," Twentieth Century Literature (Jan. 1959), 4:154-61

Kegel, Charles H., "1984": A Century of Ingsoc, Notes and Queries (1963), 10:151-52

Kessler, Martin, Power and the Perfect State; A Study in Disillusionment as Reflected in Orwell's "1984" and Huxley's "Brave New World," Political Science Quarterly (Dec. 1957), 72:565-77

Kirk, Rudolf and Charles F. Main, eds., Essays in Literary History; Presented to J. Milton French. 1960. p. 249-64

Lee, Robert E., Orwell's Fiction. 1969. p. 128-57

Lutman, Stephen, Orwell's Patriotism, Journal of Contemporary History (1967), 2:149-58

Maddison, Michael, "1984": A Burnhamite Fantasy, Political Quarterly (Jan. 1961), 32:71-79

Nott, Kathleen, Orwell "1984," The Listener (Oct. 31, 1963), 70:687-88

Oliphant, Robert, Public Voices and Wise Guys, Virginia Quarterly Review (Autumn 1961), 37:522-37

Osgerby, J. R., Set Books: "Animal Farm" and "1984," Use of English (Spring 1966), 17:237-43

Oxley, B. T., George Orwell. 1969. p. 112-25

Ranald, R. A., George Orwell and the Mad World; The Anti-universe of "1984," South Atlantic Quarterly (Autumn 1967), 66:544-53

Russell, B. R., Portraits from Memory and Other Essays. 1956. p. 221-38

Smith, Marcus, The Wall of Blackness; A Psychological Approach to "1984," Modern Fiction Studies (1968), 14:423-33

Strachey, John, The Strangled Cry and Other Unparliamentary Papers. 1962. p. 11-77

Thale, Jerome, Orwell's Modest Proposal, Critical Quarterly (Winter 1962), 4:365-68

Thompson, Frank H., Jr., Orwell's Image of the Man of Good

Will, College English (Jan. 1961), 22:235-40
West, Anthony, Principles and Persuasions; Literary Essays
of Anthony West. 1957. p. 164-76

The Road to Wigan Pier, 1937

Fyvel, T. R., George Orwell and Eric Blair; Glimpses of a
Dual Life, Encounter (July 1959), 13:60-65
Hoggart, Richard, George Orwell and the "Road to Wigan
Pier," Critical Quarterly (1965), 7:72-85
Macdonald, Dwight, Books: Varieties of Political Experience,
New Yorker (March 28, 1959), 35:135-36, 139-46, and 149-
51
Toynbee, Philip, Orwell's Passion, Encounter (August 1959),
13:81-82
Wolheim, Richard, Orwell Reconsidered, Partisan Review
(Winter 1960), 27:82-97

THOMAS LOVE PEACOCK

Crotchet Castle, 1831

Dawson, Carl, His Fine Wit; A Study of Thomas Love Peacock.
1970. p. 254-69
Hewitt, Douglas, Entertaining Ideas; A Critique of Peacock's
"Crotchet Castle," Essays in Criticism (April 1970), 20:200-
12
Mullett, C. F., "The Bee" (1790-1794); A Tour of "Crotchet
Castle," South Atlantic Quarterly (Winter 1967), 66:70-86

Gryll Grange, 1860

Dawson, Carl, His Fine Wit; A Study of Thomas Love Peacock.
1970. p. 273-82

Headlong Hall, 1816

Dawson, Carl, His Fine Wit; A Study of Thomas Love Peacock.
1970. p. 174-89

Maid Marian, 1822

Dawson, Carl, His Fine Wit; A Study of Thomas Love Peacock.
1970. p. 223-38

Melincourt, 1817

Dawson, Carl, His Fine Wit; A Study of Thomas Love Peacock.
1970. p. 192-206

The Misfortunes of Elphin, 1829

   Dawson, Carl, His Fine Wit; A Study of Thomas Love Peacock.
   1970. p. 239-53

Nightmare Abbey, 1818

   Dawson, Carl, His Fine Wit; A Study of Thomas Love Peacock.
   1970. p. 207-22
   Howells, Carol Ann, Biographia Literaria and "Nightmare
   Abbey," Notes and Queries (1969), 16:50-51

                         ANTHONY POWELL

The Acceptance World, 1956

   Hall, James, The Use of Polite Surprise; Anthony Powell,
   Essays in Literature (April 1962), 12:167-83
   Russell, John, Anthony Powell; A Quintet, Sextet, and War.
   1970. p. 129-37
   SEE ALSO Music of Time

Afternoon Men, 1962

   Bergonzi, Bernard, Anthony Powell, British Book News:
   Supps. on Writers and Their Work (1962), #144:24-40
   Russell, John, Anthony Powell; A Quintet, Sextet, and War.
   1970. p. 50-54
   Russell, John, Quintet from the Thirties: Anthony Powell,
   Kenyon Review (Autumn 1965), 27:698-726

Agents and Patients, 1936

   Russell, John, Anthony Powell; A Quintet, Sextet, and War.
   1970. p. 63-67
   Russell, John, Quintet from the Thirties: Anthony Powell,
   Kenyon Review (Autumn 1965), 27:698-726

At Lady Molly's, 1958

   Hall, James, The Tragic Comedians; Seven Modern British
   Novelists. 1963. p. 129-50
   Russell, John, Anthony Powell; A Quintet, Sextet, and War.
   1970. p. 138-46
   Webster, Harvey Curtis, A Dance of British Eccentrics, The
   New Leader (Dec. 29, 1958), 41:26-27

A Buyer's Market, 1952

   Hall, James, The Tragic Comedians; Seven Modern British

Novelists. 1963. p. 129–50
Hall, James, The Uses of Polite Surprise: Anthony Powell,
 Essays in Criticism (April 1962), 12:167–83
SEE ALSO Music of Time

Casanova's Chinese Restaurant, 1960

Hall, James, The Tragic Comedians; Seven Modern British
 Novelists. 1963. p. 129–50
Kermode, John Frank, Puzzles and Epiphanies; Essays and
 Reviews, 1958–61. 1962. p. 121–30
Russell, John, Anthony Powell; A Quintet, Sextet, and War.
 1970. p. 151–63

A Dance to the Music of Time, SEE Music of Time

From a View to a Death, 1933

Russell, John, Anthony Powell; A Quintet, Sextet, and War.
 1970. p. 59–63
Russell, John, Quintet from the Thirties; Anthony Powell,
 Kenyon Review (Autumn 1965), 27:698–726

The Kindly Ones, 1961

Hartley, L. P., Good Dog, Good Dog, Time and Tide (June 28,
 1962), 43:21–22
Karl, Frederick R., Bearers of War and Disaster, New
 Mexico Quarterly (Sept. 24, 1962), 147:21–22
Russell, John, Anthony Powell; A Quintet, Sextet, and War.
 1970. p. 163–75

The Military Philosophers, 1968

T. L. S., Essays and Reviews from The Times Literary Supplement, 1968. 1969. Vol. 7. p. 183–85

The Music of Time, 1951–64
Bergonzi, Bernard, Anthony Powell, British Book News;
 Supps. on Writers and Their Work (1962), #144:24–40
Hall, James, The Uses of Polite Surprise; Anthony Powell,
 Essays in Criticism (1962), 12:167–83
Harward, Timothy Blake, ed., European Patterns; Contempo-
 rary Patterns in European Writing. 1967. p. 49–52
Hynes, Sam, Novelist of Society, Commonweal (June 12,
 1959), 70:396–97
McCall, Raymond G., Anthony Powell's Gallery, College En-
 glish (Dec. 1965), 27:227–32

Mizener, Arthur, "A Dance to the Music of Time": The Novels
of Anthony Powell, Kenyon Review (1960), 22:79–92
Quesenbery, W. D., Jr., Anthony Powell; The Anatomy of
Decay, Critique; Studies in Modern Fiction (Spring 1964),
7:5–26
Ruoff, Gene W., Social Mobility and the Artist in "Manhattan
Transfer" and "The Music of Time," Wisconsin Studies in
Contemporary Literature (Winter–Spring 1964), 5:64–76
Shapiro, Charles, ed., Contemporary British Novelists. 1965.
p. 80–94
Vinson, James, Anthony Powell's "Music of Time," Perspec-
tive (Summer–Autumn 1958), 10:146–52
Voorhees, Richard J., "The Music of Time": Themes and
Variations, Dalhousie Review (Autumn 1962), 42:313–21
Zegerell, James J., Anthony Powell's "Music of Time," Twen-
tieth Century Literature (Oct. 1966), 12:138–46

A Question of Upbringing, 1951

Hall, James, The Uses of Polite Surprise; Anthony Powell,
Essays in Criticism (April 1962), 12:167–83
Russell, John, Anthony Powell; A Quintet, Sextet, and War.
1970. p. 112–19
SEE ALSO Music of Time

Soldier's Art, 1966

Russell, John, Anthony Powell; A Quintet, Sextet, and War.
1970. p. 184–91
T. L. S., Essays and Reviews from The Times Literary Supplement. Vol. 5. 1967. p. 74–75

Valley of Bones, 1964

Hartley, L. P., Jenkins at War, Spectator (March 20, 1964),
#7082:383
Russell, John, Anthony Powell; A Quintet, Sextet, and War.
1970. p. 184–203
T. L. S., Essays and Reviews from The Times Literary Supplement. Vol. 3. 1965. p. 105–07

Venusberg, 1932

Russell, John, Anthony Powell; A Quintet, Sextet, and War.
1970. p. 59–63
Russell, John, Quintet from the Thirties; Anthony Powell,
Kenyon Review (Autumn 1965), 27:698–726

What's Become of Waring?, 1939

Russell, John, Anthony Powell; A Quintet, Sextet, and War. 1970. p. 67-71

Russell, John, Quintet from the Thirties; Anthony Powell, Kenyon Review (Autumn 1965), 27:698-726

JOHN COWPER POWYS

Owen Glendower; An Historical Romance, 1940

Knight, G. Wilson, Owen Glendower, Review of English Literature (Jan. 1963), 4:41-52

Porius, 1951

Wilson, Angus, "Mythology" in John Cowper Powys' Novels, Review of English Literature (Jan. 1963), 4:9-24

Wolf Salent, 1929

Aiken, Conrad Potter, Reviewer's ABC; Collected Criticism of Conrad Aiken from 1916 to the Present. 1958. p. 327-29

Wilson, Angus, "Mythology" in John Cowper Powys' Novels, Review of English Literature (Jan. 1963), 4:9-24

THEODORE FRANCIS POWYS

Mr. Weston's Good Wine, 1927

Churchill, Reginald Charles, The Powys Brothers. 1962. p. 7-40

Riley, A. P., Original Ending of Mr. Weston's Good Wine, Review of English Literature (April 1967), 8:49-55

ANN RADCLIFFE

Mysteries of Udolpho, 1794

Beaty, Frederick L., Mrs. Radcliffe's Fading Gleam, Philological Quarterly (Jan. 1963), 42:126-29

Kooiman-Van Middendorp, Gerarda, The Hero in the Feminine Novel. 1966. p. 35-38

CHARLES READE

Christie Johnstone, 1853

Rathburn, Robert C. and Martin Steinmann, eds., From Jane

Austen to Joseph Conrad; Essays Collected in Memory of
James T. Hillhouse. 1958. p. 208–21

The Cloister and the Hearth, 1861

Fleichman, Avrom, The English Historical Novel; Walter
Scott to Virginia Woolf. 1971. p. 152–55   ·
Grierson, Francis, Unidentical Twins: "The Cloister and the
Hearth" and "Great Expectations," Contemporary Review
(April 1961), 199:196–98

Hard Cash, 1863

Smith, Sheila M., Propaganda and Hard Facts in Charles
Reade's Didactic Novels: A Study of "It Is Never Too Late
to Mend" and "Hard Cash," Renaissance and Modern Studies
(1960), 4:135–49

It Is Never Too Late to Mend, 1856

Eliot, George (Pseud.), Essays. 1963. p. 325–34
Smith, Sheila M., Propaganda and Hard Facts in Charles
Reade's Didactic Novels: A Study of "It Is Never Too Late
to Mend" and "Hard Cash," Renaissance and Modern Studies
(1960), 4:135–49

MARY RENAULT

The Bull from the Sea, 1961

Burns, Landon C., Jr., The Men Are Only Men; The Novels of
Mary Renault, Critique; Studies in Modern Fiction (Winter
1963–64), 6:102–21

The Charioteer, 1953

Wills, Garry, The Autosexual Novel, National Review (July 4,
1959), 7:186–87

The King Must Die, 1958

Burns, Landon C., Jr., The Men Are Only Men; The Novels of
Mary Renault, Critique; Studies in Modern Fiction (Winter
1963–64), 6:102–21
Herbert, Kevin, The Theseus Theme; Some Recent Versions,
Classical Journal (Jan. 1960), 55:173–85

The Last of the Wine, 1956

Burns, Landon C., Jr., The Men Are Only Men; The Novels of

Mary Renault, Critique; Studies in Modern Fiction (Winter
1963-64), 6:102-21

HENRY HANDEL RICHARDSON

The Fortunes of Richard Mahony, 1930

Loder, Elizabeth, "The Fortunes of Richard Mahony": Dream
and Nightmare, Southerly (1965), 25:251-63
Mares, F. H., "The Fortunes of Richard Mahony": A Reconsideration, Meanjin (March 1962), 21:64-70

Maurice Guest, 1908

Hitchcock, George, Maurice Guest, Carleton Miscellany
(Spring 1964), 5:124-27

SAMUEL RICHARDSON

Clarissa; or, The History of a Young Lady, 1747-1748

Barker, Gerard A., The Complacent Paragon; Exemplary
Characterization in Richardson, Studies in English Litera-
ture, 1500-1900 (Summer 1969), 9:503-19
Barker, Gerard A., Clarissa's Command of Her Passions;
Self-Censorship in the Third Edition, Studies in English
Literature, 1500-1900 (Summer 1970) 10:525-39
Beer, Gillian, Richardson, Milton and the Status of Evil, Re-
view of English Studies (Aug. 1968), 19:261-70
Drew, Elizabeth A., The Novel; A Modern Guide to Fifteen
English Masterpieces. 1963. p. 39-58
Dussinger, John A., Conscience and the Pattern of Christian
Perfection in "Clarissa," Modern Language Association.
Publications (1966), 81:236-45
Eaves, T. C. D. and B. D. Kimpel, Composition of "Clarissa"
and Its Revision Before Publication, Modern Language
Association. Publications (May 1968), 83:416-28
Farrell, William J., The Style and the Action in "Clarissa,"
Studies in English Literature, 1500-1900 (1963), 3:365-75
Fiedler, Leslie A., Love and Death in the American Novel.
1966. p. 62-73
Griffith, Philip Mahone, Fire Scenes in Richardson's
"Clarissa" and Smollett's "Humphrey Clinker," Tulane
Studies in English (1961), 11:39-51
Hilles, Frederick W., The Plan of "Clarissa," Philological

Quarterly (1966), 45:236–48
Kaplan, F., Our Short Story; The Narrative Devices of "Clar-
  issa," Studies in English Literature, 1500–1900 (Summer
  1971), 11:549–62
Kearney, Anthony M., "Clarissa" and the Epistolary Form,
  Essays in Criticism (1966), 16:44–56
Keast, William Rea, Two Clarissas in Johnson's Dictionary,
  Studies in Philology (July 1957), 54:429–39
Kinkead-Weekes, M., Clarissa Restored?, Review of English
  Studies (1959), 10:156–71
Konigsberg, Ira, The Tragedy of "Clarissa," Modern Language
  Quarterly (1966), 27:285–98
Preston, John M. A., The Created Self; The Reader's Role in
  Eighteenth Century Fiction. 1970. p. 38–62 and 63–93
Schmitz, R. M., Death and Colonel Modern in "Clarissa,"
  South Atlantic Quarterly (Summer 1970), 69:346–53
Sherbo, Arthur, Time and Place in Richardson's "Clarissa,"
  Boston University Studies in English (1957), 111:139–46
Spector, Robert Donald, ed., Essays on the Eighteenth Cen-
  tury Novel. 1965. p. 32–63
Winterowd, Walter Ross, The Poles of Discourse; A Study of
  Eighteenth Century Rhetoric in "Amelia" and "Clarissa,"
  Dissertation Abstracts (1965), 26:360–61

Pamela, 1740–1741

Ball, Donald L., "Pamela": A Primary Link in Richardson's
  Development as a Novelist, Modern Philology (1968), 65:
  334–42
Barker, Gerard A., The Complacent Paragon: Exemplary
  Characterization in Richardson, Studies in English Litera-
  ture, 1500–1900 (Summer 1969), 9:503–19
Battestin, M. C., On the Contemporary Reputations of Pamela,
  Joseph Andrews and Roderick Random; Remarks by an Ox-
  ford Scholar, 1748, Notes and Queries (Dec. 1968), 15:450–52
Brooks, Douglas, "Joseph Andrews" and "Pamela," Essays in
  Criticism (1969), 19:348–51
Brooks, Douglas, Richardson's "Pamela" and Fielding's
  "Joseph Andrews," Essays in Criticism (April 1967), 17:
  158–68
Chalker, John, "Virtue Rewarded": The Sexual Theme in
  Richardson's "Pamela," Literary Half-Yearly (July 1961),
  2:58–64
Costa, R. H., Epistolary Monitor in "Pamela," Modern Lan-

guage Quarterly (March 1970), 31:38–47

Detig, Joseph E., "Pamela" and Her Critics, Leyte-Samar
Studies (1968), 2:242–49

Donovan, Robert A., The Problem of Pamela or, Virtue Un-
rewarded, Studies in English Literature, 1500–1900 (1963),
3:377–95

Dussinger, J. A., What Pamela Knew; An Interpretation,
Journal of English and Germanic Philology (July 1970), 69:
377–93

Eaves, T. C. and Ben D. Kimpel, Richardson's Revisions of
"Pamela," Studies in Bibliography; Papers of the Bibliographical Society of the University of Virginia (1967), 20:
61–88

Jenkins, Owen, Richardson's "Pamela" and Fielding's "Vile
Forgeries," Philological Quarterly (1965), 44:200–210

Kaul, A. N., The Action of English Comedy; Studies in the
Encounter of Abstraction and Experience from Shakespeare
to Shaw. 1970. p. 163–68

Kearney, Anthony M., Richardson's "Pamela": The Aesthetic
Case, Review of English Literature (Leeds) (1966), 7:78–90

Lyles, Albert M., Pamela's Trials, College Language Association Journal (1965), 8:290–92

McIntosh, Carey, Pamela's Clothes, ELH (March 1968), 35:
75–83

Parker, Dorothy, The Time Scheme of "Pamela" and the
Character of B., Texas Studies in Literature and Language
(1969), 11:695–704

Reid, B. L., Justice to "Pamela," Hudson Review (1957), 9:
516–33

Schulte, Edvige, "Pamela" e le sue Origini, Annali Instituto
Universiterio Orientale, Napoli, Sezione Germanica (1964),
7:143–74

Sharrock, Roger, Richardson's "Pamela": The Gospel and the
Novel, Durham University Journal (1966), 58:67–74

Steeves, Harrison Ross, Before Jane Austen; The Shaping of
the English Novel in the Eighteenth Century. 1965. p. 53–87

Strandberg, Victor H., A Palm for Pamela; Three Studies in
the Game of Love, Western Humanities Review (Winter 1966),
20:37–47

Ten Harmsel, Henrietta, The Villain-Hero in "Pamela" and
"Pride and Prejudice," College English (1961), 23:104–08

Sir Charles Grandison, 1753-54

    Pierson, Robert C., The Revisions of Richardson's "Sir Charles Grandison," Studies in Bibliography; Papers of the Bibliographical Society of the University of Virginia (1968), 21:163-89

HENRIETTA RICHARDSON ROBERTSON

SEE

HENRY HANDEL RICHARDSON

MARK RUTHERFORD

SEE

WILLIAM HALE WHITE

SIEGFRIED SASSOON

Memoirs of an Infantry Officer, 1930

    Davidson, Donald, The Spy Glass; Views and Reviews, 1924-1930. 1963. p. 188-93

WALTER SCOTT

The Bride of Lammermoor, 1819

    Fleishman, Avrom, The English Historical Novel; Walter Scott to Virginia Woolf. 1971. p. 67-69
    Gordon, Robert C., "The Bride of Lammermoor": A Novel of Tory Pessimism, Nineteenth Century Fiction (1957), 12: 110-24
    Hook, A. D., "Bride of Lammermoor": A Reexamination, Nineteenth Century Fiction (Sept. 1967), 22:111-26
    Welsh, Alexander, A Freudian Slip in "The Bride of Lammermoor," Études Anglaises (1965), 18:134-36

The Fair Maid of Perth, 1828

    Logan, James and John E. Jordan and Northrup Frye, eds., Some British Reomantics; A Collection of Essays. 1966. p. 235-66

The Fortunes of Nigel, 1822

> Harper, Howard M., Jr. and Charles Edge, eds., The Classic
> British Novel. 1972. p. 65-84

The Heart of Midlothian, 1818

> Biggins, D., "Measure for Measure" and "The Heart of Mid-
> lothian," Études Anglaises (1961), 14:193-205
>
> Craig, David, "The Heart of Midlothian": Its Religious Basis,
> Essays in Criticism (April 1958), 8:217-25
>
> Fleishman, Avrom, The English Historical Novel; Walter
> Scott to Virginia Woolf. 1971. p. 78-101
>
> Henry, Nathanial H., Wordsworth's "Thorn": An Analogue in
> Scott's "Heart of Midlothian," English Language Notes
> (1965), 3:118-20
>
> Lynskey, Winifred, The Drama of the Elect and the Reprobate
> in Scott's "Heart of Midlothian," Boston University Studies
> in English (1960), 4:39-48
>
> Madden, William A., The Search for Forgiveness in Some
> Nineteenth Century English Novels, Comparative Literature
> Studies (1966), 3:139-53
>
> Marshall, William H., Point of View and Structure in "Heart
> of Midlothian," Nineteenth Century Fiction (1961), 16:257-62

Ivanhoe, 1820

> Simeone, William E., The Robin Hood of "Ivanhoe," Journal of
> American Folklore (1961), 74:230-34

Redgauntlet; A Tale of the Eighteenth Century, 1824

> Devlin, D. D., Scott and "Redgauntlet," Review of English Lit-
> erature (Jan. 1963), 4:91-103
>
> Fleishman, Avrom, The English Historical Novel; Walter
> Scott to Virginia Woolf. 1971. p. 73-75
>
> Rathburn, Robert C. and Martin Steinmann, eds., From Jane
> Austen to Joseph Conrad; Essays Collected in Memory of
> James T. Hillhouse. 1958. p. 46-59
>
> Smith, J. A., "Redgauntlet": The Man of Law's Tale, Times
> Literary Supplement (July 23, 1971), 70:863-64

Rob Roy, 1817

> Cadbury, William, The Two Structures of "Rob Roy," Modern
> Language Quarterly (1968), 29:42-60

Devlin, D. D., Character and Narrative in Scott; A Legend of Montrose and Rob Roy, Essays in Criticism (1968), 18:136-51

Fleishman, Avrom, The English Historical Novel; Walter Scott to Virginia Woolf. 1971. p. 69-71

Gordon, Robert C., In Defense of "Rob Roy," Essays in Criticism (1968), 18:470-75

Tillyard, Eustace M. W., Epic Strain in the English Novel. 1958. p. 59-116

St. Ronan's Well, 1823

Pike, B. A., Scott as Pessimist; A View of "St. Ronan's Well," Review of English Literature (July 1966), 7:29-38

The Waverley Novels

Fleishman, Avrom, The English Historical Novel; Walter Scott to Virginia Woolf. 1971. p. 51-77

Jauss, Hans R., ed., Nachahmung und Illusion. Kolloquium Giessen Juni 1963. p. 135-56 and 228-36

Logan, James V., John E. Jordan and Northrup Frye, eds., Some British Romantics; A Collection of Essays. 1966. p. 235-66

Meller, Horst and Hans-Joachim Zimmermann, eds., Lebende Antike; Symposion für Rudolf Sühnel. 1967. p. 348-69

Peterson, Clell T., The Writing of Waverley, American Book Collector (1967), 18:12-16

Tillyard, E. M. W., Epic Strain in the English Novel. 1958. p. 59-116

GEORGE BERNARD SHAW

Cashel Byron's Profession, 1886

Shaw, George Bernard, Selected Non-Dramatic Writings. 1965. p. 309-14

Weintraub, Stanley, The Embryo Playwright in Bernard Shaw's Early Novels, Texas Studies in Literature and Language (Autumn 1959), 1:326-55

The Irrational Knot, 1905

Shaw, George Bernard, Selected Non-Dramatic Writings. 1965. p. 309-14

Love Among the Artists, 1900

Shaw, George Bernard, Selected Non-Dramatic Writings.
1965. p. 309–14

MARY GODWIN SHELLEY

Frankenstein, 1817

Bloom, H., "Frankenstein," or The New Prometheus, Partisan
Review (Fall 1965), 32:611–18
Humanities in the Age of Science; In Honor of Peter Sammar-
tino; ed. by Charles Angoff. 1968. p. 116–38
Mays, Milton A., "Frankenstein"—Mary Shelley's Black The-
odicy, Southern Humanities Review (1969), 3:146–53
Moskowitz, Samuel, Explorers of the Infinite; Shapers of
Science Fiction. 1963. p. 33–45
Palmer, D. J. and R. E. Dowse, "Frankenstein": A Moral
Fable, Listener (Aug. 23, 1962), 68:281–84
Pollin, Burton R., Philosophical and Literary Sources of
"Frankenstein," Comparative Literature (1965), 17:97–108
Preu, James A., The Tale of Terror, The English Journal
(May 1958), 47:243–47
Rao, E. Nageswara, The Significance of "Frankenstein,"
Triveni; Journal of Indian Renaissance (1968), 37:20–26
Rieger, James, Dr. Polidori and the Genesis of "Franken-
stein," Studies in English Literature, 1500–1900 (1963),
3:461–72

PHILIP SIDNEY

The Arcadia, 1590

Anderson, D. M., Trial of the Princess in "The Arcadia," Re-
view of English Studies (Nov. 1957), n.s.8:409–12
Beaty, F. L., Lodge's "Farbonius and Prisceria" and Sidney's
"Arcadia," English Studies (Feb. 1968), 49:38–45
Brückl, O., Sir Philip Sidney's "Arcadia" as a Source for John
Webster's "The Duchess of Malfi," English Studies in Africa
(1965), 8:31–55
Challis, L., The Use of Oratory in Sidney's "Arcadia," Studies
in Philology (July 1965), 62:561–76
Cutts, John P., Dametas' Song in Sidney's "Arcadia," Renais-
sance News (1958), 11:183–88

Davis, W. R., Thematic Unity in the New "Arcadia," Studies in Philology (April 1960), 57:123-43

Dipple, Elizabeth, Captivity Episode and the New "Arcadia," Journal of English and Germanic Philology (July 1971), 70: 418-31

Dipple, Elizabeth, Harmony and Pastoral in the Old "Arcadia," ELH (Sept. 1968), 35:309-28

Dipple, Elizabeth, Metamorphosis in Sidney's "Arcadias," Philological Quarterly (Jan. 1971), 50:47-62

Dipple, Elizabeth, Unjust Justice in the Old "Arcadia," Studies in English Literature, 1500-1900 (Winter 1970), 10:83-101

Dorsten, J. A. Van, Gruterus and Sidney's "Arcadia," Review of English Studies (May 1965), n.s.16:174-77

Godshalk, W. L., Gabriel Harvey and Sidney's "Arcadia," Modern Language Review (Oct. 1964), 29:497-99

Godshalk, W. L., Sidney's Revision of the "Arcadia," Philological Quarterly (April 1964), 43:171-84

Gohn, Ernest S., Primitivistic Motifs in Sidney's "Arcadia," Papers of the Michigan Academy of Science, Arts and Letters (1960), 45:363-71

Heltzel, V. B., Arcadian Hero, Philological Quarterly (Jan. 1962), 41:173-80

Isler, A. D., Allegory of the Hero and Sidney's Two Arcadias, Studies in Philology (April 1968), 65:171-91

Isler, A. D., Heroic Poetry and Sidney's Two Arcadias, Modern Language Association. Publications (1968), 83:368-79

Kalstone, D., Transformation of "Arcadia": Sannagaro and Sir Philip Sidney, Comparative Literature (Summer 1963), 15:234-49

Lindheim, N. R., Sidney's "Arcadia"; Retrospective Narrative, Studies in Philology (April 1967), 64:159-86

Marenco, A., Double Plot in Sidney's Old "Arcadia," Modern Language Review (April 1969), 64:248-63

Marenco, Franco, Sidney e l "Arcadia" Nella Critica Letteraria, Filologia e Letteratura (1966), 12:337-76

Marenco, Franco, Per una Nuova Interpretazione dell "Arcadia" di Sidney, English Miscellany (1966), 17:10-48

McPherson, David, C., A Possible Origin for Mopas in Sidney's "Arcadia," Renaissance Quarterly (1968), 21:420-28

Rees, Joan, Fulke Greville and the Revisions of "Arcadia," Review of English Studies (Feb. 1966), 17:54-57

Taylor, A. B., A Note on Ovid in "Arcadia," Notes and Queries (Dec. 1969), 16:455

Turner, M., Heroic Ideal in Sidney's Revised "Arcadia,"
Studies in English Literature, 1500-1900 (Winter 1970), 10:
63-82

ALAN SILLITOE

The General, 1960

Rosselli, John, A Cry from the Brick Streets, Reporter (Nov.
10, 1960), 33:37-42

The Key to the Door, 1962

Caute, David, Breakthrough, Time and Tide (Sept. 21, 1961),
42:1705
McDowell, Frederick P. W., Self and Society; Alan Sillitoe's
"Key to the Door," Critique; Studies in Modern Fiction
(1963-64), 6:116-23
Penner, Allen R., Dantesque Allegory in Sillitoe's "Key to the
Door," Renascence (1968), 26:79-85 and 103

The Loneliness of the Long Distance Runner, 1960

Moody, Philippa, In the Lavatory of the Athenaeum — Post War
English Novels, Melbourne Critical Review (1963), 6:83-92
Penner, A. R., Human Dignity and Social Anarchy; Sillitoe's
"The Loneliness of the Long Distance Runner," Contempo-
rary Literature (Spring 1969), 10:253-65

Saturday Night and Sunday Morning, 1959

Allen, Walter, The Newest Voice in English Literature Is
from the Working Class, New York Times Book Review
(Dec. 20, 1959), p. 4
Burrows, John, Alan Sillitoe, John O'London's (Nov. 30,
1961), 5:596-97
Coleman, John, The Unthinkables, New Statesman (Oct.
27, 1961), p. 610-12
Gindin, James Jack, Postwar British Fiction; New Accents
and Attitudes. 1962. p. 14-33
Hurrell, John Dennis, Alan Sillitoe and the Serious Novel,
Critique; Studies in Modern Fiction (Fall-Winter 1960-61),
4:3-16
Klotz, Günther, Naturalistiche Zuge in Alan Sillitoe's Roman
"Saturday Night and Sunday Morning," Zeitschrift für Ang-
listik und Amerikanistik (1962), 10:153-61

Palievsky, P., New Name, Inostrannaya Literatura (May
1963), #5:193–97
Prince, Rod, Saturday Night and Sunday Morning, New Left
Review (Nov.–Dec. 1960), #6:14–17
Shestakov, Dmitri, Alan Sillitoe from Nottingham, Soviet Lit-
erature (1963), #9:176–79
Shestakov, Dmitri, Fifteen Million Prototypes, Inostrannaya
Literatura (Nov. 1964), #11:226–35
Staples, Hugh B., "Saturday Night and Sunday Morning": Alan
Sillitoe and the White Goddess, Modern Fiction Studies
(1964), 10:171–81
West, Anthony, Books: On the Inside Looking In, New Yorker
(Sept. 5, 1959), 35:103–04

TOBIAS SMOLLETT

The Adventures of Ferdinand, Count Fathom, SEE Ferdinand,
Count Fathom

The Adventures of Peregrine Pickle, SEE Peregrine Pickle

The Adventures of Roderick Random, SEE Roderick Random

The Adventures of Sir Launcelot Greaves, SEE Sir Launcelot
Greaves

The Expedition of Humphrey Clinker, SEE Humphrey Clinker

Ferdinand, Count Fathom, 1753

Dillingham, W. B., Melville's "Long Ghost" and Smollett's
"Count Fathom," American Literature (May 1970), 42:232–35
Martin, Harold Clark, ed., Style in Prose Fiction. 1959. p.
25–54
Paulson, Ronald, Satire in the Early Novels of Smollett, Journal of English and Germanic Philology (July 1960), 59:399–
400
Piper, William Bowman, The Large Diffused Picture of Life
in Smollett's Early Novels, Studies in Philology (Jan. 1963),
60:45–56

Humphrey Clinker, 1771

Baker, Sheridan, "Humphrey Clinker" as Comic Romance,
Papers of the Michigan Academy of Science, Arts and Letters (1961), 46:645–54

Boggs, W. Arthur, Dialectal Ingenuity in "Humphrey Clinker,"
  Papers on English Language and Literature (1965), 1:327–37
Evans, David L., "Humphrey Clinker": Smollett's Tempered
  Augustanism, Criticism (1967), 9:257–74
Garron, Scott, A Study of the Organization of Smollett's "The
  Expedition of Humphrey Clinker," Southern Quarterly (1966),
  4:349–63 and 5:22–46
Gassman, Byron, The "Briton" and "Humphrey Clinker,"
  Studies in English Literature, 1500–1900 (1963), 3:397–414
Gassman, Byron, Religious Attitudes in the World of "Hum-
  phrey Clinker," Brigham Young University Studies (1965),
  6:65–72
Griffith, P. M., Fire Scenes in Richardson's "Clarissa" and
  Smollett's "Humphrey Clinker"; A Study of Literary Rela-
  tionship in the Structure of the Novel, Tulane Studies in
  English (1961), 11:39–51
Hopkins, Robert, The Function of Grotesque in "Humphrey
  Clinker," Huntington Library Quarterly (1969), 32:163–77
Iser, Wolfgang, The Generic Control of the Aesthetic Re-
  sponse: An Examination of Smollett's "Humphrey Clinker,"
  Southern Humanities Review (1969), 3:243–57
Park, William, Fathers and Sons: "Humphrey Clinker," Lit-
  erature and Psychology (1966), 16:166–74
Paulson, Ronald, Satire in the Early Novels of Smollett,
  Journal of English and Germanic Philology (July 1960), 59:
  381–402
Preston, Thomas P., Smollett and the Benevolent Misanthrope
  Type, Modern Language Association. Publications (1964),
  79:51–57
Reid, Benjamin Lawrence, The Long Boy and Others; Wherein
  Will Be Found a Gathering of Essays, Written to Divert and
  Entertain and at the Same Time to Instruct, Concerning Div-
  ers Occupations and Wit; Newly Imprinted for Scholarly In-
  spection. 1969. p. 78–99
Rousseau, George S., Matt Bramble and the Sulphur Contro-
  versy in the Eighteenth Century Medical Background of
  "Humphrey Clinker," Journal of the History of Ideas (1967),
  28:577–89
Spector, Robert Donald, ed., Essays on the Eighteenth Century
  Novel. 1965. p. 154–64
Wagoner, Mary, On the Satire in "Humphrey Clinker," Papers
  on Language and Literature (1966), 2:109–16

Peregrine Pickle, 1751

> Paulson, Ronald, Satire in the Early Novels of Smollett,
> Journal of English and Germanic Philology (July 1960), 59:
> 393-397

> Paulson, Ronald, Smollett and Hogarth; The Identity of Pallet,
> Studies in English Literature, 1500—1900 (Summer 1964), 4:
> 351-59

> Piper, William Bowman, The Large Diffused Picture of Life
> in Smollett's Early Novels, Studies in Philology (Jan. 1963),
> 60:45-56

Roderick Random, 1740

> Alter, Robert, Rogue's Progress; Studies in the Picaresque
> Novel. 1964. p. 58-79

> Battestin, Martin C., On the Contemporary Reputations of
> Pamela, Joseph Andrews and Roderick Random; Remarks
> by an Oxford Scholar, 1748, Notes and Queries (Dec. 1968),
> 15:450-52

> Brack, O. M., Jr. and J. B. Davis, Smollett's Revisions of
> "Roderick Random," Bibliographical Society of America.
> Papers (July 1970), 64:295-311

> Paulson, Ronald, Satire in the Early Novels of Smollett, Jour-
> nal of English and Germanic Philology (July 1960), 59:381-
> 402

> Piper, William Bowman, The Large Diffused Picture of Life
> in Smollett's Early Novels, Studies in Philology (Jan. 1963),
> 60:45-56

> Spector, Robert Donald, ed., Essays on the Eighteenth Century
> Novel. 1965. p. 131-53

> Underwood, G. N., Linguistic Realism in "Roderick Random,"
> Journal of English and Germanic Philology (Jan. 1970), 69:
> 32-40

Sir Launcelot Greaves, 1762

> Paulson, Ronald, Satire in the Early Novels of Smollett,
> Journal of English and Germanic Philology (July 1960), 59:
> 400-02

CHARLES PERCY SNOW

The Affair, 1960

> Kermode, John Frank, Puzzles and Epiphanies; Essays and

Reviews 1958-61. 1962. p. 155-63

Kvam, Ragnar, Ny Engelsk Prosa, Samtiden (Nov. 1960), 69: 549-57

Millgate, Michael, Strangers and Brothers, Commentary (July 1960), 30:76-79

Nelson, Bryce E., The Affair, Audit (March 1961), 1:11-15

Corridors of Power, 1964

Burgess, Anthony, Powers that Be, Encounter (Jan. 1965), 24: 71-76

Enright, D. J., Easy Lies the Head, New Statesman (Nov. 6, 1964), p. 698-99

Ludlow, George, The Power of C. P. Snow: "Corridors of Power," Time and Tide (Nov. 1964), 5/11:20

Macdonald, Alastair, The Failure of Success, Dalhousei Review (Winter 1964-65), 44:494-500

Shils, Edward, The Charismatic Centre: "Corridors of Power," Spectator (Nov. 6, 1964), #7115:608-09

Death Under Sail, 1932

Mayne, Richard, The Reub Armchair, Encounter (Nov. 1963), 21:76-82

The Masters, 1951

Noon, William T., Satire: Poison and the Professor, English Record (Fall 1960), 11:53-56

Sutherland, W. O. S., ed., Six Contemporary Novels. 1962. p. 46-57

The New Men, 1954

Watson, Kenneth, C. P. Snow and "The New Men," English (1965), 15:134-39

The Sleep of Reason, 1968

T. L. S., Essays and Reviews from The Times Literary Supplement, 1968. 1969. Vol. 7. p. 175-77

Time of Hope, 1949

Moody, Philippa, In the Lavatory of the Athenaeum—Post War English Novels, Melbourne Critical Review (1963), 6:83-92

Strangers and Brothers

Dobree, Bonamy, The Novels of C. P. Snow, Literary Half-

Yearly (Jan. 1963), 4:28-34

Hall, William F., The Humanism of C. P. Snow, Wisconsin
Studies in Contemporary Literature (Spring-Summer 1963),
4:199-208

Ivasheva, V., Illusion and Reality about the Work of Charles
P. Snow, Inostrannaya Literatura (June 1960), #6:198-203

Mayne, Richard, The Club Armchair, Encounter (Nov. 1963),
21:76-82

Millgate, Michael, Structure and Style in the Novels of C. P.
Snow, Review of English Literature (April 1960), 1:34-41

O'Connor, Frank, The Girl at the Goal Gate, Review of English Literature (April 1960), 1:25-33

Stanford, Raney, The Achievement of C. P. Snow, Western
Humanities Review (Winter 1962), 16:43-52

Thale, Jerome, C. P. Snow: The Art of Worldliness, Kenyon
Review (Autumn 1960), 22:621-34

Turner, Ian, Above the Snow Line, Overland (Aug. 1960), #18:
37-43

MURIEL SPARK

The Bachelors, 1960

Updike, John, Creatures of the Air, New Yorker (Sept. 30,
1961), 37:161-67

The Comforters, 1957

Kermode, Frank, The Prime of Miss Muriel Spark, New
Statesman (Sept. 27, 1963), 66:398-99

The Girls of Slender Means, 1963

Kermode, Frank, The Prime of Miss Muriel Spark, New
Statesman (Sept. 27, 1963), 66:398-99

Kostelanetz, Richard, ed., On Contemporary Literature; An
Anthology of Critical Essays on the Major Movements and
Writers of Contemporary Literature. 1964. p. 591-96

Raven, Simon, Heavens Below, Spectator (Sept. 20, 1963),
#7056:354

Soule, George, Must a Novelist Be an Artist?, Carleton Miscellany (Spring 1964), 5:92-98

T. L. S., Essays and Reviews from The Times Literary Supplement. Vol. 2. 1963. p. 100-02

The Mandelbaum Gate, 1964

Bedford, Sybille, Frontier Region: "The Mandelbaum Gate,"
Spectator (Oct. 29, 1965), p. 555–56

Berthoff, Warner, Fictions and Events; Essays in Criticism
and Literary History. 1971. p. 118–54

Enright, D. J., Public Doctrine and Private Judging: "The
Mandelbaum Gate," New Statesman (Oct. 15, 1965), 70:563–
66

T. L. S., Essays and Reviews from The Times Literary Supplement. Vol. 4. 1966. p. 34–36

The Prime of Miss Jean Brodie, 1961

Dobie, Ann B., "The Prime of Miss Jean Brodie": Muriel
Spark Bridges the Credibility Gap, Arizona Quarterly
(1969), 25:217–28

Lodge, David, The Uses and Abuses of Omniscience; Method
and Meaning in Muriel Spark's "The Prime of Miss Jean
Brodie," Critical Quarterly (Autumn 1970), 12:235–57

Robinson, 1958

Ohmann, Carol B., Muriel Spark's "Robinson," Critique;
Studies in Modern Fiction (1965), 8:70–84

CHRISTINA STEAD

The Man Who Loved Children, 1944

Katz, Alfred H., Some Psychological Themes in a Novel by
Christina Stead, Literature and Psychology (Fall 1965), 15:
210–15

JAMES STEPHENS

The Crock of Gold, 1912

Martin, Augustine, "The Crock of Gold": Fifty Years After,
Colby Library Quarterly (1962), Ser. 6:148–58

Deirdre, 1923

McFate, Patricia Ann, James Stephens' "Deirdre," Eire-Ireland (Autumn 1969), 4:87–93

LAURENCE STERNE

The Life and Opinions of Tristram Shandy, Gentleman, SEE
Tristram Shandy

Sentimental Journey, 1768

Alvarez, A., The Delinquent Aesthetic, Hudson Review
(Autumn 1966), 19:590–600

Fasano, Pino, L"Amicizia" Foscolo-Sterne e la Traduzione
Didimea del "Sentimental Journey," English Miscellany
(1963), 14:115–69

Stout, G. D., Jr., Yorick's "Sentimental Journey": A Comic
Pilgrim's Progress for the Man of Feeling, ELH (Dec.
1963), 30:395–412

Thomson, J. E. P., Contrasting Scenes and Their Part in the
Structure of "A Sentimental Journey," Aumla (Nov. 1969),
#32:206–13

Woolf, Virginia, Collected Essays. 1967. Vol. 1. p. 95–101

Tristram Shandy, 1760

Alter, Robert, "Tristram Shandy" and the Game of Love,
American Scholar (Sept. 1968), 37:316–23

Anderson, Howard, Associationism and Wit in "Tristram
Shandy," Philological Quarterly (1969), 48:27–41

Anderson, Howard and John S. Shea, eds., Studies in Criticism and Aesthetics, 1660–1800: Essays in Honor of
Samuel Holt Monk. 1967. p. 315–31

Anderson, Howard P., A Version of Pastoral; Class and
Society in "Tristram Shandy," Studies in English Literature,
1500–1900 (Summer 1967), 7:509–29

Brissenden, R. F., ed., Studies in the Eighteenth Century;
Papers Presented at the David Michal Smith Memorial
Seminar, Canberra, 1966. 1968. p. 133–54

Burckhardt, S., "Tristram Shandy's" Law of Gravity, ELH
(March 1961), 28:70–88

Camden, Charles Carroll, ed., Restoration and Eighteenth
Century Literature; Essays in Honor of Alan Dugall
McKillop. 1963. p. 49–68

Cash, Arthur Hill, Lockean Psychology of "Tristram Shandy,"
ELH (June 1955), 22:125–35

Cash, Arthur Hill, The Sermon in "Tristram Shandy," ELH
    (1964), 31:395–417
Chatterjee, Ambarnath, Dramatic Technique in "Tristram
    Shandy," Indian Journal of English Studies (1965), 6:33–43
Chatterjee, Ambarnath, The Humour of "Tristram Shandy,"
    Bulletin of the Department of English (Calcutta University)
    (1968–69), 4:40–50
Cook, Albert Spaulding, The Meaning of Fiction. 1960. p.
    24–37
Cook, Albert Spaulding, Reflexive Attitudes; Sterne, Gogol,
    Gide, Criticism (Spring 1960), 2:164–74
Davies, R. A., Annotating Sterne with the Cyclopaedia;
    Towards a Scholarly Edition of "Tristram Shandy," Notes
    and Queries (Feb. 1971), 18:56–58
Day, W. G., Some Source Passages from "Tristram Shandy,"
    Notes and Queries (Feb. 1971), 18:58–60
Drew, Elizabeth A., The Novel; A Modern Guide to Fifteen
    English Masterpieces. 1963. p. 75–94
Dyson, A. E., Sterne: The Novelist as Jester, Critical Quar-
    terly (Winter 1962), 4:309–20
Farrell, W. J., Nature Versus Art as a Comic Pattern in
    "Tristram Shandy," ELH (March 1963), 30:16–35
Faurot, R. M., Mrs. Shandy Observed, Studies in English Lit-
    erature, 1500–1900 (Summer 1970), 10:579–89
Gerlach-Nielsen, Merete, Hans Hertel and Morten Nøjgaard,
    eds., Romanproblemer. Theorier og Analyser; Festskrift
    til Hans Sørensen den 28. September 1968. 1968. p. 152–61
Gold, Joel J., "Tristram Shandy" at the Ambassador's Chapel,
    Philological Quarterly (1969), 48:421–24
Goodin, George, The Comic as a Critique of Reason; "Tris-
    tram Shandy," College English (Dec. 1967), 29:206–23
Hafter, Ronald, Garrick and "Tristram Shandy," Studies in
    English Literature, 1500–1900 (1967), 7:475–89
Hall, J. J., Hobbyhorsical World of "Tristram Shandy," Mod-
    ern Language Quarterly (June 1963), 24:131–43
Harper, Howard M., Jr. and Charles Edge, eds., The Classic
    British Novel. 1972. p. 22–35
Hicks, John H., The Critical History of "Tristram Shandy,"
    Boston University Studies in English (1956), 2:65–84
Hnatko, Eugene, "Tristram Shandy's" Wit, Journal of English
    and Germanic Philology (1966), 65:47–64
Holtz, William, Time's Chariot and "Tristram Shandy," Mich-
    igan Quarterly (Spring 1966), 5:197–203

Isaacs, Neil D., The Autoerotic Metaphor in Joyce, Sterne,
Lawrence, Stevens, and Whitman, Literature and Psychology
(Spring 1965), 15:92–106
James, Overton Philip, The Relation of "Tristram Shandy" to
the Life of Sterne, Dissertation Abstracts (1963), 23:3888
Kleinstück, Johannes, Zur Form und Methode der "Tristram
Shandy," Archiv für das Studium der Neueren Sprachen und
Literaturen (1957), 194:122–37
Laird, John, Philosophical Incursions into English Literature.
1962. p. 74–91
Landow, George P., "Tristram Shandy" and the Comedy of
Context, Brigham Young University Studies (1966), 7:208–24
McMaster, J., Experience to Expression; Thematic Character
Contrasts in "Tristram Shandy," Modern Language Quarterly
(March 1971), 32:42–57
Mazzeo, Joseph Anthony, ed., Reason and the Imagination;
Studies in the History of Ideas, 1600–1800. 1962. p. 255–77
Nassar, Eugene Paul, The Rape of Cinderella; Essays in Lit-
erary Continuity. 1970. p. 87–99
Petrie, G., Rhetoric as Fictional Technique in "Tristram
Shandy," Philological Quarterly (Oct. 1969), 48:479–84
Petrie, G., A Rhetorical Topic in "Tristram Shandy," Modern
Language Review (April 1970), 65:261–66
Piper, William Bowman, Tristram Shandy's Tragi-Comical
Testimony, Criticism (Summer 1961), 3:171–85
Piper, William Bowman, Tristram Shandy's Digressive
Artistry, Studies in English Literature, 1500–1900 (Summer
1961), 1:65–76
Pons, Christian, Laurence Sterne ou le Génie de l'Humour,
Cahiers du Sud (July–Aug. 1962), 53:425–46
Preston, John M. A., The Created Self; The Reader's Role in
Eighteenth Century Fiction. 1970. p. 133–64, 165–95, and
196–211
Price, Martin, To the Palace of Wisdom; Studies in Order and
Energy from Dryden to Blake. 1964. p. 312–41
Reid, Benjamin Lawrence, The Long Boy and Others; Wherein
will be Found a Gathering of Essays, Written to Divert and
Entertain and at the Same Time, to Instruct, Concerning
Several Distinguished Gentlemen of Divers Occupation and
Wit; Newly Imprinted for Scholarly Inspection. 1969. p.
100–27
Reid, Benjamin Lawrence; Sterne and the Absurd Homunculus,
Virginia Quarterly Review (Winter 1967), 43:71–95

Ryan, Marjorie, "Tristram Shandy" and the Limits of Satire, Kansas Quarterly (1969), 1:58-63

Seidlin, Oskar, Essays in German and Comparative Literature. 1961. p. 182-202

Shackford, John B., Sterne's Use of Catachresis in "Tristram Shandy," Iowa English Yearbook (Fall 1963), #8:74-79

Singleton, Marvin K., Deduced Knowledge as Shandean Nub: Paracelsian Hermetic as Metaphoric Bridge in "Tristram Shandy," Zeitschrift für Anglistik und Amerikanistik (1968), 16:274-84

Singleton, Marvin K., Trismegistic Tenor and Vehicle in Sterne's "Tristram Shandy," Papers on Language and Literature (1968), 4:158-69

Stedmond, J. M., Genre and "Tristram Shandy," Philological Quarterly (Jan. 1959), 38:37-51

Stedmond, J. M., Satire and "Tristram Shandy," Studies in English Literature, 1500-1900 (Summer 1961), 1:53-63

Stedmond, J. M., Style and "Tristram Shandy," Modern Language Quarterly (Sept. 1959), 20:243-51

Theobald, D. W., Philosophy and Imagination; An Eighteenth Century Example, Personalist (Summer 1966), 47:315-27

Wagoner, Mary S., Satire of the Reader in "Tristram Shandy," Texas Studies in Literature and Language (1966), 8:337-44

The Winged Skull; Papers from the Laurence Sterne Bicentenary Conference at the University of York and Sponsored by McMaster University, The University of York, and the New Paltz College of the State University of New York; ed. by Arthur N. Cash and John M. Stedmond. 1971. p. 3-18, 21-41, 59-75, 97-111, 124-31, 145-55, 194-209, and 237-69

ROBERT LOUIS STEVENSON

The Black Arrow, 1888

Faurot, R. M., From Records to Romance; Stevenson's "The Black Arrow" and the Paston Letters, Studies in English Literature, 1500-1900 (Autumn 1965), 5:677-90

Dr. Jekyll and Mr. Hyde, SEE The Strange Case of Dr. Jekyll and Mr. Hyde

Kidnapped, 1886

Watt, Ian Pierre, ed., The Victorian Novel; Modern Essays in Criticism. 1971. p. 373-89

The Master of Ballantrae, 1889

Bonds, Robert E., The Mystery of "The Master of Ballantrae,"

English Literature in Transition (1880–1920) (1964), 7:8–11

Egan, Joseph J., From History to Myth; A Symbolic Reading of "The Master of Ballantrae," Studies in English Literature, 1500–1900 (1968), 8:699–710

Kilroy, James F., Narrative Technique in "The Master of Ballantrae," Studies in Scottish Literature (Oct. 1967), 5: 98–106

Wright, Austin, ed., Victorian Literature; Modern Essays in Criticism. 1961. p. 284–94

The Strange Case of Dr. Jekyll and Mr. Hyde, 1886

Aring, Charles D., The Case Becomes Less Strange, American Scholar (Winter 1960–61), 30:67–78

Egan, Joseph J., The Relationship of Theme and Art in "The Strange Case of Dr. Jekyll and Mr. Hyde," English Literature in Transition (1880–1920) (1966), 9:28–32

Masood, Rahila, The Appeal of Stevenson, Venture (March 1960), 1:38–57

Miyoshi, Masso, Dr. Jekyll and the Emergence of Mr. Hyde, College English (1966), 27:470–74 and 479–80

Treasure Island, 1883

Golding, William Gerald, The Hot Gates and Other Occasional Pieces. 1966. p. 106–10

Masood, Rahila, The Appeal of Stevenson, Venture (March), 1:38–57

Watt, Ian Pierre, ed., The Victorian Novel; Modern Essays in Criticism. 1971. p. 373–89

BRAM STOKER

Dracula, 1897

Richardson, Maurice, The Psychoanalysis of Ghost Stories, Twentieth Century (Dec. 1959), 166:419–31

Wasson, Richard, The Politics of "Dracula," English Literature in Transition (1880–1920) (1966), 9:24–27

JONATHAN SWIFT

Gulliver's Travels, 1726

Banks, Ley Otis, Moral Perspective in "Gulliver's Travels" and "Candide"; Broadsword and Rapier, Forum (Houston) (Summer 1965), 4:4–8

Barroll, John Leeds, Gulliver and the Struldbruggs, Modern

Language Association. Publications (March 1958), 73:43–50

Barroll, John Leeds, Gulliver in Luggnagg; A Possible Source, Philological Quarterly (Oct. 1957), 36:504–08

Barzun, Jacques, Energies of Art; Studies of Authors, Classic and Modern. 1956. p. 81–100

Bentman, R., Satiric Structure and Tone in the Conclusion of "Gulliver's Travels," Studies in English Literature, 1500–1900 (Summer 1971), 11:535–48

Byers, John R., Jr., Another Source for "Gulliver's Travels," Journal of English and Germanic Philology (Jan. 1958), 57:14–20

Carnochan, W. B., Complexity of Swift: Gulliver's Fourth Voyage, Studies in Philology (Jan. 1963), 60:23–44

Carnochan, W. B., "Gulliver's Travels": An Essay on the Human Understanding, Modern Language Quarterly (March 1964), 25:5–21

Carnochan, W. B., Some Roles of Lemuel Gulliver, Texas Studies in Literature and Language (1964), 5:520–29

Corder, Jim, Gulliver in England, College English (Nov. 1961), 23:98–103

Crane, Ronald Simon, The Idea of the Humanities and Other Essays Critical and Historical. Vol. 2. 1967. p. 261–82

Danchin, Pierre, The Text of "Gulliver's Travels," Texas Studies in Literature and Language (Summer 1960), 2:233–50

Dickenson, H. T., Popularity of "Gulliver's Travels" and "Robinson Crusoe," Notes and Queries (May 1967), 14:172

Dircks, Richard J., Gulliver's Tragic Rationalism, Criticism (1960), 2:134–49

Downs, Robert Bingham, ed., Molders of the Modern Mind. 1960. p. 115–19

Dyson, Anthony Edward, The Crazy Fabric; Essays in Irony. 1965. p. 1–13

Ehrenpreis, Irvin, The Meaning of Gulliver's Last Voyage, Review of English Literature (July 1962), 3:18–38

Ehrenpreis, Irvin, Origins of "Gulliver's Travels," Modern Language Association. Publications (Dec. 1957), 72:880–99

English Association. Essays and Studies, 1958. 1958. p. 53–67

Fitzgerald, R. P., Allegory of Luggnagg and the Struldbruggs in "Gulliver's Travels," Studies in Philology (July 1968), 65:657–76

Gill, J. E., Beast over Man; Theriophilic Paradox in Gulliver's Voyage to the Country of the Houyhnhnms, Studies in Philology (Oct. 1970), 67:532–49

Goldgar, Bertrand A., Satires on Man and the Dignity of Human Nature, Modern Language Association. Publications (1965), 80:535–41

Gray, James, The Modernism of Jonathan Swift, Queen's Quarterly (Spring 1960), 67:11–17

Greenberg, Robert A., Gulliver's Travels, Explicator (1957), 16:Item 2

Hart, Jeffrey, The Ideologue as Artist; Some Notes on "Gulliver's Travels," Criticism (Spring 1960), 2:125–33

Halewood, W. H., Gulliver's Travels, ELH (Dec. 1966), 33:422–33

Halewood, W. H., Plutarch in Houyhnhnmland: A Neglected Source for Gulliver's Fourth Voyage, Philological Quarterly (April 1965), 44:185–94

Hitt, Ralph E., Antiperfectionism as a Unifying Theme in "Gulliver's Travels," Mississippi Quarterly (1962), 15:161–69

Jacobson, Richard, A Biblical Allusion in "Gulliver's Travels," Notes and Queries (Aug. 1970), 17:286–87

Jenkins, Clauston, The Ford Changes and the Text in "Gulliver's Travels," Papers of the Bibliographical Society of America (Jan. 1968), 62:1–23

Johnson, Maurive, Remote Regions of Man's Mind: The Travels of Gulliver, University of Kansas City Review (June 1961), 27:299–303

Jonathan Swift, 1667–1967; A Dublin Tercentenary Tribute; ed. by Roger McHugh and Philip Edwards. 1968. p. 78–93

Kirk, Rudolf and Charles Frederick Main, eds., Essays in Literary History; Presented to J. Milton French. 1960. p. 113–25

Leyburn, Ellen Douglass, Gulliver's Clothes, Satire Newsletter (Spring 1964), 1:35–40

McGeeney, Patrick, Gulliver's Travels, Use of English (Summer 1963), 14:244–49

McManmon, John J., The Problem of a Religious Interpretation of Gulliver's Fourth Voyage, Journal of the History of Ideas (Jan.–March 1966), 27:59–72

Mazzeo, Joseph Anthony, Reason and the Imagination; Studies in the History of Ideas, 1600–1800. 1962. p. 231–53

Milburn, Daniel Judson, The Age of Wit, 1650–1750. 1966. p. 120–52

Miller, Henry Knight, Eric Rothstein and G. S. Rousseau, eds.,

The Augustan Milieu; Essays Presented to Louis A. Landa.
    1970. p. 155-73
Munro, J. M., Book III of "Gulliver's Travels" Once More,
    English Studies (Oct. 1968), 49:429-36
Orwell, George, The Collected Essays, Journalism and Let-
    ters of George Orwell. Vol. 4. 1968. p. 205-23
Orwell, George, Orwell Reader; Fiction, Essays and Report-
    age. 1956. p. 283-300
Passon, Richard H., Legal Satire in "Gulliver" from John
    Bull, American Notes and Queries (1967), 5:99-100
Preu, James A., The Case of the Mysterious Manuscript,
    English Journal (Nov. 1963), 52:579-86
Price, Martin, To the Palace of Wisdom; Studies in Order and
    Energy from Dryden to Blake. 1964. p. 179-203
Quinlan, M. J., Lemuel Gulliver's Ships, Philological Quar-
    terly (July 1967), 46:412-17
Read, Herbert Edward, Selected Writings; Poetry and Criti-
    cism. 1964. p. 117-37
Reichard, Hugo M., Gulliver the Pretender, Papers on English
    Language and Literature (Autumn 1965), 1:316-26
Reisner, Thomas A., Swift's "Gulliver's Travels," Explicator
    (Jan. 1968), 26:Item 38
Reiss, Edmund, The Importance of Swift's Glubbdubdrib Epi-
    sode, Journal of English and Germanic Philology (April
    1960), 59:223-28
Rosenheim, E., Jr., Fifth Voyage of Lemuel Gulliver; A Foot-
    note, Modern Philology (Nov. 1962), 60:103-19
Schuster, Sister Mary Faith, Clothes Philosophy in "Gulliver's
    Travels," American Benedictine Review (Sept. 1964), 15:
    316-26
Seelye, John D., Hobbes' "Leviathan" and the Giantism Com-
    plex in the First Book of "Gulliver's Travels," Journal of
    English and Germanic Philology (April 1961), 68:228-39
Seronsy, Cecil C., Some Proper Names in "Gulliver's Trav-
    els," Notes and Queries (1957), 4:470-71
Sherburn, George, The "Copies of Verses" About Gulliver,
    Texas Studies in Literature and Language (1961), 3:3-7
Sherburn, George, Errors Concerning Houyhnhnms, Modern
    Philology (Nov. 1958), 56:92-97
Smith, Don N., The Structural Scheme of "Gulliver's Travels,"
    Marab: A Review (Spring/Summer 1965), 1:43-52
Speck, W. A., Swift. 1970. p. 100-37
Stavron, C. N., Gulliver's Voyage to the Land of Dubliners,

South Atlantic Quarterly (Fall 1960), 59:490-99

Steeves, Harrison Ross, Before Jane Austen; The Shaping of the English Novel in the Eighteenth Century. 1965. p. 43-52

Sturm, Norbert A. S. M., Gulliver; The Benevolent Linguist, University of Dayton Review (1967), 4:43-54

Suits, Conrad, The Role of the Horses in "A Voyage to the Houyhnhnms," University of Toronto Quarterly (Jan. 1965), 34:118-32

Sutherland, John Hale, Reconsideration of Gulliver's Third Voyage, Studies in Philology (Jan. 1957), 54:45-52

Sutherland, William Owen Sheppard, The Art of the Satirist; Essays on the Satire of Augustan England. 1965. p. 108-25

Tallman, Warren, Swift's Fool; A Comment upon Satire in "Gulliver's Travels," Dalhousie Review (1961), 40:470-78

Taylor, Dick, Jr., Gulliver's Pleasing Visions; Self-Deception as Major Theme in "Gulliver's Travels," Tulane Studies in English (1962), 12:7-61

Tilton, John W., "Gulliver's Travels" as a Work of Art, Bucknell Review (Dec. 1959), 8:246-59

Tracy, Clarence, The Unity of "Gulliver's Travels," Queen's Quarterly (Winter 1962), 68:597-609

Tuveson, Ernest Lee, ed., Swift; A Collection of Critical Essays. 1964. p. 55-89, 111-14, and 127-42

Tyne, J. L., Gulliver's Maker and Gullibility, Criticism (Spring 1965), 7:151-67

Van Tine, James, The Risks of Swiftian Sanity, University Review (March 1966), 32:235-40 and (June 1966), 32:275-81

Voight, Milton, Swift and Psychoanalytic Criticism, Western Humanities Review (Autumn 1962), 16:361-67

Wasiolek, Edward, Relativity in "Gulliver's Travels," Philological Quarterly (Jan. 1958), 37:110-16

Williams, Kathleen, ed., Swift; The Critical Heritage. 1970. p. 8-22, 66-70, 77-89, 121-27, 233-43, and 305-14

Wilson, James R., Swift, the Psalmist, and the Horse, Tennessee Studies in Literature (1958), 3:17-23

Wood, James O., Gulliver and the Monkey of Tralee, Studies in English Literature, 1500-1900 (Summer 1969), 9:415-26

Yunck, John A., The Skeptical Faith of Jonathan Swift, Personalist (Autumn 1961), 42:533-54

Zimansky, Curt A., Gulliver, Yahoos and Critics, College English (Oct. 1965), 27:45-49

Zoeman, W. E., The Houyhnhnm as Menippean Horse, College

English (1966), 27:449-54

WILLIAM MAKEPEACE THACKERAY

Catherine, 1839-40

Colby, Robert A., "Catherine": Thackeray's Credo, Review of
English Studies (Nov. 1964), 15:381-96
Kleis, John Christopher, Dramatic Irony in Thackeray's
"Catherine," Victorian Newsletter (Spring 1968), #33:50-53
Salerno, Nicholas A., "Catherine": Theme and Structure,
American Imago (Summer 1961), 18:159-66

The History of Henry Esmond, 1852

Donnelly, Jerome, Stendhal and Thackeray; The Source of
"Henry Esmond," Revue de Littérature Comparée (1965),
39:372-81
Fleishman, Avrom, The English Historical Novel; Walter
Scott to Virginia Woolf. 1971. p. 127-48
Marshall, William H., Dramatic Irony in "Henry Esmond,"
Revue des Langues Vivantes (1961), 27:35-42
Ridley, M. R., Thackeray's "Esmond," Time and Tide (April
25-May 1, 1963), p. 27
Smith, David J., The Arrested Heart; Familial Love and
Psychic Conflict in Five Mid-Victorian Novels, Dissertation
Abstracts (1966), 27:1839A
Sutherland, J., "Henry Esmond" and the Virtues of Careless-
ness, Modern Philology (May 1971), 68:345-54
Talon, H. A., Time and Memory in Thackeray's "Henry Es-
mond," Review of English Studies (May 1962), n.s.13:147-56
Watt, Ian Pierre, ed., The Victorian Novel; Modern Essays in
Criticism. 1971. p. 266-72
Williams, Ioan M., Thackeray. 1969. p. 96-102
Williamson, Karina, A Note on the Function of Castlewood in
"Henry Esmond," Nineteenth Century Fiction (June 1963),
18:71-77
Worth, George J., The Unity of "Henry Esmond," Nineteenth
Century Fiction (March 1961), 15:345-53

The History of Pendennis, SEE Pendennis

The Newcomes, 1854

McMaster, Juliet, Theme and Form in "The Newcomes,"
Nineteenth Century Fiction (1968), 23:177-88

Pendennis, 1848

> DeBruyn, John, Tom Jones and Arthur Pendennis, <u>Lit</u> (Spring
> 1966), #7:81−88
> Fido, Martin, "The History of Pendennis": A Reconsideration,
> <u>Essays in Criticism</u> (Oct. 1964), 14:363−79
> Smith, David J., The Arrested Heart; Familial Love and
> Psychic Conflict in Five Mid-Victorian Novels, <u>Dissertation</u>
> <u>Abstracts</u> (1966), 27:1839A
> Williams, Ioan M., <u>Thackeray</u>. 1969. p. 77−90

Philip, 1862

> Baker, Joseph E., Thackeray's Recantation, <u>Modern Language</u>
> <u>Association. Publications</u> (Dec. 1962), 77:586−94

The Virginians; A Tale of the Last Century, 1857

> Hubbell, Jay Broadus, <u>South and Southwest; Literary Essays</u>
> <u>and Reminiscences</u>. 1965. p. 153−73
> Shain, Charles E., The English Novelists and the Civil War,
> <u>American Quarterly</u> (Fall 1962), 14:399−421
> Williams, Ioan M., <u>Thackeray</u>. 1969. p. 102−07

Vanity Fair, 1847

> Blodgett, H., Necessary Presence; The Rhetoric of the Narra-
> tor in "Vanity Fair," <u>Nineteenth Century Fiction</u> (Dec. 1967),
> 22:211−23
> Bort, Barry D., Dove or Serpent? The Imposter in "Vanity
> Fair," <u>Discourse</u> (Autumn 1966), 9:482−91
> Brophy, Brigid, <u>Don't Never Forget; Collected Views and Re-</u>
> <u>Reviews</u>. 1967. p. 209−16
> Butterfield, Stephen, The Charades of "Vanity Fair," <u>Massa-</u>
> <u>chusetts Studies in English</u> (1968), 1:94−95
> Craig, G. Amour, On the Style of "Vanity Fair," <u>English Insti-</u>
> <u>tute Essays</u> (1958), p. 87−113
> Drew, Elizabeth A., <u>The Novel; A Modern Guide to Fifteen</u>
> <u>English Masterpieces</u>. 1963. p. 111−26
> Dyson, Anthony Edward, <u>The Crazy Fabric; Essays in Irony</u>.
> 1965. p. 72−95
> Dyson, Anthony Edward, "Vanity Fair": An Irony Against
> Heroes, <u>Critical Quarterly</u> (Spring 1964), 6:11−31
> Fleishman, Avrom, <u>The English Historical Novel; Walter</u>
> <u>Scott to Virginia Woolf</u>. 1971. p. 146−48
> Fraser, Russell A., Pernicious Casuistry; A Study of Char-

acter in "Vanity Fair," Nineteenth Century Fiction (1957),
    12:137–47
Greene, D. J., Becky Sharp and Lord Steyne — Thackeray or
    Disraeli?, Nineteenth Century Fiction (Sept. 1961), 16:157–64
Hagan, John, A Note on the Napoleonic Background of "Vanity
    Fair," Nineteenth Century Fiction (March 1961), 15:358–61
Harden, Edgar F., The Discipline and Significance of Form in
    "Vanity Fair," Modern Language Association. Publications
    (Dec. 1967), 82:530–41
Harden, Edgar F., The Fields of Mars in "Vanity Fair," Ten-
    nessee Studies in Literature (1965), 10:123–32
Hibbard, G. R., ed., Renaissance and Modern Essays Pre-
    sented to Vivian de Sola Pinto in Celebration of His Seven-
    tieth Birthday. 1966. p. 119–27
Houston, Neal B., A Brief Inquiry into the Morality of Amelia
    in "Vanity Fair," Victorian Newsletter (1966), 30:23–24
Howe, Irving, ed., Modern Literary Criticism. 1958. p.
    183–96
Janssens, Marcel, Functies van Schrijver en Lezer in W. M.
    Thackerays "Vanity Fair," Revue Belge de Philologie et
    d'Histoire (1962), 40:729–88
Johnson, E. D. H., "Vanity Fair" and "Amelia"; Thackeray in
    the Perspective of the Eighteenth Century, Modern Philology
    (Nov. 1961), 59:100–13
Karl, Frederick Robert, An Age of Fiction; The Nineteenth
    Century British Novel. 1964. p. 177–203
Keech, James M., Make 'Em Wait; Installment Suspense in
    Thackeray's "Vanity Fair," Serif (1966), 3:9–12
Knoepflmacher, U. C., Laughter and Despair; Readings in Ten
    Novels of the Victorian Age. 1971. p. 50–83
Kronenberger, Louis, The Polished Surface; Essays in the
    Literature of Worldliness. 1969. p. 201–16
Lapart, C., La Morale du Sentiment dans "The Newcomes" et
    "Vanity Fair," Caliban (1964), #1:139–47
McCullen, Maurice L., Jr., Sentimentality in Thackeray's
    "Vanity Fair," Cithara (Nov. 1969), 9:56–66
Martin, Harold C., ed., Style in Prose Fiction. 1959. p. 87–
    113
Mathison, John K., The German Sections of "Vanity Fair,"
    Nineteenth Century Fiction (Dec. 1963), 18:235–46
Miller, Joseph Hillis, ed., Aspects of Narrative; Selected
    Papers from the English Institute. 1971. p. 1–45
Nelson, Raymond A., The Rhythmical Structure of "Vanity

Fair," Discourse (Jan. 1958), 1:175–98

Paris, Bernard J., The Psychic Structure of "Vanity Fair,"
Victorian Studies (June 1967), 10:389–410

Patten, R. L., Fight at the Top of the Tree; "Vanity Fair"
versus "Dombey and Son," Studies in English Literature,
1500–1900 (Autumn 1970), 10:759–73

Peake, Charles, Thackeray's Waterloo, Literary Half-Yearly
(July 1961), 2:48–57

Plunkett, P. M., Thackeray's "Vanity Fair," Explicator (Nov.
1964), 23:Item 19

Quennell, Peter, Casanova in London. 1971. p. 97–109

Sharp, M. C., Sympathetic Mockery; A Study of the Narrator's
Character in "Vanity Fair," ELH (Sept. 1962), 29:324–36

Steig, M., "Barnaby Rudge" and "Vanity Fair": A Note on a
Possible Influence, Nineteenth Century Fiction (Dec. 1970),
25:353–54

Stevens, Joan, Thackeray's "Vanity Fair," Review of English
Studies (Jan. 1965), 6:19–38

Stevens, Joan, "Vanity Fair" and the London Skyline, Journal
of the Australasian Universities Language and Literature
Association (May 1967), 27:18–36

Stewart, David H., "Vanity Fair": Life in the Void, College
English (Dec. 1963), 25:209–14

Taube, Myron, The Character of Amelia in the Meaning of
"Vanity Fair," Victorian Newsletter (1960), #18:1–8

Taube, Myron, Contract as a Principle of Structure in "Vanity
Fair," Nineteenth Century Fiction (1963), 18:119–35

Taube, Myron, The George-Amelia-Dobbin Triangle in the
Structure of "Vanity Fair," Victorian Newsletter (1966),
#29:9–18

Taube, Myron, The Parson-Snob Controversy and "Vanity
Fair," Victorian Newsletter (1968), 34:25–29

Taube, Myron, The Puppet Frame of "Vanity Fair," ELH
(1968), 6:40–42

Taube, Myron, The Race for the Money in the Structure of
"Vanity Fair," Victorian Newsletter (Fall 1963), #24:12–17

Taube, Myron, Thackeray and the Reminiscential Vision,
Nineteenth Century Fiction (Dec. 1963), 18:247–59

Taube, Myron, Thackeray at Work: The Significance of Dele-
tions from "Vanity Fair," Nineteenth Century Fiction (1963),
18:273–79

Thompson, Leslie M., "Vanity Fair" and the Johnsonian Tradition in Fiction, New Rambler (1969), C7:45–49

Tillotson, Kathleen Mary, Novels of the Eighteen-Forties.
1961. p. 224-56
Tillyard, Eustace M., Epic Strain in the English Novel. 1958.
p. 117-25
Von Hendy, Andrew, Misunderstandings about Becky's Char-
acterization in "Vanity Fair," Nineteenth Century Fiction
(Dec. 1963), 18:279-83
Watt, Ian Pierre, ed., The Victorian Novel; Modern Essays in
Criticism. 1971. p. 248-65
Wilkinson, Ann Y., Tomeavesian Way of Knowing the World;
Technique and Meaning in "Vanity Fair," ELH (Sept. 1965),
32:370-87
Williams, Ioan M., Thackeray. 1969. p. 57-76
Worth, G. J., More on the German Sections of "Vanity Fair,"
Nineteenth Century Fiction (March 1965), 19:402-04
Wright, Austin, ed., Victorian Literature; Modern Essays in
Criticism. 1961. p. 342-57

JOHN RONALD REUEL TOLKIEN

The Lord of the Rings, 1954

Auden, Systan Hugh, Good and Evil in "The Lord of the Rings,"
Critical Quarterly (Spring-Summer 1968), 10:138-42
Auden, Wystan Hugh, The Quest Hero, Texas Quarterly (Win-
ter 1961), 4:81-93
Barber, Dorothy K., The Meaning of "The Lord of the Rings,"
Mankato State College Studies (Feb. 1967), 2:38-50
Beatie, Bruce A., Folk Tale, Fiction and Saga in J. R. R.
Tolkien's "The Lord of the Rings," Mankato State College
Studies (Feb. 1967), 2:1-17
Fifield, Merle, Fantasy in and for the Sixties, English Journal
(1966), 55:841-44
Fuller, Edmund, Books with Men Behind Them. 1962. p.
169-96
Grebstein, Sheldon Norman, ed., Perspectives in Contempo-
rary Criticism; A Collection of Recent Essays by American,
English and European Literary Critics. 1968. p. 370-81
Hayes, Noreen and Robert Renshaw, Of Hobbits: "The Lord of
the Rings," Critique; Studies in Modern Fiction (1967), 9:
58-66
Hillegas, Mark R., ed., Shadows of Imagination; The Fantasies
of C. S. Lewis, J. R. R. Tolkien, and Charles Williams.
1969. p. 59-110

Isaacs, Neil David and Rose A. Zimbardo, eds., Tolkien and
the Critics; Essays on J. R. R. Tolkien's "The Lord of the
Rings." 1968. p. 12-288

Levitin, Alexis, The Hero in J. R. R. Tolkien's "The Lord of
the Rings," Mankato State College Studies (Feb. 1967), 2:
25-37

Miesel, Sandra L., Some Motifs and Sources for "Lord of the
Rings," Riverside Quarterly (1968), 3:125-28

Miesel, Sandra L., Some Religious Aspects of "Lord of the
Rings," Riverside Quarterly (1968), 3:209-13

Norwood, W. D., Tolkien's Intention in "The Lord of the
Rings," Mankato State College Studies (Feb. 1967), 2:18-24

Rang, Jack C., Two Servants, Mankato State College Studies
(Feb. 1967), 2:84-94

Reilly, Robert J., Romantic Religion; A Study of Barfield,
Lewis, Williams and Tolkien. 1971. p. 190-211

Reilly, Robert J., Tolkien and the Fairy Story, Thought
(Spring 1963), 38:89-106

Spacks, Patricia Meyer, Ethical Pattern in "The Lord of the
Rings," Critique; Studies in Modern Fiction (Spring-Fall
1959), 3:30-42

Thomson, G. H., "Lord of the Rings": The Novel as Traditional Romance, Wisconsin Studies in Contemporary Literature (Winter 1967), 8:43-59

Urang, Gunnar, Shadows of Heaven; Religion and Fantasy in
the Writing of C. S. Lewis, Charles Williams and J. R. R.
Tolkien. 1971. p. 93-130

Wilson, Emund, The Bit Between My Teeth; A Literary
Chronicle of 1950-1965. 1965. p. 326-32

ANTHONY TROLLOPE

The American Senator, 1877

Hagan, John, The Divided Mind of Anthony Trollope, Nineteenth Century Fiction (June 1959), 14:1-26

Barchester Towers, 1857

Kincaid, J. R., "Barchester Towers" and the Nature of Con-
servative Comedy, ELH (Dec. 1970), 37:595-612

Knoepflmacher, U. C., Laughter and Despair; Readings in Ten
Novels of the Victorian Age. 1971. p. 25-49

Kronenberger, Louis, The Polished Surface; Essays in the
Literature of Worldliness. 1969. p. 217-32

Pope-Hennessey, James, Anthony Trollope. 1971. p. 158-60
Shaw, W. David, Moral Drama in "Barchester Towers," Nine-
teenth Century Fiction (June 1964), 19:45-54
Watt, Ian Pierre, ed., The Victorian Novel; Modern Essays in
Criticism. 1971. p. 347-61

Can You Forgive Her?, 1864

Chamberlain, David S., Unity and Irony in Trollope's "Can
You Forgive Her?," Studies in English Literature, 1500-
1900 (Autumn 1968), 8:669-80
Pope-Hennessey, James, Anthony Trollope. 1971. p. 254-57

Cousin Henry, 1878

Polhemus, Robert M., "Cousin Henry": Trollope's Note from
Underground, Nineteenth Century Fiction (March 1966), 20:
385-89

Dr. Thorne, 1858

Hagan, John, The Divided Mind of Anthony Trollope, Nine-
teenth Century Fiction (June 1959), 14:1-26
Williams, Raymond, The English Novel; From Dickens to
Lawrence. 1970. p. 84-86

Dr. Wortle's School, 1881

Maxwell, J. C., Cockshut on "Dr. Wortle's School," Nineteenth
Century Fiction (1958), 13:153-59

The Duke's Children, 1880

Hagan, John H., "The Duke's Children": Trollope's Psychological Masterpiece, Nineteenth Century Fiction (1958), 13:
1-21
Kenney, Blair Gates, The Two Isabels; A Study in Distortion,
Victorian Newsletter (Spring 1964), #25:15-17

The Eustace Diamonds, 1873

Pope-Hennessey, James, Anthony Trollope. 1971. p. 300-05

Framley Parsonage, 1861

Bićanić, Sonia, Some New Facts about the Beginning of Trollope's "Framley Parsonage," Studia Romanica et Anglica
Zagrabiensia (1960), #9-10:171-76
Pope-Hennessey, James, Anthony Trollope. 1971. p. 186-88
and 207-11

The Last Chronicle of Barset, 1867

> Harper, Howard M., Jr. and Charles Edge, eds., The Classic
> British Novel. 1972. p. 121-42
> Thale, Jerome, The Problem of Structure in Trollope, Nine-
> teenth Century Fiction (Sept. 1960), 15:147-57

Orley Farm, 1886

> Pope-Hennessey, James, Anthony Trollope. 1971. p. 244-48
> Rathburn, Robert C. and Martin Steinmann, Jr., eds., From
> Jane Austen to Joseph Conrad; Essays Collected in Memory
> of James T. Hillhouse. 1958. p. 146-59

Phineas Farm, The Irish Member, 1869

> Pope-Hennessey, James, Anthony Trollope. 1971. p. 278-82

The Prime Minister, 1814

> Pope-Hennessey, James, Anthony Trollope. 1971. p. 328-31
> Skilton, David, The Spectator's Attack on Trollope's "Prime
> Minister": A Mistaken Attribution, Notes and Queries (Nov.
> 1968), 15:420-21

The Vicar of Bullhampton, 1870

> Cadbury, William, The Uses of the Village; Form and Theme
> in Trollope's "The Vicar of Bullhampton," Nineteenth Cen-
> tury Fiction (Sept. 1963), 18:151-63

The Warden, 1855

> Best, G. F. A., The Road to Hiram's Hospital; A Byway of
> Early Victorian History, Victorian Studies (Dec. 1961), 5:
> 135-50
> Goldberg, M. A., Trollope's "The Warden": A Commentary on
> the "Age of Equipoise," Nineteenth Century Fiction (June
> 1963), 18:381-90
> Pope-Hennessey, James, Anthony Trollope. 1971. p. 147-49
> Sharp, R. L., Trollope's Mathematics in "The Warden," Nine-
> teenth Century Fiction (1962), 17:288-89
> Watt, Ian Pierre, ed., The Victorian Novel; Modern Essays in
> Criticism. 1971. p. 337-46

The Way We Live Now, 1875

> Edwards, P. D., The Chronology of "The Way We Live Now,"
> Notes and Queries (1969), 16:214-16

Edwards, P. D., Trollope Changes His Mind; The Death of
Melmotte in "The Way We Live Now," Nineteenth Century
Fiction (June 1963), 18:89-91

Nathan, Sabine, Anthony Trollope's Perception of the Way We
Live Now, Zeitschrift für Anglistik und Amerikanistik
(1962), 10:259-78

Pope-Hennessey, James, Anthony Trollope. 1971. p. 326-28

Tanner, Tony, Trollope's "The Way We Live Now": Its Modern Significance, Critical Quarterly (Autumn 1967), 9:256-71

JOHN WAIN

Born in Captivity, SEE Hurry On Down

Hurry On Down, 1953

Harkness, Bruce, The Lucky Crowd; Contemporary British
Fiction, English Journal (Oct. 1958), 47:387-97

Strike the Father Dead, 1962

Davenport, Guy, Jungles of the Imagination, National Review
(Oct. 9, 1962), 13:273-74

EDGAR WALLACE

Mr. Justice Maxwell, n.d.

Barr, Donald, I've Been Reading: Anthony Hope and Edgar
Maxwell, as a Matter of Fact, Columbia University Forum
(Winter 1960), 3:38-41

HORACE WALPOLE

Castle of Otranto, 1764

Preu, James A., The Tale of Terror, English Journal (May
1958), 47:243-47

Steeves, Harrison Ross, Before Jane Austen; The Shaping of
the English Novel in the Eighteenth Century. 1965. p. 243-71

EVELYN WAUGH

Black Mischief, 1932

Hall, James, The Tragic Comedians; Seven Modern British

Novelists. 1963. p. 45-65
Mooney, Harry J., Jr. and Thomas F. Staley, eds., The Shapeless God; Essays on Modern Fiction. 1968. p. 70-73

Brideshead Revisited, 1945

Bergonzi, Bernard, Evelyn Waugh's Gentleman, Critical
Quarterly (1963), 5:23-36
Bergonzi, Bernard, The Situation of the Novel. 1970. p. 109-
13
Churchill, Thomas, The Trouble with "Brideshead Revisited,"
Modern Language Quarterly (March 1967), 28:213-28
Cogley, John, Revisiting Brideshead, Commonweal (April 17,
1964), 80:103-06
Coleman, John, No Room for Hooper, Spectator (July 29,
1960), #6892:187
D'Avanzo, M. L., Truth and Beauty in "Brideshead Revisited,"
Modern Fiction Studies (Summer 1965), 11:140-52
Davis, R. M., Serial Version of "Brideshead Revisited," Twen-
tieth Century Literature (April 1969), 15:35-43
Doyle, Paul A., Waugh's "Brideshead Revisited," Explicator
(March 1966), 26:Item 57
Eagleton, Terry, Exiles and Émigrés; Studies in Modern Lit-
erature. 1970. p. 57-67
Gardiner, Harold Charles, In All Conscience; Reflections on
Books and Culture. 1959. p. 89-91 and 91-96
Gleason, James, Evelyn Waugh and the Stylistics of Commit-
ment, Wisconsin Studies in Literature (1965), #2:70-74
Harty, E. R., "Brideshead" Re-Read: A Discussion of Some
of the Themes of Evelyn Waugh's "Brideshead Revisited,"
Unisa English Studies (1967), 3:66-74
Kellogg, Gene, The Vital Tradition; The Catholic Novel in a
Period of Convergence. 1970. p. 108-10
Kermode, John Frank, Puzzles and Epiphanies; Essays and
Reviews, 1958-1961. 1962. p. 164-75
LaFrance, Marston, Context and Structure of Evelyn Waugh's
"Brideshead Revisited," Twentieth Century Literature
(April 1964), 10:12-18
Mooney, Harry J., Jr. and Thomas F. Staley, eds., The Shape-
less God; Essays on Modern Fiction. 1968. p. 74-80
Oppel, Horst, ed., Der Moderne Englische Roman; Interpreta-
tionen. 1965. p. 301-27
Reinhardt, Kurt Frank, The Theological Novel of Modern

Europe; An Analysis of Masterpieces by Eight Authors.
1969. p. 203-16

Sykes, Christopher, et al, A Critique of Waugh, Listener
(Aug. 31, 1967), 78:267-69

Voorhees, Richard J., Evelyn Waugh's War Novels, Queen's
Quarterly (Spring 1958), 65:53-63

Vredenburgh, Joseph L., Further Contributions to a Study of
the Incest Object, American Imago (Fall 1959), 16:263-68

Wooton, Carl, Evelyn Waugh's "Brideshead Revisited": War
and Limited Hope, Midwest Quarterly (July 1969), 10:359-75

Decline and Fall, 1928

Doyle, P. A., "Decline and Fall": Two Versions, Evelyn
Waugh Newsletter (1967), 2:4-5

Eagleton, Terry, Exiles and Émigrés; Studies in Modern Literature. 1970. p. 42-50

Tysdahl, Björn, The Bright Young Things in the Early Novels
of Evelyn Waugh, Edda (1962), 62:326-34

The End of the Battle, 1961

O'Donovan, Patrick, Evelyn Waugh's Opus of Disgust, New
Mexico Quarterly (Feb. 12, 1962), 146:21-22

A Handful of Dust, 1934

Bergonzi, Bernard, Evelyn Waugh's Gentleman, Critical Quar-
Quarterly (1963), 5:23-36

Bergonzi, Bernard, The Situation of the Novel. 1970. p. 105-
08

Brophy, Brigid, Don't Never Forget; Collected Views and Re-
Reviews. 1967. p. 156-58

Eagleton, Terry, Exiles and Émigrés; Studies in Modern Literature. 1970. p. 53-57

Ellis, A. E., Hetton Revisited: "A Handful of Dust," Spectator
(March 20, 1964), p. 392-93

Green, Peter, Du Côté de Chez Waugh, Review of English Literature (April 1961), 2:89-100

Hall, James, The Tragic Comedians; Seven Modern British
Novelists. 1963. p. 45-65

Marković, Vida E., The Changing Face; Disintegration of
Personality in the Twentieth Century British Novel, 1900-
1950. 1970. p. 70-81

Wasson, Richard, "A Handful of Dust": Critique of Victorian-
ism, Modern Fiction Studies (Winter 1961), 7:327-37

Helena, 1950

Mooney, Harry J., Jr. and Thomas F. Staley, eds., The Shapeless God; Essays on Modern Fiction. 1968. p. 81-83

Men at Arms, 1952

Raven, Simon, Waugh's Private Wars, Spectator (June 12,
1964), #7094:798
Voorhees, Richard J., Evelyn Waugh's War Novels, Queen's
Quarterly (Spring 1958), 65:53-63

Officers and Gentlemen, 1955

Raven, Simon, Waugh's Private Wars, Spectator (June 12,
1964), #7094:798
Voorhees, Richard J., Evelyn Waugh's War Novels, Queen's
Quarterly (Spring 1958), 65:53-63

The Ordeal of Gilbert Pinfold, 1957

Mooney, Harry J., Jr. and Thomas F. Staley, eds., The Shapeless God; Essays on Modern Fiction. 1968. p. 83-85

Sword of Honor, 1952-61

Bergonzi, Bernard, The Situation of the Novel. 1970. p. 114-
18

Unconditional Surrender, 1961

Bergonzi, Bernard, Evelyn Waugh's Gentleman, Critical
Quarterly (1963), 5:23-36
Burrows, L. R., Scenes de la Vie Militaire, Westerly (1962),
#7:3-6
Engelborghs, M., Evelyn Waugh Besluit Zijn Trilogie, Kul-
tuurleven (Feb. 1962), 29:135-37
Raven, Simon, Waugh's Private Wars, Spectator (June 12,
1964), #7094:798

Vile Bodies, 1930

Eagleton, Terry, Exiles and Émigrés; Studies in Modern Lit-
erature. 1970. p. 50-53
Hall, James, The Tragic Comedians; Seven Modern British
Novelists. 1963. p. 45-65
Jervis, S. A., Evelyn Waugh, "Vile Bodies" and the Younger
Generation, South Atlantic Quarterly (Summer 1967), 66:
440-48

Linck, Charles E., Jr. and Robert M. Davis, The Bright
Young People in "Vile Bodies," Papers on Language and
Literature (1969), 5:80-90
Tysdahl, Björn, The Bright Young Things in the Early Novels
of Evelyn Waugh, Edda (1962), 62:326-34

MARY WEBB

Precious Bane, 1924

Sanders, Charles, Webb's "Precious Bane," Explicator (1966),
25:Item 10

HERBERT GEORGE WELLS

Ann Veronica; A Modern Love Story, 1909

Borrello, Alfred, H. G. Wells; Author in Agony. 1972. p.
47-49
Parrinder, Patrick, H. G. Wells. 1970. p. 91-94

First Men on the Moon, 1901

Borrello, Alfred, H. G. Wells; Author in Agony. 1972. p.
67-70
Hillegas, Mark, R., Cosmic Pessimism in H. G. Well's
Scientific Romances, Papers of the Michigan Academy of
Science, Arts and Letters (1961), 46:655-63

History of Mr. Polly, 1910

Borrello, Alfred, H. G. Wells; Author in Agony. 1972. p.
30-32
Parrinder, Patrick, H. G. Wells. 1970. p. 65-86
Ray, Gordon N., H. G. Wells Tries to Be a Novelist, English
Institute Essays (1959), p. 106-59

In the Days of the Comet, 1906

Borrello, Alfred, H. G. Wells; Author in Agony. 1972. p.
51-53

The Invisible Man, 1897

Borrello, Alfred, H. G. Wells; Author in Agony. 1972. p.
59-62
Hillegas, Mark R., Cosmic Pessimism in H. G. Wells'
Scientific Romances, Papers of the Michigan Academy of

Science, Arts and Letters (1961), 46:655-63
Parrinder, Patrick, H. G. Wells. 1970. p. 24-26

The Island of Dr. Moreau, 1896

Hillegas, Mark R., Cosmic Pessimism in H. G. Wells'
Scientific Romances, Papers of the Michigan Academy of
Science, Arts and Letters (1961), 46:655-63
Parrinder, Patrick, H. G. Wells. 1970. p. 26-28
Pritchett, Victor Sawdon, The Living Novel and Later Appre-
ciations. 1964. p. 160-69

Joan and Peter; The Story of an Education, 1918

Borrello, Alfred, H. G. Wells; Author in Agony. 1972. p.
36-39

Kipps; The Story of a Simple Soul, 1905

Ray, Gordon N., H. G. Wells Tries to Be a Novelist, English
Institute Essays (1959), p. 106-59
Wilson, H., Death of Masterman; A Repressed Episode in
H. G. Wells' "Kipps," Modern Language Association. Pub-
lications (Jan. 1971), 86:63-69

Love and Mr. Lewisham, 1900

Borrello, Alfred, H. G. Wells; Author in Agony. 1972. p.
21-23
Parrinder, Patrick, H. G. Wells. 1970. p. 50-52
Ray, Gordon N., H. G. Wells Tries to Be a Novelist, English
Institute Essays (1959), p. 106-59

Men Like Gods, 1923

Borrello, Alfred, H. G. Wells; Author in Agony. 1972. p.
84-88
Leeper, Geoffrey, The Happy Utopias of Aldous Huxley and
H. G. Wells, Meanjin (1965), 24:120-24

Mr. Blettsworthy on Rampole Island, 1928

Borrello, Alfred, H. G. Wells; Author in Agony. 1972. p.
95-99

The Passionate Friends, 1913

Borrello, Alfred, H. G. Wells; Author in Agony. 1972. p.
44-46

The Time Machine; An Invention, 1895

> Bergonzi, Bernard, The Publication of "The Time Machine":
> 1894–95, Review of English Studies (1960), 11:42–51
> Bergonzi, Bernard, "The Time Machine": An Ironic Myth,
> Critical Quarterly (Winter 1960), 2:293–305
> Borrello, Alfred, H. G. Wells; Author in Agony. 1972. p.
> 9–12
> Hillegas, Mark R., Cosmic Pessimism in H. G. Wells'
> Scientific Romances, Papers of the Michigan Academy of
> Science, Arts and Letters (1961), 46:655–63
> Parrinder, Patrick, H. G. Wells. 1970. p. 16–23
> Philmus, Robert M., "The Time Machine": Or, Fourth Dimen-
> sion as Prophecy, Modern Language Association. Publica-
> tions (May 1969), 84:530–35

Tono-Bungay, 1909

> Borrello, Alfred, H. G. Wells; Author in Agony. 1972. p.
> 23–28
> Costa, Richard H., H. G. Wells' "Tono-Bungay": Review of
> New Studies, English Literature in Transition (1880–1920)
> (1967), 10:89–96
> Lodge, David, Language of Fiction; Essays in Criticism and
> Verbal Analysis of the English Novel. 1966. p. 214–42
> Newell, Kenneth B., The Structure of H. G. Wells' "Tono-
> Bungay," English Literature in Transition (1880–1920)
> (1961), 4:1–8
> Parrinder, Patrick, H. G. Wells. 1970. p. 65–86
> Poston, Lawrence III, "Tono-Bungay": Wells' Unconstructed
> Tale, College English (March 1965), 26:433–38
> Ray, Gordon N., H. G. Wells Tries to Be a Novelist, English
> Institute Essays (1959), p. 106–59

The War of the Worlds, 1898

> Hillegas, Mark R., Cosmic Pessimism in H. G. Wells'
> Scientific Romances, Papers of the Michigan Academy of
> Science, Arts and Letters (1961), 46:655–63
> Hughes, David Y., "The War of the Worlds" in the Yellow
> Press, Journalism Quarterly (1966), 43:639–46
> Parrinder, Patrick, H. G. Wells. 1970. p. 28–33
> Solomon, Eric, Prophetic War Novels, Notes and Queries
> (Jan. 1959), 6:36–37

When the Sleeper Awakes, 1899

   Borrello, Alfred, H. G. Wells; Author in Agony. 1972. p.
   88–90

The Wonderful Visit, 1895

   Borrello, Alfred, H. G. Wells; Author in Agony. 1972. p.
   61–64

WILLIAM HALE WHITE

Autobiography of Mark Rutherford, 1881

   Davies, Horton, A Mirror of the Ministry in Modern Novels.
   1959. p. 51–78

Clara Hopgood, 1896

   Thomson, Patricia, The Novels of Mark Rutherford, Essays
   in Criticism (1964), 14:256–67

Revolution in Tanner's Lane, 1887

   Rayson, R. J., Is "Revolution in Tanner's Lane" Broken-
   Backed?, Essays in Criticism (Jan. 1970), 20:71–80

OSCAR WILDE

The Picture of Dorian Gray, 1891

   Baker, H. A., Jr., Tragedy of the Artist; "The Picture of
   Dorian Gray," Nineteenth Century Fiction (Dec. 1969), 24:
   349–55
   Beebe, Maurice, Ivory Towers and Sacred Founts; The Artist
   as Hero in Fiction from Goethe to Joyce. 1964. p. 114–71
   Brown, Robert D., Suetonius, Symonds and Gibbon in "The
   Picture of Dorian Gray," Modern Language Notes (April
   1956), 71:264
   Goetsch, Paul, Bemerkungen zur Urfassung von Wildes "The
   Picture of Dorian Gray," Die Neueren Sprachen (1966), 15:
   324–32
   Gordon, Jan B., Hebraism, Hellenism and "The Picture of
   Dorian Gray," Victorian Newsletter (Spring 1968), 33:36–38
   Gordon, Jan B., "Parody as Initiation": The Sad Education of
   Dorian Gray, Criticism (1967), 9:355–71

Nickerson, C. C., Vivian Grey and Dorian Gray, Times Literary Supplement (Aug. 14, 1969), 68:909

Poteet, L. J., Dorian Gray and the Gothic Novel, Modern Fiction Studies (Summer 1971), 17:239–48

Saagpakk, Paul F., Psychological Elements in British Novels from 1890–1930, Dissertation Abstracts (1966), 27:782A

Spivey, Ted R., Damnation and Salvation in "The Picture of Dorian Gray," Boston University Studies in English (Autumn 1960), 4:162–70

JOHN ANTHONY BURGESS WILSON

SEE

ANTHONY BURGESS

ANGUS WILSON

Anglo-Saxon Attitudes, 1956

Halio, Jay L., The Novels of Angus Wilson, Modern Fiction Studies (Summer 1962), 8:171–81

Scott-Kilvert, Ian, Angus Wilson, Review of English Literature (April 1960), 1:42–53

Hemlock and After, 1952

Cockshut, A. O. J., Favored Sons; The Moral World of Angus Wilson, Essays in Criticism (Jan. 1959), 9:50–60

Cox, C. B., The Humanism of Angus Wilson: A Study of "Hemlock and After," Critical Quarterly (Autumn 1961), 3:227–37

Halio, Jay L., The Novels of Angus Wilson, Modern Fiction Studies (Summer 1962), 8:171–81

Scott-Kilvert, Ian, Angus Wilson, Review of English Literature (April 1960), 1:42–53

Late Call, 1964

Bergonzi, Bernard, The Situation of the Novel. 1970. p. 157–59

Burgess, Anthony, Powers that Be, Encounter (Jan. 1965), 24:71–76

Shaw, Valerie A., "The Middle Age of Mrs. Eliot" and "Late Call": Angus Wilson's Traditionalism, Critical Quarterly

(Spring 1970), 12:9−27
T. L. S., Essays and Reviews from The Times Literary Supplement, 1964. 1965. Vol. 3. p. 103−05

The Middle Age of Mrs. Eliot, 1958

Halio, Jay L., The Novels of Angus Wilson, Modern Fiction
Studies (Summer 1962), 8:171−81
Kermode, John Frank, Puzzles and Epiphanies; Essays and
Reviews, 1958−1961. 1962. p. 193−97
Meg Eliot Surprised, Times Literary Supplement (Nov. 21,
1958), p. 672
Oppel, Horst, ed., Der Moderne Englische Roman; Interpre-
tationen. 1965. p. 359−73
Scott-Kilvert, Ian, Angus Wilson, Review of English Litera-
ture (April 1960), 1:42−53
Shaw, Valerie A., "The Middle Age of Mrs. Eliot" and "Late
Call": Angus Wilson's Traditionalism, Critical Quarterly
(Spring 1970), 12:9−27

No Laughing Matter, 1967

Bergonzi, Bernard, The Situation of the Novel. 1970. p.
159−61
Gillie, Christopher, The Shape of Modern Fiction; Angus
Wilson's "No Laughing Matter," Delta (June 1968), #43:18−
23
Servotte, Herman, Experiment en Traditie: Angus Wilson's
"No Laughing Matter," Dietsche Warande en Belfort (1968),
113:324−35
Servotte, Herman, A Note on the Formal Characteristics of
Angus Wilson's "No Laughing Matter," English Studies
(Feb. 1969), 50:58−64
T. L. S., Essays and Reviews from The Times Literary Sup-
plement, 1967. 1968. Vol. 6. p. 201−04

The Old Men at the Zoo, 1961

Lindberg, Margaret, Angus Wilson: "The Old Men at the Zoo"
as Allegory, Iowa English Yearbook (Fall 1969), #14:44−48
Pritchett, V. S., Bad-Hearted Britain, New Statesman and
Nation (Sept. 29, 1961), p. 429−30
Symons, Julian, Politics and the Novel, Twentieth Century
(Winter 1962), 170:147−54

VIRGINIA WOOLF

Between the Acts, 1941

Basham, C., Between the Acts, Durham University Journal
(1960), 21:87-94

Cowley, Malcolm, Think Back on Us; A Contemporary Chronicle of the Nineteen Thirties. 1967. p. 382-84

Fleishman, Avrom, The English Historical Novel; Walter
Scott to Virginia Woolf. 1971. p. 246-55

Francis, Hubert E., Jr., Virginia Woolf and "The Moment,"
Emory University Quarterly (Fall 1960), 16:139-51

Love, Jean O., Worlds in Consciousness; Mythopoetic Thought
in the Novels of Virginia Woolf. 1970. p. 222-37

Richter, Harvena, Virginia Woolf; The Inward Voyage. 1970.
p. 60-63, 159-61, 229-31, and 237-40

Summerhayes, Don, Society, Morality, Analogy; Virginia
Woolf's World "Between the Acts," Modern Fiction Studies
(1964), 9:329-37

Watkins, R., Survival in Discontinuity; Virginia Woolf's "Between the Acts," Massachusetts Review (Spring 1969), 10:
356-76

Jacob's Room, 1922

Briffault, Herma, Virginia Woolf y la Revolucion Novelistica,
Torre (July-Sept. 1963), 11:121-40

Gindin, James, Harvest of a Quiet Eye; The Novel of Compassion. 1971. p. 187-90

Love, Jean O., Worlds in Consciousness; Mythopoetic Thought
in the Novels of Virginia Woolf. 1970. p. 125-44

Richter, Harvena, Virginia Woolf; The Inward Voyage. 1970.
p. 83-86 and 107-10

Mrs. Dalloway, 1925

Beja, Morris, Matches Struck in the Dark; Virginia Woolf's
Moments of Vision, Critical Quarterly (1964), 6:137-52

Benjamin, A. S., Towards an Understanding of the Meaning of
Virginia Woolf's "Mrs. Dalloway," Wisconsin Studies in Contemporary Literature (Summer 1965), 6:214-27

Eagleton, Terry, Exiles and Émigrés; Studies in Modern Literature. 1970. p. 33-37

Fortin, René E., Sacramental Imagery in "Mrs. Dalloway,"
Renascence (Autumn 1965), 18:23-31

Francis, Herbert E., Jr., Virginia Woolf and "The Moment,"
Emory University Quarterly (Fall 1960), 16:139–51

Friedman, Norman, Criticism and the Novel; Hardy, Hemingway, Crane, Woolf, and Conrad, Antioch Review (Fall 1958),
18:343–70

Gamble, Isabel, The Secret Sharer in "Mrs. Dalloway,"
Accent (1956), 16:235–51

Garnett, David, Virginia Woolf, American Scholar (1965),
36:371–86

Gelfant, Blanche, Love and Conversion in "Mrs. Dalloway,"
Criticism (1966), 8:229–45

Gindin, James, Harvest of a Quiet Eye; The Novel of Compassion. 1971. p. 192–99 and 201–03

Harper, Howard M., Jr. and Charles Edge, eds., The Classic
British Novel. 1972. p. 220–37

Hoffmann, C. G., From Short Story to Novel; The Manuscript
Revisions of Virginia Woolf's "Mrs. Dalloway," Modern
Fiction Studies (Summer 1968), 14:171–86

Hoffmann, C. G., Real Mrs. Dalloway, University of Kansas
City Review (March 1956), 22:204–08

Hungerford, Edward A., My Tunneling Process; The Method
of Mrs. Dalloway, Modern Fiction Studies (1957), 3:164–67

Karl, Frederick R. and Marvin Magalaner, A Reader's Guide
to Great Twentieth Century English Novels. 1959. p. 128–49

Latham, Jacqueline, The Origins of "Mrs. Dalloway," Notes
and Queries (March 1966), 13:98–99

Latham, Jacqueline, Thessaly and the Colossal Figure in
"Mrs. Dalloway," Notes and Queries (July 1969), 16:263–65

Lewis, A. J., From the Hours to "Mrs. Dalloway," British
Museum Quarterly (1964), 28:15–18

Love, Jean O., Worlds in Consciousness; Mythopoetic Thought
in the Novels of Virginia Woolf. 1970. p. 145–60

Marković, Vida E., The Changing Face; Disintegration of Personality in the Twentieth Century British Novel, 1900–1950.
1970. p. 54–69

Millach, Francis L., Thematic and Structural Unity of "Mrs.
Dalloway," Thoth (Winter 1964), 5:62–73

Moody, A. A., The Unmasking of Clarissa Dalloway, Review
of English Literature (Jan. 1962), 3:67–79

Oppel, Horst, ed., Der Moderne Englische Roman. Interpretationen. 1965. p. 160–200

Page, Alex, A Dangerous Day; Mrs. Dalloway Discovers Her
Double, Modern Fiction Studies (Summer 1961), 7:115–24

Richter, Harvena, Virginia Woolf; The Inward Voyage. 1970.
    p. 51–58, 118–21, 139–42, 190–92, and 217–19
Roll-Hansen, Diderik, Peter Walsh's Seven League Boots: A
    Note on "Mrs. Dalloway," English Studies (1969), 50:301–04
Rosenberg, S., Match in the Crocus; Obtrusive Art in Virginia
    Woolf's "Mrs. Dalloway," Modern Fiction Studies (Summer
    1967), 13:211–20
Saagpakk, Paul F., Psychological Elements in British Novels
    from 1890–1930, Dissertation Abstracts (1966), 27:782A
Samuelson, Ralph, The Theme of "Mrs. Dalloway," Chicago
    Review (Winter 1958), 11:57–76
Schoff, Francis G., Mrs. Dalloway and Mrs. Ramsay, Iowa
    English Yearbook (1964), 9:54–60
The Shaken Realist; Essays in Modern Literature in Honor of
    Frederick J. Hoffman; ed. by Melvin J. Friedman and John
    B. Vickery. 1970. p. 100–27
Simon, Irene, Some Aspects of Virginia Woolf's Imagery,
    English Studies (June 1960), 41:180–96
Wallace, A. Doyle and Woodburn O. Ross, eds., Studies in
    Honor of John Wilcox by Members of the English Depart-
    ment, Wayne State University. 1958. p. 239–50
Weber, Robert W., Die Glocken von Big Ben. Zur Struktur-
    funktion der Uhrzeit in "Mrs. Dalloway," Deutsche Viertel-
    jahrsschrift für Literaturwissenschaft und Geistesgeschichte
    (June 1965), 39:246–58

Night and Day, 1919

Love, Jean O., Worlds in Consciousness; Mythopoetic Thought
    in the Novels of Virginia Woolf. 1970. p. 107–24

Orlando, 1928

Bowen, Elizabeth, Seven Winters; Memories of a Dublin Child-
    hood and After-Thoughts; Pieces on Writing. 1962. p. 130–39
Fleishman, Avrom, The English Historical Novel; Walter
    Scott to Virginia Woolf. 1971. p. 237–45
German, Howard and Sharon Kaehele, The Dialectic of Time
    in "Orlando," College English (1962), 24:35–41
Graham, John, The Caricature Value of Parody and Fantasy
    in "Orlando," University of Toronto Quarterly (July 1961),
    30:345–66
Hoffmann, Charles G., Fact and Fantasy in "Orlando": Vir-
    ginia Woolf's Manuscript Revisions, Texas Studies in Lit-
    erature and Language (1968), 10:435–44

McIntyre, Clara F., Is Virginia Woolf a Feminist?, Person-
alist (April 1960), 41:176-84
Miller, Walter James and Dorothy Dinnerstein, Woolf's
"Orlando," Explicator (March 1961), 19:Item 37
Richter, Harvena, Virginia Woolf; The Inward Voyage. 1970.
p. 72-74, 85-87, 115-17, 150-60, and 189-93
Samuelson, Ralph, Virginia Woolf: "Orlando" and the Femi-
nist Spirit, Western Humanities Review (1961), 15:51-58

A Room of One's Own, 1929

McIntyre, Clara F., Is Virginia Woolf a Feminist?, Personalist (April 1960), 41:176-84

Three Guineas, 1938

McIntyre, Clara F., Is Virginia Woolf a Feminist?, Personalist (April 1960), 41:176-84

To the Lighthouse, 1927

Baldanza, Frank, "To the Lighthouse" Again, Modern Lan-
guage Association. Publications (June 1955), 70:548-52
Beja, Morris, Matches Struck in the Dark; Virginia Woolf's
Moments of Vision, Critical Quarterly (1964), 6:137-52
Brogan, Howard O., Science and Narrative Structure in
Austen, Hardy and Woolf, Nineteenth Century Fiction (March
1957), 11:276-87
Cohn, Ruby, Art in "To the Lighthouse," Modern Fiction
Studies (Summer 1962), 8:127-36
Drew, Elizabeth A., The Novel; A Modern Guide to Fifteen
English Masterpieces. 1963. p. 262-79
Francis, Herbert E., Jr., Virginia Woolf and "The Moment,"
Emory University Quarterly (Fall 1960), 16:139-51
Fromm, Harold, "To the Lighthouse": Music and Sympathy,
English Miscellany (1968), 19:181-95
Gindin, James, Harvest of a Quiet Eye; The Novel of Com-
passion. 1971. p. 182-85 and 197-203
Hashmi, Shahnaz, Indirect Style in "To the Lighthouse," Indian
Journal of English Studies (1961), 2:112-20
Kaehele, Sharon and Howard German, "To the Lighthouse":
Symbol and Vision, Bucknell Review (May 1962), 10:328-46
Karl, Frederick R. and Marvin Magalaner, eds., A Reader's
Guide to Great Twentieth Century English Novels. 1959.
p. 128-49
Liberto, Sarah, The "Perpetual Pageant" of Art and Life in

"To the Lighthouse," Descant (Winter 1965), 9:35-43

Love, Jean O., Worlds in Consciousness; Mythopoetic Thought in the Novels of Virginia Woolf. 1970. p. 161-79 and 180-94

Maekawa Shunichi Kyōju Kanreki Kinen-Ronbunshū. (Essays and Studies in Commemoration of Professor Shunichi Maekawa's Sixty-First Birthday.) 1968. p. 53-64

May, Keith M., The Symbol of Painting in Virginia Woolf's "To the Lighthouse," Review of English Literature (April 1971), 8:91-98

Osgerby, J. R., Virginia Woolf's "To the Lighthouse," Use of English (Winter 1963), 15:116-24

Pedersen, Glenn Malvern, Vision in "To the Lighthouse," Modern Language Association. Publications (Dec. 1958), 73:585-600

Perez Gallego, Candido, "To the Lighthouse" y la Estructura de las Novelas de Virginia Woolf, Filologia Moderna (1967), 6:115-31

Proudfit, S. W., Lily Briscoe's Painting; A Key to Personal Relationships in "To the Lighthouse," Criticism (Winter 1971), 13:26-38

Richter, Harvena, Virginia Woolf; The Inward Voyage. 1970. p. 66-68, 70-76, 164-67, 180-87, 211-15, and 219-26

Schoff, Francis G., Mrs. Dalloway and Mrs. Ramsay, Iowa English Yearbook (1964), 9:54-60

Schorer, Mark, ed., Modern British Fiction. 1961. p. 391-417

Simon, Irene, Some Aspects of Virginia Woolf's Imagery, English Studies (June 1960), 41:180-96

Vickery, John B., ed., Myth and Literature; Contemporary Theory and Practice. 1966. p. 243-55

Warner, John M., Symbolic Patterns of Retreat and Reconciliation in "To the Lighthouse," Discourse (1969), 12:376-92

Voyage Out, 1915

Love, Jean O., Worlds in Consciousness; Mythopoetic Thought in the Novels of Virginia Woolf. 1970. p. 86-106

Richter, Harvena, Virginia Woolf; The Inward Voyage. 1970. p. 24-26, 92-98, and 123-25

The Waves, 1931

DeRigo, Giorgio, "The Waves" (Le Onde) di Virginia Woolf, Letteràture Moderne (1962), 12:167-81

Francis, Herbert E., Jr., Virginia Woolf and "The Moment,"

Emory University Quarterly (Fall 1960), 16:139–51

Gindin, James, Harvest of a Quiet Eye; The Novel of Compassion. 1971. p. 199–203

Hampshire, Stuart N., Modern Writers and Other Essays.
1970. p. 38–46

Karl, Frederick R. and Marvin Magalaner, eds., A Reader's
Guide to Great Twentieth Century English Novels. 1959.
p. 128–49

King, M. P., Androgynous Mind and "The Waves," University
Review (March 1964), 30:221–24

Love, Jean O., Worlds in Consciousness; Mythopoetic Thought
in the Novels of Virginia Woolf. 1970. p. 195–221

McConnell, Frank D., "Death Among the Apple Trees": "The
Waves" and the World of Things, Bucknell Review (1968),
16:23–39

Payne, Michael, The Eclipse of Order; The Ironic Structure
of "The Waves," Modern Fiction Studies (Summer 1969),
15:209–18

Rantavaara, Irma, Ing-Forms in the Service of Rhythm and
Style in Virginia Woolf's "The Waves," Neuphilologische
Mitteilungen (1960), 61:79–97

Richter, Harvena, Virginia Woolf; The Inward Voyage. 1970.
p. 58–60, 89–92, 100–02, 113–15, 120–22, 125–28, 132–36,
144–46, 164–72, and 194–99

The Years, 1937

Hoffmann, Charles G., Virginia Woolf's Manuscript Revisions
of "The Years," Modern Language Association. Publications
(Jan. 1969), 84:79–89

Marder, Herbert, Beyond the Lighthouse: "The Years," Bucknell Review (1967), 15:61–70

HENRY VINCENT YORK

SEE

HENRY GREEN

LIST OF BOOKS INDEXED

Abercrombie, Lascelles, Thomas Hardy; A Critical Study. London: Martin Secker. 1912.

Adams, Robert Martin, James Joyce; Common Sense and Beyond. New York: Random House. 1967.

Aiken, Conrad Potter, Reviewer's ABC: Collected Criticism of Conrad Aiken, from 1916 to the Present. New York: Meridian Books. 1958.

Aldington, Richard, Literary Studies and Reviews. New York: Dial. 1924.

Alldritt, Keith, The Visual Imagination of D. H. Lawrence. Evanston: Northwestern University Press. 1971.

Allen, Walter, The English Novel. London: Phoenix House. 1954.

———, Reading a Novel. London: Phoenix House. 1956.

Allott, Kenneth and Miriam Farris, The Art of Graham Greene. London: Hamish Hamilton. 1951.

Allsop, Kenneth, Angry Decade; A Survey of the Cultural Revolt of the 1950's. Elmsford, N. Y. 1959.

Alter, Robert, Rogue's Progress; Studies in the Picaresque Novel. (Harvard Studies in Comparative Literature, 26.) Cambridge, Mass.: Harvard University Press. 1964.

Altick, Richard, The Scholar Adventurers. New York: Macmillan. 1950.

Anderson, David, The Tragic Protest; A Christian Study of Some Modern Literature. Richmond, Va.: John Knox Press. 1970.

Anderson, Howard and John S. Shea, eds., Studies in Criticism and Aesthetics, 1660–1800: Essays in Honor of Samuel Holt Monk. Minneapolis: University of Minnesota Press. 1967.

Anderson, Margaret, ed., The Little Review Anthology. New York: Hermitage House. 1953.

Anderson, Warren D. and Thomas D. Clareson, eds., Victorian Essays; A Symposium; Essays on the Occasion of the Centennial of the College of Wooster in Honor of Emeritus Professor Waldo H. Dunn. Kent, Ohio: Kent State University Press. 1967.

Andreach, Robert J., Studies in Structure; The Stages of the Spiritual Life in Four Modern Authors. New York: Fordham University Press. 1964.

Andreas, Osborne, Joseph Conrad; A Study in Non-Conformity. New York: Philosophical Library. 1959.

Arnold, Armin, James Joyce. Berlin: Colloquium Verlag. 1963.

Atlantic Monthly, Jubilee: One Hundred Years of the "Atlantic."
    Selected and edited by Edward Weeks and Emily Flint.
    Boston, Mass.: Little, Brown and Co. 1957.
Auden, Wystan Hugh, The Dyer's Hand and Other Essays. New
    York: Random House. 1962.
Auster, Henry, Local Habitations; Regionalism in the Early
    Novels of George Eliot. Cambridge, Mass.: Harvard Uni-
    versity Press. 1970.
Babb, Howard S., The Novels of William Golding. Columbus,
    Ohio: Ohio State University Press. 1970.
Baines, Jocelyn, Joseph Conrad: A Critical Biography. New
    York: McGraw-Hill Pub. Co. 1960.
Bajarlia, Juan Jacobo, Literatura de Vanguardia—Del "Ulysses"
    de Joyce y las Escuelas Poeticas. Buenos Aires: Collec-
    tión Universal. 1946.
Baker, Ernest A., The History of the English Novel. Vol. 9.
    London: Witherly. 1938.
Bancroft, William Wallace, Joseph Conrad: His Philosophy of
    Life. Philadelphia: University of Pennsylvania Press.
    1931.
Barnard, G. C., Samuel Beckett; A New Approach. London:
    Dent. 1970.
Barzun, Jacques, Energies of Art; Studies of Authors, Classic
    and Modern. New York: Harper and Row. 1956
Beach, Joseph Warren, The Twentieth Century Novel: Studies in
    Technique. New York: Appleton-Century Crofts Co. 1932.
Beebe, Maurice, Ivory Towers and Sacred Founts; The Artist as
    Hero in Fiction from Goethe to Joyce. New York: New
    York University Press. 1964.
Beer, Gillian, Meredith; A Change of Masks; A Study of the
    Novels. London: University Press. 1970.
Bendz, Ernst, Joseph Conrad; An Appreciation. Gothenburg:
    N. J. Grumpert. 1923.
Bentley, Eric, A Century of Hero Worship. New York: Lippin-
    cott Pub. Co. 1944.
_____, ed., The Importance of Scrutiny. New York: George
    Stewart. 1948.
Bergonzi, Bernard, Heroes' Twilight; A Study of the Literature
    of the Great War. New York: Coward-McCann, Inc. 1966.
_____, The Situation of the Novel. London: Macmillan Co. 1970.
Bersani, Leo, Balzac to Beckett; Center and Circumference in
    French Fiction. New York: Oxford University Press.
    1970.

Berthoff, Warner, Fictions and Events; Essays in Criticism and
    Literary History. New York: Dutton Pub. Co. 1971.
Blackmur, Richard Palmer, Eleven Essays in the European
    Novel. New York: Harcourt, Brace, and Janovich. 1964.
    _____, A Primer of Ignorance. New York: Harcourt, Brace and
    Janovich. 1967.
Blunden, Edmund, Thomas Hardy. London: Macmillan Co. 1942.
Bogan, Louise, Selected Criticism; Prose, Poetry. New York:
    Noonday Press. 1955
Böckmann, Paul, ed., Stil-und Formprobleme in der Literatur.
    Heidelberg: Carl Winter. 1959.
Booth, Wayne, The Rhetoric of Fiction. Chicago: University of
    Chicago Press. 1961.
Borges, Jorge Luis, Other Inquisitions, 1937-1952. Austin:
    University of Texas Press. 1964.
Borrello, Alfred, H. G. Wells; Author in Agony. Carbondale:
    Illinois University Press. 1972.
Bowen, Elizabeth, Seven Winters; Memories of a Dublin Child-
    hood and After-Thoughts; Pieces on Writing. New York:
    Alfred A. Knopf. 1962.
Bradbrook, M. C., Joseph Conrad: Poland's English Genius.
    New York: Cambridge University Press. 1942.
Braybrooke, Patrick, Thomas Hardy and His Philosophy. Lon-
    don: C. W. Daniel. 1924
Brissenden, R. F., ed., Studies in the Eighteenth Century; Papers
    Presented at the David Nichol Smith Memorial Seminar,
    Canberra, 1966. Canberra: Australian National University
    Press. 1968.
Brooks, Gilbert Benjamin, Crescent and Green; A Miscellany of
    Writings on Pakistan. London: Cassell Pub. Co. 1955.
Brooks, Jean R., Thomas Hardy; The Poetic Structure. Ithaca:
    Cornell University Press. 1971.
Brophy, Brigid, Don't Never Forget; Collected Views and Re-
    Reviews. New York: Holt, Rinehard, and Winston, Inc.
    1967.
Brower, Reuben Arthur and William Richard Poirrier, eds., In
    Defense of Reading; A Reader's Approach to Literary Crit-
    icism. New York: E. P. Dutton and Co., Inc. 1962.
Brown, Douglas, Thomas Hardy. London: Longmans, Green and
    Co. 1954.
Brown, E. K., Rhythm in the Novel. Toronto: University of
    Toronto Press. 1950.
Brown, Francis, ed., Highlights of Modern Literature. New York:

New American Library. 1954.
Browne, Ray Broadus, William John Roscelli and Richard J.
    Loftus, eds., The Celtic Cross; Studies in Irish Culture
    and Literature. Lafayette, Ind.: Purdue University Press.
    1964.
Bullett, Gerald, Modern English Fiction. London: Jenkins Pub.
    Co. 1926.
Burgess, Anthony, Re Joyce. New York: W. W. Norton and Co.
    1965.
Burgum, Edwin Berry, The Novel and the World's Dilemma.
    New York: Oxford University Press. 1947.
Burke, Kenneth, Language as Symbolic Action; Essays on Life,
    Literature and Method. Los Angeles: University of Cali-
    fornia Press. 1966.
Bush, Douglas, Engaged and Disengaged. Cambridge, Mass.:
    Harvard University Press. 1966.
Butt, John, ed., Of Books and Humankind; Essays and Poems
    Presented to Bonamy Dobrée. London: Routledge and
    Kegan Paul. 1964.
Byatt, A. S., Degrees of Freedom; The Novels of Iris Murdoch.
    London: Chatto and Windus. 1965.
Camden, Charles Carroll, ed., Restoration and Eighteenth Cen-
    tury Literature; Essays in Honor of Alan Dugald McKillop.
    Chicago, Ill.: University of Chicago Press. 1963.
Canby, Henry Seidel, Definitions; Essays in Contemporary Criti-
    cism. New York: Harcourt, Brace, and Janovich. 1924.
Carroll, David, ed., George Eliot; The Critical Heritage. New
    York: Barnes and Noble. 1971.
Cary, Joyce, Art and Reality; Ways of the Creative Process.
    New York: Harper and Row. 1958
Cecil, Lord David, Fine Art of Reading; And Other Literary
    Studies. Indianapolis: Bobbs-Merrill Co. 1957.
_____, Poets and Storytellers. New York: Macmillan Co. 1949.
_____, Victorian Novelists; Essays in Revaluation. Chicago:
    University of Chicago Press. 1958.
Charles Dickens, 1812-1870; A Centennial Volume; ed. by
    E. W. F. Tomlin. New York: Simon and Schuster. 1969.
Charques, R. D., Contemporary Literature and Social Revolution.
    London: Secker Pub. Co. 1933.
Chesterton, Gilbert Keith, The Spice of Life and Other Essays.
    Chester Springs, Penn.: Dufour Editions, Inc. 1966.
Chew, Samuel C., Thomas Hardy; Poet and Novelist. New York:
    Alfred A. Knopf, Inc. 1928.

Child, Harold H., Essays and Reflections. New York: Cambridge University Press. 1948.

Churchill, Reginald Charles, The Powys Brothers. London: Longsman Green Co. 1962.

Clifford, James Lowry, ed., Eighteenth Century English Literature; Modern Essays in Criticism. New York: Oxford University Press. 1959.

Cohen, Morton, Rider Haggard; His Life and Works. London: Hutchinson Pub. Co. 1960.

Colby, Robert Alan, Fiction with a Purpose; Major and Minor Nineteenth Century Novels. Bloomington: Indiana University Press. 1967.

Coleridge, Samuel Taylor, Coleridge on the Seventeenth Century. Durham, N. C.: Duke University Press. 1955.

Collins, Joseph, The Doctor Looks at Literature. New York: George H. Doran. 1923.

Connolly, Thomas Edmund, Joyce's "Portrait"; Criticisms and Critiques. New York: Appleton-Century-Crofts. 1962.

Cook, Albert, The Dark Voyage and the Golden Mean; A Philosophy of Comedy. Cambridge, Mass.: Harvard University Press. 1949.

_____, The Meaning of Fiction. Detroit, Mich.: Wayne State University Press. 1960.

Cowley, Malcolm, Think Back on Us; A Contemporary Chronicle of the 1930's. Carbondale: Southern Illinois University Press. 1967.

Cox, R. G., ed., Thomas Hardy; The Critical Heritage. New York: Barnes and Noble. 1970.

Craik, W. A., The Brontë Novels. London: Methuen. 1968.

Crane, Ronald Simon, The Idea of the Humanities and Other Essays Critical and Historical. Chicago: University of Chicago Press. 1967.

Crankshaw, Edward, Joseph Conrad; Some Aspects of the Art of the Novel. London: John Lane. 1936.

Crews, Frederick, ed., Psychoanalysis and Literary Process. Cambridge; Winthrop Pub. Co. 1970.

Cronin, Anthony, A Question of Modernity. London: Secker and Warburg. 1966.

Cunliffe, J. W., English Literature in the Twentieth Century. New York: Macmillan Co. 1933.

Curle, Richard, Joseph Conrad and His Characters. London: Heinemann. 1957.

Curran, Constantine, James Joyce Remembered. New York:

Oxford University Press. 1968.

Daiches, David, The Novel and the Modern World. Rev. ed.
Chicago: University of Chicago Press. 1960.

_____, The Novel and the Modern World. Chicago: University
of Chicago Press. 1964. (Paperback)

Davenport, William Henry, ed., Voices in Court; A Treasury of
the Bench, the Bar and the Courtroom. New York: Macmillan Co. 1958

Davidson, Donald, The Spyglass; Views and Reviews, 1924-1930.
Nashville, Tenn.: Vanderbilt University Press. 1963.

_____, Still Rebels; Still Yankees, and Other Essays. Baton
Rouge, La.: Louisiana State University Press. 1957.

Davies, Horton, A Mirror of the Ministry in Modern Novels.
New York: Oxford University Press. 1959.

Dawson, Carl, His Fine Wit; A Study of Thomas Love Peacock.
Berkeley; University of California Press. 1970.

Deutscher, Isaac, Russia in Transition and Other Essays. New
York: Coward-McCann Inc. 1957.

The Dial, A Dial Miscellany; ed. by William Wasserstrom.
Syracuse, New York: Syracuse University Press. 1963.

Dobree, Bonamy, The Lamp and the Lute; Studies in Six Modern
Authors. London: Clarendon Press. 1929.

_____, Modern Prose Style. London: Oxford University Press.
1934.

Dolezel, Lubomir and Richard W. Bailey, eds., Statistics and
Style. New York: American Elsevier Pub. Co. 1969.

Dowden, Wilfred S., Joseph Conrad; the Imaged Style. Nashville,
Tenn.: Vanderbilt University Press. 1970.

Downs, Robert Bingham, Molders of the Modern Mind; One Hundred Eleven Books that Shaped Western Civilization. New
York: Barnes and Noble. 1961.

_____, ed., First Freedom; Liberty and Justice in the World of
Books and Reading. Chicago: American Library Association. 1960.

Draper, R. P., ed., D. H. Lawrence; The Critical Heritage.
London: Routledge and Kegan Paul. 1970.

Drew, Elizabeth A., The Novel; A Modern Guide to Fifteen English Masterpieces. New York: W. W. Norton and Co.
1963.

D'Souza, Frank and Jagdish Shivpuri, eds., Siddha III. Bombay:
Siddharth College of Arts and Science. 1968.

Duckworth, Alistair M., The Improvement of the Estate; A Study
of Jane Austen's Novels. Baltimore: Johns Hopkins Uni-

versity Press. 1971.

Dyson, Anthony Edward, The Crazy Fabric; Essays in Irony.
New York: St. Martin's Press, Inc. 1965.

_____, The Inimitable Dickens; A Reading of the Novels. London:
Macmillan Co. 1970.

Eagleton, Terry, Exiles and Émigrés; Studies in Modern Literature. New York: Schocken Books, Inc. 1970.

East, Sara Toll, ed., Law in American Society. New York: H. W.
Wilson Co. 1964.

Eco, Umberto, Diario Minimo. Milan: Mondadori. 1963.

_____, Le Poetiche di Joyce: Dalla "Summa" al "Finnegan's
Wake." Milan: Bompiana Co. 1966.

Edgar, Pelham, The Art of the Novel. New York: Macmillan Co.
1933.

Egoff, Sheila, G. T. Stubbs and L. F. Ashley, eds., Only Connect;
Readings on Children's Literature. New York: Oxford
University Press. 1969.

Eliot, George, pseud., Essays; ed. by Thomas Pinney. New York:
Columbia University Press. 1963.

Ellis, Havelock, From Marlowe to Shaw; The Studies, 1876–1936
in English Literature. London: Williams and Norgate.
1950.

Ellmann, Richard, ed., Edwardian and Late Victorians: English
Institute Essays, 1959. New York: Columbia University
Press. 1960.

Enck, John Jacob, Elizabeth T. Forter and Alvin Whitley, eds.,
The Comic in Theory and Practice. New York: Appleton-
Century-Crofts. 1960.

Encounter, Encounters; An Anthology from the First Ten Years
of "Encounter" Magazine. New York: Basic Books. 1963.

English Association. Essays and Studies. New York: Transat-
lantic Press. 1958.

_____, Essays and Studies. New York: Humanities Press. 1966.

Enright, Dennis Joseph, Conspirators and Poets. Chester
Springs, Penna.: Dufour Eds., Inc. 1966.

Evans, B. Ifor, English Literature Between the Wars. London:
Methuen. 1949.

Evans, Joan, ed., The Flowering of the Middle Ages. New York:
McGraw-Hill Book Co. 1966.

Evans, Robert O., ed., Graham Greene; Some Critical Considerations. Lexington: University of Kentucky Press. 1963.

Fadiman, Clifton, Party of One; The Selected Writings of Clifton
Fadiman. New York: World Pub. Co. 1955.

Feibleman, James K., In Praise of Comedy. London, Allen and
 Unwin. 1939.
Feldman, Gene and Max Gartenberg, eds., Beat Generation and
 the Angry Young Men. New York: Citadel Press, Inc.
 1958.
Fiedler, Leslie Aaron, ed., Art of the Essay. New York:
 Thomas Y. Crowell. 1958.
_____, Love and Death in the American Novel. New York: Cri-
 terion Books. 1960.
_____, Love and Death in the American Novel. Rev. ed. New
 York: Stein and Day. 1966.
Flanagan, Thomas James Bonner, Irish Novelists, 1800–1850.
 New York: Columbia University Press. 1959.
Fleishman, Avrom, The English Historical Novel; Walter Scott
 to Virginia Woolf. Baltimore, Md.: Johns Hopkins Univer-
 sity Press. 1971.
Fletcher, Ian, ed., Romantic Mythologies. London: Routledge
 and Kegan Paul. 1967.
Ford, Boris, ed., The Pelican Guide to English Literature.
 Baltimore: Penguin Books. 1958.
The Forties; Fiction, Poetry, Drama; ed. by Warren French.
 Deland, Fla.: Everett-Edwards, Inc. 1969.
Fowler, Alastair, ed., Silent Poetry; Essays in Numerological
 Analysis. New York: Barnes and Noble. 1970.
Fowlie, Wallace, Love in Literature; Studies in Symbolic Ex-
 pression. Bloomington: University of Indiana Press.
 1965.
Frank, Joseph, The Widening Gyre. New Brunswick, N. J.: Rut-
 gers University Press. 1963.
Freeman, John, The Moderns; Essays in Literary Criticism.
 London: Robert Scott. 1916.
Freeman, Mary, D. H. Lawrence; A Basic Study of His Ideas.
 Gainesville: University of Florida Press. 1955.
French, Warren, ed., The Forties; Fiction, Poetry, Drama.
 Deland, Fla.: Everett-Edwards, Inc. 1969.
Freund, Philip, How to Become a Literary Critic. New York:
 Beechhurst Press. 1940.
Friedman, Alan, The Turn of the Novel. New York: Oxford Uni-
 versity Press. 1966.
Frye, Northrop, Fables of Identity; Studies in Poetic Mythology.
 New York: Harcourt, Brace, and Janovich, Inc. 1963.
_____, ed., Sound and Poetry. New York: Columbia University
 Press. 1956.

Fuller, Edmund, Books with Men Behind Them. New York:
    Random House. 1962.
Gabrieli, Vittorio, ed., Friendship's Garland; Essays Presented
    to Mario Praz on His Seventieth Birthday. Rome: Edizioni
    di Storia e Letteratura. 1966.
Ganz, Margaret, Elizabeth Gaskell; The Artist in Conflict. New
    York: Twayne Pub., Inc. 1969.
Gardiner, Harold Charles, In All Conscience; Reflections on
    Books and Culture. Boston: Hanover House. 1959.
Garnett, Edward, Friday Nights. London: Cape. 1922.
Gass, William H., Fiction and the Figures of Life. New York:
    Alfred A. Knopf. 1971.
Gerin, Winifred, Anne Brontë. London: Thomas Nelson and
    Sons. 1959.
Gerlach-Nielsen, Merete, Hans Hertel and Morten Nøjgaard,
    eds., Romanproblemer. Theorier og Analyser; Festskrift
    til Hans Sørensen den 28. September 1968. Odense: Uni-
    versitetsfarlaget. 1968.
Gillie, Christopher, Character in English Literature. London:
    Chatto and Windus. 1965.
Gillon, Adam, The Eternal Solitary; A Study of Joseph Conrad.
    New York: Bookman Asso. 1960.
Gindin, James, Harvest of a Quiet Eye; The Novel of Compassion.
    Bloomington: Indiana University Press. 1971.
_____, Postwar British Fiction; New Accents and Attitudes.
    Berkeley: University of California Press. 1962.
Givens, Seon, ed., James Joyce; Two Decades of Criticism. New
    York: Vanguard Press, Inc. 1948.
Glicksberg, Charles I., The Self in Modern Literature. Univer-
    sity Park, Penna.: Pennsylvania State University Press.
    1963.
Godfrey, Denis, E. M. Forster's Other Kingdom. Edinburgh:
    Oliver and Boyd. 1968.
Goldberg, S. L., James Joyce. New York: Grove Press. 1962.
Goldfarb, Russell Marshall, Sexual Repression and Victorian
    Literature. Lewisburg: Bucknell University Press. 1970.
Golding, Louis, James Joyce. London: Thornton Butterworth,
    Ltd. 1933.
Golding, William Gerald, ed., The Hot Gates and Other Occasional
    Pieces. New York: Harcourt, Brace, and Janovich, Inc.
    1966.
Goldman, Arnold, James Joyce. London: Routledge and Kegan
    Paul. 1968.

_____, The Joyce Paradox; Form and Freedom in His Fiction.
Evanston: Northwestern University Press. 1966.

Goldring, Douglas, South Lodge; Reminiscences of Violet Hunt,
Ford Madox Ford and "The English Review" Circle. London: Constable. 1943.

Gooneratne, Yasmine, Jane Austen. New York: Cambridge University Press. 1970.

Gordan, John D., Joseph Conrad; The Making of a Novelist.
Cambridge, Mass.: Harvard University Press. 1940.

Gorman, Herbert, James Joyce; His First Forty Years. New
York: Huebsch Pub. 1924.

Gould, Gerald, The English Novel Today. London: Castle. 1924.

Grebstein, Sheldon Norman, ed., Perspectives in Contemporary
Criticism; A Collection of Recent Essays by American,
English and European Literary Critics. New York: Harper
and Row. 1968.

Greene, Graham, Collected Essays. New York: Viking Press.
1969.

Gregory, Horace, D. H. Lawrence: Pilgrim of the Apocalypse.
New York: Grove Press. 1957.

Grimsditch, Herbert B., Character and Environment in the Novels
of Thomas Hardy. London: Witherby. 1925.

Grossvogel, David I., Limits of the Novel; Evaluations of a Form
from Chaucer to Robbe Grillet. Ithaca, N. Y.: Cornell
University Press. 1968.

Guerard, Albert J., Conrad the Novelist. Cambridge, Mass.:
Harvard University Press. 1958.

_____, Thomas Hardy; The Novels and Stories. Cambridge,
Mass.: Harvard University Press. 1949.

Guetti, James L., Jr., The Rhetoric of Joseph Conrad; Amherst
Honors Theses #2. Amherst, Mass.: Amherst College
Press. 1960.

Guidi, Augusto, Il Primo Joyce. Rome: Edizioni di Storia e
Letteratura. 1954.

Gurko, Leo, Joseph Conrad; Giant in Exile. New York: Macmillan Co. 1962.

Hall, J., The Lunatic Giant in the Drawing Room. Bloomington:
Indiana University Press. 1968.

_____, The Tragic Comedians; Seven Modern British Novelists.
Bloomington: Indiana University Press. 1963.

Hamill, Elizabeth, These Modern Writers. Melbourne: Georgian
House. 1946.

Hardy, Barbara, ed., Critical Essays on George Eliot. London:

Routledge and Kegan Paul. 1970.

_____, The Moral Art of Dickens, New York: Oxford University
Press. 1970.

Hardy, Evelyn, Thomas Hardy; A Critical Biography. London:
Hogarth Press. 1954.

Hardy, Florence Emily, The Early Life of Thomas Hardy, 1840–
1891. New York: Macmillan Co. 1928.

_____, The Later Years of Thomas Hardy, 1892–1928. New York:
Macmillan Co. 1930.

Harper, Howard M., Jr. and Charles Edge, eds., The Classic
British Novel. Athens: University of Georgia Press.
1972.

Harrison, Ada and Derek Stanford, Anne Brontë; Her Life and
Work. London: Methuen and Co. 1959.

Hartt, Julian N., The Lost Image of Man. Baton Rouge, La.:
Louisiana State University Press. 1963.

Harward, Timothy Blake, ed., European Patterns; Contemporary
Patterns in European Writing; A Series of Essays by Bruce
Arnold and others. Chester Springs, Penna.: Dufour Eds.,
Inc. 1967

Haugh, Robert F., Joseph Conrad; Discovery in Design. Norman:
University of Oklahoma Press. 1957.

Häusermann, H. W., The Genevese Background. London: Routledge and Kegan Paul. 1952.

Hay, Eloise Knapp, The Political Novels of Joseph Conrad.
Chicago: University of Chicago Press. 1963.

Hayden, Donald E. and E. Alworth, eds., Classics in Semantics.
New York: Philosophical Library, Inc. 1965.

Hayman, David, Joyce et Mallarme. Paris: Lettres Modernes.
1956.

Heath, William, Elizabeth Bowen; An Introduction to Her Novels.
Madison: University of Wisconsin Press. 1961.

Hesla, David H., The Shape of Chaos; An Interpretation of the
Art of Samuel Beckett. Minneapolis: University of Minnesota Press. 1971.

Hibbard, G. R., ed., Renaissance and Modern Essays Presented
to Vivian de Sola Pinto in Celebration of His Seventieth
Birthday. London: Routledge and Kegan Paul. 1966.

Heppenstall, Rayner, The Fourfold Tradition. London: Barrie
and Rockliff. 1961.

Hesse, Eva, ed., New Approaches to Ezra Pound; A Coordinated
Investigation of Pound's Poetry and Ideas, Berkeley: University of California Press. 1969.

Hillegas, Mark R., ed., Shadows of Imagination; The Fantasies
    of C. S. Lewis, J. R. R. Tolkien and Charles Williams.
    Carbondale: Southern Illinois University Press. 1969.
Hoare, Dorothy M., Some Studies in the Modern Novel. London:
    Chatto and Windus. 1938.
Hochman, Baruch, Another Ego; The Changing View of Self and
    Society in the Work of D. H. Lawrence. Columbia: Uni-
    versity of South Carolina Press. 1970.
Hodgart, Matthew and Mabel Worthington, Song in the Work of
    James Joyce. New York: Columbia University Press.
    1959.
Hoffman, Frederick J., The Mortal No; Death and the Modern
    Imagination. Princeton: Princeton University Press.
    1964.
Hoggart, Richard, Speaking to Each Other; Essays. New York:
    Oxford University Press. 1970.
Holloway, John, The Charted Mirror; Literary and Critical
    Essays. London: Routledge and Kegan Paul. 1960.
Holmes, Charles M., Aldous Huxley and the Way to Reality.
    Bloomington: Indiana University Press. 1970.
Hommage à Paul Dottin. Caliban #3. Special Issue. Toulouse:
    Faculté des Lettres et Sciences Humaines de Toulouse.
    1966.
Hornback, Bert G., The Metaphor of Chance; Vision and Tech-
    nique in the Works of Thomas Hardy. Athens: Ohio Uni-
    versity Press. 1971.
Hough, Graham, The Dark Sun: A Study of D. H. Lawrence. New
    York: Macmillan Co. 1957.
Howard, David, et al, Tradition and Tolerance in Nineteenth Cen-
    tury Fiction; Critical Essays on Some English and Ameri-
    can Novels. New York: Barnes and Noble. 1967.
Howe, Irving, ed., Modern Literary Criticism; An Anthology.
    Boston: Beacon Press. 1958.
Howells, William Dean, Criticism and Fiction and Other Essays.
    New York: New York University Press. 1959.
Hoyt, Charles Alva, ed., Minor British Novelists. Carbondale:
    Southern Illinois University Press. 1967.
Hubbell, Jay Broadus, South and Southwest; Literary Essays and
    Reminiscences. Durham, N. C.: Duke University Press.
    1965.
Humanities in the Age of Science; In Honor of Peter Sammartino;
    ed. by Charles Angoff. Rutherford, N. J.: Fairleigh Dick-
    enson University Press. 1968.

Hunt, Leigh, Leigh Hunt's Literary Criticism. New York:
    Columbia University Press. 1956.
Huntley, H. Robert, The Alien Protagonist: Ford Madox Ford.
    Chapel Hill, N. C.: University of North Carolina Press.
    1970.
Hyman, Stanley Edgar, Standards; A Chronicle of Books for Our
    Time. New York: Horizon Press. 1966.
Illinois University English Department, Studies by Members of
    the English Department, University of Illinois, in Memory
    of John Jay Parry. Urbana: University of Illinois Press.
    1955.
Image of the Work; Essays in Criticism by Bertram Evans and
    Others. Berkeley; University of California Press. 1955.
Isaacs, Neil David and Rose A. Zimbardo, eds., Tolkien and the
    Critics; Essays on J. R. R. Tolkien's "The Lord of the
    Rings." Notre Dame: University of Notre Dame Press.
    1968.
Jaffe, Adrian H. and Herbert Weisinger, eds., The Laureate
    Fraternity; An Introduction to Literature. Evanston: Row,
    Peterson and Co. 1960.
James, Henry, Literary Reviews and Essays; On American, En-
    glish and French Literature. New York: Twayne Pub.,
    Inc. 1957.
Jauss, Hans R., ed., Nachahmung und Illusion. Kolloquium
    Giessen Juni 1963. Munchen: Eidos. 1964.
_____, and Dieter Schaller, eds., Medium Aevum Vivum; Fest-
    schrift für Walther Bulst. Heidelberg: Winter. 1960.
Jefferson, D. W., ed., The Morality of Art; Essays Presented to
    G. Wilson Knight by His Colleagues and Friends. London:
    Routledge and Kegan Paul. 1969.
Johnson, Bruce, Conrad's Models of Mind. Minneapolis: Uni-
    versity of Minnesota Press. 1971.
Jonathan Swift, 1667–1967; A Dublin Tercentenary Tribute; ed.
    by Roger McHugh and Philip Edwards. Chester Springs,
    Penna.: Dufour Eds. Inc. 1968.
Jones, R. T., George Eliot. New York: Cambridge University
    Press. 1970.
Josipovici, Gabriel, The World and the Book; A Study of Modern
    Fiction. Stanford: Stanford University Press. 1971.
Kaplan, Harold J., The Passive Voice; An Approach to Modern
    Fiction. Athens: Ohio University Press. 1966.
Karl, Frederick Robert, An Age of Fiction; The Nineteenth Cen-
    tury British Novel. New York: Farrar, Straus and Girous.
    1964.

_____, A Reader's Guide to Joseph Conrad. New York: Noonday
        Printing Co. 1960.

_____, and Marvin Magalaner, A Reader's Guide to Great Twen-
        tieth Century English Novels. New York: Noonday Printing
        Co. 1959.

Kaul, A. N., The Action of English Comedy; Studies in the En-
        counter of Abstraction and Experience from Shakespeare
        to Shaw. New Haven: Yale University Press. 1970.

Kazin, Alfred, Contemporaries. New York: Little, Brown and
        Co. 1962.

Keating, George T., A Conrad Memorial Library. Garden City:
        Doubleday and Co. 1929.

Kellett, E. E., Reconsiderations; Literary Essays. New York:
        Cambridge University Press. 1928.

Kellogg, Gene, The Vital Tradition; The Catholic Novel in a
        Period of Convergence. Chicago: Loyola University
        Press. 1970.

Kenner, Hugh, Dublin's Joyce. Bloomington: Indiana University
        Press. 1956.

_____, Gnomon; Essays on Contemporary Literature. New York:
        McDowell, Obolensky. 1958.

_____, Flaubert, Joyce and Beckett; The Stoic Comedians. Bos-
        ton: Beacon Press. 1962.

Kermode, John Frank, Puzzles and Epiphanies; Essays and Re-
        views 1958-1961. New York: Chilmark Press. 1962.

Kingsmill, Hugh, The Life of D. H. Lawrence. New York: Dodge
        Pub. Co. 1938.

Kirk, Rudolf and C. F. Main, eds., Essays in Literary History
        Presented to J. Milton French. New Brunswick: Rutgers
        University Press. 1960.

Kirschner, Paul, Conrad; the Psychologist as Artist. Edinburgh:
        Oliver and Boyd. 1968.

Knies, Earl A., The Art of Charlotte Brontë. Athens: Ohio Uni-
        versity Press. 1969.

Knight, George Wilson, Neglected Powers; Essays on Nineteenth
        and Twentieth Century Literature. New York: Barnes and
        Noble. 1971.

Knoepflmacher, Ulrich Camillus, Laughter and Despair; Readings
        in Ten Novels of the Victorian Age. Berkeley: University
        of California Press. 1971.

_____, Religious Humanism and the Victorian Novel; George
        Eliot, Walter Pater and Samuel Butler. Princeton, N. J.:
        Princeton University Press. 1965.

Cape. 1953.

_____, Robert, A Treatise on the Novel. London: Jonathan Cape.
    1947.

Lingner, Erika, et al, Essays in Honour of William Gallacher.
    Berlin: Humboldt Co. 1966.

Literary Monographs; ed. by Eric Rothstein and Thomas K.
    Dunseath. Madison: University of Wisconsin Press. 1967.

Litz, Walton, Art of James Joyce; Method and Design in "Ulysses"
    and "Finnegan's Wake." London: Oxford University Press.
    1961.

_____, Walton, James Joyce. New York: Twayne Pub. Co. 1966.

Lodge, David, Language of Fiction; Essays in Criticism and Ver-
    bal Analysis of the English Novel. New York: Columbia
    University Press. 1966.

Logan, James V., John E. Jordan and Northrop Frye, eds., Some
    British Romantics; A Collection of Essays. Columbus:
    Ohio State University Press. 1966.

Loomis, Roger Sherman, Studies in Medieval Literature; A
    Memorial Collection of Essays. Philadelphia: Franklin
    Pub. Co. 1970.

Love, Jean O., Worlds in Consciousness; Mythopoetic Thought in
    the Novels of Virginia Woolf. Berkeley: University of
    California Press. 1970.

Lovett, Robert M. and Helen S. Hughes, The History of the Novel
    in England. Boston: Houghton Mifflin Co. 1932.

Lynd, Robert, Books and Writers. London: Dent. 1952.

McAlpin, E. A., Old and New Books as Life Teachers. Garden
    City: Doubleday Pub. Co. 1928.

McCarthy, Mary Therese, The Writing on the Wall and Other
    Literary Essays. New York: Harcourt, Brace, and Jano-
    vich. 1970.

McConkey, James, The Novels of E. M. Forster. Ithaca: Cornell
    University Press. 1957.

McCormack, Thomas, ed., Afterwords; Novelists on Their Novels.
    New York: Harper and Row. 1968.

McCormick, John, Catastrophe and Imagination; A Re-Interpre-
    tation of the Recent English and American Novel. London:
    Longmans Green. 1957.

McDowall, Arthur, Thomas Hardy; A Critical Study. London:
    Faber and Faber. 1931.

McIntosh, Angus and Michael A. K. Halliday, Patterns of Lan-
    guage; Papers in General, Descriptive and Applied Lin-
    guistics. (Indiana University Studies in the History and

Theory of Linguistics.) Bloomington: Indiana University
    Press. 1967.
Mack, Maynard and Ian Gregor, eds., Imagined Worlds; Essays
    on Some English Novels and Novelists in Honour of John
    Butt. London: Methuen Press. 1968.
Maekawa Shunichi Kyōju Kanreki Kinen-Ronbunshū. (Essays and
    Studies in Commemoration of Professor Shunichi Maekawa's
    Sixty-First Birthday.) Tokyo: Eihōsha. 1968.
Magalaner, Marvin, ed., A James Joyce Miscellany. New York:
    James Joyce Society. 1957.
_____, A James Joyce Miscellany. 2nd Series. Carbondale:
    Southern Illinois University Press. 1959.
Mais, Stuart P., Why We Should Read. London: Grant Richards.
    1921.
Majault, Joseph, James Joyce. Paris: Editions Universitaires.
    1963.
Manheim, Leonard F. and Eleanor B. Manheim, eds., Hidden
    Patterns; Studies in Psychoanalytic Literary Criticism.
    New York: Macmillan Co. 1966.
Mann, Thomas, Past Masters and Other Papers. London: Secker
    and Warburg. 1933.
Mansfield, Katherine, Novels and Novelists. New York: Alfred
    A. Knopf. 1930.
Marković, Vida E., The Changing Face; Disintegration of Per-
    sonality in the Twentieth Century British Novel, 1900–1950.
    Carbondale: Southern Illinois University Press. 1970.
Martin, Harold Clark, ed., Style in Prose Fiction. (English Insti-
    tute Essays, 1958), New York: Columbia University Press.
    1959.
Mason, Eudo C., Exzentrische Bahnen; Studien zum Dichterbe-
    wusstsein der Neuzeit. Göttingen: Vandenhoeck and
    Ruprecht. 1963.
Maugham, William Somerset, Art of Fiction; An Introduction to
    Ten Novels and Their Authors. Garden City: Doubleday
    Pub. Co. 1955.
_____, Selected Prefaces and Introductions of W. Somerset
    Maugham. Garden City: Doubleday Pub. Co. 1963.
Mazzeo, Joseph Anthony, ed., Reason and the Imagination; Studies
    in the History of Ideas, 1600–1800. New York: Columbia
    University Press. 1962.
Megroz, R. L., Joseph Conrad's Mind and Method; A Study of
    Personality and Art. London: Faber and Faber. 1931.
Meixner, John A., Ford Madox Ford's Novels; A Critical Study.

Minneapolis: University Press. 1962.
Meller, Horst and Hans-Joachim Zimmermann, eds., Lebende
    Antike; Symposion für Rudolf Sühnel. Berlin: E. Schmidt.
    1967.
Mercanton, Jacques, Poètes de L'Univers. Paris: Editions
    Albert Skira. 1947.
Mercier, Vivian, The Irish Comic Tradition. London: Oxford
    University Press. 1962.
Michigan Academy of Science, Arts and Letters. Papers; ed. by
    Sheridan Baker. Ann Arbor: University of Michigan
    Press. 1960.
Milburn, Daniel Judson, The Age of Wit, 1650–1750. New York:
    Macmillan Co. 1966.
Miller, Henry Knight and Eric Rothstein and G. S. Rousseau, eds.,
    The Augustan Milieu; Essays Presented to Louis A. Landa.
    London: Oxford University Press. 1970.
Miller, Joseph Hillis, ed., Aspects of Narrative; Selected Papers
    from the English Institute. New York: Columbia University
    Press. 1971.
_____, Thomas Hardy; Distance and Desire. Cambridge, Mass.:
    Harvard University Press. 1970.
Miller, Milton L., Nostalgia; A Psychoanalytic Study of Marcel
    Proust. Boston: Houghton, Mifflin Pub. Co. 1956.
Miller, Norbert, ed., Romananfänge; Versuch zu einer Poetik des
    Romans. Berlin: Literarisches Colloquium. 1965.
Millgate, Michael, Thomas Hardy; His Career as a Novelist. New
    York: Random House. 1971.
Misra, B. P., Indian Inspiration of James Joyce. Agra, India:
    Gaya Prasad and Sons. n.d.
Mizener, Arthur, The Sense of Life in the Modern Novel. Boston:
    Houghton Mifflin Co. 1964.
Moholy-Nagy, L., Vision in Motion. Chicago: Paul Theobald.
    1947.
Mooney, Harry J., Jr. and Thomas F. Satley, eds., The Shapeless
    God; Essays on Modern Fiction. Pittsburgh: University of
    Pittsburgh. 1968.
Moore, Harry Thornton, ed., D. H. Lawrence Miscellany. Car-
    bondale: Southern Illinois University Press. 1959.
_____, The Intelligent Heart; The Story of D. H. Lawrence. New
    York: Farrar, Straus, and Young. 1954.
_____, The Life and Works of D. H. Lawrence. New York:
    Twayne Pub. 1951.
Mordell, Albert, ed., Notorious Literary Attacks. New York:

Boni and Liveright. 1926.

More, Paul Elmer, On Being Human. Princeton, N. J.: Princeton University Press. 1936.

Morse, J. Mitchell, The Sympathetic Alien; James Joyce and Catholicism. New York: New York University Press. 1959.

Moseley, Edwin M., Pseudonyms of Christ in the Modern Novel; Motifs and Methods. Pittsburgh: University of Pittsburgh Press. 1963.

Moseley, Virginia, Joyce and the Bible. DeKalb: Northern Illinois University Press. 1967.

Moser, Thomas, Joseph Conrad; Achievement and Decline. Cambridge, Harvard University Press. 1957.

Moskowitz, Samuel, Explorers of the Infinite; Shapers of Science Fiction. New York: World Pub. Co. 1963.

Mudrick, Marvin, ed., Conrad; A Collection of Critical Essays. Englewood Cliffs, N. J.: Prentice-Hall Pub. Co. 1966.

Mueller, William Randolph, Prophetic Voices in Modern Fiction. New York: Association Press. 1959.

Muir, Edwin, The Structure of the Novel. London: Hogarth Press. 1928.

Muller, Herbert J., Modern Fiction; A Study of Values. New York: Funk and Wagnall Pub. Co. 1937.

Murry, John Middleton, Reminiscences of D. H. Lawrence. London: Jonathan Cape. 1933.

_____, Son of Woman; The Story of D. H. Lawrence. London: Jonathan Cape. 1931.

Naganowski, Egon, Telemach w Labiryncie Swiata; O Twórczosei James Joyce 'a. Warsaw: Czytelnik. 1962.

Nassar, Eugene Paul, The Rape of Cinderella; Essays in Literary Continuity. Bloomington: Indiana University Press. 1970.

Newhouse, Neville H., Joseph Conrad. New York: Arco Pub. Co., Inc. 1969.

Nin, Anais, D. H. Lawrence; An Unprofessional Study. Paris: E. W. Titus. 1932.

Noon, William T., Joyce and Aquinas. New Haven: Yale University Press. 1957.

O'Brien, Darcy, The Conscience of James Joyce. Princeton, N. J.: Princeton University Press. 1967.

O'Brien, Justin, The French Literary Horizon. New Brunswick: Rutgers University Press. 1967.

O'Connor, Frank, The Mirror in the Roadway; A Study of the Modern Novel. New York: Alfred A. Knopf. 1956.

O'Connor, William Van, ed., Forms of Modern Fiction. Minne-
    apolis: University of Minnesota Press. 1948.
_____, The New University Wits and the End of Modernism.
    Carbondale: Southern Illinois University Press. 1963.
Oliver, Harold J., The Art of E. M. Forster. Melbourne: Mel-
    bourne University Press. 1960.
O'Neill, Judith, ed., Critics on Charlotte and Emily Brontë;
    Readings in Literary Criticism. Coral Gables, Fla.: Uni-
    versity of Miami Press. 1968.
Oppel, Horst, ed., Der Moderne Englische Roman; Interpreta-
    tionen. Berlin: E. Schmidt. 1965.
Orvis, Mary, The Art of Writing Fiction. Englewood Cliffs,
    N. J.: Prentice-Hall Pub. Co. 1948.
Orwell, George, The Collected Essays, Journalism and Letters
    of George Orwell. New York: Harcourt, Brace, and Jano-
    vich, Inc. 1968.
_____, Orwell Reader; Fiction, Essays and Reportage. New
    York: Harcourt, Brace, and Janovich, Inc. 1956.
Oxley, B. T., George Orwell. New York: Arco Pub. Co. 1969.
Parrinder, Patrick, H. G. Wells. Edinburgh, Oliver, and Boyd.
    1970.
Partlow, Robert B., Jr., ed., Dickens the Craftsman; Strategies
    of Presentation. Carbondale: Southern Illinois University
    Press. 1970.
Pearce, Richard A., Stages of the Clown; Perspectives on Mod-
    ern Fiction from Dostoyevsky to Beckett. Carbondale:
    Southern Illinois University Press. 1970.
Pearce, Roy Harvey, ed., Experience in the Novel; Selected
    Papers from the English Institute. New York: Columbia
    University Press. 1968.
Perspectives in Literary Symbolism; ed. by Joseph Strelka.
    University Park, Penna.: Pennsylvania State University
    Press. 1968.
Phillips, William, ed., Art and Psychoanalysis. New York:
    Criterion Books. 1957.
Pinguentini, Gianni, James Joyce in Italia. Firenze: Liberia
    Commissionaria Sansoni. 1963.
Pope-Hennessey, James, Anthony Trollope. Boston: Little,
    Brown and Co. 1971.
Porter, Katherine Anne, The Collected Essays and Occasional
    Writings of Katherine Anne Porter. New York: Delacorte
    Press. 1970.
Potter, Stephen, D. H. Lawrence; A First Study. London:

Jonathan Cape. 1930.

Prescott, Joseph, Exploring James Joyce. Carbondale: Southern Illinois University Press. 1964.

Prescott, Orville, In My Opinion. Indianapolis: Bobbs-Merrill Co. 1952.

Preston, John M. A., The Created Self; The Reader's Role in Eighteenth Century Fiction. New York: Barnes and Noble. 1970.

Price, Martin, To the Palace of Wisdom; Studies in Order and Energy from Dryden to Blake. New York: Doubleday and Co. 1964.

Pritchett, Victor Sawdon, In My Good Books. London: Chatto and Windus. 1942.

_____, The Living Novel and Later Appreciations. New York: Random House. 1964.

Quennell, Peter, Casanova in London. New York: Stein and Day. 1971.

Raskin, Jonah, The Mythology of Imperialism. New York: Random House. 1971.

Rathburn, Robert C. and Martin Steinmann, eds., From Jane Austen to Joseph Conrad; Essays Collected in Memory of James T. Hillhouse. Minneapolis: University of Minnesota Press. 1958.

Read, Herbert Edward, Selected Writings; Poetry and Criticism. New York: Horizon Press. 1964.

Reck, Rima D., ed., Explorations of Literature. Baton Rough, La.: Louisiana State University Press. 1966.

Rees, Richard, Brave Men; A Study of D. H. Lawrence and Simone Weil. London: Gollanz. 1958.

Reid, Benjamin Lawrence. The Long Boy and Others; Wherein Will Be Found a Gathering of Essays, Written to Divert and Entertain and at the Same Time to Instruct, Concerning Several Distinguished Gentlemen of Divers Occupation and Wit; Newly Imprinted for Scholarly Inspection. Athens: University of Georgia Press. 1969.

Reilly, Robert J., Romantic Religion; A Study of Barfield, Lewis, Williams and Tolkien. Athens: University of Georgia Press. 1971.

Reinhardt, Kurt Frank, The Theological Novel of Modern Europe; An Analysis of Masterpieces by Eight Authors. New York: Frederick Ungar Pub. Co. 1969.

Rexroth, Kenneth, Classics Revisited. Westminster, Md.: Quadrangle Books. 1968.

Richter, Harvena, Virginia Woolf; The Inward Voyage. Princeton, N. J.: Princeton University Press. 1970.

Riesner, Dieter and Helmut Gneuss, eds., Festschrift für Walter Hübner. Berlin: Schmidt. 1964.

Robinson, Michael, The Long Sonata of the Dead; A Study of Samuel Beckett. London: Rupert Hart-Davis. 1969.

Røstvig, Maren-Sofie, et al, The Hidden Sense and Other Essays. New York: Humanities Press. 1963.

Rothstein, Eric and Thomas K. Dunseath, Literary Monographs I. Madison: University of Wisconsin Press. 1967.

Roussel, Royal, The Metaphysics of Darkness; A Study in the Unity and Development of Conrad's Fiction. Baltimore: Johns Hopkins University Press. 1971.

Rowse, Alfred Leslie, The English Spirit; Essays in Literature and History. Rev. ed. New York: Funk, Inc. 1967.

Rupp, Ernest Gordon, Six Makers of English Religion, 1500-1700. New York: Harper and Row. 1957.

Russell, Bertrand Russell, Portraits from Memory and Other Essays. New York: Simon and Schuster. 1956.

Russell, John, Anthony Powell; A Quintet, Sextet and War. Bloomington: Indiana University Press. 1970.

Rutherford, Andrew, ed., Kipling's Mind and Art; Selected Critical Essays. Stanford: Stanford University Press. 1964.

Rutland, W. R., Thomas Hardy; A Study of His Writings and Their Background. Oxford: Basil Blackwell. 1938.

Ryf, Robert S., A New Approach to Joyce; "A Portrait of the Artist" as a Guidebook. Berkeley: University of California Press. 1962.

Saturday Review, Saturday Review Treasury; A Volume of Good Reading Selected from the Complete Files. New York: Simon and Schuster. 1957.

Savage, D. S., The Withered Branch; Studies in the Modern Novel. London: Fyre and Spottiswoode. 1950.

Schilling, Bernard Nicholas, The Comic Spirit; Boccaccio to Thomas Mann. Detroit: Wayne State University Press. 1965.

Scholes, Robert, The Fabulators. New York: Oxford University Press. 1967.

Schorer, Mark, ed., Modern British Fiction. London: Oxford University Press. 1961.

_____, The World We Imagine; Selected Essays. New York: Farrar, Straus and Giroux. 1968.

Seidlin, Oskar, Essays in German and Comparative Literature.

(North Carolina University Studies in Comparative Literature.) Chapel Hill: University of North Carolina Press.
1961.

Seligmann, Herbert J., D. H. Lawrence; An American Interpretation. New York: Thomas Seltzer. 1924.

Semmler, Clement, For the Uncanny Man; Essays Mainly Literary. London: Angus and Robertson. 1963.

The Shaken Realist; Essays in Modern Literature in Honor of
Frederick J. Hoffman; ed. by Melvin J. Friedman and John
B. Vickery. Baton Rouge, La.: Louisiana State University
Press. 1970.

Shalvi, Alice and A. A. Mendilow, ed., Studies in English Language and Literature. Jerusalem: Hebrew University.
1966.

Shapiro, Charles, ed., Contemporary British Novelists. Car-
bondale: Southern Illinois University Press. 1965.
_____, Twelve Original Essays on Great English Novels.
Detroit: Wayne State University Press. 1960.

Shaw, George Bernard, Selected Non-Dramatic Writings. Boston: Houghton, Mifflin. 1965.

Sheed, Wilfred, The Morning After; Selected Essays and Reviews. New York: Farrar, Straus, and Giroux, Inc. 1971.

Sheppard, John T., Music at Belmont and Other Essays and Addresses. New York: Haughton Pub. Co. 1951.

Sherry, Norman, Charlotte and Emily Brontë. London: Evans
Bros., Ltd. 1969.
_____, Jane Austen. New York: Arco Pub. Co. 1969.

Shine, Hill, ed., Booker Memorial Studies. Chapel Hill: University of North Carolina Press. 1950.

Simon, Irène, Formes du Roman Anglais de Dickens à Joyce.
Liege: Faculté de Philosophie et Lettres. 1949.

Singh, Bhupal, A Survey of Anglo-Indian Fiction. London: Oxford University Press. 1934.

Slater, Michael, ed., Dickens 1970; Centenary Essays. New
York: Stein and Day. 1970.

Slatoff, Walter J., With Respect to Readers; Dimensions of Literary Response. Ithaca: Cornell University Press. 1970.

Soupault, Philippe, Souvenirs de James Joyce. Paris: Charlot.
1945.

Speck, W. A., Swift. London: Evans Bros. 1970.

Spector, Robert Donald, ed., Essays on the Eighteenth Century
Novel. Bloomington: Indiana University Press. 1965.

Spender, Stephen, The Struggle of the Modern. Berkeley: University of California Press. 1963.

Spilka, Mark, The Love Ethic of D. H. Lawrence. Bloomington:
   Indiana University Press. 1955.

Sprague, Rosemary, George Eliot; A Biography. New York:
   Chilton Book Co. 1968.

Squire, John C., Books in General. London: Heinemann. 1919.

_____, Life and Letters. London: Heinemann. 1921.

Staley, Thomas F. and Bernard Benstock, eds., Approaches to
   Ulysses; Ten Essays. Pittsburgh: University of Pittsburgh Press. 1970.

Staley, Thomas F., ed., James Joyce Today; Essays on the Major
   Works; Commemorating the Twenty-Fifth Anniversary of
   His Death. Bloomington: Indiana University Press. 1966.

Stallman, Robert Wooster, Art of Joseph Conrad; A Critical
   Symposium. East Lansing: Michigan State University
   Press. 1960.

_____, The Houses that James Built and Other Literary Studies.
   East Lansing: Michigan State University Press. 1961.

Stanford, Donald Edwin, ed., Nine Essays in Modern Literature.
   (L. S. U. Studies. Humanities Series #15.) Baton Rouge,
   La.: Louisiana State University Press. 1965.

Stanford, W. B., The Ulysses Theme; A Study in the Adaptability
   of a Traditional Hero. Oxford: Basil Blackwell. 1954.

Stanzel, Franz, Die Typischen Erzählsituationen im Roman.
   Wien: W. Bräumuller. 1955.

Starr, G. A., Defoe and Casuistry. Princeton, N. J.: Princeton
   University Press. 1971.

Steeves, Harrison Ross, Before Jane Austen; The Shaping of the
   English Novel in the Eighteenth Century. New York: Holt,
   Rinehart, and Winston, Inc. 1965.

Steiner, George, Language and Silence; Essays on Language,
   Literature and the Inhuman. New York: Atheneum Pub.
   1967.

Stephens, James, James, Seumas and Jacques; Unpublished
   Writings of James Stephens. New York: Macmillan Co.
   1964.

Stewart, J. I. M., Eight Modern Writers. New York: Oxford
   University Press. 1963.

_____, James Joyce. London: Longmans, Green. 1957.

Stoll, John E., The Novels of D. H. Lawrence. Columbia: University of Missouri Press. 1971.

Stone, Donald David, Novelists in a Changing World; Meredith,
   James, and the Transformation of English Fiction in the

1880's. Cambridge, Mass.: Harvard University Press.
     1972.
Strachey, John, The Strangled Cry and Other Unparliamentary
     Papers. New York: William Sloane Asso. 1962.
Strelka, Joseph, ed., Perspectives in Literary Symbolism.
     (Yearbook of Comparative Criticism, 1.) University Park:
     Pennsylvania State University Press. 1968.
Strong, Leonard Alfred George, Personal Remarks. New York:
     Liveright Pub. Co. 1953.
Sutherland, William Owen Sheppard, The Art of the Satirist;
     Essays on the Satire of Augustan England. Austin: Uni-
     versity of Texas Press. 1965.
_____, ed., Six Contemporary Novels. Austin: University of
     Texas Press. 1962.
Swados, Harvey, A Radical's America. Boston: Little, Brown
     and Co. 1962.
Swinnerton, Frank Arthur, A Galaxy of Fathers. Garden City:
     Doubleday Pub. Co. 1966.
_____, The Georgian Scene. New York: Farrar and Rinehart.
     1931.
T. L. S., Essays and Reviews from The Times Literary Supple-
     ment. London: Oxford University Press (various dates)
Thackeray, William Makepeace, Contributions to the Morning
     Chronicle; Now First Reprinted. Urbana; University of
     Illinois Press. 1955.
Thale, Jerome, Novels of George Eliot. New York: Columbia
     University Press. 1959.
Tillotson, Kathleen Mary, Novels of the Eighteen-Forties. Lon-
     don: Oxford University Press. 1961.
Tillyard, Eustace Mandeville Wetenhall, Epic Strain in the En-
     glish Novel. Fair Lawn, N. J.: Essential Books. 1958.
Tindall, William York, The Literary Symbol. New York:
     Columbia University Press. 1955.
Tiverton, Father William, D. H. Lawrence and Human Existence.
     London: Rockliff. 1951.
Trilling, Lionel, Beyond Culture; Essays on Literature and
     Learning. New York: Viking Press, Inc. 1965.
_____, Opposing Self; Nine Essays in Criticism. New York:
     Viking Press, Inc. 1955.
Troy, William, William Troy; Selected Essays. New Brunswick,
     N. J.: Rutgers University Press. 1967.
Tuveson, Ernest Lee, ed., Swift; A Collection of Critical Essays.
     Englewood Cliffs, N. J.: Prentice-Hall Pub. Co. 1964.

Tynan, Kenneth, Curtains; Selections from the Drama Criticism
    and Related Writings. New York: Atheneum Pubs. 1961.
Tyrmand, Leopold, ed., Kultura Essays. Albany: State Univer-
    sity of New York. 1970.
Tysdahl, B. J., Joyce and Ibsen; A Study in Literary Influence.
    New York: Humanities Press. 1968.
Unterecker, John Eugene, ed., Approaches to the Twentieth Cen-
    tury Novel. New York: Crowell Pubs., Inc. 1965.
Urang, Gunnar, Shadows of Heaven; Religion and Fantasy in the
    Writing of C. S. Lewis, Charles Williams and J. R. R.
    Tolkien. Philadelphia: Pilgrim Press. 1971.
Ussher, Hermut, Three Great Irishmen: Shaw, Yeats and Joyce.
    New York: Devin-Adair. 1953.
Van Dyke, Henry, The Man Behind the Book; Essays in Under-
    standing. New York: Charles Scribner Pub. Co, 1929.
Verschoyle, Derek, ed., The English Novelists. London: Chatto
    and Windus. 1936.
Vickery, John B., ed., Myth and Literature; Contemporary
    Theory and Practice. Lincoln: University of Nebraska
    Press. 1966.
Virginia University Bibliographical Society, Studies in Bibliog-
    raphy; Papers of the Bibliographical Society of the Univer-
    sity of Virginia. Charlottesville: The Society. 1961-69.
Visiak, E. H., The Mirror of Conrad. New York: Philosophical
    Library. 1956.
Wagenknecht, Edward Charles, Dickens and the Scandalmongers;
    Essays in Criticism. Norman: University of Oklahoma
    Press. 1965.
Wain, John, Essays on Literature and Ideas. New York: St.
    Martins Press, Inc. 1963.
Wallace, A. Doyle and Woodburn O. Ross, eds., Studies in Honor
    of John Wilcox by Members of the English Department,
    Wayne State University. Detroit: Wayne State University
    Press. 1958.
Warner, Oliver, Joseph Conrad. London: Longmans, Green.
    1951.
Warren, Austin, Rage for Order; Essays in Criticism. Chicago:
    University of Chicago Press. 1948.
Warren, Robert Penn, Selected Essays. New York: Random
    House. 1958.
Watt, Ian Pierre, ed., The Victorian Novel; Modern Essays in
    Criticism. London: Oxford University Press. 1971.
Wayne State University, Detroit, Studies in Honor of John Wilcox

by Members of the English Department, Wayne State University. Detroit: Wayne State University Press. 1958.

Webb, Eugene, Samuel Beckett; A Study of his Novels. Seattle: University of Washington Press. 1970.

Weber, Carl J., Hardy of Wessex; His Life and Literary Career. New York: Columbia University Press. 1940.

Weber, L. Sherwood, et al, From Homer to Joyce; A Study Guide to Thirty-Six Great Books. New York: Holt Pub. Co. 1939.

Webster, Harvey Curtis, On a Darkling Plain; The Art and Thought of Thomas Hardy. Chicago: University of Chicago Press. 1947.

West, Anthony, D. H. Lawrence. London: Barker Pub. Co. 1950.

_____, Principles and Persuasions; The Literary Essays of Anthony West. New York: Harcourt, Brace, and Janovich. 1957.

West, Ray B., Jr. and R. W. Stallman, The Art of Modern Fiction. New York: Rinehart Pub. Co. 1949.

Wethered, Herbert Newton, Curious Art of Autobiography; From Benvenuto Cellini to Rudyard Kipling. New York: Philosophical Library. 1956.

Whitbread, Thomas Bacon, ed., Seven Contemporary Authors; Essays on Cozzens, Miller, West, Golding, Heller, Albee and Powers. Austin: University of Texas Press. 1966.

Wiley, Paul, Novelist of Three Worlds: Ford Madox Ford. Syracuse: Syracuse University Press. 1962.

Will, Frederic, ed., Hereditas; Seven Essays on the Modern Experience of the Classical. Austin: University of Texas Press. 1964.

Williams, Charles, Image of the City and Other Essays. London: Oxford University Press. 1958.

Williams, Ioan M., Thackeray. New York: Arco Pub. Co. 1969.

Williams, Raymond, The English Novel; From Dickens to Lawrence. London: Chatto and Windus. 1970.

_____, Modern Tragedy. Stanford: Stanford University Press. 1966.

Williams, William Carlos, Selected Essays. New York: Random House. 1954.

Wilson, Edmund, The Bit Between My Teeth; A Literary Chronicle of 1950–1965. New York: Farrar, Straus, and Giroux. 1965.

The Winged Skull; Papers from the Laurence Sterne Bicentenary

Conference at the University of York and Sponsored by
McMaster University, The University of York, and the
New Paltz College of the State University of New York.
Kent, Ohio: Kent State University Press. 1971.

Wolfe, Peter, The Disciplined Heart; Iris Murdoch and Her Novels. Columbia: University of Missouri Press. 1966.

Woolf, Virginia, Collected Essays. New York: Harcourt, Brace,
and Janovich. 1957

Wright, Austin, ed., Victorian Literature; Modern Essays in
Criticism. London: Oxford University Press. 1961.

Wright, Walter F., Romance and Tragedy in Joseph Conrad.
Lincoln: University of Nebraska Press. 1949.

Young, Kenneth, Ford Madox Ford. London: Longmans, Green.
1956.

Yudhishtar, Conflict in the Novels of D. H. Lawrence. Edinburgh: Oliver and Boyd. 1969.

Zabel, Morton Dauwen, Craft and Character: Texts, Methods
and Vocation in Modern Fiction. New York: Viking Press,
Inc. 1957.

_____, ed., Literary Opinion in America; Essays Illustrating the
Status, Methods and Problems of Criticism in the United
States in the Twentieth Century. 3rd ed. rev. New York:
Harper and Row. 1962.

LIST OF JOURNALS INDEXED

AUMLA; A Journal of Literary Criticism, Philology and Linguistics. Townsville, Australia: James Cook University
of North Queensland.

Accent. Urbana, Ill.

Akzente; Zeitschrift für Literatur. Munich, W. Ger.

Alphabet. London, Ontario, Canada.

America. New York.

American Benedictine Review. Atchinson, Kansas.

American Book Collector. Chicago, Ill.

American Imago. Detroit, Mich: Wayne State University.

American Literature; A Journal of Literary History, Criticism,
and Bibliography. Durham: Duke University.

American Notes and Queries. New Haven, Conn.

American Quarterly. Philadelphia, Penna.

American Scholar; A Quarterly for the Independent Thinker.
Washington, D. C.

Analyst. Scarsdale, N. Y.

Anglia; Zeitsschrift für Englische Philologie. Tübingen, Ger.

Anglo-Soviet Journal. London, England.

Anglo-Welsh Review. Pembroke Dock, Wales.

Annales de la Faculté des Lettres d'Aix. Aix-en-Provence.

Annales de l'Université de Paris. Paris.

Annali Istituto Universitario Orientale, Napoli, Sezione Germanica. Naples, Italy.

Annuale Mediaevale. Pittsburgh, Penna.

Antaios. Stuttgart.

Antioch Review. Yellow Springs, Ohio.

L'Approdo. Naples, Italy.

Arcadia. Berlin, W. Ger.

Archiv für das Studium der Neueren Sprachen und Literaturen.
Braunschweig, W. Ger.

Archives des Lettres Modernes; Etudes de Critique et d'Histoire
Littéraire. Paris.

Arizona Quarterly. Tucson, Ariz.: University of Arizona.

Aspect. Somerville, Mass.

Atlantic Monthly. Boston, Mass.

Audit. Buffalo, N. Y.

Babel. Australia.

Balcony. Sydney, Australia.

Ball State Teacher's College Forum. Muncie, Inc.: Ball State
University.

Ball State University Forum. (Formerly: Ball State Teacher's
College Forum.) Muncie, Ind.: Ball State University.

Barat Review; A Journal of the Liberal Arts. Lake Forest, Ill.:
    Barat College.
Belfagor; Rassegna di varia Umanita. Florence, Italy.
Bibliographical Society of America. Papers. New York.
Black Orpheus. Ibadan, Africa.
Blackfriars. Oxford, England.
Blackmore Studies. London, England.
Bookman. New York.
Bookman's Journal and Print Collector; The Paper for All Liter-
    ary Men and Collectors. London, England.
Books Abroad; An International Literary Quarterly. Norman,
    Okla.: University of Oklahoma.
Books at Iowa. Iowa City: University of Iowa.
Boston University. Studies in English. Boston, Mass.
Brigham Young University Studies. Provo, Utah.
British Book News; Supps. on Writers and Their Work. London,
    England.
British Museum Quarterly. London, England.
Brno Studies in English. Praha, Czechoslovakia.
Brontë Society Transactions. Keighley, England.
Broom. Arcola, Ill.
Bucknell Review. Lewisburg, Penna.: Bucknell University.
Bulletin Bibliographique de la Societé Internationale Arthurienne.
    Paris.
Bulletin of the Department of English. Calcutta, India: Calcutta
    University.
Bulletin of the New York Public Library. New York.
Busara. Nairobi, Kenya: Dept. of English, University College.
CEA Critic. Shreveport, La.: Centenary College.
CLA Journal. Baltimore, Md.: Morgan State College.
Cahiers du Sud. Marseilles.
Cairo Studies in English; Bicentenary Essays on "Rasselas"; A
    Supp. Cairo, Egypt.
Caliban. Toulouse.
Cambridge Journal. Cambridge, England.
Cambridge Quarterly. Cambridge, England.
Canadian Forum. Toronto, Ontario, Canada.
Canadian Literature/Litterature Canadienne; A Quarterly of
    Criticism and Review. Vancouver, B. C.: University of
    British Columbia.
Canadian Slavonic Papers. Ottawa, Canada: Carleton University.
Carleton Miscellany. Northfield, Minn.
Carnegie Series in English. Pittsburgh, Penna.: Carnegie Insti-
    tute of Technology.

Carnegie Studies in English. Pittsburgh, Penna.
Catholic World. New York.
Centennial Review. East Lansing, Mich.: Michigan State University.
Centennial Review of Arts and Science. (See Centennial Review)
Changing World. London, England.
Character and Personality. (Now: Journal of Personality.) Durham, N. C.
Chelsea; A Magazine for Poetry, Plays, Stories and Translations. Chelsea Station, N. Y.
Chicago Review. Chicago, Ill.: University of Chicago.
Christian Scholar. New Haven, Conn.
Church History. Oreland, Penna.
Circle. Berkeley, Calif.
Cithara; Essays in Judaeo-Christian Tradition. St. Bonaventure, N. Y.
Classical Bulletin. St. Louis, Mo.: St. Louis University.
Classical Journal. Iowa City, Iowa: University of Iowa.
Colby Library Quarterly. Waterville, Maine: Colby College Library.
College English. Champagne, Ill.: National Council of Teachers of English.
College Language Association Journal. Baltimore, Md.: Morgan State College.
The Colophon; A Quarterly for Bookmen. New York.
Colorado Quarterly. Boulder, Colo.: University of Colorado.
Columbia University Forum; A Journal of Fact and Opinion. New York: Columbia University.
Commentary. New York: American Jewish Committee.
Commonweal. New York.
Comparative Literature. Eugene, Ore.: University of Oregon.
Comparative Literature Studies. Urbana, Ill.: University of Illinois.
Connecticut Review. Hartford, Conn.
Conradiana. Abilene, Texas: McMurry College.
Contemporary Literature. Madison, Wis.: University of Wisconsin.
Contemporary Reviews. London, England
Convivium. Barcelona, Spain.
Cornell Library Journal. Ithaca, N. Y.
The Critic; A Catholic Review of Books. Chicago, Ill.
Critical Quarterly. London: Oxford University.
Critical Review. Victoria, Australia: University of Melbourne.
Criticism. Detroit, Mich.: Wayne State University.

Critique. Paris.
Critique; Studies in Modern Fiction. Minneapolis, Minn.
Cuadernos Americanos. Mexico.
Cuadernos Hispanoamericanos. Madrid.
Cultura. San Salvador, El Salvador.
Daedalus. Boston, Mass.
Dalhousie Review; A Canadian Quarterly of Literature and
    Opinion. Halifax, N. S.: Dalhousie University.
Delta. Cambridge, England.
Denver Quarterly. Denver, Colo.: University of Denver.
Descant. Fort Worth, Texas: Texas Christian University.
Deutsche Vierteljahrschrift für Literaturwissenschaft und
    Geistesgeschichte. W. Ger.
Dialectics; A Marxist Literary Journal. New York.
Dickensian. London, England.
Dickens Studies. Boston: Emerson College.
Dietsche Warende en Belfort. Antwerp, Belgium.
Discourse; A Review of the Liberal Arts. Moorhead, Minn.:
    Concordia College.
Dissertation Abstracts. Ann Arbor, Mich.
Downside Review; A Quarterly of Catholic Thought. Bath,
    England.
Dubliner, Dublin, Ireland.
Durham University Journal, Durham, England: University of
    Durham.
ELH. Baltimore, Md.: Johns Hopkins University.
Eckart; Ein Deutsches Literaturblatt. Berlin.
Edda. Oslo, Norway.
Edita. Havana.
Eighteenth Century Studies. Berkeley, Calif.: University of
    California.
Eire-Ireland; Journal of Irish Studies. St. Paul, Minn.
Emory University Quarterly. Atlanta, Ga.
Encounter. London, England.
Englische Studien. Leipzig.
English. London, England.
English Institute Essays. New York.
English Journal. Champaign, Ill.
English Language Notes. Boulder, Colo.: University of Colorado.
English Literature in Transition (1880—1920). DeKalb, Ill.:
    Northern Illinois University.
English Miscellany. Rome, Italy.
English Record. Binghamton, N. Y.: New York State English
    Council.

English Review. London, England.
English Studies; A Journal of English Letters and Philology.
      Netherlands.
English Studies in Africa. Johannesburg.
Envoy. Pittsburgh, Penna.: Duquesne University.
Esquire. New York.
Essays.
Essays and Studies. London, England.
Essays and Studies by Members of the English Association.
      (See: Essays and Studies.)
Essays by Divers Hands; Being the Transactions of the Royal
      Society of Literature. London, England.
Essays in Criticism; A Quarterly Journal of Literary Criticism.
      Oxford, England.
Etudes. Paris.
Etudes Anglaises. Paris.
Etudes Anglaises et Americaines.
Etudes de Lettres. Lausanne, Switzerland: Université de
      Lausanne.
Evelyn Waugh Newsletter. Garden City, N. Y.: State University
      of New York.
Evergreen Review. New York.
Explicator. Richmond, Va.: Richmond Professional Institute.
Extrapolation. Wooster, Ohio.
Figaro Littéraire. Paris.
Filologia e Letteratura. Naples, Italy.
Filologia Moderna. Madrid, Spain.
First Person. Rockport, Mass.
Foreground; A Creative and Critical Quarterly. Cambridge,
      Mass.
Fortnightly. London, England. (Incorporated into Contemporary
      Review.)
Forum. Houston.
Four Quarters. Philadelphia, Penna.: LaSalle College.
French Review. Ypsilanti, Mich.: Eastern Michigan University.
Fresco. Detroit, Mich.: University of Detroit.
Furman Studies. Greenville, S. C.
Geist und Zeit. Duesseldorf.
General Magazine and Historical Chronicle. Philadelphia,
      Penna.: University of Pennsylvania.
Georgia Review. Athens, Ga.: University of Georgia.
German Life and Letters. Oxford, England.
Germanisch-Romanische Monatsschrift. Heidelberg.
Giornale Critico della Filosofia Italiana. Florence, Italy.

Graffiti. New York.
The Guardian. Rangoon.
Harvard Library Bulletin. Cambridge, Mass.: Harvard University Library.
Hibbert Journal. London, England.
History Today. London, England.
Hollins Critic. Hollins, Va.: Hollins College.
Horisont. Stockholm, Sweden.
Horizon. New York.
Hudson Review. New York.
Humanist. London, England.
Humanities Association Bulletin. Canada: University of Alberta.
Huntington Library Quarterly. San Marino, Calif.
Ibadan. Ibadan, Nigeria: University of Ibadan.
Indian Journal of English Studies. Calcutta, India.
Inostrannaya Literatura. Moscow.
International Literary Annual. London, England.
Inventario; Rivista Trimestrale. Florence, Italy.
Iowa English Yearbook. Ames, Iowa: Iowa State University.
Irish Digest. Dublin.
Italica. New York: American Assn. of Teachers of Italian; Columbia University.
Izraz. Sarajevo, Yugoslavia.
James Joyce Quarterly. Tulsa, Okla.: University of Tulsa.
Jewish Frontier. New York.
John O'London's; Books of the Month. London, England.
Journal of Aesthetics and Art Criticism. Detroit, Mich.: Wayne State University.
Journal of American Folklore. Austin, Texas: University of Texas.
Journal of Asian Studies. Coral Gables, Fla.: University of Miami.
Journal of Contemporary History. London, England.
Journal of English and Germanic Philology. Urbana, Ill.: University of Illinois.
Journal of General Education. University Park, Penna.: Pennsylvania State University.
Journal of General Psychology. Provincetown, Mass.
Journal of Popular Culture. Bowling Green, Ohio: Bowling Green University.
Journal of Religion. Chicago, Ill.: University of Chicago.
Journal of Australasian Universities Language and Literature Association. New Zealand.

Journal of the History of Ideas; A Quarterly Devoted to Cultural
    and Intellectual History. Philadelphia, Penna.: Temple
    University.
Journalism Quarterly. Minneapolis, Minn.: University of Min-
    nesota.
Jubilee. Chicago, Ill. (Now: U. S. Catholic and Jubilee.)
Kansas Quarterly. Lawrence, Kansas: University of Kansas.
Keats-Shelley Journal. New York.
Kenyon Review. Gambier, Ohio: Kenyon College.
Kerygma. Stockholm, Sweden.
Kipling Journal. London, England.
Komma. The Hauge.
Kultuurleven. Leuven, Belgium.
Kwartalnik Neofilologiczny. Warsaw.
Les Langues Modernes. Paris.
Letteràture Moderne; Rivista di Varia Umanita. Milan.
Lettres Nouvelles. Paris.
Les Lettres Romanes. Louvain: Université Catholique.
Leuvense Bijdragen; Tijdschrift voor Germaanse Filologie.
    Leuven, Belgium.
Leyte-Samar Studies. Tacloban City, Philippines: Divine Word
    University.
Library Chronicle of the University of Texas. Austin: Univer-
    sity of Texas Library.
Listener. London.
Lit. Swarthmore, Penna.: Swarthmore College.
Literary Criterion. Mysore, India; University of Mysore.
Literary Half-Yearly. Mysore, India.
Literary Monographs. Madison, Wisconsin.
Literary Review. Teaneck, N. J.: Fairleigh Dickinson Univer-
    sity.
Literature and Psychology. Hartford, Conn.
Lock Haven Review. Lock Haven, Penna.: Lock Haven State
    College.
London Magazine. London, England.
London Times Literary Supplement. London, England.
Mad River Review. Dayton, Ohio.
Malahat Review. Victoria, B. C., Canada: University of Victoria.
Manchester Review. Manchester, England.
Mankato State College Studies. Mankato, Minn.: Mankato State
    College.
Marab; A Review. Heidelberg, Ger.
Massachusetts Review. Amherst, Mass.: University of Massa-
    chusetts.

Massachusetts Studies in English. Amherst, Mass.: University
 of Massachusetts.
Meanjin Quarterly. Australia: University of Melbourne.
Medieval Studies. New York.
Melbourne Critical Review. Victoria, Australia: University of
 Melbourne.
Memoirs of Osaka Gakugei University. Osaka.
Memoirs of Osaka Kyoiku University. Osaka.
Michigan Academy of Science, Arts and Letters. Papers.
 (Superseded by Michigan Academician.) Ann Arbor, Mich.
Mid-Century. New York.
Midwest Quarterly. Pittsburg, Kansas: Kansas State College.
Midwest Review. Wayne, Nebraska: Nebraska State Teachers
 College at Wayne.
Minnesota Review. St. Paul, Minn.
Mississippi Quarterly. State College, Miss.
Modern Age. Chicago, Ill.
Modern Fiction Studies. Lafayette, Ind.: Purdue University.
Modern Language Association. Publications. New York.
Modern Language Notes. Baltimore, Md.: Johns Hopkins Uni-
 versity.
Modern Language Quarterly. Seattle, Wash.: University of
 Washington.
Modern Language Review. London, England.
Modern Philology. Chicago, Ill.: University of Chicago.
Modern Quarterly; A Journal of Radical Opinion. Baltimore, Md.
Modern Review. Calcutta, India.
Moderna Sprak. Stockholm, Sweden.
Month. London, England.
Mosaic; A Journal for the Comparative Study of Literature and
 Ideas. Manitoba, Canada: University of Manitoba.
Names. Potsdam, N. Y.: State University College.
Nation. New York.
National Review. New York.
Neophilologus. Groningen, Netherlands.
Neue Rundschau. Berlin.
Die Neueren Sprachen. Berlin.
Neuphilologische Mitteilungen. Helsinki, Finland: Porthania
 University.
New Colophon. New York.
New Directions.
New Leader. New York.
New Left Review. London, England.

New Mexico Quarterly. Albuquerque, New Mexico: University
of New Mexico.
New Orleans Review. New Orleans, La.: Loyola University.
New Rambler. London: Johnson Society.
New Republic. Washington, D. C.
New Society. London, England.
New Statesman. London, England.
New Statesman and Nation. London, England.
New York Times Book Review. New York.
New Yorker. New York.
Nineteenth Century and After. London, England.
Nineteenth Century Fiction. Berkeley: University of California
North Dakota Quarterly. Grand Forks, N. D.: University of
North Dakota.
Northwest Review. Eugene, Oregon.
Notes and Queries. London, England.
Notre Dame English Journal. South Bend, Ind.: Notre Dame
English Assn.
La Nouvelle Revue. Paris.
Nouvelle Revue Française. Paris.
Novel; A Forum on Fiction. Providence, R. I.: Brown University
November Review. New York: Brooklyn College.
Orbis Litterarum; Revue Internationale d'Etudes Littéraires.
Copenhagen, Denmark.
Orient/West. Tokyo, Japan.
Overland. Melbourne, Australia.
PMLA (See Modern Language Association. Publications.)
Pacific Spectator; A Journal of Interpretation. Stanford, Calif.
Papers of the Michigan Academy of Science, Arts and Letters.
(See Michigan Academy of Science, Arts and Letters.
Papers.)
Papers on English Language and Literature. (See Papers on
Language and Literature.)
Papers on Language and Literature. Edwardsville, Ill.: South-
ern Illinois University. (Formerly: Papers on English
Language and Literature.)
Partisan Review. New Brunswick, N. J.: Rutgers University.
Paunch. Buffalo, N. Y.
Personalist; An International Review of Philosophy. Los
Angeles: University of Southern California.
Perspective; A Magazine of Modern Literature. St. Louis, Mo.:
Washington University.
Philologica Pragensia. Prague, Czechoslovakia.

Philological Quarterly. Iowa City, Iowa: University of Iowa.
Police College Magazine. Warwickshire, England.
Polish Review. New York: Polish Institute of Arts and Science
    in America.
Political Quarterly. London, England.
Political Science Quarterly. New York.
Il Ponte; Rivista di Politica e Letteratura. Florence, Italy.
Prairie Schooner. Lincoln, Nebraska: University of Nebraska.
Preuves. Paris.
Princeton University Library Chronicle. Princeton, N. J.:
    Princeton University Library.
Psychoanalysis and Psychoanalytic Review. New York.
Psychoanalytic Review. New York.
Quadrant. Sydney, Australia.
Quarterly Bulletin. Chicago: Northwestern University Medical
    School.
Quarterly Review. Washington, D. C.
Quarterly Review of Literature. Princeton, N. J.
Queen's Quarterly. Kingston, Ontario, Canada.
Renaissance and Modern Studies. England: University of Not-
    tingham.
Renaissance News. (See Renaissance Quarterly.)
Renaissance Quarterly. New York.
Renascence; A Critical Journal of Letters. Milwaukee, Wis.
Reporter; The Magazine of Facts and Ideas. New York.
Research Studies. Pullman: Washington State University.
Research Studies of the State College of Washington. (See Re-
    search Studies.)
Review of English Literature. Leeds.
Review of English Studies; A Quarterly Journal of English Lit-
    erature and English Language. London: Oxford University.
Revue Belge de Philologie et d'Histoire. Brussels, Belgium.
Revue de Littérature Comparée. Paris.
Revue de Paris. Paris.
Revue de l'Université d'Ottawa. Ottawa, Canada.
Revue des Langues Vivantes; Tidjdschrift voor Levende Talen.
    Bruxelles.
Revue des Lettres Modernes; Histoire des Idées et des Littéra-
    tures. Paris.
Revue Nouvelle. Brussels, Belgium.
Rice University Studies; Writings in All Scholarly Disciplines.
    Houston, Texas

Rice Institute Pamphlets. Houston, Texas.
Riverside Quarterly. Saskatchewan, Canada: University of
     Saskatchewan.
Revista Peruana de Cultura. Lima, Peru.
Revista do Livro. Rio de Janeiro.
Romance Notes. Chapel Hill: University of North Carolina.
Romanic Review. Irvington-on-Hudson, N. Y.: Columbia Uni-
     versity.
Samtiden; Tidsskrift fur Politikk, Litteratur og Samfunnsspors-
     mal. Oslo, Norway.
Satire Newsletter. Oneonta, N. Y.: State University College.
Saturday Review. New York.
Science and Society. New York.
Serif. Kent, Ohio: Kent State University.
Sewanee Review. Sewanee, Tenn.: University of the South.
Shaw Review. University Park: Pennsylvania State University.
Shenandoah; Washington and Lee University Review. Lexington,
     Va.
Shippensburg State College Review. Shippensburg, Penna.
Sinn und Form; Beiträge zur Literatur. Berlin, E. Ger.
South Atlantic Quarterly. Durham, N. C.: Duke University.
South Dakota Review. Vermillion, S. D.: University of South
     Dakota.
Southerly; A Review of Australian Literature. Sydney, Australia.
Southern Folklore Quarterly. Gainesville, Fla.: University of
     Florida.
Southern Humanities Review. Auburn, Ala.: Auburn University.
Southern Quarterly; A Scholarly Journal in the Humanities and
     Social Sciences. Hattiesburg, Miss.: University of South-
     ern Mississippi.
Southern Review. Adelaide, Australia.
Southern Review. Baton Rouge, Louisiana.
Southwest Review. Dallas, Texas: Southern Methodist University.
Soviet Literature. Moscow.
Spectator. London, England.
Spectrum. Santa Barbara, Calif.: University of California.
Speculum; A Journal of Mediaeval Studies. Cambridge, Mass.
Spieghel Historiael van de Bond van Gentske Germanisten. Ghent.
Standpunte. Capetown, S. Africa.
Studia Germanica Gandensia. Ghent.
Studia Neophilologica. Stockholm, Sweden.
Studia Romanica et Anglica Zagrabiensia. Zagreb, Yugoslavia.

Studies. Dublin, Ireland.

Studies in Bibliography; Papers of the Bibliographical Society of the University of Virginia. New York.

Studies in Burke and His Time. Rockford, Ill.: Rockford College.

Studies in English Literature. Tokyo: English Literary Society of Japan, University of Tokyo.

Studies in English Literature, 1500–1900. Houston, Texas: Rice University.

Studies in Philology. Chapel Hill: University of North Carolina.

Studies in Romanticism. (Formerly: Boston University Studies in English.) Boston: Boston University.

Studies in Scottish Literature. Columbia, S. C.: University of South Carolina.

Studies in Short Fiction. Newberry, S. C.: Newberry College.

Studies in the Literary Imagination. Atlanta: Georgia State College.

Studies in the Novel. Denton: North Texas State University.

Studies in the Twentieth Century; A Scholarly and Critical Journal. Troy, N. Y.

Style. Fayetteville, Ark.: University of Arkansas.

Susquehanna University Studies. Selinsgrove, Penna.

Symposium; A Quarterly Journal of Modern Foreign Literature. Syracuse, N. Y.: Syracuse University.

Tamarack Review. Toronto, Canada.

Tel Quel; Science-Litterature. Paris.

Temps Modernes. Paris.

Tennessee Folklore Society Bulletin. Murfreesboro, Tenn.: Middle Tennessee State University.

Tennessee Studies in Literature. Knoxville, Tenn.: University of Tennessee.

Terzo Programma. Rome.

Texas Quarterly. Austin, Texas: University of Texas.

Texas Studies in English. Austin, Texas.

Texas Studies in Literature and Language. Austin, Texas: University of Texas.

Theoria. Natal, S. Africa.

Thoth. Syracuse, N. Y.: Syracuse University.

Thought. Bronx, N. Y.: Fordham University.

Threshold. Belfast, Ireland.

Time and Tide. London, England.

Times Literary Supplement. London, England.

Torre; Revista General de la Universidad de Puerto Rico. San Juan, Puerto Rico.

Trace. London, England.
Transition. Glendale, Calif.
Triveni; Journal of Indian Renaissance. Machilipatnam, India.
Tulane Studies in English. New Orleans, La.: Tulane University.
Twentieth Century. London, England.
Twentieth Century Literature; A Scholarly and Critical Journal.
    Los Angeles, Calif.
Twentieth Century Studies. Canterbury, England: University of
    Kent.
Two Cities; La Revue Bilingue de Paris. Paris.
Union. Havana.
Unisa English Studies. Pretoria, S. Africa.
University Libertarian.
University of Ceylon Review. Peradenija, Ceylon.
University of Dayton Review. Dayton, Ohio: University of Dayton.
University of Kansas City Review. (See University Review.)
University of Mississippi Studies in English. University, Miss.
University of Portland Review; Journal of Arts and Sciences.
    Portland, Ore.
University of Toronto Quarterly. Toronto, Canada.
University Review. Dublin, Ireland.
University Review. (Formerly: University of Kansas City Re-
    view.) Kansas City, Mo.
Use of English. London, England.
Veltro. Rome.
Venture. Wheaton, Ill.
Victorian Newsletter. New York.
Victorian Studies; A Journal of the Humanities, Arts and Sci-
    ences. Bloomington: Indiana University.
Vinduet: Gyldendals Tidsskrift for Literatur. Oslo, Norway.
Virginia Quarterly Review; A National Journal of Literature and
    Discussion. Charlottesville, Va.: University of Virginia.
Visvabharati Quarterly. West Bengal, India.
De Vlaamse Gids. Brussels, Belgium.
Voprosi Literaturi. Moscow.
Wake Newsletter. Newcastle University College, N. S. W.
Wascana Review. Regina, Saskatchewan, Canada.
West Virginia University Philological Papers. Morgantown,
    West Virginia.
Westerly. Nedlands, Western Australia; University of Western
    Australia.
Western American Literature. Fort Collins, Colo.: Colorado
    State University.

<u>Western Humanities Review</u>. Salt Lake City; University of
  Utah.
<u>Wisconsin Studies in Contemporary Literature</u>. (See <u>Contem-</u>
  <u>porary Literature</u>.)
<u>Wisconsin Studies in Literature</u>. Oshkosh, Wis.
<u>Wiseman Review</u>. London, England.
<u>X, A Quarterly Review</u>. London, England.
<u>Yale Literary Magazine</u>. New Haven, Conn.
<u>Yale Review</u>. New Haven, Conn.: Yale University.
<u>Zeitschrift fur Anglistik und Amerikanistik</u>. East Berlin, Ger.

INDEX